D0153112

The Critical Response to Eudora Welty's Fiction

Recent Titles in
Critical Responses in Arts and Letters

The Critical Response to Mark Twain's *Huckleberry Finn*
Laurie Champion, editor

The Critical Response to Nathaniel Hawthorne's *The Scarlet Letter*
Gary Scharnhorst, editor

The Critical Response to Tom Wolfe
Doug Shomette, editor

The Critical Response to Ann Beattie
Jaye Berman Montresor, editor

The Critical Response to Eugene O'Neill
John H. Houchin, editor

The Critical Response to Bram Stoker
Carol A. Senf, editor

The Critical Response to John Cheever
Francis J. Bosha, editor

The Critical Response to Ann Radcliffe
Deborah D. Rogers, editor

The Critical Response to Joan Didion
Sharon Felton, editor

The Critical Response to Tillie Olsen
Kay Hoyle Nelson and Nancy Huse, editors

The Critical Response to George Eliot
Karen L. Pangallo, editor

The Critical Response to Eudora Welty's Fiction

Edited by
Laurie Champion

Critical Responses in Arts and Letters, Number 12
Cameron Northouse, Series Adviser

Greenwood Press
Westport, Connecticut • London

Library of Congress Cataloging-in-Publication Data

The Critical response to Eudora Welty's fiction / edited by Laurie Champion.
p. cm.—(Critical responses in arts and letters, ISSN 1057–0993; no. 12)
Includes bibliographical references and index.
ISBN 0–313–28596–9 (alk. paper)
1.Welty, Eudora, 1909– —Criticism and interpretation.
I. Champion, Laurie. II. Series.
PS3545.E6Z635 1994
813′.52—dc20 93–43709

British Library Cataloguing in Publication Data is available.

Library of Congress Catalog Card Number: 93–43709
ISBN: 0–313–28596–9
ISSN: 1057–0993

First published in 1994

Greenwood Press, 88 Post Road West, Westport, CT 06881
An imprint of Greenwood Publishing Group, Inc.

Printed in the United States of America

The paper used in this book complies with the Permanent Paper Standard Issued by the National Information Standards Organization (Z39.48–1984).

10 9 8 7 6 5 4 3 2

Copyright Acknowledgments

The editor and publisher gratefully acknowledge permission for use of the following material:

Louise Bogan, "The Gothic South," *The Nation* magazine, The Nation Co., Inc., 1941.

Neil D. Isaacs, "Life for Phoenix," first published in Vol. 71, No. 1, *Sewanee Review*, 1963. Reprinted by permission of the editor.

Charles E. May, "Why Sister Lives at the P.O." Copyright © 1978. Reprinted by permission of Charles E. May.

Lionel Trilling, "American Fairy Tale," *The Nation* magazine, The Nation Co., Inc., 1942.

Merrill Maguire Skaggs, "The Uses of Enchantment in Frontier Humor and *The Robber Bridegroom*." Reprinted from *Studies in American Humor* 3 (October 1976): 96-102.

Barbara Harrell Carson, "Eudora Welty's Dance with Darkness: *The Robber Bridegroom*," first appeared in *The Southern Literary Journal* 20 (Spring 1988): 51-68. Reprinted by permission of *The Southern Literary Journal*.

Diana Trilling, "Fiction in Review," *The Nation* magazine, The Nation Co., Inc., 1943.

Peggy W. Prenshaw, "Persephone in Eudora Welty's 'Livvie,'" *Studies in Short Fiction* 17.2 (Spring 1980): 149-55. Reprinted by permission of *Studies in Short Fiction* and Newberry College.

Mary Alice Bookhart, "Eudora Welty." Review of *Delta Wedding*, by Eudora Welty. *The Clarion-Ledger*, 28 April 1946: 8. Reprinted by permission of *The Clarion-Ledger*, Jackson, Mississippi.

Diana Trilling, "Fiction in Review." Review of *Delta Wedding*, by Eudora Welty. *The Nation* magazine, The Nation Co., Inc., 1946.

Frank Hains, "Eudora Welty Talks about Her New Book, *Losing Battles*," *The Clarion-Ledger* 5 April 1970: 6F. Reprinted by permission of *The Clarion-Ledger*, 1970.

Louis Dollarhide, "Eudora Welty's *Losing Battles* Is Magnificent Feast." Review of *Losing Battles*, by Eudora Welty. *Mississippi Library News* (June 1970): 96-98. Reprinted with permission, *Mississippi Library News* (now *Mississipi Libraries*).

Louis D. Rubin, Jr., "Everything Brought out in the Open: Eudora Welty's *Losing Battles*." Reprinted from *The Hollins Critic* (June 1970), by permission.

Robert Drake, "Miss Welty's Wide World." Review of *Losing Battles*, by Eudora Welty. Copyright 1970 Christian Century Foundation. Reprinted by permission from the June 17, 1970 issue of *The Christian Century*.

James Boatwright, "Speech and Silence in *Losing Battles*," *Shenandoah* 25.3 (Spring 1974): 3-14. Copyright 1974 by Washington & Lee University, reprinted from *Shenandoah*: The Washington & Lee University Review, with the permission of the Editor.

James Boatwright, "The Continuity of Love." Review of *The Optimist's Daughter*, by Eudora Welty. *New Republic* 10 June 1972. Reprinted by permission of *The New Republic*, © 1972, The New Republic, Inc.

Cleanth Brooks, "The Past Reexamined: *The Optimist's Daughter*," first printed in *The Mississippi Quarterly*, Vol. 26, No.4, (Fall, 1973).

Elmo Howell, "Eudora Welty and the Use of Place in Southern Fiction," *Arizona Quarterly* 28 (Autumn 1972): 248-56. Reprinted by permission of *Arizona Quarterly*.

John A. Allen, "Eudora Welty: The Three Moments," *The Virginia Quarterly Review* 51.4 (Autumn 1975): 605-27. Reprinted by permission of *The Virginia Quarterly Review*.

Anne Tyler, "The Fine, Full World of Welty." Review of *The Collected Stories of Eudora Welty*, by Eudora Welty. *Washington Evening Star*, 26 October 1980: D1+. Reprinted by permission of the author.

Walter Clemons, "Songs of the South," from *Newsweek* 3 November 1980: 85-86. ©1980, Newsweek, Inc. All rights reserved. Reprinted by permission.

Jennifer Uglow, "Journeys out of Separateness." Review of *The Collected Stories of Eudora Welty*, by Eudora Welty. *The Times Literary Supplement*, 8 Jan. 1982. ©Times Newspapers Ltd (London) 1982: 26. Reproduced from *The Times Literary Supplement* by kind permission.

Anne Tyler, "A Visit with Eudora Welty," *The New York Times Book Review*, 2 November 1980: 33-34. Copyright 1980 by The New York Times Company. Reprinted by permission. Reprinted by permission of Anne Tyler.

Robert Drake, "The Loving Vision." Review of *The Collected Stories of Eudora Welty*, by Eudora Welty. *Modern Age* 27.1 (Winter 1983): 96-97. Reprinted by permission of *Modern Age*.

Sara McAlpin BVM, "Family in Eudora Welty's Fiction," *The Southern Review*. Used with permission of Sara McAlpin BVM; essay first published in *The Southern Review* 18.3 (July 1982): 480-94.

Harriet Pollack, "On Welty's Use of Allusion: Expectations and Their Revision in 'The Wide Net,' *The Robber Bridegroom*, and 'At The Landing,'" *The Southern Quarterly* 29.1 (Fall 1990): 5-31. Reprinted with permission from *The Southern Quarterly*.

Alice Walker, "At First," in *Good Night Willie Lee, I'll See You in the Morning*. Excerpt reprinted by permission of Doubleday, a division of Bantam, Doubleday, Dell Publishing Group, Inc.

Excerpts from Robert Graves's "To Juan at the Winter Solstice" and "Ulysses" reprinted by permission of A.P. Watt Ltd on behalf of The Trustees of the Robert Graves Copyright Trust. Graves, Robert. "To Juan at the Winter Solstice." *Collected Poems 1975*. New York: Oxford UP, 1975. 137. Graves Robert. "Ulysses." *Collected Poems 1975*. New York: Oxford University Press, 1975. 56. Reprinted by permission of Oxford University Press.

Excerpts from "A Worn Path" in *A Curtain of Green and Other Stories*, copyright © 1941 by Eudora Welty, © renewed 1969 by Eudora Welty, reprinted by permission of Harcourt Brace & Company and by permission of Russell & Volkening as agents for the author.

Excerpts from "At The Landing," in *The Wide Net and Other Stories*, copyright © 1943 by Eudora Welty, © renewed 1971 by Eudora Welty, reprinted by permission of Harcourt Brace & Company and by permission of Russell & Volkening as agents for the author.

Excerpts from *Delta Wedding*, copyright © 1946, 1945, © renewed 1974, 1973 by Eudora Welty, reprinted by permission of Harcourt Brace & Company and by permission of Russell & Volkening as agents for the author.

Excerpts from *Losing Battles* by Eudora Welty. Copyright © 1970 by Eudora Welty, reprinted by permission of Random House, Inc. and by permission of Russell & Volkening as agents for the author.

Excerpts from *The Optimist's Daughter* by Eudora Welty. Copyright © 1969, 1972 by Eudora Welty, reprinted by permission of Random House, Inc. and by permission of Russell & Volkening as agents for the author.

Excerpts from *The Ponder Heart* by Eudora Welty, copyright © 1954, 1953 and © renewed 1982, 1981 by Eudora Welty, reprinted by permission of Harcourt Brace & Company and by permission of Russell & Volkening as agents for the author.

Excerpts from *The Robber Bridegroom* by Eudora Welty, copyright © 1942, © renewed 1970 by Eudora Welty, reprinted by permission of Harcourt Brace & Company and by permission of Russell & Volkening as agents for the author.

Every reasonable effort has been made to trace the owners of copyright materials in this book, but in some cases this has proven impossible. The author and publisher will be glad to receive information leading to more complete acknowledgments in subsequent printings of the book and in the meantime extend their apologies for any omissions.

Contents

Losing Battles **1970**

The Optimist's Daughter **1972**

General Criticism 1972-1979

The Collected Stories of Eudora Welty **1980**

General Criticism 1980-1993

Series Foreword

Critical Responses in Arts and Letters is designed to present a documentary history of highlights in the critical reception to the body of work of writers and artists and to individual works that are generally considered to be of major importance. The focus of each volume in this series is basically historical. The introductions to each volume are themselves brief histories of the critical response an author, artist, or individual work has received. This response is then further illustrated by reprinting a strong representation of the major critical reviews and articles that have collectively produced the author's, artist's, or work's critical reputation.

The scope of *Critical Responses in Arts and Letters* knows no chronological or geographical boundaries. Volumes under preparation include studies of individuals from around the world and in both contemporary and historical periods.

Each volume is the work of an individual editor, who surveys the entire body of criticism on a single author, artist, or work. The editor then selects the best material to depict the critical response received by an author or artist over his/her entire career. Documents produced by the author or artist may also be included when the editor finds that they are necessary to a full understanding of the materials at hand. In circumstances where previous, isolated volumes of criticism on a particular individual or work exist, the editor carefully selects material that better reflects the nature and directions of the critical response over time.

In addition to the introduction and the documentary section, the editor of each volume is free to solicit new essays on areas that may not have been adequately dealt with in previous criticism. Also, for volumes on living writers and artists, new interviews may be included, again at the discretion of the volume's editor. The volumes also provide a supplementary bibliography and are fully indexed.

While each volume in *Critical Responses to Arts and Letters* is unique, it is also hoped that in combination they form a useful, documentary history of the critical response to the arts, and one that can be easily and profitably employed by students and scholars.

Cameron Northouse

The Critical Response to Eudora Welty's Fiction

Introduction

Eudora Welty holds a prominent position among Southern writers, receiving critical attention in publications that scan a wide range of interests. Journals that specialize in American literature, journals that publish general essays, and journals that focus on Southern literature frequently include articles about Welty's works.

Although Welty has not written a biography, in *One Writer's Beginnings*, she describes her childhood. *One Writer's Beginnings* is taken from a series of lectures Welty gave at Harvard University, consisting of three essays: "Listening," "Learning to See," and "Finding a Voice." Welty has also written scholarly essays and published her photography. Welty's major works of fiction include four collections of short stories, three short novels, and two full-length novels.

Welty's collections of short stories are reprinted in *The Collected Stories of Eudora Welty*, which contains all the stories in *A Curtain of Green*, *The Wide Net*, *The Golden Apples*, *The Bride of the Innisfallen*, and two previously uncollected stories. Many of Welty's stories are included in short story, American literature, and Southern literature anthologies. Welty's works have also been adapted for the stage and for television. Joseph Fields and Jerome Chodorov's 1956 stage adaptation of *The Ponder Heart* was a Broadway success. The WPA Theatre produced "The Hitch-Hikers" for the stage, and "Why I Live at the P.O." and "The Wide Net" have been filmed as part of the American Short Stories film series.

A Curtain of Green and Other Stories 1941

In 1941, Doubleday published *A Curtain of Green and Other Stories*. In her introduction to this collection, Katherine Anne Porter begins with a brief biographical summary of Welty. She relates Welty's life to her writing career:

> But there is an ancient system of ethics, an unanswerable, indispensable moral law, on which she is grounded firmly, and this, it would seem to me is ample domain enough; these laws have never been the peculiar property of any party or creed or nation, they relate to that true and human world of which the artist is a living part; and when he dissociates himself from it in favor of a set of political, which is to say, inhuman, rules, he cuts himself away from his proper society—living men.[1]

More specifically, she describes the stories in *A Curtain of Green*: "In all of these stories, varying as they do in excellence, I find nothing false or labored, no diffusion of interest, no wavering of mood—the approach is direct and simple in method, though the themes and moods are anything but simple, and there is even in the smallest story a sense of power in reserve which makes me believe firmly that, splendid beginning that this is, it is only the beginning."

In his 1941 essay, Dale Mullen sums up the initial response to *A Curtain of Green*. He observes that "Welty's *A Curtain of Green* has received a critical attention such as has been accorded to no other first book by a Mississippian in the last decade."[2] Many of the early reviewers comment on the grotesque elements reflected in the stories. Both the *Time* reviewer and John Lane, writing for *Times Literary Supplement*, praise Welty's talents as a short story writer but view the grotesque elements as flaws in the stories. The *Times* reviewer says, "she has a strong taste for melodrama, and is preoccupied with the demented, the deformed, the queer, the highly spiced. Of the 17 pieces, only two report states of experience which could be called normal, only one uses the abnormal to illuminate any human mystery deeper than its own."[3] John Lane says Welty has "a leaning towards the bizarre, a fondness for the afflicted in mind or body and for strange violences of behavior, that needs to be held in check."[4] *New York Times* critic Marianne Hauser and *Accent* critic Arthur J. Carr see the grotesque elements as strengths in these stories. Hauser observes the stories as "dark, weird and often unspeakably sad in mood, yet there is no trace of personal in them, neither harshness nor sentimental resignation; but an alert, constant awareness of life as a whole, and that profound, intuitive understanding of life which enables the artist to accept it."[5] Carr sees the grotesque as one element in Welty's multidimensional theme of moral paradox. He says that because the characters do not understand fully the action Welty portrays, they act "'unconsciously,' even deterministically," and with this portrayed attitude, Welty fashions both comic and tragic interpretations.[6]

In their reviews, Kay Boyle and Louise Bogan compare Welty with other writers. Boyle's "Full-Length Portrait" begins with a discussion of Porter's introduction, then compares Welty with Emily Dickinson. She adds that Welty is "one of the most gifted and interesting short-story writers of our time."[7] Bogan's "The Gothic South" compares Welty's ability to describe details with Gogol's penchant for detail. She commends Welty's method of writing, complimenting her as "mistress of her material."[8]

Critical approaches to *The Curtain of Green* include Fredrick Brantley's "A Curtain of Green: Themes and Attitudes," Robert Griffin's "Eudora Welty's *A Curtain of Green*," and Michael Kreyling's "Modernism in Welty's *A Curtain of Green and Other Stories*." Brantley examines themes such as the characters' isolation and the secrets that control the protagonists.[9] Griffin explicates the stories in terms of Welty's use of poetic language,[10] and Kreyling traces the relationship between the stories and "the modern period that envelops [Welty's] Southern material."[11]

Many of the stories in *A Curtain of Green* have appeared in anthologies and have received extensive critical attention as individual short stories. Neil D. Isaacs focuses his discussion on "A Worn Path," and Charles E. May concentrates on "Why I Live at the P.O." Isaacs, in "Life for Phoenix," examines the meaning of "A Worn Path" that is strengthened by Welty's technique. Among other things, he discusses the plot, setting, and various symbols and metaphors in terms of Christian themes. More broadly, his analysis reveals themes that concern the meaning of life.[12] In "Why Sister Lives at the P.O.," May looks at the characterization of Sister in terms of R.D. Laing's "unembodied self." He comments on the characters' lack of effective communication, and he illustrates ironies in the story.[13]

The Robber Bridegroom 1942

In 1942, Doubleday published Welty's first novel, *The Robber Bridegroom*. Most early reviewers remark on the fairly-tale motifs of the story, noting its allusions to Grimm's Fairy Tales, particularly Grimm's *Robber Bridegroom*. Marianne Hauser, writing for *New York Times Book Review*, calls it

> an American fairy tale, and if we think of America in the old terms of gigantic forests, savage Indians, heavy-fisted pioneers and roving highwaymen, it seems no surprise that "The Robber Bridegroom" outdoes in its fantastic exuberance any of the fairy tales collected by the Brothers Grimm from the folklore of old Germany's elfin woods.
>
> And yet Miss Welty has transplanted many elements from those stories into her book, has taken themes from the Brothers Grimm's "Robber Bridegroom," from their "Goosegirl," and even from "Snow White." She has done this with her tongue in her cheek, as if to say: Just watch and see what happens to those fairytales if I let them run

wild in the big woods of the old Natchez country, with Indians lurking behind the bushes.[14]

According to Charles Shattuck, "Miss Welty has toned down the jadish bloodthirstiness of the story as the Grimm brothers recorded it, and vastly heightened the decorative and the marvelous. It is a playful book, thematically delicate and elusive, on pleasure bent. The main pleasure perhaps, lies in the skillful weaving-in of dozens of fragments and motifs from dozens of other folk-tales that hover distantly on the edge of memory. . . . This rich synthesis I take to be the main pleasure, at least for anyone who, like the author, loves old legends."[15]

Alfred Kazin, writing for *New York Herald Tribune Books*, says Welty

is writing out of a joy in the world she has restored, and with an eye toward the comedy and poetry embedded in it.

That joy is the great thing in "The Robber Bridegroom," and explains why it is cast as a fairy tale. We have moved here into a world where the image we all carry of the past has been restored to a pure frame of myth. . . .

Every myth we tell each other today, or try to restore, is only the symbol of our own longing, and turns upon itself. Not the smallest part of Miss Welty's rather exquisite achievement is the skill with which she reminds us that the enchanted forest is for us to recapture—and is forever dead.[16]

Although many reviewers favor Welty's allusion to fairy tales in *The Robber Bridegroom*, Lionel Trilling's "American Fairy Tale" implies that Welty's allusions may not be quite so successful. He disapproves of the prose style Welty uses, calling it "conscious simplicity."[17]

John Peale Bishop, in "The Violent Country," comments on Welty's allusions to the Grimm fairy tale, but suggests the Cupid and Psyche myth as a stronger derivative for *The Robber Bridegroom*. He points out the identity question as one of the strongest themes in the book.[18]

Later critical response to *The Robber Bridegroom* includes two 1973 essays by Charles C. Clark and Gordon E. Slethaug. In "*The Robber Bridegroom*: Realism and Fantasy on the Natchez Trace," Clark says the novella uses irony to portray a fictional combination of history, frontier humor, folklore, and fairy tale to express "the predicament of man, a creature both blessed and cursed with a dual nature."[19] In "Initiation in Eudora Welty's *The Robber Bridegroom*," Slethaug argues that external events lead to Clement and Rosamond's internal questions that involve the nature of evil and good. Both Clement and Rosamond are initiated into life's complexity, as manifested in their having "a deeper awareness of themselves" and a more intense "understanding and acceptance of life, including an acceptance of the inextricability of good and evil."[20]

More recent critical views of *The Robber Bridegroom* include Merrill Maguire Skaggs's 1976 essay "The Uses of Enchantment in Frontier Humor and *The Robber Bridegroom*," Warren French's 1979 essay "'All Things are Double': Eudora Welty as a Civilized Writer," Michael Kreyling's 1979 essay "Clement and the Indians: Pastoral and History in *The Robber Bridegroom*," and Barbara Harrell Carson's 1988 essay "Eudora Welty's Dance With Darkness: *The Robber Bridegroom*." As the title suggests, Skaggs's essay examines *The Robber Bridegroom* in terms of elements of enchantment found in frontier humor. Skaggs also relates Bruno Bettelheim's discussion of fairy tales to elements found in southwestern humor.[21] French relates *The Robber Bridegroom* to the European fairy tale, the American folk tale, and numerous modern works.[22] Kreyling looks at history and pastoral and their rivalry as reflected in elements of theme and style.[23] Carson's essay also appears in her book *Eudora Welty: Two Pictures at Once in Her Frame*. In her essay, she builds on earlier criticism that examines "the relationship between fairy tale and reality in . . . *The Robber Bridegroom*." She examines the book from a "larger metaphysical scheme—one which suggests that the moral weight of the tale comes down on the side of recognizing and accepting the unity of contraries in life . . . ." She sees fairy tale and history as merging to create a conflict between "the human impulse to simplify life" and the complexity of life.[24]

In "The *Robber Bridegroom* as a Capitalist Fable," Ellen L. Walker and Gerda Seaman demonstrate Welty's use of legend, fairy tale, and history to create her "comic retelling" of American culture's central experience: "the transformation of the forest to the market place."[25]

The Wide Net and Other Stories 1943

In 1943, Harcourt Brace published Welty's second collection of stories, *The Wide Net and Other Stories*. Among initial reviews are Eugene Armfield's and Katherine Woods's highly favorable reviews. Armfield, writing for *New York Times Book Review*, notes that "Not the least of Miss Welty's qualities is the fineness of her descriptive writing, her evocations of a gleaming fish, a bird, a battered house, a sunlit field filled with butterflies. The people are disarmingly 'ordinary' and the events have an air of casualness. . . . Most of the people you have met before, in real life or in other books. It is the touch of a very real talent which gives them life and variety and meaning."[26] Katherine Woods compares Welty's talent to Isak Dinesen's "in the sweep of its imagination, its communication of the dreamlike and the anachronistic, its ability to transport the reader alike into fantasy or realism, its complete fitness of form and substance which makes perfection of style." She adds that Welty's work has more gusto and that "there is a sound folk quality; the mind's reach may be distant, and subtle, but it is never nebulous, or strained. The book's quality is native, to the country and to the artist. And here we touch the limit of any comparison: beauty and fantasy are the artist's own approach to reality, the quest, that is forever individual, for fundamental truth."[27]

Some initial reviewers did not review *The Wide Net* so favorably. The *Time* reviewer says, "At her best, 34-year-old Miss Welty runs a photo-finish with the finest prose artists of her time and displays a delicateness of sensibility which borders at once on genius and indecency. Yet her finest writing is nearly always marred by such Celtic locutions as 'a sure man, very sure and tender'; and the sensibility is seldom grounded in anything remotely sensible."[28] Jean Stafford, writing for *Partisan Review*, remarks that Welty, "warily picking her way through meanings and the amorphous produce of the soul, or rocketing out of sight in a burst of fantasy, loses her humor, eaves fissures in her masonry, forgets her breeding, and writes eight stories in a language so vague that not only actual words but syntax itself have the improbable inexactitude of a verbal dream. Nor is the landscape any more precise, nor have the characters more than the most general physiognomy, the most uniform speech and attitudes and meditations."[29] In her review for *Nation*, Diana Trilling calls *The Wide Net* "a book of ballets, not of stories. . . ." She compares Welty's stories to Dali's paintings, referring to both artists as creators of "a myth of modern femininity."[30] Issac Rosenfield, in his review for *New Republic*, says that "A Still Moment" is "perfectly successful" yet suggests an implied anxiety causes Welty to force "a compensatory poetry upon her prose."[31]

More recent analyses of *The Wide Net* include essays by critics such as Garven Davenport, Jr., Albert J. Devlin, and Victor Thompson, who use various historical approaches in their assessments of the stories. Davenport, in "Renewal and Historical Consciousness in *The Wide Net*," illustrates that at least one character in each of the stories in *The Wide Net* faces a dark, mysterious, or dreamlike situation, which leads to renewed potentials for emotional enrichment. He says, "characters experience isolation and renewal and in doing so embody a concept of historical consciousness. . . . [Welty's] approach is through individual and very private characters who move often within rather limited horizons between isolation and inclusion in a universal network of human needs and desires."[32] In "Eudora Welty's Historicism: Method and Vision," Devlin concentrates primarily on "A Still Moment" and "First Love" to demonstrate Welty as historian. He shows how Welty "assimilates, selects, and transforms historical matter into satisfying aesthetic forms."[33] Thompson also discusses historical elements in "A Still Moment" and "First Love." In "The Natchez Trace in Eudora Welty's 'A Still Moment,'" Thompson concludes that Welty incorporates history and legend in "A Still Moment," modifying "them to conform to the theme of her story."[34] In "Aaron Burr in Eudora Welty's 'First Love,'" he compares Welty's Aaron Burr to the historical Aaron Burr.[35]

St. George Tucker Arnold, Jr. and Suzanne Marrs also consider history in their interpretations of "First Love." Arnold explicates "First Love" in terms of Welty's portrayal of regional history. He says Welty leads readers to identify with someone who participated in an historical event, thus confronting both "the region's collective experience and the very private, personal progress of the individual character in his attempt to deal with the happening." Thus, Welty transforms "historical abstraction to dramatic actuality."[36] Marrs demonstrates that the concluding paragraphs of "First Love" are based on historical fact.[37]

Pearl Amelia McHaney, in "Historical Perspectives in 'A Still Moment,'" offers historical background information that enhances readers' understanding of "A Still Moment." She gives details that demonstrate that Welty models "A Still Moment" after "three historical characters: Lorenzo Dow, Methodist minister; James Murrell, bandit of the southwest; and John James Audubon, ornithologist and painter."[38]

Peggy Whitman Prenshaw's "Persephone in Eudora Welty's 'Livvie'" presents an evaluation that concentrates on a specific story in the collection *The Wide Net*. As her title suggests, Prenshaw demonstrates the parallels between characters in "Livvie," especially Livvie, and the Persephone myth.

General Criticism 1943-1945

In 1944, Robert Penn Warren wrote "The Love and Separateness in Miss Welty." In this seminal essay, Warren responds to Diana Trilling's review of *The Wide Net*. He discusses "the special tone and mood, the special perspective, the special sensibility" of the stories in *The Wide Net*. He says almost all characters in the stories are isolated, and it is this condition of isolation that yields the situation of the stories. These characters either try to escape their isolation, or the characters or the reader come to recognize the characters' isolated states. He says the fundamental theme is "'Innocence and Experience'" and that contradictions "are understood not in mechanical but vital terms: the contrasts provide the terms of human effort, for the dream must be carried to, submitted to, the world, innocence to experience, love to knowledge, knowledge to the fact, individuality to communion."[39]

Warren's influential essay introduced new critical approaches to Welty's work and is essential for Welty scholars. It is not included in this volume because it is reprinted in his collection of essays and in two Welty anthologies and is therefore easily available to scholars.[40]

Delta Wedding 1946

In 1946, Harcourt Brace published Welty's first full-length novel, *Delta Wedding*. Initially, the novel received mixed reviews. Some reviewers, such as Sterling North, Issac Rosenfield and Diana Trilling do not review the novel favorably. North, writing for *Atlanta Constitution*, says the novel is obscure and describes Welty's style as that of an amateur.[41] In his *New Republic* review, Rosenfield objects to the dullness of the novel, saying Welty deals with the sensations of a society, not truly a society.[42] Diana Trilling's review for *Nation* discusses Welty's novel in terms of her continued interest in regional literature. Others, such as the *Christian Century* reviewer, comment on the weak plot.[43]

Other reviewers praise Welty's accomplishments. The *Minneapolis Sunday Tribune* reviewer, Hamilton Basso, Paul Engle, and Mary Alice Bookhart defend the plot. The *Minneapolis Sunday Tribune* reviewer comments on Welty's use of a Jamesian technique to create a mosaic-like portrait of people. He says, "Nothing of big moment happens, but in this kind of story nothing needs to."[44] Basso says that even though "nothing 'happens' in *Delta Wedding*, . . . *everything* happens." He calls her portrayal of the Southern family "nothing short of wonderful" and her use of dialogue "a minor triumph."[45] Engle says that the merit of the novel is that it cannot be summarized. He says Welty's style presents characters psychologically and adds that the novel is "as solid writing as you will read this year."[46] Bookhart says Welty seems more concerned with creating the mood than with the plot. She commends Welty's clearly presented observations and her attention to detail.[47] John Crowe Ransom considers *Delta Wedding* a "full-length formal novel, with a content which is really capable of sustained presentation. [Welty] writes here according to some of the solidest canons of fiction." He compares her with Virginia Woolf, then addresses the critics who "will not be able to give credence to her exhibit of so exotic a minority culture in action down in the South." He sees the plot as moving between "drama of dialogue and external action, on the one hand, and interior monologue on the other," creating complexity and richness.[48] Charles Poore, writing for *New York Times Book Review*, observes that Welty presents her distinctive perception of the South. He says *Delta Wedding* shares "the excellencies of her short stories with all the advantages of a wider pattern. It gives her a chance to tell us more about her people and their ways of life; it gives us the pleasure of seeing a full drama rather than a one-act play.

And, beyond that, it is true to human life as you will find it at a considerable distance from the Mississippi Delta."[49]

Later critical response to *Delta Wedding* includes critiques by John Edward Hardy and Elmo Howell. In "Delta Wedding as Region and Symbol," Hardy analyzes the novel in terms of its formal structure—"a version of pastoral," but with "fully *conscious* exploring of the implications of the mode . . . for the *mores* of the society which produced it." He demonstrates the complex theme and structure and notes the "poetic order—of recurrent themes, symbols, and motives of symbolic metaphor."[50] Howell, in "Eudora Welty's Comedy of Manners," calls *Delta Wedding* Welty's "most impressive accomplishment." He views character and incident as subordinate to the mood the novel evokes. He provides a genealogy of the Fairchild family, saying, "the purpose of the novel is to show the importance of family ties and the way one generation impinges on another."[51]

More recent criticism of *Delta Wedding* includes Peggy Prenshaw's "Cultural Patterns in Eudora Welty's *Delta Wedding* and 'The Demonstrators,'" M.E. Bradford's "Fairchild as Composite Protagonist in *Delta Wedding*, and Douglas Messerli's "The Problem of Time in Welty's *Delta Wedding*." Prenshaw argues that Welty often draws material for her fiction from her own Mississippi environment, thus her fictional work "is remarkable not only for structural and thematic features, but for its portrayal and interpretation of the South." She says the Fairchilds "serve as a microcosm of the agrarian life—the dependence on the seasons as a regulatory force on one's life, the isolation from the world at large, the family unity, and the strong ties to the land and to a sense of history."[52] Bradford argues that the "composite protagonist" of the novel is the Fairchild family. The central action is the struggle for the Fairchilds to maintain the social bonds that connect individuals to the family and the inward feelings of the individuals that comprise the family.[53] Messerli argues that *Delta Wedding* reflects Welty's "preoccupation with time" more than any of her other novels. Among other things, he discusses the ways the characters perceive time in terms of the past, the present, and the future.[54]

Even more recent analyses include interpretations by Barbara Ladd, Albert J. Devlin, and Sharlee Mullins Glenn. In "'Coming Through': The Black Initiate in *Delta Wedding*," Ladd examines the changes the black characters in the novel experience. She concludes that Welty desires for these characters to have "the same impulse to love and separateness as well as the same power to change the community that she claims for her white characters."[55] In "Meeting the World in *Delta Wedding*," Devlin examines *Delta Wedding* as it reflects Welty's "artistic maturity" and the "internal dynamics of [her] distinguished literary career."[56] Glenn's "In and Out the

Circle: The Individual and the Clan in Eudora Welty's *Delta Wedding*" portrays the "conflict between the need for individual autonomy and the equally powerful need for community and family" as one of the main themes in the novel. The circle is a metaphor to explore the relationship between the individual and the clan; those inside the circle represent members of the Fairchild clan, those outside the circle represent individuals outside the clan, and those in intersecting circles represent those who are both part of the clan and an individual outside the clan.[57]

General Criticism 1946-1948

In "Fantasy in the Fiction of Eudora Welty," Eunice Glenn argues that it seems that the significance of Miss Welty's method would be "in the interrelationship of the external and internal—reality and imagination." Glenn compares Welty's stories to Hawthorne, while discussing the way magnified reality becomes fantasy in Welty's stories. In Welty's stories, the dream, which reflects the irrational world, fuses with logic and produces a reconciliation. Fantasy enhances and contributes to the interpretation of ordinary experiences.[58]

The Golden Apples 1949

In 1949, Harcourt Brace published *The Golden Apples*. Initially, many reviewers such as Francis Steegmuller, John Farrelly, and Lee E. Cannon comment on *The Golden Apples* as a unified collection of stories. Steegmuller, writing for *New York Times Book Review* says, "The whole thing is a 'good story' made up of countless 'good stories'. . . . Thanks to the unity of its parts, this book passes beyond any need of being evaluated on the crowded, dreary judging stand of the contemporary short story. It is a work of art at once eloquent and entertaining, whose very form is in a lovely, nonspectacular way the original creation of an invaluable artist."[59] Farrelly says *The Golden Apples* should be read as a novel. He sees time as "the really important character."[60] Cannon says *Delta Wedding* is a novel in a Pickwickian sense. Cannon comments on Welty's skill in characterization and phrasing, adding that she creates "a philosophical significance."[61]

Initial reviewers Hershell Brickell and Hamilton Basso remark on the mythical allusions in *The Golden Apples*. Brickell notes that readers must read the entire book to understand the "full impact" of the stories. . . . He observes, "Miss Welty is writing at two levels, of things as they are, and of their relationship to classical and medieval mythology. . . ."[62] Basso remarks that Welty's Morgana is "just as real" as Faulkner's

Yoknapatawpha County. "Her book is best described as the chronicle of a small Southern town" that represents "the whole Deep South. . . ." *The Golden Apples* "is in no sense a 'regional' novel." The characters are Southern just as the characters in Gogol's 'Dead Souls' are Russian, but "their problems and preoccupations, their joys and sorrows are basic everywhere." He praises the way Welty handles the children and her "eye for significant detail, a nice sense of the comic and the bizarre, and, above everything else, a gift for language."[63]

Margaret Marshall criticizes Welty's use of an "'our town'" device, a device she says has the fatal disadvantage of neglecting to portray characters other than "as 'characters' in 'our town'. . . ."[64] However, Louis D. Rubin, Jr. sees the characters in *The Golden Apples* as "superb creatures of fiction." He says the characters "seem almost to take on a mythlike aura."[65]

Critics of *The Golden Apples* continue to analyze the structural unity of the stories and Welty's allusions to myth in the stories. Wendell V. Harris, in "The Thematic Unity of Welty's *The Golden Apples*," concentrates on the complex technical devices in the collection of stories. He examines distinct techniques that produce various themes.[66] William M. Jones, in "The Plot as Search," argues that both author and reader search for plot. He says Welty takes readers "with her on the plot search, [but] she also seems to regard the entire collection of stories as a psychotherapeutic exercise." Readers are never really sure whether their own imaginations form meanings of the book as a whole or whether Welty consciously shapes their interpretations, combining the mythic and the real and making them seem a unified whole.[67] In "Technique as Myth: The Structure of *The Golden Apples*," Danièle Pitavy-Souques demonstrates the depth of *The Golden Apples*, relating the Perseus myth to Welty's artistic technique.[68] Thomas L. McHaney, in "Eudora Welty and the Multitudinous Golden Apples," provides a comprehensive study of mythical allusions in *The Golden Apples*. He shows the "almost symphonic orchestration of closely related parallels between old myth and modern reality" as the form of the book, a form that "structures, and thus properly reveals several meanings of the golden apples."[69]

Critics also discuss perception, duality, disruption of unity, mistaken identity, and Welty's artistic patterns as elements in *The Golden Apples*. In "Seeing Double in *The Golden Apples*," J.A. Bryant, Jr. discusses the perception of the characters that somewhat necessitates the "total vision." He observes that when these characters continue in this perception, it sometimes motivates them "to go on strange quests or otherwise wander from the patterns of normal behavior."[70] "The Duality of Morgana: The Making of Virgie's Vision, the Vision of *The Golden Apples*," reflects Elaine Upton Pugh's examination of Cassie and Virgie in light of conflicting phases of the sun and moon. She relates these conflicts to aspects of *The Golden Apples*.[71] Susan V. Donaldson, in "Recovering Otherness in *The Golden Apples*," says Welty draws "our attention to the art of storytelling in . . . Morgana—and by implication in the South as well. . . ." Welty offers a two-fold revelation—Morgana appropriates storytelling to establish "communal unity" and recovering the otherness within Morgana's stories possibly to disrupt that unity.[72] Lowry Pei's "Dreaming the Other in *The Golden Apples*" demonstrates the narrative techniques of *The Golden Apples* as an expression of elusive realities that forces readers to develop thoughts and images. Similes move the reader toward "the linguistic equivalent of the 'mistaken' identities. . . ." Welty uses these arbitrary comparisons, challenging readers to imagine their own meaningful explanations.[73] Merrill Maguire Skaggs's, "Eudora Welty's 'I' of Memory" integrates "The Eye of Memory" television program with Welty's role as an artist. In "The Eye of Memory," Welty and other writers discuss Katherine Anne Porter. Welty offers "shrewd literary and psychological insights" about Porter and her work. Skaggs focuses on how Welty's comments reveal insights about "herself and her own work." She examines *The Golden Apples* in terms of "Welty's strengths and the practice of her own artistic ideals."[74]

General Criticism 1949-1953

Granville Hicks's 1952 essay "Eudora Welty" states that Welty is not merely a regional writer—her art is part of the Western literary tradition, an art that transcends mere Southern geographical borders. He says events in her stories do not matter so much as the effect these events have on people—she is concerned with "states of mind," and she emphasizes "emotional states."[75]

In his 1953 essay "The World of Eudora Welty," Robert Daniel discusses wilderness, farm, small town, and metropolitan scenes of various works by Welty. He says parallels between Welty and Faulkner's scenes and historical periods result from their shared Mississippi heritage as much as from any direct influence. Eudora Welty's best work allows readers to feel "the form and pressure of a coherently organized view of the world," a view Welty possibly inherited from Faulkner. But her unique achievement is her portrayal of her characters' "deep, inward response" to conditions of their existence, an artistic gift that does not resemble any other writer's fiction.[76]

The Ponder Heart 1954

Harcourt Brace published *The Ponder Heart* in 1954. It won the William Dean Howells Medal of the Academy of Arts and Letters. Initially, *The*

Ponder Heart was one of Welty's most widely received books. Reviewers often remark that *The Ponder Heart* is a work that everyone can understand and read, and they comment on Welty's use of monologue and humor. The *Atlantic* reviewer says, "This is Edna Earle's story and she tells it in a rhythmical Southern monologue, confiding, defending, condemning, the honeysuckle flavoring of her words so beautifully at odds with her native shrewdness."[77] V.S. Pritchett praises Welty for creating Edna Earle's speech that reflects "headlong garrulity." He commends Welty's dialogue, saying her "first person singular has been caught, word by awful word, in all its affectionate self-importance, by a writer with a wonderful ear."[78] The *Jackson Daily News* reviewer says, "To some 'The Ponder Heart' will be no more than an amusing tale of extravagantly peculiar characters in a small Southern town. To others it will show the wistful remnants of a past era, rich inhumanity and lost emotions, whose sense of values is a fantasia of the inconsequential."[79] Granville Hicks says Welty avoids sentimentality, praising her great wisdom, humanity, and literary skill, which enable her to portray Uncle Daniel as a comic character who has below average intelligence without suggesting condescension or bad taste.[80] Although Shirley Barker says the climax marrs *The Ponder Heart*, she admires the humor, calling it "pure fun."[81] John Chapman does not review *The Ponder Heart* so favorably. He says the introduction is too long and that the "real reason for the whole story is the remarkable and truly comic courtroom scene."[82]

Much of the more recent criticism follows the pattern of the early reception of *The Ponder Heart*, discussing the humor and dialogue in the novel. In "Dialogue as a Reflection of Place in *The Ponder Heart*," Robert B. Holland demonstrates that the structure of the characters' dialogue vocalizes their culture.[83] Gerda Seaman and Ellen L. Walker, in "'It's All in a Way of Speaking': A Discussion of *The Ponder Heart*," suggest that Edna Earle tells about Uncle Daniel, but in doing so, she reveals her own story. Her narrative account reveals different perspectives, yet she acts as a "'self-justifying historian.'" She tells her tale "to justify the world as she sees it and to hide the world she does not wish to see."[84] Rachel V. Weiner's "Eudora Welty's *The Ponder Heart*: The Judgment of Art" sees Edna Earle as a realistic spokesperson for the Ponders, Clay, and the rural South. Edna Earle is "the rare historian of such places who is both personal and detached, indulgent and questioning, always watchful and yet well-spoken when the moment for openness is at hand."[85] Lynn Snyder, in "Rhetoric in *The Ponder Heart*," analyzes Edna Earle's speech as a rhetorical oral presentation that defends Uncle Daniel. The formal rhetoric of the courtroom fails to defend Uncle Daniel, but Edna Earle, "is a most persuasive advocate for Daniel, drawing her listener into her tale, arguing through the force of her own character, and intensifying the listener's and reader's emotional response."[86] In "Edna Earle Ponder's Good Country People," John L. Idol, Jr. discusses the characterization of Edna Earle in terms of her "small-town pugnacity and self-conceit, her image of herself as a member of the landed gentry now absorbed into the life of a small Southern town. . . ."[87]

Other topics for discussion of *The Ponder Heart* include Michael Kreyling's look at *The Ponder Heart* in terms of the Dionysian-Apollonian conflict.[88] Barbara Harrell Carson's "In the Heart of Clay: Eudora Welty's *The Ponder Heart*" presents Carson's conclusion that Edna Earle shifts and combines feelings, thoughts, and actions, without "hierarchical ordering"; Edna Earle represents "the whole human self."[89]

Jermone Chodorev and Joseph Field's 1956 adaptation of *The Ponder Heart* was a Broadway success. Frank Hains, writing for Jackson's *Clarion-Ledger*, says that the adaptation is done as well as could be done, given the limitations of the stage; however, he says the novel overshadows the adaptation.[90] Bette E. Barber's "Eudora Welty's *The Ponder Heart* Gets Rave Notices at Broadway" summarizes New York newspaper reviews of this production. She outlines reviews from *New York Herald Tribune*, *New York Times*, and *New York Daily News*, all favorable reviews.[91]

The Bride of the Innisfallen and Other Stories 1955

In 1955, Harcourt Brace published Welty's fourth collection of short stories, *The Bride of the Innisfallen and Other Stories*. Some reviewers such as Frances Gaither, Edward Weeks, and Thomas Arp comment on Welty's use of characters and settings from outside Mississippi. Gaither, writing for *New York Times Book Review* notes that three of the stories "concern journeys in latitudes where unfamiliar manners and idioms prevail. Miss Welty's talents, invested in these foreign ventures, have, however, suffered no adverse sea-change."[92] Weeks says Welty "is just as deft with Irishmen and Italians as with her own neighbors."[93] Arp, in his review for *San Francisco Chronicle*, says Welty departs from her usual Mississippi setting, demonstrating her use of various techniques, points-of-view, and types of characters. Arp also discusses a thematic thread that runs through all the stories, saying they all involve either a stated or an implied search for qualities such as love, happiness, knowledge, understanding, or identity.[94] Arthur Shay and Warren Beck praise elements of the individual stories and the overall collection. In *Chicago Sun Times*, Shay observes, "Eudora Welty stands about midway between those writers of first rank whose stories have beginnings, middles and ends, and those who offer meaty slices of life. Her stories are all center slices, all extremely well done."[95] In *Chicago Tribune*, Beck calls the collection "a fruition of sheer genius. Its vein is poetic, scrupulously conveying essences of experience in a subtle realism but uniquely accented and tinged by imagination."[96]

William Peden, in *Saturday Review*, also praises the collection as a whole, yet he does not review the title story so favorably. He says it seems more a "highly *private* game" than a story. However, he says the collection as a whole is remarkable, demonstrating that Welty stands in a class almost by herself, for "sheer virtuosity and variety."[97] In his review for *Shenandoah*, Fred Bornhauser discusses, among other things, Robert Penn Warren's theme of love and separateness in terms of *The Bride of the Innisfallen*.[98] Frank Hains's review for Jackson's *Clarion-Ledger* comments on the particular mood of each of the stories, saying the stories reflect warmth, tenderness, and humor.[99] The reviewer for the *Virginia Quarterly Review* also comments on the mood of the collection of stories. This reviewer says that *The Bride of the Innisfallen* may not be Welty's best work, yet he praises her as a "greatly gifted writer."[100]

The Bride of the Innisfallen has received less critical attention than some of Welty's works. Among this criticism are essays by Andrea Goudie, Noel Polk, and Alun R. Jones. Goudie, in "Eudora Welty's Circe: A Goddess Who Strove with Men," examines the allusions to myth and the mythic structure.[101] Polk, in "Water, Wanderers, and Weddings: Love in Eudora Welty," looks at water, wanderers, and weddings as symbols that reflect "the entire spectrum of things having to do with love relationships."[102] In "A Frail Travelling Coincidence: Three Later Stories of Eudora Welty," Jones concentrates on "The Bride of the Innisfallen," "No Place for You, My Love," and "Going to Naples." He identifies "An Odyssean wandering in search of lost happiness and innocence, a conviction that home is that state of mind, instantly recognized, when we are momentarily flooded with a sense of meaningful peace, of knowing that we are, if only momentarily, at home. When two people find that elusive sense of peaceful belonging together then we can say that they have found love."[103]

In an essay written for this collection, Albert J. Devlin focuses on "No Place for You, My Love." He analyzes the story in terms of its daring aesthetics, demonstrating it as "a special ferment in [Welty's] career."

General Criticism 1954-1969

The years 1954-1969 mark the beginning of extensive Welty scholarship. Essays on Welty's works in general include assessments by William M. Jones, Chester Eisinger, and Alun R. Jones. William M. Jones, in "Name and Symbol in the Prose of Eudora Welty," illustrates that because of her complex use of symbols and allusions to myth, Welty transcends mere regional writing. He analyzes Welty's works through *The Bride of the Innisfallen* and presents parallels between Welty's fiction and myth and folklore.[104] In his 1963 essay "Eudora Welty and the Triumph of the Imagination," Eisinger calls Welty's work "a major contribution to American literature of the twentieth century." He analyzes Welty's works as her development of a "new school of fiction" and her dedication "to the power and mystery of the imagination. . . ."[105] Alun R. Jones, in his 1963 essay "The World of Love: The Fiction of Eudora Welty," comments that although Welty explores the Southern world in her fiction, her exploration of "human nature and the human dilemma" make her art distinctive. He says that Welty "restores our illusions about the world of love, concluding that "an elegant and correct compassion" characterizes her fiction.[106]

In the '60s, before the publication of *Losing Battles* or *The Optimist's Daughter*, critics such as Ruth M. Vande Kieft, Alfred Appel, Jr., J.A. Bryant, and Neil Isaacs wrote books or pamphlets on Welty's works. The most important of these are Vande Kieft's book and Isaacs's pamphlet. Published in 1962, Vande Kieft's influential *Eudora Welty* was published as a volume in Twayne's United States Authors Series. Vande Kieft's *Eudora Welty* was then and still is the best introduction to Welty's fiction. In 1987, Vande Kieft expanded and revised the first edition to include Welty's works since 1962. Most critics consider Vande Kieft's *Eudora Welty* among the most important contributions to Welty scholarship.[107]

Isaacs's *Eudora Welty* appeared in the Steck-Vaughn Southern Writers Series. Among other things, Isaacs discusses Welty's allusions to myth in terms of the opposing forces of the summer king and the winter king. He also categorizes some of Welty's stories as "performances," demonstrating that Welty presents the performances from the point of view of adopted characters who are clearly removed "from her own."[108]

Alfred Appel, Jr.'s *A Season of Dreams: The Fiction of Eudora Welty* was published in 1965, a volume in the Southern Literary Studies Series.[109] Appel's most important chapters discuss Welty's technique and her portrayal of Negro characters. J.A. Bryant, Jr.'s *Eudora Welty*, a 1968 pamphlet in the Minnesota Pamphlets on American Writers Series, provides a general introduction to Welty's works.[110]

In 1969, James Boatwright edited a special Welty issue of *Shenandoah*. Distinguished writers such as Malcolm Cowley, Martha Graham, Walker Percy, Allen Tate, and Robert Penn Warren pay a special tribute to Welty. Reynolds Price's "The Onlooker, Smiling: An Early Reading of *The Optimist's Daughter*," Alun Jones's "A Frail Travelling Coincidence: Three

Later Stories of Eudora Welty," and essays by Eudora Welty, Nash K. Burger, Diarmuid Russell, R. B. Heilman, Ashley Brown, and Joyce Carol Oates also appear in the issue.

Losing Battles 1970

In 1970, Random House published Welty's second full-length novel, *Losing Battles*. *Losing Battles* was Welty's first major fictional work in fifteen years and was given almost unanimous favorable reviews. James Boatwright, Joyce Carol Oates, Reynolds Price, and Louis Dollarhide comment on the humor of the novel. Boatwright, writing for *New York Times Book Review*, says *Losing Battles* proves that Welty has the "surest comic sense of any American writer alive." He says her comedy "takes no easy liberties, . . . presents character without fake compassion or amused condescension, a comedy that releases, illuminates, renews our own seeing, that moves in full knowledge of lose, bondage, panic and death."[111] In *Atlantic*, Joyce Carol Oates says the novel depends "upon interludes of comedy and charm" because the "serious social and psychological concerns are muted. . . ."[112] Reynolds Price, in his *Washington Post* review, compares the depth of the novel with *The Tempest*, *The Winter's Tale*, *War and Peace* and equates the humor of the novel to the humor of *Huckleberry Finn*.[113] In his review for *Mississippi Library News*, Dollarhide comments on the broad range of Welty's humor in the novel. He points out the multifarious humor, a humor comprised of situation, character, and conversation.[114]

Linda Kuehl groups Welty with writers such as Conrad, Virginia Woolf, James Joyce, Faulkner and Beckett, who she says write fiction that "defies intellectual restatement," providing indescribable and elusive experiences.[115] Jack Kroll and Howard Moss allude to the epic-like nature of the novel in their reviews. Kroll, writing for *Newsweek*, says Welty handles the novel "as if it were the stuff of an epic, which in a sense it certainly is."[116] Moss, in his *New Yorker* review, observes that Welty unifies folk tale, metaphor, and realism to create "an epic of kin rather than a family chronicle."[117] In his essay-review for *Hollins Critic*, Louis D. Rubin, Jr. calls Welty "a major writer, one of the three or four most important writers to come out of twentieth-century America." Along with his discussion of *Losing Battles*, he provides a brief discussion of *Delta Wedding* and a more in-depth discussion of *The Golden Apples*, the work he calls Welty's "masterpiece."[118] In his review for *Christian Century*, Robert Drake says that he does not place *Losing Battles* in the front rank of Welty's fiction, yet he refers to Welty as "one of the most distinguished of 20th century American writers of fiction."[119]

Frank Hains presents his interview with Eudora Welty in "Eudora Welty Talks about Her New Book, *Losing Battles*." In this interview, Hains quotes Welty as saying, "I'm content with the way I wrote [*Losing Battles*]—it's the only way I can. . . ." She also says she hopes that the novel is a comedy and remarks that she does not intend for the title to be pessimistic.[120]

Losing Battles has received much critical attention since its publication. Some topics for discussion have been on interpretations that focus on the family and on analyses that concentrate on the multifarious conflicts in the novel. William E. McMillen and Peggy Prenshaw discuss the conflicts in *Losing Battles*. In "Conflict and Resolution in Welty's *Losing Battles*," McMillen discusses the subtle movements that do not always lead to definite conclusions. He traces the events that lead to Jack and Gloria's reconciliation with their psychological conflicts.[121] Prenshaw's "The Harmonies of *Losing Battles*" begins with a survey of the critics' initial response to *Losing Battles*. She then focuses on how Welty juxtaposes opposite forces in much of her work. She analyzes the theme and form of *Losing Battles* in light of its "pattern of reconciliation and balance," what she calls harmonies.[122]

As his title suggests, in "Speech and Silence in *Losing Battles*," James Boatwright presents his discussion of the significance of speech and silence in *Losing Battles*.[123] Larry J. Reynolds, in "Enlightening Darkness: Theme and Structure in Eudora Welty's *Losing Battles*," demonstrates how Welty's subtly reveals her narrative, relying heavily on dialogue, dramatic event, and a restricted use of imagery to expose serious issues that involve human existence.[124] Prenshaw's anthology *Eudora Welty: Critical Essays* includes five essays that concentrate primarily on *Losing Battles*.[125]

The Optimist's Daughter 1972

A shorter version of *The Optimist's Daughter* first appeared in a 1969 issue of *New Yorker*. Reynolds Price's bases his essay "The Onlooker Smiling: An Early Reading of *The Optimist's Daughter*" on this *New Yorker* version. Price argues that Welty maintains the position of the onlooker and identifies vision as a main concern of the novel. He calls *The Optimist's Daughter* Welty's "strongest, richest work." Price's essay first appeared in the *Shenandoah* special issue and is reprinted in Turner and Harding's anthology, Harold Bloom's anthology, and in Price's own collection of essays, *A Common Room*.[126]

In 1972, Random House published the novel version of *The Optimist's Daughter*. *The Optimist's Daughter*, like *Losing Battles*, received almost unanimously favorable reviews. Reviewers such as Howard Moss and Granville Hicks comment on Welty's universal appeal. Moss, writing for

New York Times Book Review, praises it as Welty's best book. Moss says, "Known as a 'Southern regionalist,' Miss Welty is too good for pigeonholing labels." In the novel, "Two kinds of people, two versions of life, two contending forces in America collide in 'The Optimist's Daughter.'"[127] Hicks points out that Welty reaches the universal level through the regional level: "*The Optimist's Daughter* is not so much about Mount Salus as about . . . the human condition."[128] The reviewer for *Hudson Review* views Welty's subject as the connection "between feeling and perception." This reviewer says Welty combines "Chekhovian understatement with Faulknerian verve" and adds that *The Optimist's Daughter* demonstrates Welty's "powers at their best."[129] The *Time* reviewer thinks that *The Optimist's Daughter* is Welty's most "inward, contemplative book."[130] James Boatwright calls Welty "a master of narrative" in his review for *Shenandoah*. He provides a summary of the plot and says the scene where Laurel spends her last night home is the "strongest and most mysterious scene in the book. . . ."[131]

Cleanth Brooks, in his influential essay "The Past Reexamined: *The Optimist's Daughter*," discusses the plot of *The Optimist's Daughter* in terms of Laurel's psychological journey into her past. He traces events that lead to Laurel's understanding of her past and her discoveries about herself.[132]

Critical essays on *The Optimist's Daughter* include examinations that involve discussions of symbolism, imagery, and recurring patterns in the novel. John F. Desmond, Robert L. Phillips, Marilyn Arnold, Noaka Fuwa Thorton, and Gail Mortimer take this approach in their analyses. John F. Desmond's "Pattern and Vision in *The Optimist's Daughter*" portrays his insights that Welty's main subject is "vision itself—the whole range of perception and blindness, feeling and insensitivity. . . ." He explores the "images of patterns" that appear within the larger patterns of Welty's structure.[133] Robert L. Phillips, in "Patterns of Vision in Welty's *The Optimist's Daughter*," considers Welty's use of imagery as the reflection of a somewhat undefinable development in her characters and in her readers.[134] Marilyn Arnold's "Images of Memory in Eudora Welty's *The Optimists Daughter*" examines the images and symbols in the novel as they are relevant to "the elusive character of Welty's idea."[135] In "Medusa-Perseus Symbolism in Eudora Welty's *The Optimist's Daughter*," Noaka Fuwa Thorton views the symbolism in *The Optimist's Daughter* as Welty's allusions to Greek myth, specifically the characters Medusa and Perseus.[136] Gail Mortimer, in "Image and Myth in Eudora Welty's *The Optimist's Daughter*," observes Welty's narrative strategies in terms of the enhanced implications of the images in the novel.[137]

Kim Martin Long takes a similar approach to *The Optimist's Daughter* in her essay written for this volume, "'The Freed Hands': The Power of

Images in Eudora Welty's *The Optimist's Daughter.*" She examines symbols such as flowers, birds, hands, and time, revealing connective links between the patterns of imagery these symbols convey.

General Criticism 1970-1979

In 1973, Lewis P. Simpson edited a special *Mississippi Quarterly* Welty issue. He writes an introduction and includes essays by Welty, Charles East, William F. Buckley, Ruth M. Vande Kieft, Thomas H. Landess, Nell Ann Pickett, Cleanth Brooks, Thomas L. McHaney, Charles C. Clark, Michael Kreyling, Carol A. Moore, and M.E. Bradford. Noel Polk's valuable Welty checklist also appears in this special issue.

Critical assessments of Welty's fiction in general include essays by Elmo Howell, John A. Allen, and Lucinda H. Mackethan. Howell, in "Eudora Welty and the City of Man," comments that Welty "feels very keenly the plight of the individual who pursues his own dream, never quite going the whole way perhaps but suffering from loneliness even while playing his part in the family life."[138] In "Eudora Welty and the Use of Place in Southern Fiction," Howell discusses various settings in Welty's fiction. He explores Welty's regionally distinct settings, calling her Faulkner's "feminine counterpart."[139] Allen focuses on Welty's novels in his essay "Eudora Welty: The Three Moments." He explores Welty's notion of heroism, suggesting that specific male characters in her novels are not true heroes.[140] In "To See Things in Their Time: The Act of Focus in Eudora Welty's Fiction," MacKethan observes characters in *Delta Wedding*, *The Golden Apples*, *Losing Battles*, and *The Optimist's Daughter* as Objects, Insiders, Outsiders, and Seers, four groups of characters defined by their abilities to "'stand still' and see themselves in proper relation to their worlds."[141]

General assessments written during this time period also include a book by Zelma Turner Howard and anthologies edited by John F. Desmond, Louis Dollarhide and Ann J. Abadie, and Peggy Whitman Prenshaw. Howard, in *The Rhetoric of Eudora Welty's Short Stories*, relates the stories in *A Curtain of Green*, *The Wide Net*, and *The Golden Apples* to rhetorical devices representative of Wayne Booth's methods.[142] In *A Still Moment: Essays on the Art of Eudora Welty*, Desmond presents ten essays intended to help readers understand Welty's vision.[143] Dollarhide and Abadie present the proceedings of a symposium to honor Eudora Welty at the 1977 inauguration of the Center for the Study of Southern Culture at the University of Mississippi.[144] Prenshaw presents 27 previously unpublished critical essays in her collection *Eudora Welty: Critical Essays*.[145]

The Collected Stories of Eudora Welty 1980

The Collected Stories of Eudora Welty, a collection of 41 stories, includes all the stories in *A Curtain of Green and Other Stories*, *The Wide Net and Other Stories*, *The Golden Apples*, and *The Bride of the Innisfallen and Other Stories*. "Where Is the Voice Coming From?" and "The Demonstrators," two previously uncollected stories, are also in *The Collected Stories*.

Reviewers almost unanimously praise *The Collected Stories*, many whom reappraise Welty's canon and provide an overview of her career. Whitney Balliett, in *New Yorker*, gives an overview of the publication of Welty's fiction, concluding that "Welty is, particularly in her short stories, an experimenter."[146] Maureen Howard, writing for *New York Times Book Review*, finds pleasure tracing Welty's writing performance through the years. She sees Welty not as regional writer but as a Southern writer. She praises her rich talent, comparing her with Chekhov and Porter. Through her life spent observing, Welty produces stories with vigilance. The magnificent and entertaining stories respond to their historical times, verifying the present and preserving the past.[147] Walter Clemons compares Welty with John Cheever and Hawthorne, referring to her as "one of the most ambitious romancers . . . in the history of American writing."[148]

Robert Drake's review points out thematic themes that run throughout the stories. He says, "Love, wonder, awe—I think these are Miss Welty's great concerns. . . ."[149] In his review for *New Republic*, Reynolds Price says the best news is that Welty's stories are available in a single package. These stories stand as good on their own merit, and no short story writer since Hemingway has influenced the aspirations of other short stories more than Welty. He praises her for not revising the stories, yet he wonders if the anthology, exclusive of *The Golden Apples*, should have been organized in order of Welty's original composition.[150] However, Jennifer Uglow, writing for *Times Literary Supplement*, applauds the unchanged arrangement of the stories. She says each collection of short stories has "shape and coherence."[151] In his review published in *Time*, Paul Gray says Welty gives an imaginative account of her observations, reminding us that her personal visions have become part of the public domain.[152]

Anne Tyler presents an interview with Welty and a review of *The Collected Stories*. In her review, she remarks on Welty's talent for placing and naming, concluding that "this collection is something to be treasured."[153] Her interview, appearing in *New York Times Book Review*, reveals details about Welty's writing habits, her attitudes toward writing, and her friendships with other writers.[154]

General Criticism 1980-1993

Since 1980, Welty's works have received much critical attention. Many scholarly articles continue to explicate individual stories, along with analyses that concentrate on specific books or collections of stories. Scholars write many books that focus on Welty's fiction, and chapters on Welty appear in anthologies that provide general interpretations of contemporary writers.

In the early '80s, Michael Kreyling, Elizabeth Evans, Jennifer Lynn Randisi, and Albert J. Devlin wrote books on Welty's works. Kreyling, in *Eudora Welty's Achievement of Order*, demonstrates the chronological development of Welty's insights and methods to locate "a unique and integrating vision" in her works.[155] Evans, in *Eudora Welty*, a volume in the Ungar Modern Literature Series, discusses Welty as a woman of letters, analyzes her fiction, and concludes with a chapter on "The High Art of Eudora Welty."[156] Randisi's *A Tissue of Lies: Eudora Welty and the Southern Romance*, represents her treatment of Welty's novels in relation to the tradition of Southern Romance.[157] In *Eudora Welty's Chronicle: A Story of Mississippi Life*, Devlin examines Welty's works in chronological order of publication, focusing on her "complex historical imagination."[158]

Peggy Prenshaw edited a special Welty issue of *Southern Quarterly*, and she edited *Conversations With Eudora Welty*. In the Summer 1982 special issue of *Southern Quarterly*, she includes an interview, an essay by Albert J. Devlin, and four articles that Welty scholars Ruth M. Vande Kieft, Michael Kreyling, Elizabeth Evans, and W.U. McDonald, Jr. read at the special Welty session of the South Atlantic Modern Language Association in 1981. In *Conversations With Eudora Welty*, she presents a collection of twenty-six interviews with Eudora Welty.[159]

Sara McAlpin BVM begins her 1982 essay "Family in Eudora Welty's Fiction" with a brief explanation of the emphasis on the family as one defining feature of Southern literature. She focuses on the distinct portrayal of the family found in Welty's fiction, concentrating her discussion on *Delta Wedding* and *Losing Battles*.[160]

In the mid-'80s, Carol S. Manning's *With Ears Opening Like Morning Glories: Eudora Welty and the Love of Storytelling* was published. Manning studies Welty's fiction as the reflection of creativity that the Southern storytelling tradition sparks.[161] In *Sacred Groves and Ravaged Gardens: The Fiction of Eudora Welty, Carson McCullers, and Flannery O'Connor*, Louise Westling views these three writers in context of the historical tradition of Southern women writers.[162] In 1986, Albert J. Devlin edited a special Welty issue of *Mississippi Quarterly*, celebrating the fiftieth anniversary of her initial publication. The essays that appear in the special issue are reprinted in Devlin's 1987 book *Welty: A Life in Literature.*[163]

Harold Bloom's 1986 anthology *Eudora Welty*, a volume in Modern Critical Views Series, contains thirteen previously published essays.[164] Editors W. Craig Turner and Lee Emling Harding, in their 1989 anthology *Critical Essays on Eudora Welty*, reprint essays on Welty's major works of fiction. The volume also includes new essays by Pearly McHaney, Albert Devlin, Merrill Skaggs, and Suzanne Marrs.[165] Also in 1989, Dawn Trouard edited *Eudora Welty: Eye of the Storyteller*. Trouard's collection includes sixteen essays selected from a 1987 conference on Welty held at the University of Akron.[166]

More recently, Franziska Gygax, in *Serious Daring from Within: Female Narrative Strategies in Eudora Welty's Novels*, takes a feminist critical approach to *Delta Wedding*, *The Golden Apples*, *Losing Battles*, and *The Optimist's Daughter*.[167] Michael Kreyling's *Author and Agent: Eudora Welty and Diarmund Russell* offers a narrated account of the correspondence from 1940 to 1973 between Welty and her agent, Diarmuid Russell.[168] In *The Heart of the Story: Eudora Welty's Short Fiction*, Peter Schmidt gives intriguing analyses of Welty's short stories, departing from the formalist approaches and the many examinations that involve mythical interpretations of Welty's stories.[169] Barbara Harrell Carson's recent *Eudora Welty: Two Pictures at Once in Her Frame* examines Welty's fiction in terms of Welty's "holistic vision," pointing out feminist aspects, psychological insights, ethical positions, and rhetorical strategies reflected in Welty's fiction.[170]

In the Summer 1991 special issue of *Southern Quarterly*, *Natchez Literary Celebration*, Michael Kreyling contributes his essay "The Natchez Trace in Eudora Welty's Fiction." He argues that the Natchez Trace represents Welty's metaphorical journey from her as she considers life's possibilities to her as she realizes that the life of a writer was the only life for her.[171]

The Fall 1993 special issue of *Southern Quarterly*, *The World of Eudora Welty*, presents four papers and the round-table discussion by scholars from Moscow's Gorky Institute who participated in the 1991 symposium "The Artistic World of Eudora Welty." Scholars Marilyn Arnold, Deborah Wilson, Axel Nissen, and Ruth D. Weston also contribute to *The World of Eudora Welty*.

Bibliographies of Welty primary and secondary sources include works by Victor H. Thompson, Bethany C. Swearingen, Noel Polk, Pearl Amelia McHaney, and W.U. McDonald. Thompson's *Eudora Welty: A Reference Guide* lists critical works and bibliographical studies, including periodical and newspaper articles, essays and addresses, and interviews.[172] Swearingen's *Eudora Welty: A Critical Bibliography, 1936-1958* provides extensive annotations of early critical responses to Welty's fiction. She includes a section of "First Appearance of Stories," reviews and criticism of Welty's writings, and "Selected Local Material."[173] Noel Polk's "A Eudora Welty Checklist" provides listings through 1973,[174] and Pearl Amelia McHaney's "A Eudora Welty Checklist: 1973-1986" continues his bibliography.[175] W.U. McDonald's "Works By Welty: A Continuing Checklist," in the Winter issues of *Eudora Welty Newsletter* and McHaney's "Checklist of Welty Scholarship," in the Summer issues of the *Eudora Welty Newsletter* provide up-to-date bibliographical sources. Welty scholars appreciate Noel Polk's 1993 *Eudora Welty: A Bibliography of Her Work*, published by the University Press of Mississippi. Polk provides a complete bibliography of Welty's works, including physical characteristics of the books, dust jackets, descriptive bibliography, essays, and book reviews.

Peggy Prenshaw and W.U. McDonald offer valuable bibliographical essays for Welty scholars. Prenshaw's Welty chapter in *American Women Writers: Bibliographical Essays* assesses editions, manuscripts, and Welty scholarship through 1981.[176] McDonald's 1986 treatment of Welty in *Contemporary Authors: Bibliographical Series* provides a checklist and an extensive, evaluative discussion of secondary works.[177] Suzanne Marrs's valuable *The Welty Collection*, provides an annotated listing of all the manuscripts in the Welty Collection located at the Mississippi Department of Archives and History.[178]

Welty scholars have recently formed a Eudora Welty Society to promote and foster Welty scholarship. The coordinating committee consists of prominent Welty scholars. Membership dues are minimal, and inquiries should be sent to Dawn Trouard at The University of Akron.

As this survey indicates, Welty has been the topic for extensive critical discussions. Scholars have analyzed her works from various critical perspectives, including traditional and non-traditional approaches to literature. Scholars continue to use traditional approaches to Welty's works, and they demonstrate new critical directions in recent explorations of her work. Harriet Pollack's recent "On Welty's Use of Allusion: Expectations and Their Revision in 'The Wide Net,' *The Robber Bridegroom* and 'At The Landing,'" goes beyond a mere outline of allusions found in these three works; she explores the unique text that Welty creates by simultaneously exposing more than one narrative to her readers.[179] Pollack's essay is an abbreviated version of a chapter from her forthcoming book, *Words Between Strangers: Reading Eudora Welty's Fiction*, to be published by the University Press of Mississippi. This full-length study addresses questions that involve whether author or reader determine the meaning of a text and explores the ways meanings of a text are made. Patricia Yaeger's recent analyses that apply Bakhtinian and Lacanian theories to Welty's fiction are particularly reflective of new critical directions.[180] In her essay written for this anthology, "Diverting Swine: The Magical Relevancies of Eudora Welty's Ruby Fisher and Circe," Dawn Trouard demonstrates new critical approaches to Welty's works. Trouard challenges the view that Ruby Fisher and Circe play roles that allow them to become hostage to male roles. She sees "Circe" as Welty's most feminist story, building on feminist analysis by Yaeger and Peter Schmidt. Yet Trouard more "*aggressively* locates powers" in the characters Ruby Fisher and Circe.

Welty continues to attract attention from critics all over the world. She lives in Jackson Mississippi and frequently gives interviews and public appearances. She often gives talks on the radio and on television, and she gives public readings and frequently attends literary conferences. Scholars who interview her often remark about her pleasant and warm personality. Scholars consider Welty's gifts to humanity among the most important gifts of any living Southern writer. Her works will surely remain in the literary canon as the mark of one of America's most talented writers.

NOTES

[1]Katherine Anne Porter, "Introduction," *A Curtain of Green* (New York: Doubleday, 1941) ix-xix.

[2] Dale Mullen, "Some Notes on the Stories of Eudora Welty," *Mississippi Literary Review* (1941): 21-24.

[3]"New Writer," *Time* 24 Nov. 1941: 110-11.

[4]John Lane, "An Original Newcomer," *Times Literary Supplement* 17 July 1943: 341.

[5]Marianne Hauser, "'A Curtain of Green' and Other New Works of Fiction," *New York Times Book Review* 16 Nov. 1941: 6.

[6]Arthur J. Carr, "Among Recent Books," *Accent* 2 (1942): 188-89.

[7]Kay Boyle, "Full-Length Portrait," *New Republic* 24 Nov. 1941: 707-08.

[8]Louise Bogan, "The Gothic South," *Nation* 6 Dec. 1941: 572.

[9]Fredrick Brantley, "*A Curtain of Green*: Themes and Attitudes," *American Prefaces* 7 (1942): 241-51.

[10]Robert J. Griffin, "Eudora Welty's *A Curtain of Green*," *The Forties: Fiction, Poetry, Drama*, ed. Warren French (Deland, FL: Everett/Edwards, 1969) 101-10.

[11]Michael Kreyling, "Modernism in Welty's *A Curtain of Green and Other Stories*," *Southern Quarterly* 20 (1982): 40-53.

[12]Neil D. Isaacs, "Life for Phoenix," *Sewanee Review* 71.1 (1963): 75-81.

[13]Charles E. May, "Why Sister Lives at the P.O.," *Southern Humanities Review* 12 (1978): 243-49.

[14]Marianne Hauser, "Miss Welty's Fairy Tale," *New York Times Book Review* 1 Nov. 1942: 6-7.

[15]Charles Shattuck, "Eudora Welty: *The Robber Bridegroom*," *Accent* 3 (1944): 124.

[16]Alfred Kazin, "An Enchanted World in America," *New York Herald Tribune Books* 25 Oct. 1942: Sec. viii, p.19.

[17]Lionel Trilling, "American Fairy Tale," *Nation* 19 Dec. 1942: 687.

[18]John Peale Bishop, "The Violent Country," *New Republic* 16 Nov. 1942: 646-47.

[19]Charles C. Clark, "*The Robber Bridegroom*: Realism and Fantasy on the Natchez Trace," *Mississippi Quarterly* 26 (1973): 625-28.

[20]Gordon E. Slethaug, "Initiation in Eudora Welty's *The Robber Bridegroom,*" *Southern Humanities Review* 7 (1973): 77-87.

[21]Merrill Maguire Skaggs, "The Uses of Enchantment in Frontier Humor and *The Robber Bridegroom,*" *Studies in American Humor* 3 (1976): 96-102.

[22]Warren French, "'All Things are Double': Eudora Welty as a Civilized Writer," Prenshaw, *Critical Essays* 179-88.

[23]Michael Kreyling, "Clement and the Indians: Pastoral and History in *The Robber Bridegroom,*" Dollarhide and Abadie 25-45.

[24]Barbara Harrell Carson, "Eudora Welty's Dance with Darkness: *The Robber Bridegroom,*" *Southern Literary Journal* 20.2 (1988): 51-68.

[25] Ellen L. Walker and Gerda Seaman, "*The Robber Bridegroom* as a Capitalist Fable," *Southern Quarterly* 26.4 (1988): 57-68.

[26] Eugene Armfield, "Short Stories by Eudora Welty," *New York Times Book Review* 26 Sept. 1943: 3.

[27]Katherine Woods, "*The Wide Net*" *Tomorrow* 3 (1943): 54.

[28]"Sense and Sensibility," *Time* 27 Sept. 1943: 100-101.

[29]Jean Stafford, "Empty Net," *Partisan Review* 11 (1944): 114-15.

[30]Diana Trilling, "Fiction in Review," *Nation* 2 Oct. 1943: 386-87.

[31]Issac Rosenfield, "Consolations of Poetry," *New Republic* 18 Oct. 1943: 525-26.

[32]Garvin F. Davenport, Jr., "Renewal and Historical Consciousness in *The Wide Net,*" Prenshaw, *Critical Essays* 189-200.

[33]Albert J. Devlin, "Eudora Welty's Historicism: Method and Vision," *Mississippi Quarterly* 30 (1977): 213-34.

[34]Victor H. Thompson, "The Natchez Trace in Eudora Welty's 'A Still Moment,'" *Southern Literary Journal* 6.1 (1973): 59-69.

[35]Victor H. Thompson, "Aaron Burr in Eudora Welty's 'First Love,'" *Notes on Mississippi Writers* 8 (1976): 75-83.

[36]St. George Tucker Arnold, Jr., "Eudora Welty's 'First Love' and the Personalizing of Southern Regional History," *Journal of Regional Cultures* 1 (1981): 97-105.

[37]Suzanne Marrs, "The Conclusion of Eudora Welty's 'First Love': Historical Backgrounds," *Notes on Mississippi Writers* 13 (1981): 73-98.

[38]Pearl Amelia McHaney, "Historical Perspectives in 'A Still Moment,'" Turner and Harding 52-69.

[39]Robert Penn Warren, "The Love and Separateness in Miss Welty," *Kenyon Review* 6 (1944): 246-59.

[40]It is reprinted in Robert Penn Warren, *Collected Essays* (New York: Random, 1958): 156-69; Bloom 19-28; Turner and Harding 42-51.

[41]S[terling N[orth], "Miss Welty Needs to Be Untangled," *Atlanta Constitution* 21 April 1946: B10.

[42]Issac Rosenfield, "Double Standard," *New Republic* 29 April 1946: 633-34.

[43]"*Delta Wedding, A Novel,*" *Christian Century* 63 (22 May 1946): 657-58.

[44]"A Mississippi Mosaic," *Minneapolis Sunday Tribune* 19 May 1946: G17.

[45]Hamilton Basso, "Look Away, Look Away, Look Away," *New Yorker* 11 May 1946: 89.

[46]Paul Engle, "Miss Welty's Full Charm in First Novel," *Chicago Tribune* 14 April 1946: 3, 12.

[47]Mary Alice Bookhart, "Eudora Welty," *Clarion-Ledger* 28 April 1946: 8.

[48]John Crowe Ransom, "*Delta Wedding,*" *Kenyon Review* 8 (1946): 503-07.

[49]Charles Poore, "A Fine Novel of the Deep South," *New York Times Book Review* 14 April 1946: 1, 41.

[50]John Edward Hardy, "*Delta Wedding* as Region and Symbol," *Sewanee Review* 60 (1952): 397-417.

[51] Elmo Howell, "Eudora Welty's Comedy of Manners," *South Atlantic Quarterly* 69 (1970): 469-79.

[52]Peggy Prenshaw, "Cultural Patterns in Eudora Welty's *Delta Wedding* and 'The Demonstrators,'" *Notes on Mississippi Writers* 3 (1979): 51-70.

[53]M.E. Bradford, "Fairchild as Composite Protagonist in *Delta Wedding*," Prenshaw, *Critical Essays* 201-207.

[54]Douglas Messerli, "The Problem of Time in Welty's *Delta Wedding*," *Studies in American Fiction* 5 (1977): 227-40.

[55]Barbara Ladd, "'Coming Through': The Black Initiate in *Delta Wedding*," *Mississippi Quarterly* 41 (1988): 541-51.

[56]Albert J. Devlin, "Meeting the World in *Delta Wedding*," Turner and Harding 90-109. See also Devlin's "Modernity and the Literary Plantation: Eudora Welty's *Delta Wedding*," *Mississippi Quarterly* 43 (1990): 163-72.

[57]Sharlee Mullins Glenn, "In and Out the Circle: The Individual and the Clan in Eudora Welty's *Delta Wedding*," *Southern Literary Journal* 22.1 (1989): 50-60.

[58]Eunice Glenn, "Fantasy in the Fiction of Eudora Welty," *A Southern Vanguard*, ed. Allen Tate (New York: Prentice, 1947) 78-91.

[59]Frances Steegmuller, "Small-Town Life," *New York Times Book Review* 21 Aug. 1949: 5.

[60]John Farrelly, "The Long Afternoon," *New Republic* 22 Aug. 1949: 19-20.

[61]Lee E. Cannon, "Main Street in Dixie," *Christian Century* 7 Sept. 1949: 1039-40.

[62]Hershell Brickell, "Dragons in Mississippi," *Saturday Review of Literature* 23 (27 Aug. 1949): 9.

[63]Hamilton, Basso, "Books: Morgana Mississippi," *New Yorker*, 3 Sept. 1949: 63-64.

[64]Margaret Marshall, "Notes by the Way," *Nation* 10 Sept. 1949: 256.

[65]Louis D. Rubin, Jr., "Five Southerners," *Hopkins Review* 3 (1950): 44-45.

[66]Wendell V. Harris, "The Thematic Unity of Welty's *The Golden Apples*," *Texas Studies in Literature and Language* 6 (1964): 92-95.

[67]William M. Jones, "The Plot as Search," *Studies in Short Fiction* 5 (1967): 37-43.

[68]Danièle Pitavy-Souques, "Technique as Myth: The Structure of *The Golden Apples*," Prenshaw, *Critical Essays* 258-68.

[69]Thomas L. McHaney, "Eudora Welty and the Multitudinous Golden Apples," *Mississippi Quarterly* 26 (1973): 589-624.

[70]J.A. Bryant, Jr., "Seeing Double in *The Golden Apples*," *Sewanee Review* 82 (1974): 300-15.

[71]Elaine Upton Pugh, "The Duality of Morgana: The Making of Virgie's Vision, the Vision of *The Golden Apples*," *Modern Fiction Studies* 28 (1982): 435-51.

[72]Susan V. Donaldson, "Recovering Otherness in *The Golden Apples*," *American Literature* 63 (1991): 489-506.

[73]Lowry Pei, "Dreaming the Other in *The Golden Apples*," *Modern Fiction Studies* 28 (1982): 415-33.

[74]Merrill Maguire Skaggs, "Eudora Welty's 'I' of Memory," Turner and Harding 153-65.

[75]Granville Hicks, "Eudora Welty," *English Journal* 41 (1952): 461-68.

[76]Robert Daniel, "The World of Eudora Welty," *Hopkins Review* 6 (1953): 49-58.

[77]"Good as Gold," *Atlantic* 193 (Feb. 1954): 78.

[78]V.S. Pritchett, "Bossy Edna Earle Had a Word for Everything," *New York Times Book Review* 10 Jan. 1954: 5.

[79]"Eudora Welty's Latest Novel Is Given Review," *Jackson Daily News* 12 Jan. 1954: 12.

[80]Granville Hicks, "Two Novels About Youth and Age By Jessamyn West and Eudora Welty," *New Leader* 11 Jan. 1954: 16.

[81]Shirley Barker, rev. of *The Ponder Heart*, *Library Journal* 77 (15 Dec. 1953): 2213.

[82]John Chapman, "Witless on the Delta," *Dallas Morning News* 10 Jan. 1954: Sec. vi, p.15.

[83]Robert B. Holland, "Dialogue as a Reflection of Place in *The Ponder Heart*," *American Literature* 35 (1963): 352-58.

[84]Gerda Seaman and Ellen L. Walker, "'It's All in a Way of Speaking': A Discussion of *The Ponder Heart*," *Southern Literary Journal* 23.2 (1991): 65-76.

[85]Rachel V. Weiner, "Eudora Welty's *The Ponder Heart*: The Judgment of Art," *Southern Studies* 19 (1980): 261-73.

[86]Lynn Snyder, "Rhetoric in *The Ponder Heart*," *Southern Literary Journal* 21.2 (1989): 17-26.

[87]John L. Idol, Jr., "Edna Earle Ponder's Good Country People," *Southern Quarterly* 20.3 (1982): 66-75.

[88] Michael Kreyling, *Eudora Welty's Achievement of Order* (Baton Rouge: Louisiana State UP, 1980) 106-17.

[89]Barbara Harrell Carson, "In the Heart of Clay: Eudora Welty's *The Ponder Heart*," *American Literature* 59 (1987): 609-25.

[90]Frank Hains, "*Ponder Heart* Now Out in Dramatic Version," *Clarion-Ledger* 27 May 1956: Sec. iv, p.6.

[91]Bette E. Barber, "Eudora Welty's *The Ponder Heart* Gets Rave Notices at Broadway," *Clarion-Ledger* 19 Feb. 1956: Sec. i, p.6.

[92]Frances Gaither, "Of the South and Beyond," *New York Times Book Review* 10 April 1955: 4.

[93]Edward Weeks, "Miss Welty's World," *Atlantic* 195.5 (1955): 76, 78.

[94]Thomas Arp, "Welty's New Book of Short Stories," *San Francisco Chronicle* 3 April 1955: 16.

[95]Arthur Shay, "Seven Slices of Life Served With Perfection," *Chicago Sun Times* 10 April 1955: 4.

[96]Warren Beck, "The Realization of Sheer Genius," *Chicago Tribune* 10 April 1955: 3.

[97]William Peden, "The Incomparable Welty," *Saturday Review* 38 (9 April 1955): 18.

[98]Fred Bornhauser, "*The Bride of the Innisfallen*," *Shenandoah* 7 (1955): 71, 77-81.

[99]Frank Hains, "Miss Welty Magnificent in Newest Short Pieces," *Clarion-Ledger* 10 April 1955: Sec. iv, p.6.

[100]"*The Bride of the Innisfallen*," *Virginia Quarterly Review* 31 (1955): lxviii.

[101]Andrea Goudie, "Eudora Welty's Circe: A Goddess Who Strove with Men," *Studies in Short Fiction* 13 (1976): 481-89.

[102]Noel Polk, "Water, Wanderers, and Weddings: Love in Eudora Welty," Dollarhide and Abadie 95-122.

[103]Alun R. Jones, "A Frail Travelling Coincidence: Three Later Stories of Eudora Welty," *Shenandoah* 20 (1969): 40-53.

[104]William M. Jones, "Name and Symbol in the Prose of Eudora Welty," *Southern Folklore Quarterly* 2 (Dec. 1958): 173-85.

[105]Chester Eisinger, "Eudora Welty and the Triumph of the Imagination," *Fiction of the Forties*, by Eisinger (Chicago: U of Chicago P, 1963) 258-83.

[106]Alun R. Jones, "The World of Love: The Fiction of Eudora Welty," *The Creative Present*, ed. Nona Balakian and Charles Simmons (New York: Doubleday, 1963) 175-92.

[107]Ruth M. Vande Kieft, *Eudora Welty* (Boston: Twayne, 1962).

[108]Neil Isaacs, *Eudora Welty* (Austin, TX.: Steck-Vaughn, 1969).

[109]Alfred Appel, Jr., *A Season of Dreams: The Fiction of Eudora Welty* (Baton Rouge: Louisiana State UP, 1965).

[110]J.A. Bryant, Jr., *Eudora Welty* (Minneapolis: U of Minnesota P, 1968).

[111]James Boatwright, "*Losing Battles*," *New York Times Book Review* 12 April 1970: 32-34.

[112]Joyce Carol Oates, "Eudora's Web," *Atlantic* 225 (April 1970): 118-120, 122.

[113]Reynolds Price, "'Frightening Gift,'" *Washington Post* 17 April 1970: C1, 4.

[114]Louis Dollarhide, "Eudora Welty's *Losing Battles* Is Magnificent Feast," *Mississippi Library News* June 1970: 96-98.

[115]Linda Kuehl, "Back to Backwoods Mississippi for Granny's 90th Birthday," *Commonweal* Sept. 18, 1970: 465-66.

[116]Jack Kroll, "The Lesson of the Master," *Newsweek* 13 April 1970: 90, 92.

[117]Howard Moss, "The Lonesomeness and Hilarity of Survival," *New Yorker* 4 July 1970: 74-75.

[118]Louis D. Rubin, Jr., "Everything Brought out in the Open," *Hollins Critic* 7.3 (1970): 1-12.

[119]Robert Drake, "Miss Welty's Wide World," *Christian Century* 17 June 1970: 766-67.

[120]Frank Hains, "Eudora Welty Talks about Her New Book, *Losing Battles*," *Clarion-Ledger* 5 April 1970: F6.

[121]William E. McMillen, "Conflict and Resolution in Welty's *Losing Battles*," *Critique* 15 (1973): 110-24.

[122]Peggy Prenshaw, "The Harmonies of *Losing Battles*," *Modern American Fiction: Form and Function*, ed. Thomas Daniel Young (Baton Rouge: Louisiana State UP, 1989) 184-97.

[123]James Boatwright, "Speech and Silence in *Losing Battles*," *Shenandoah* 25.3 (1974): 3-14.

[124]Larry J. Reynolds, "Enlightening Darkness: Theme and Structure in Eudora Welty's *Losing Battles*," *Journal of Narrative Technique* 8 (1978): 113-40.

[125]Mary Anne Ferguson, "*Losing Battles* as a Comic Epic in Prose," 305-324; Louise Y. Gossett, "*Losing Battles*: Festival and Celebration," 341-50; Seymour L. Gross, "A Long Day's Living: The Angelic Ingenuities of *Losing Battles*," 325-40; Robert B. Heilman, "Losing Battles and Winning the War," 269-304; Douglas Messerli, "'A Battle with Both Sides Using the Same Tactics': The Language of Time in *Losing Battles*," 351-366.

[126]Reynolds Price, "The Onlooker Smiling: An Early Reading of *The Optimist's Daughter*," *Shenandoah* 20 (1969): 58-73; *Things Themselves: Essays and Scenes* (New York: Atheneum, 1972) 114-38; *A Common Room* (New York: Atheneum, 1987) 54-69; Turner and Harding 225-37; Bloom 75-88.

[127]Howard Moss, "Eudora Welty's New Novel About Death and Class," *New York Times Book Review* 21 May 1972: 1, 18.

[128]Granville Hicks, "Universal Regionalist," *New Leader* 55 (7 Aug. 1972): 19.

[129]*Hudson Review* 25 (1972): 508-10.

[130]M.D., "The Limits of Love," *Time* 5 June 1972: 88, 90.

[131]James Boatwright, "The Continuity of Love," *New Republic* 10 Aug. 1972: 24-25.

[132]Cleanth Brooks, "The Past Reexamined: *The Optimists Daughter*," *Mississippi Quarterly* 26 (1973): 577-87.

[133]John F. Desmond, "Pattern and Vision in *The Optimist's Daughter*," Desmond 18-38.

[134]Robert L. Phillips, "Patterns of Vision in Welty's *The Optimist's Daughter*," *Southern Literary Journal* 14.1 (1981): 10-23.

[135]Marilyn Arnold, "Images of Memory in Eudora Welty's *The Optimists Daughter*," *Southern Literary Journal* 14.2 (1982): 28-38.

[136]Noaka Fuwa Thorton, "Medusa-Perseus Symbolism in Eudora Welty's *The Optimist's Daughter*," *Southern Quarterly* 23.4 (1985): 64-76.

[137]Gail Mortimer, "Image and Myth in Eudora Welty's *The Optimist's Daughter*," *American Literature* 62 (1990): 616-33.

[138]Elmo Howell, "Eudora Welty and the City of Man," *Georgia Review* 33 (1979): 770-82.

[139]Elmo Howell, "Eudora Welty and the Use of Place in Southern Fiction," *Arizona Quarterly* 28 (1972): 248-56.

[140]John A. Allen, "Eudora Welty: The Three Moments," *Virginia Quarterly Review* 51.4 (1975): 605-27.

[141]Lucinda H. MacKethan, "To See Things in Their Time: The Act of Focus in Eudora Welty's Fiction," *American Literature* 50 (1978): 258-75.

[142]Zelma Turner Howard, *The Rhetoric of Eudora Welty's Short Stories* (Jackson: U and College P of Mississippi, 1973).

[143]John F. Desmond, *A Still Moment: Essays on the Art of Eudora Welty* (Metuchen, N.J.: The Scarecrow Press, 1978).

[144]Louis Dollarhide and Ann J. Abadie, eds., *Eudora Welty: A Form of Thanks* (Jackson: UP of Mississippi, 1979).

[145]Peggy Whitman Prenshaw, ed., *Eudora Welty: Critical Essays* (Jackson: UP of Mississippi, 1979).

[146]Whitney Balliett, "Making the Jump," *New Yorker* 5 Jan. 1981: 89.

[147]Maureen Howard, "A Collection of Discoveries," *New York Times Book Review* 2 Nov. 1980: 1, 31-32.

[148]Walter Clemons, "Songs of the South," *Newsweek* 3 Nov. 1980: 85-86.

[149]Robert Drake, "The Loving Vision," *Modern Age* 27.1 (1983): 96-97.

[150]Reynolds Price, "*The Collected Stories of Eudora Welty*," *New Republic* 183 (1 Nov. 1980): 31-34.

[151]Jennifer Uglow, "Journeys out of Separateness," *Times Literary Supplement* 8 Jan. 1982: 26.

[152]Paul Gray, "Life, with a Touch of the Comic," *Time* 3 Nov. 1980: 110.

[153]Anne Tyler, "The Fine, Full World of Welty," *Washington Evening Star* 26 Oct. 1980: D1+.

[154]Anne Tyler, "A Visit with Eudora Welty," *New York Times Book Review* 2 Nov. 1980: 33-34.

[155]Michael Kreyling, *Eudora Welty's Achievement of Order* (Baton Rouge: Louisiana State UP, 1980).

[156]Elizabeth Evans, *Eudora Welty* (New York: Frederick Ungar 1981).

[157]Jennifer Lynn Randisi, *A Tissue of Lies: Eudora Welty and the Southern Romance* (Washington: UP of America, 1982).

[158]Albert J. Devlin, *Eudora Welty's Chronicle: A Story of Mississippi Life* (Jackson: UP of Mississippi, 1983).

[159]Prenshaw, Peggy Whitman, ed., *Conversations with Eudora Welty* (Lafayette: Mississippi UP, 1984).

[160]Sara McAlpin BVM, "Family in Eudora Welty's Fiction," *Southern Review* 18.3 (1982): 480-94.

[161]Carol S. Manning, *With Ears Opening Like Morning Glories: Eudora Welty and the Love of Storytelling*. Westport, CT: Greenwood, 1985.

[162]Louise Westling, *Sacred Groves and Ravaged Gardens: The Fiction of Eudora Welty, Carson McCullers, and Flannery O'Connor* (Athens, GA: U of Georgia P, 1985).

[163]Albert J. Devlin, ed., *Welty: A Life in Literature* (Jackson: UP of Mississippi, 1987).

[164]Harold Bloom, *Eudora Welty* (New York: Chelsea, 1986).

[165]W. Craig Turner and Lee Emling Harding, eds., *Critical Essays on Eudora Welty* (G.K. Hall, 1989).

[166]Dawn Trouard, ed., *Eudora Welty: Eye of the Storyteller* (Ohio: Kent State UP, 1989).

[167]Franziska Gygax, *Serious Daring from Within: Female Narrative Strategies in Eudora Welty's Novels* (Westport, CT: Greenwood, 1990).

[168] Michael Kreyling, *Author and Agent: Eudora Welty and Diarmund Russell* (New York: Farrar, 1991).

[169]Peter Schmidt, *The Heart of the Story* (Jackson: UP of Mississippi, 1991).

[170]Barbara Harrell Carson, *Eudora Welty: Two Pictures at Once in Her Frame* (Troy, N.Y.: Whitston Publishing Co., 1992).

[171]Michael Kreyling, "The Natchez Trace in Eudora Welty's Fiction," *Southern Quarterly* 29.4 (1991): 161-70.

[172]Victor H. Thompson, *Eudora Welty: A Reference Guide* (Boston: G.K. Hall, 1976).

[173]Bethany C. Swearingen, *Eudora Welty: A Critical Bibliography, 1936-1958* (Jackson UP of Mississippi, 1984).

[174]Noel Polk, "A Eudora Welty Checklist," *Mississippi Quarterly* 26 (1973): 663-93.

[175]Pearl Amelia McHaney, "A Eudora Welty Checklist: 1973-1986," *Mississippi Quarterly* 39 (1986): 651-97.

[176]Peggy Whitman Prenshaw, "Eudora Welty," *American Women Writers: Bibliographical Essays*, ed. Maurice Duke, Jackson R. Bryer, and M. Thomas Inge (Westport, CT: Greenwood, 1983) 233-67.

[177]W.U. McDonald, Jr., "Eudora Welty," *American Novelists*, ed. James J. Martine (Detroit: Gale, 1986) 383-421, vol. 1 of *Contemporary Authors: Bibliographical Series*.

[178]Suzanne Marrs, *The Welty Collection: A Guide to the Eudora Welty Manuscripts and Documents at the Mississippi Department of Archives and History* (Jackson: UP of Mississippi, 1988).

[179]Harriet Pollack, "On Welty's Use of Allusion: Expectations and Their Revision in 'The Wide Net,' *The Robber Bridegroom* and 'At The Landing,'" *Southern Quarterly* 29.1 (1990): 5-31.

[180]Patricia Yaeger, "Toward a Feminine Sublime," *Gender and Theory: Dialogues on Feminist Criticism*, ed., Linda Kauffman (Oxford, UK: Basil Blackwell, 1989) 191-212; "The Case of the Dangling Signifier: Phallic Imagery in Eudora Welty's 'Moon Lake,'" *Twentieth Century Literature* 28 (1982): 431-52.

A Curtain of Green and Other Stories
1941

Full-Length Portrait

Kay Boyle

In her introduction to Eudora Welty's collection of short stories, Katherine Anne Porter has said a number of profoundly true and sensitive things. She has said them of Miss Welty, whom she describes as "a quiet, tranquil-looking, modest girl" who was brought to visit her one hot midsummer evening in Louisiana; and she says them of Miss Welty as a writer with a writer's responsibility and problem to consider; and lastly, she says them of the actual writing Miss Welty has done. I speak of these remarks of Miss Porter's here because they seem to me to offer as good a set of standards to bring to the evaluation of writers and writing as any I have seen.

Miss Porter tells us that Miss Welty spends "an immense amount of time" writing, although the fact that she does write is either not known or, if known, dismissed as of little importance in the Mississippi town where Miss Welty has spent the relatively few years of her life. We learn that she listens to music, cultivates flowers and leads the "normal social life" which exists in any medium-sized town; we learn, too, that she was never in any hurry either to be published or acclaimed, and that she possessed that happy and "instinctive knowledge that writing cannot be taught, but only learned, and learned by the individual in his own way, at his own pace, and in his own time." To complete this gravely and brilliantly executed portrait, Miss Porter adds that Miss Welty has been spared a "militant social consciousness," which Miss Porter believes can only serve to narrow, not to widen, the creative artist's way. When the artist "disassociates himself from the human world in favor of a set of political, which is to say, inhuman rules," Miss Porter writes, "he cuts himself away from his proper society—living men."

Here then is Miss Welty's equipment, and it is a singularly uncorrupt equipment in much the same way that Emily Dickinson's was. Add to it what Miss Porter defines as "an active and disciplined imagination," and we are, in "A Curtain of Green," brought face to face with one of the most gifted and interesting short-story writers of our time. The parallel between Emily Dickinson and Eudora Welty need not, I feel, be dropped here. They are both American women writers of exceptional distinction who, each in her own century and in her own conditions, instinctively mistrusted the outer paraphernalia of literary contacts and activity who, each in her own way, sought and found in silence an inner and almost mystical tongue. That Eudora Welty has just won a prize for her story, "A Worn Path," in the O. Henry Memorial Collection is interesting to note, but it is of little importance. She is working out something for herself which none of us can have any part in, and whatever honors come must be simply by the way. In the same sense, what small pieces of criticism one might write down are of little importance, for Eudora Welty has probably recognized the weaknesses already and is proceeding beyond them. The first one is her tendency to carry objectivity so far that at times her characters are seen from such a distance and at such an angle that they lose all human proportions, and the approach of the author herself deteriorates into something as unworthy as the spectator's point of view. This manifests itself notably in the first three stories in the book, and I deplore that they should have been placed where they are. I should like to have seen the collection start off with "Keela, the Outcast Indian Maiden," "Powerhouse" and the "Hitch-Hikers," printed with equal importance and somehow side by side.

It is characteristic of Miss Porter's own active and disciplined mind that she does not let matters rest here but enters boldly and admirably into the question of the compunction which Miss Welty or any other short-story writer should feel about writing a novel—the publisher's trap, Miss Porter calls it, which he lays for every short-story writer of any gifts at all. "She can very well become a master of the short story," Miss Porter writes. "It is quite possible that she can never write a novel, and there is no reason why she should." In considering this statement I have attempted to project Miss Welty's "case against realism" into a vehicle which would demand more continuity of thought and more development of act. Although I feel that her short stories are (and here is my second critical note) not unlike paintings in that they are absolutely halted as they stand, I foresee no way of failure for her written or unwritten novel. On the contrary, I feel that Eudora Welty could "at her own pace, and in her own time" do whatever she set out to do.

From *The New Republic* 105 (24 November 1941): 707.

The Gothic South

Louise Bogan

The definite Gothic quality which characterizes so much of the work of writers from the American South has puzzled critics. Is it the atmosphere of the *roman noir*, so skillfully transferred to America by Poe? Or is it a true and indigenous atmosphere of decaying feudalism? Faulkner treats the horrifying and ambiguous situations thrown up by a background which has much in common with nineteenth-century Russia in a style darkened and convoluted by, it would seem, the very character of his material. Eudora Welty, who is a native and resident of Mississippi, in the stories of this volume has instinctively chosen another method which opens and widens the field and makes it more amenable to detached observation. She proceeds with the utmost simplicity and observes with most delicate terseness. She does not try mystically to transform or anonymously to interpret. The parallel forced upon us, particularly by those of Miss Welty's stories which are based on an oblique humor, is her likeness to Gogol.

The tramp musicians, the inhabitants of a big house (either mad, drunk, or senile), the idiots and ageless peasant women, the eccentric families tyrannized over by an arch-eccentric, the pathetic and ridiculous livers of double lives, even the Negro band leader with his sadism and delusion of grandeur—all these could come out of some broken-down medieval scene, and all could be treated completely successfully—with humorous detachment, combined with moments of tenderness and roaring farce—by the author of "The Inspector General" and "Dead Souls." Like Gogol, Miss Welty opens the doors and describes the setting, almost inch by inch. She adds small detail to small detail: the fillings in people's teeth, the bright mail-order shirts of little boys, the bottles of Ne-Hi, the pictures of Nelson Eddy hung up like icons. We see what happens to representatives of an alien commercial world—here, traveling salesmen: how they become entangled against their will in this scene, which goes on under its own obscure decomposing laws; or dissolve back into it, symbolically enough, in delirium and death. Even the women in the beauty parlor have a basic place in the composition; they are not so much modernly vulgar as timelessly female—calculating, shrewd, and sharp. Miss Welty's method can get everything in; nothing need be scamped, because of romantic eagerness, or passed over, because of rules of taste. Temperamentally and by training she has become mistress of her material by her choice of one exactly suitable kind of treatment, and a final test of a writer's power—as we read her, we are made to believe that she has hit upon the only possible kind. But it is a method, in Miss Welty's hands, only suitable for her Southern characters on their own ground. The one story dealing with the North, Flowers for Marjorie, goes completely askew.

Katherine Anne Porter, in her preface, surveys with much insight the nature and scope of and the dangers attendant upon the specialized talent of the writer of short stories. She warns against "the novel," a form held up to the short-story writer as a baited trap. She does not warn against the other trap, the commercial short story, and the other tempter, "the agent." It seems impossible that Miss Welty, equipped as she is, should fall into line and produce the bloated characters and smoothed-out situations demanded by "commercial" publications. But other finely equipped persons have given in. As for the novel, she needs only the slenderest unifying device, something analogous to "a smart *britchka*, a light spring-carriage of the sort affected by bachelors, retired lieutenant colonels, staff captains, landowners possessed of about a hundred souls," to produce one whenever she wishes.

From *The Nation* 153 (6 December 1941): 572.

Life for Phoenix

Neil D. Isaacs

The first four sentences of "A Worn Path"[1] contain simple declarative statements using the simple past of the verb "to be": "It was Decem-ber. . . ," ". . . there was an old Negro woman. . . ," "Her name was Phoenix Jackson," "She was very old and small. . . ." The note of simplicity thus struck is the keynote of Eudora Welty's artistic design in the story. For it is a simple story (a common reaction is "simply beautiful"). But it is also a story which employs many of the devices which can make of the modern short story an intricate and densely complex form. It uses them, however, in such a way that it demonstrates how a single meaning may be enriched through the use of various techniques. Thus, instead of various levels of meaning, we have here a single meaning reinforced on several levels of perception. Moreover, there is no muddying of levels and techniques; they are neatly arranged, straightforwardly presented, and simply perceived.

The plot-line follows Phoenix Jackson, who is graphically described in the second paragraph, on her long walk into Natchez where she has to get medicine for her grandson. The trek is especially difficult because of her age, and in the process of struggling on she forgets the reason for the struggle. At the end she has remembered, received the medicine, and decided to buy the child a Christmas present with the ten cents she has acquired during the day.

What makes this a story? It barely appears to fulfill even Sidney Cox's generous criterion of "turning a corner or at least a hair."[2] But it does belong to a specific story-teller's genre familiar from Homer to Fielding to

[1]References are to Eudora Welty, *A Curtain of Green*, Garden City, N. Y. (Doubleday, Doran and Company), 1943.

[2]Familiar words to a generation of students at Darmouth College.

Kerouac—"road" literature. This form provides a ready-made plot pattern with some inherent weaknesses. The story concerns the struggle to achieve a goal, the completion of the journey; and the story's beginning, middle, and end are the same as those of the road. The primary weakness of this structure is its susceptibility to too much middle.

A traditional concept of road literature, whether the mythical journey of the sun across the heavens or a boy's trip down the Mississippi or any other variation, is its implicit equation with life: the road of life, life's journey, ups and downs, the straight and narrow, and a host of other clichés reflect the universality of this primitive metaphor. "A Worn Path" makes explicit, beginning with the very title, Eudora Welty's acceptance of the traditional equation as a basic aspect of the story. In fact, the whole meaning of "A Worn Path" will rely on an immediate recognition of the equation—the worn path equals the path of life—which is probably why it is so explicit. But we needn't start with a concept which is metaphorical or perhaps primitively allegorical. It will probably be best for us to begin with the other literal elements in the story: they will lead us back to the sub- or supra-literal eventually anyway.

An important part of the setting is the time element, that is, the specific time of the year. We learn immediately that it is "a bright frozen day" in December, and there are several subsequent, direct statements which mark it more precisely as Christmas time. The hunter talks about Santa Claus and the attendant at the hospital says that "It's Christmas time," echoing what the author has said earlier. There are several other references and images forming a pattern to underline the idea of Christmas time, such as "Up above her was a tree in a pearly cloud of *mistletoe*." [Italics in this paragraph all mine.] Notice especially the elaborate color pattern of red, green, and silver, the traditional colors of Christmas. It begins with Phoenix's head "in a *red* rag, coming along a path through the pinewoods" (which are green as well as Christmas trees). Later she sees "a wagon track, where the *silver grass* blew between the *red* ruts" and "little strings of trees *silver* in their dead leaves" (reddish brown?). This pattern comes to a climax in the description of the city and the lady's packages, which also serves to make explicit its purpose, return it to the literal: "There were red and green electric lights strung and crisscrossed everywhere. . . . . . . an armful of red-, green-, and silver-wrapped presents."

From the plot-line alone the idea of Christmas doesn't seem to be more than incidental, but it is obvious from the persistent references that Christmas is going to play an important part in the total effect of the story. Besides the direct statements already mentioned, there proliferates around the pattern throughout the story a dense cluster of allusions to and suggestions of the Christmas myth at large and to the *meanings* of Christmas in particular. For instance, as Phoenix rests under a tree, she has a vision of a little boy offering her a slice of marble-cake on a little plate, and she says, "That would be acceptable." The allusion here is to Communion and Church ritual. Later, when a bird flies by, Phoenix says, "God watching me the whole time." Then there are references to the Eden story (the ordering of the species, the snake in summer to be avoided), to the parting of the Red Sea (Phoenix walking through the field of corn), to a sequence of temptations, to the River Jordan and the City of Heaven (when Phoenix gets to the river, sees the city shining, and hears the bells ringing; then there is the angel who waits on her, tying her shoes), to the Christ-child in the manger (Phoenix describing her grandson as "all wrapped up" in "a little patch quilt . . . like a little bird" with "a sweet look"). In addition, the whole story is suggestive of a religious pilgrimage, while the conclusion implies that the return trip will be like the journey of the Magi, with Phoenix following a star (the marvelous windmill) to bring a gift to the child (medicine, also windmill). Moreover, there's the hunter who is, in part, a Santa Claus figure himself (he carries a big sack over his shoulder, he is always laughing, he brings Phoenix a gift of a nickel).

The richness of all this evocation of a Christianity-Christmas frame of reference heightens the specific points about the meanings of Christmas. The Christmas spirit, of course, is the Christian ethic in its simplest terms: giving, doing for others, charity. This concept is made explicit when the nurse says of Phoenix, "She doesn't come for herself." But it had already been presented in a brilliant piece of ironic juxtaposition [Italics mine]:

> She entered a door, and there she saw *nailed up on the wall* the document that had been stamped with the *gold seal* and framed in the *gold frame* which *matched the dream that was hung up in her head.*
>
> *"Here I be,"* she said. There was a *fixed and ceremonial stiffness* over her body.
>
> "A *charity* case, I suppose," said an attendant. . . .

Amid the Christmas season and the dense Christmas imagery, Phoenix, with an abiding intuitive faith, arrives at the shrine of her pilgrimage, beholds a symbolic crucifixion, presents herself as a celebrant in the faith, and is recognized as an embodiment of the message of the faith. This entire scene, however, with its gold trimming and the attitude of the attendant, is turned ironically to suggest greed, corruption, cynicism—the very opposite of the word used, charity. Yet the episode, which is Phoenix's final and most severe trial, also results in her final emergence as a redeemer and might be called her Calvary.

Perhaps a better way to get at the meaning of Christmas and the meaning of "A Worn Path" is to talk about life and death. In a sense, the meaning of Christmas and that of Easter are the same—a celebration of life out of death. (Notice that Phoenix refers to herself as a *June* bug and that the woman with the packages "gave off perfume like the *red roses in hot summer*.") [Italics mine.] Christ is born in the death of the year and in a near-dead nature-society situation in order to rejuvenate life itself, naturally and spiritually. He dies in order that the life of others may be saved. He is reborn out of death, and so are nature, love, and the spirit of man. All this is the potent Christian explanation of the central irony of human existence, that life means death and death is life. One might state the meaning of "A Worn Path" in similar terms, where Phoenix endures a long, agonizing dying in order to redeem her grandson's life. So the medicine, which the nurse calls charity as she makes a check in her book, is a symbol of love and life. The windmill represents the same duality, but lighter sides of both aspects. If the path is the path of life, then its end is death and the purpose of that death is new life.

It would be misleading, however, to suggest that the story is merely a paralleling of the Christian nature-myth. It is, rather, a miniature nature-myth of its own which uses elements of many traditions. The most obvious example is the name Phoenix from the mythological Egyptian bird, symbol of immortality and resurrection, which dies so that a new Phoenix may emerge from its ashes. There is a reference to the Daedalus labyrinth myth when Phoenix walks through the corn field and Miss Welty puns: "'Though the maze now,' she said, for there was no path." That ambivalent figure of the hunter comes into play here as both a death figure (killer, bag full of slain quail) and a life figure (unconscious giver of life with the nickel, banisher of Cerberus-like black dog who is attacking Phoenix), but in any case a folk-legend figure who can fill "the whole landscape" with his laugh. And there are several references to the course of the sun across the sky which gives a new dimension to the life-road equation; e.g., "Sun so high! . . . The time getting all gone here."

The most impressive extra-Christian elements are the patterns that identify Phoenix as a creature of nature herself and as a ritual-magic figure. Thus, Phoenix makes a sound "like the chirping of a solitary little bird," her hair has "an odor like copper," and at one point "with [her] mouth drawn down, [she] shook her head once or twice in a little strutting way." Even more remarkable is the "fixed and ceremonial stiffness" of her body, which moves "like a festival figure in some parade." The cane she carries, made from an umbrella, is tapped on the ground like a magic wand, and she uses it to "switch at the brush as if to rouse up any hiding things." At the same time she utters little spells:

> Out of my way, all you foxes, owls, beetles, jack rabbits, coons, and wild animals! . . . Keep out from under these feet, little bob-whites. . . . Keep the big wild hogs out of my path. Don't let none of those come running my direction. . . . Ghost, . . . who be you the ghost of ? . . . Sweetgum makes the water sweet. . . . Nobody know who made this well for it was here when I was born. . . . Sleep on, alligators, and blow your bubbles.

Other suggestions of magic appear in the whirling of cornhusks in streamers about her skirts, when she parts "her way from side to side with the cane, through the whispering field," when the quail seem "unseen," and when the cabins are "all like old women under a spell sitting there." Finally, ironically, when Phoenix swings at the black dog, she goes over "in the ditch, like a little puff of mile-weed."

More or less remote, more or less direct, all these allusions are used for the same effect as are the references to Christianity, to reinforce a statement of the meaning of life. This brings us back to the basic life-road equation of the story, and there are numerous indications that the path is life and that the end of the road is death and renewal of life. These suggestions are of three types; statements which relate the road, the trip, or Phoenix to time: Phoenix walks "with the balanced heaviness and lightness of a pendulum in a grandfather clock"; she tells the hunter, "I bound to go. . . . The time come around"; and the nurse says "She makes these trips just as regular as clockwork." Second (the most frequent type), there are descriptions of the road or episodes along the way which are suggestive of life, usually in a simple metaphorical way: "I got a long way" (ambiguously referring to past and future); "I in the thorny bush"; "up through pines. . . . Now down through oaks"; "This the easy place. This the easy going." Third, there are direct references to death, age, and life: Phoenix says to a buzzard, "Who you watching?" and to a scarecrow, "Who be you the ghost of? For I have heard of nary death close by"; then she performs a little dance of death with the scarecrow after she says, "My senses is gone. I too old. I the oldest people I ever know."

This brings us full circle in an examination of the design of the story, and it should be possible now to say something about the total meaning of "A Worn Path." The path is the path of life, and the story is an attempt to probe the meaning of life in its simplest, most elementary terms. Through the story we arrive at a definition of life, albeit a teleological one. When the hunter tells Phoenix to "take my advice and stay home, and nothing will happen to you," the irony is obvious and so is the metaphor: don't live and you can't die. When Phoenix forgets why she has made the arduous trek to Natchez,[3] we understand that it is only a rare person who knows the meaning of his life, that living does not imply knowing. When Phoenix describes the Christ-like child waiting for her and says, "I not going to forget him again, no, the whole enduring time. I could tell him from all the others in creation," we understand several things about it: her life is almost over, she sees clearly the meaning of life, she has an abiding faith in that meaning, and she will share with her grandson this great revelation just as together they embody its significance. And when Phoenix's "slow step began on the stairs, going down," as she starts back to bring the boy the medicine and the windmill, we see a composite symbol of life itself, dying so that life may continue. Life is a journey toward death, because one must die in order that life may go on.

[3]p. 283: "It was my memory had left me. . . . I forgot it in the coming."

From *Sewanee Review* 71.1 (1963): 75-81.

Why Sister Lives at the P.O.

Charles E. May

Often in literary studies a well-known artist will turn critic briefly and make an offhand comment about the work of a fellow writer that becomes solidified into dogma and thus creates a critical or interpretative dead end. Such seems to be the case with the one-liner that Katherine Anne Porter tossed off over thirty years ago about Eudora Welty's popular little family comedy, "Why I Live at the P.O." Porter's classifying of the story as a "terrifying case of dementia praecox" seems so "right" that no one has ever bothered to examine or challenge her judgment.[1] If the story is a case study, albeit an hilarious one, of paranoia in action, then little is left for the critic to do except nod his head with a knowing smile.

However, this alone does not account for the lack of discussion of one of the most anthologized stories of a writer whose other stories are discussed widely. Another reason for critical silence on the work is that it is comic. No interpretation can fully account for what makes it so funny, and no one wants the thankless task of explaining a joke. One could point out, as Ruth M. Vande Kieft has, that the narrator of the story nicely illustrates Bergson's notion that mechanical rigidity in human beings is laughable.[2] There is certainly nothing flexible about Sister's persecution obsession. One could suggest, as Sean O'Faolain has, that the story, like most good humor, is a very mixed affair and thus hides a groan somewhere behind the joke.[3] Again, it seems clear that if we laugh because the characters of the story seem so obsessed with trivia, we also despair to think that people *can* be so obsessed with trivia. After making these general comments, critics have found little else to say about the humor of the story except to admire Welty's ability to capture a particular humorous verbal idiom. Everyone agrees that the story is a *tour de force*.

An additional problem that faces Welty critics who would interpret "Why I Live at the P.O." is the fact that its tone and technique seem radically different from Welty's usual fictional milieu. Best known and most discussed for stories that take place in a "Season of Dreams" where reality is transformed into fantasy and fable, and, as R.P. Warren has noted in a famous essay, the logic of things is not the logic of ordinary daylight life, Welty, in this, one of her most widely-read stories, creates a season that is not one of dream at all; the reality of things seems to remain stubbornly, almost militantly, real. Warren has suggested that the dream-like effect of the typical Welty story seems to result from her ability to squeeze meaning from the most trivial details.[4] However, here in a story that depends on the triviality of things, there is no dream-like effect; the trivial details are comically allowed to remain trivial. They are never transformed into hierophanic entities the way they are in such typical Welty fables as "First Love," "Livvie," "Death of a Traveling Salesman," or "A Worn Path." No one has dared to try to show how Sister's green-tomato pickle or Stella-Rondo's flesh-colored kimono are transformed from the profane into the sacred.

For these reasons the story seems almost impervious to critical analysis. Aside from Robert Drake's interesting but inconclusive analysis of the story as a "cater-cornered epic" several years ago in *The Mississippi Quarterly*, the only comments that have been made about the form of the story are the suggestions made by several readers that it is a monologue similar to Ring Lardner's "Haircut," for Sister reveals more about her moral status than she intends to or is aware of.[5] Drake never makes clear just what the nature of the "cater-cornered epic" genre is. He suggests that it involves the exalting of the everyday and the familiar to the level of the heroic and epic; yet the result is not mock-heroic, but rather something harder to define than that. Somehow, the cater-cornered nature of the story is related to a multiple point of view in which sister seems inwardly aware of the absurdity of her position in the P.O., but must justify her position anyway.[6] Because Drake does not make the connection between Sister's psyche and the story's structure clear, I am left unsure about how the work is epical, cater-cornered, butt-ended, parallel-parked, or otherwise geometrically arranged.

I have reviewed these desultory comments about Welty's little story at such length because they illustrate certain basic interpretative problems about the work. The problem of calling Sister a schizophrenic is the resulting temptation to leave the issue there and thus ignore both the structural implications the phenomenon has for the story and the phenomenological implications it has for the characters. The problem of making such general comments about the story's monologue genre, its insane logic, its geometrical design, or its trivia-saturated detail is that all these remarks seem to be critical dead ends. None lead to a unified interpretation of the story or an appreciation of the complexity of its human content and artistic structure. R.P. Warren says that Welty's typical fictional character is, in one way or another, isolated from the world. Around this character, Warren further suggests, Eudora Welty creates either the drama of the isolated person's attempt to escape into the real world, or the drama of the discovery, either by the isolated character or by the reader, of the nature of the particular predicament.[7] Of these two types, "Why I Live at the P.O." seems clearly to belong to the latter. Moreover, it seems equally clear that since Sister is less interested in discovering than justifying her situation, the drama of the story resides in the reader's gradual discovery of just exactly why Sister does live at the P.O. Consequently, although the story, by its very nature, seems to resist interpretation, by its very nature also it requires interpretation. The drama of the story exists as the drama of the reader's analysis of sister's basic situation as she herself describes it.

To make this discovery, I suggest the reader play the role of phenomenologist rather than psychoanalyst. To say that Sister's motives, actions, and intentions are other than those she proclaims is to indulge in the obvious and get nowhere. To attempt to analyze Sister's phenomenological situation in relation to her family, particularly her relation to her sister, Stella-Rondo, is to participate in the drama of discovery that Welty's story demands. R.D. Laing rather than Freud seems to be the best guide here. If Sister is indeed a schizophrenic, whatever that means, her predicament should not be analyzed *in vacuo*, but within the family nexus itself. I don't pretend that the method developed by R.D. Laing and Aaron Esterson in *Sanity, Madness and the Family* for analyzing families of schizophrenics can be adopted whole cloth to apply to the situation of "Why I Live at the P.O." After all, we do only have Sister's word on everything that happens, and, as everyone agrees, she is not to be trusted. Moreover, we are dealing here with the static, closed form of the art work, not the open, dynamic situation of existential reality. Yet, to use Laing's Sartrean terminology, we cannot make "intelligible" what the basic situation of the story is until we very carefully retrace the steps from what is going on (the "process") to who is doing what (the "praxis").[8] If the action of the story, or Sister's recounting of it, is "cater-cornered," circular, "one-sided," or "cut on the bias," then we must determine the existential source of both Sister's logic and the story's geometry.

A close look at the events of Sister's momentous Fourth of July indicates that she is an example of what Laing has termed the "unembodied self."[9] She does nothing directly, but rather observes and criticizes what the body experiences and does. More specifically, in this story, Sister is one who does things subjectively rather than objectively. Welty dramatizes Sister's divided self by splitting her quite neatly into a subjective side, Sister herself, and an objective side, Stella-Rondo, who is "exactly twelve months to the day younger." Stella-Rondo acts out everything that Sister subjectively thinks or feels. In this sense Sister is right when she insists throughout the story that she does nothing, that everything is Stella-Rondo's fault. Yet the reader is also right in suspecting that everything that happens is Sister's doing. It is Sister who first dates Mr. Whitaker, but it is Stella-Rondo who marries him and moves away from the family; both are desires which Sister harbors but cannot act out. Stella-Rondo did not break up Sister and Mr. Whitaker by telling him that she was "one-sided," or as Sister says, "bigger on one side than the other." Rather, Stella-Rondo's action dramatizes that the one side which is sister is the subjective side that cannot act.

According to Sister, Stella-Rondo turns the other members against her one by one. However, what Stella-Rondo really does throughout the story is act out Sister's subjective feelings. First, Sister says that Shirley-T is the "spit-image of Papa-Daddy if he'd cut off his beard." A bit later at the table, Stella-Rondo turns Papa-Daddy against Sister by telling him, "Sister says she fails to understand why you don't cut off your beard." Although Sister's defense—"I did not say any such of a thing, the idea!"—is literally true; that is, she did not say these exact words, it is obvious that "the idea" was indeed hers. Next, when Uncle Rondo appears in Stella-Rondo's flesh-colored kimono, Sister says he looks like a "half-wit" in it. Later, Stella-Rondo echoes Sister by saying that Uncle Rondo "looks like a fool." At supper, Stella-Rondo thus articulates Sister's feelings when she tells Uncle Rondo that Sister said he looked like a fool in the pink kimono. Again, although Sister did not use these exact words, she thought what Stella-Rondo voices. When Sister asks the imaginary listener, "Do you remember who it was really said that?" the listener should remember all too well.

Sister communicates everything in this oblique, cater-cornered way; she does not express her feelings directly, but rather diagonally through Stella-Rondo. Consequently, she can cause a great many events to occur, yet disclaim responsibility for any of them. She can sit in the post office, proclaiming, "I didn't do anything," and thereby believe that she preserves her freedom, her individuality, her blamelessness, and her inviolate self. R.D. Laing's description of the schizoid individual indicates the nature and result of Sister's self justification: she tries to preserve the self by withdrawing into a central citadel and writing off everything else except the self. The tragic paradox of this situation, says Laing, is that the more the schizoid person tries thusly to defend the self, the more he or she destroys it. The real danger stems not from the "enemies" outside, but rather from the destructive defensive maneuvers inside.

Once we see that Stella-Rondo is the objective side of Sister's subjective self, the inevitability of Sister's being driven out of the house precisely because she urges the exile of Stella-Rondo becomes clear. If Stella-Rondo is a female version of the prodigal son returned, then like the good and faithful son who stayed home, Sister resents the fact that Stella-Rondo has failed in the prodigality of the venture that Sister's subjective side has sent her out on. M.H. Abrams, in his study, *Natural Supernaturalism*, has reminded us that the prodigal son story is a figure for life as a circular rather than a linear journey. The leaving of home is a fall from unity into self-dividedness; the return is the circularity of the return to union.[10] It is precisely this union of subjectivity and objectivity that Sister does not want.

Sister now desires to remain safe at home where she can manipulate the family from her position as dutiful daughter. However, given her subjective/objective split, the very existence of this desire means that Stella-Rondo will become the favorite while Sister becomes the exile. The psychological mechanism here is similar to that which Edgar Allan Poe describes as the "perverse"—that "radical, primitive, irreducible sentiment" often overlooked by moralists and psychologists alike.

Thus, in a very complex way the story illustrates the schizoid self-deception of the unembodied self. Moreover, it also dramatizes the results of a complete failure of communication when people not only refuse to listen to each other, but refuse to listen to themselves as well. The basic irony of the story is that although Sister spends the whole tale explaining why she lives at the P.O., she really does not know why. Although she talks, talks, talks, no one listens to what she says, not even herself. In fact, no one listens to anyone else in the story; the motif is constant throughout. When Sister denies that she said Papa-Daddy should shave off his beard, Stella-Rondo says, "Anybody in the world could have heard you, that had ears." And the more Sister protests, the less Papa-Daddy listens; "he acts like he just don't hear me," says Sister. "Papa-Daddy must of gone stone deaf." When Sister warns Uncle Rondo not to go near Papa-Daddy, he ignores her and goes on "zigzagging right on out to the hammock" anyway.

Sister, of course, is the character most guilty of not listening in the story, even though she is always accusing others of this. She tells Mama that if it had been her that had run away to Illinois and returned, Mama would not have been so overjoyed to see her. When Mama insists that she would have, Sister says, "she couldn't convince me though she talked till she was blue in the face." The last words of the story further emphasize Sister's refusal to listen, and sum up her situation: "And if Stella-Rondo should come to me this minute, on bended knees, and *attempt* to explain the incidents of her life with Mr. Whitaker, I'd simply put my fingers in both my ears and refuse to listen." The fact is, Sister has been telling the whole story with her fingers figuratively in both ears. She will not listen to Stella-Rondo because she will not listen to herself. Consequently, she will go to her grave denying the facts of life, as she claims Stella-Rondo will do. Our response to Sister as we read the story might best be expressed in the Southern colloquialism, "I just wish you could hear yourself talk." It is precisely the point of the story that Sister cannot.

A speech to a listener that the speaker cannot actually hear, a speech in which the speaker reveals herself unawares, is, of course, the kind of utterance that we often attribute to the dramatic monologue form. However, Welty's story poses an important difference. The monologue speakers in Robert Browning's poems, for example, have dramatized listeners to whom they speak, with definite strategies in mind. Andrea del Sarto, Fra Lippo Lippi, the infamous Duke, all either have certain aims in speaking as they do to their listeners, or else they speak as a way to discover just what their situation is. A closer analogue to "Why I Live at the P.O." is Browning's "Soliloquy of the Spanish Cloister." The poem is not a soliloquy in the sense that it is a set speech, a delivery of feelings or ideas previously arrived at by the speaker, but rather a soliloquy in the sense that it is spoken to no one. The particular ironic nature of the "Soliloquy of the Spanish Cloister" which makes it closer to "Why I live at the P.O." than the work with which it is usually compared, Ring Lardner's "Haircut," is that the speaker in Browning's poem is "guilty" precisely of those sins which he attributes to Brother Lawrence. Consequently, he damns himself even as he believes he is damning Brother Lawrence. No one hears him, not even himself, but he is damned nevertheless. Similarly, Sister alienates herself from the family in the very act of trying to alienate Stella-Rondo.

However, the literary character that Sister resembles even more is Dostoevsky's Underground Man. As it is for Dostoevsky's nameless antihero, Sister's logic is not so much insane as it is the rational pushed to such an extreme that it becomes irrational and perverse. Sister's story, an apologia, but not an apology, is an argument that becomes nonsense. The whole story that Sister tells (not the story Welty creates) is nonsense, not because of the triviality of objects and concerns that the argument seems to be about, but rather because the subjective is completely cut off from objective reality. If the story is about schizophrenia, this is the nature of the pathology. Although, as is typical of her, Sister accuses the members of her family of "cutting off your nose to spite your face," this is exactly what she does to herself. By pulling herself into her underground P.O., by casting off everything except her own subjectivity, Sister, like Dostoevsky's underground man, becomes involved in a constant verbal defense of the autonomy of the self that only serves to further destroy the self, to eat it up with its own subjectivity.

At the end of the story when Sister's "revolution" against the family on the Fourth of July has divided up the whole town into two camps that correspond to her own divided self, she believes she has established a separate peace. "Peace, that's what I like. . . . I want the world to know I'm happy." But as long as everything in Sister's life is "cater-cornered," which is indeed the way she likes things, she will never have peace. Like the Ancient Mariner, she will grab every Wedding Guest who enters the P.O. and once again tell her oblique and slanted story, therefore never uniting her ghost-like subjective self with the objective world of others. The real drama of the story is the reader's discovery of the logical and phenomenological circle in which Sister is trapped.

NOTES

[1]"Introduction," *Selected Stories of Eudora Welty* (New York: The Modern Library, 1943), p. xx.

[2]*Eudora Welty* (New York: Twayne, 1962), p. 67.

[3]*Short Stories* (Boston: Little, Brown and Co., 1961), p. 279.

[4]"Love and Separateness in Eudora Welty," *Selected Essays* (New York: Random House, 1951), p. 169.

[5]J.A. Bryant, Jr., *Eudora Welty* (Minneapolis: University of Minnesota Press, 1968), p. 8. Alfred Appel, Jr., *A Season of Dreams* (Baton Rouge: Louisiana State University Press, 1965), p. 48.

[6]"Comments on Two Eudora Welty Stories," *The Mississippi Quarterly*, 13 (Summer 1960), 130.

[7]Warren, p. 161.

[8]R.D. Laing and A. Esterson, *Sanity, Madness, and the Family* (London: Penguin Books, 1970), p. 22.

[9]R.D. Laing, *The Divided Self* (London: Penguin Books, 1965), p. 69.

[10]*Natural Supernaturalism* (New York: W. W. Norton & Co., Inc., 1971), p. 165. William Jones, "Name and Symbol in the Prose of Eudora Welty," *Southern Folklore Quarterly*, 22 (Dec., 1958), 178, notes that the name "Rondo," a musical composition in which a central theme is restated again and again, reflects the circular movement of the static situation in the story.

From *Southern Humanities Review* 12 (1978): 243-49.

The Robber Bridegroom
1942

The Violent Country

John Peale Bishop

Murder is as soundless as a spout of blood, as regular and rhythmic as sleep. Many find a skull and a little branching of bones between two floors of leaves. In the sky is a perpetual wheel of buzzards. A circle of bandits counts out gold, with bending shoulders more slaves mount the block and go down, a planter makes a gesture of abundance with his riding whip, a flatboatman falls back from the tavern to the river below with scarcely time for a splash, a rope descends from a tree and curls into a noose. And all around again are the Indians.

Such is the violent country in which Eudora Welty has laid "The Robber Bridegroom," as it is described by Clement Musgrove, the innocent, gullible planter, who stands close to the center of her tale. The scene is that dank primitive forest of Louisiana, some way above New Orleans, between the muddy Mississippi and the old murderous Natchez Trace, which even today, where it lasts, has the appearance of going back to the beginning of time. At the end of the eighteenth century, when it was just beginning to be cut into plantations by Americans coming in before the Spanish had resigned their claims of sovereignty to the French, it must have been a place of fear. To its natural terrors were added, not only the Indians with their scalping knives and tortures, but the white bandits who worked up and down its trails.

It is not difficult to understand how Miss Welty was attracted to it as background for a fairy tale, which is, at least in part, a reworking of the plot of the older "Robber Bridegroom." Out of all Grimm's Fairy Tales, none more intensely conveys the early terror of the forest. Out of another story of Grimm come Clement's daughter, the fair Rosamond, who is as beautiful as day, and her wicked stepmother, who is as ugly as night. Mike Fink, the fabulously strong flatboatman, is a creature of the folklore of the Lower Mississippi and so is Little Harp, who carries Big Harp's severed and still speaking head around with him in a trunk, though the Harps had, I believed, an actual historical existence along the Natchez Trace. Jamie Lockhart, the robber bridegroom, is harder to place as to source; at first sight, he might well be what he appears, a New Orleans gentleman, though through the greater part of the story he is a bandit, with his face so thoroughly stained by berry juice that even Rosamond, though she shares his bed, does not discover his identity. Their relations derive in part from Grimm, though more, I should say, from the myth of Cupid and Psyche.

The fascination of the genuine fairy tale is that it allows us, for a time, to penetrate the minds of our remotest ancestors and to recognize, as we cannot through any other imaginative medium, their terrors and their beliefs. The modern fairy tale cannot do this. It aims at arriving by fantasy at an end which we can accept as sound and true. It will bring together, things which mere observation could never find in one place, in order to discover their hidden connection. Since it assumes at the start a suspension of credibility, it must disarm by an air of simplicity and persuade by its charm. And this Miss Welty does. But what her tale adds up to, I cannot be sure. Rosamond and her wicked stepmother are incongruous in Louisiana and though the dangers, as we well know, were real enough under the live oaks, where the light is drowned and the Spanish moss drifts like seaweed in the submarine shade, we are never made to feel that terror of the forest which is always present in the tale of Grimm.

If Miss Welty meant to establish that our tall tale is our equivalent of the European folk tale she fails to do so. Her deepest interest in "The Robber Bridegroom" would seem to be in the question of identity. Nothing is what it seems. All bridegrooms, she seems to be saying, are robbers; their love is brought under a mask and they never call anything by its true name, so that they destroy a woman's faith and their own honor by taking that love which is a woman's right to bestow freely. But in time, the hurt is healed and at last the robber bridegroom is seen as a prosperous gentleman of the world. The predatory lover becomes the respectable father of twins and nothing is easier than the transfer of a bandit into a merchant. This, I take it, is the moral of "The Robber Bridegroom"; but it is to be found in words rather than in the narrative.

From *The New Republic* 107 (16 November 1942): 646-47.

American Fairy Tale

Lionel Trilling

Eudora Welty's little fairy-tale novel has been greeted with considerable reserve. The reviewers have given it the respect obviously due a book by the author of "A Curtain of Green," and they have expressed great admiration for its prose. But most of them have been disappointed, and some of them have attributed Miss Welty's lack of success to the impossibility or the impropriety of what she has tried to do. For "The Robber Bridegroom" translates the elements of European fairy tales into the lore of the American frontier—its princess is a Mississippi girl who gathers pot herbs at the edge of the indigo field, its mild father-king is a planter, its bridegroom with a secret that must not be pried into is a river bandit, its giant is the fabulous flatboatman Mike Fink, its Rumpelstiltskinesque creature of earth is a white-trash boy, its spirits of air are Indians.

It seems to me that we cannot judge on principle the possibility or the propriety of this transmogrification. To be sure, there is a hint of quaintness in the conception; still, if it were well done it could be done, and if it has not been well done by Miss Welty it might yet be done by someone else who thought it worth trying. But what I find disappointing in the book is not its conception but its manner—exactly that element which has been generally exempted from blame, Miss Welty's prose. This is in the fashion of sophisticated Celtic simplicity—the jacket blurb speaks accurately of its connection with "the Crock of Gold"—and it aims at an added piquancy by introducing American idioms. It is sometimes witty, it is always lucid and graceful, and it has the simplicity of structure that is no doubt the virtue of modern prose. But its lucidity, its grace, and its simplicity have a quality that invalidates them all—they are too conscious, especially the simplicity, and nothing can be falser, more purple and "literary," than conscious simplicity. This is prose whose eyes are a little too childishly wide; it is a little too conscious of doing something daring and difficult. Miss Welty is being playful and that is perfectly all right, but she is also aware of how playful she is and that is wearisome. She has used the manner of a secret archly shared but (ah!) even more archly not shared, for although she seems to have attached no specific meanings to her fantastic episodes, the whole work has the facetious air of having a profound meaning for herself. In short, she has written one of those fabrications of fantasy which have so tempted two other gifted women of our time—Elinor Wylie with her "The Venetian Glass Nephew" and her "Mr. Hazard and Mr. Hodge," and Virginia Woolf with her "Orlando," very artful and delicate works, very remote and aloof, though passionately connected, in secret ways, with the lives of the authors themselves, and very exasperating in their inevitably coy mystification.

From *The Nation* 155 (19 December 1942): 686-87.

The Uses of Enchantment in Frontier Humor and *The Robber Bridegroom*

Merrill Maguire Skaggs

Looking back on *The Robber Bridegroom* some thirty years after its publication, Eudora Welty told the Mississippi Historical Society, "I made our local history, . . . legend and the fairy tale into working equivalents. It was my firm intention to bind them together."[1] In citing two of Grimm's tales as sources of her "double character of the title,"[2] she invited a comparison of her story to the folk tales of Europe. In stressing as part of her historical material the "legendary folk hero"[3] of frontier humor, Mike Fink, she invited her audience to identify the similarities between fairy tales and tall tales. And in insisting that hers was a *historical* novel,[4] she invited a look at the connections between historical facts and fairy stories.

One easily guesses what historical facts might have provoked a desire to escape into fantasy in 1942 when Welty published her novella. But Welty also hints at the kinds of events which might have triggered frontier tall tales when she sets her novella on the Natchez Trace. Most of her details about the Trace, once known as The Devil's Backbone, can be found in Robert Coates' popular history of 1930, *The Outlaw Years*. One can read in Coates, for example, that early innkeepers often had clipped ears betraying their former thefts;[5] or that Mike Fink, the hero of the flatboatmen, drank a gallon of whiskey a day;[6] or that Fink's habitual boast was, "I can out-run, out-hop, out-jump, throw down, drag out, and lick any man in the country!";[7] or that berry stains were used to disguise a robber named Hare, who worked the Trace but was also known in New Orleans as a great dandy;[8] or that robbers often congregated at Cave-in-Rock; or that the Spanish passports used by brigands to escape English authority could be obtained only through the recommendation of a respectable landed gentleman;[9] or that Samuel Mason once obtained such a passport by conning a fellow traveler; or that the robber Little Harpe was finally apprehended when he tried to claim a reward by presenting another robber's severed head, preserved in blue clay.[10]

In including Little Harpe as a character in *The Robber Bridegroom*, however, Welty provides the strongest evidence of the link she first imagined and then forged between the southwestern frontier and fairy tales. The historical Harpe brothers, Big Harpe and Little Harpe, taught other robbers that the most effective means of disposing of corpses was to disembowel them, fill them with stones, and dump them in the nearest body of water. And this was a practice Samuel Mason later emulated.

I, at least, first heard of similar acts in fairy tales such as "The Little Red Hen" or in some versions of "Little Red Riding Hood." But my happily limited experience suggests my first hypothesis: that the perverse impulse to disembowel an enemy and then sink his stone-filled body has usually been projected onto a creature imagined operating in a remote fantasy world. When such an event occurs in one's own real world, however, its horror makes one wish to be an enchanted, superhuman, invulnerable power oneself—something like a half-horse, half-alligator, with a bit of snapping turtle thrown in.

In his recent study, *The Uses of Enchantment*, Bruno Bettelheim claims that if one takes fairy stories "as descriptions of reality, then the tales are indeed outrageous in all respects—cruel, sadistic, and whatnot. But as symbols of psychological happenings or problems, these stories are quite true."[11] Bettelheim argues that fairy tales function valuably to relieve "severe inner pressures" and to "offer examples of both temporary and permanent solutions to pressing difficulties."[12] They provide a cultural escape valve while they consistently encourage their hearers to engage in "the hazardous struggles without which one can never achieve true identity."[13] The typical fairy tale promises "that if a child dares to engage in this fearsome and taxing search [for an identity], benevolent powers will come to his aid and he will succeed."[14] Bettelheim feels that the most important ingredient of all fairy tales is the promise of success, of simpleton's or everyman's eventually inheriting the kingdom he lives in.

Against the background of the frontier's horror, one can understand that many of the purposes Bettelheim identifies in fairy tales might be served by southwestern humor stories told by a "ring-tailed roarer." Both use extravagance or enchantment to confront basic fears and anxieties. Only in the age of the intended audience, in fact, do frontier roarer stories and fairy tales differ significantly, for roarer stories are fairy tales for adults. Their verbal humor—their rhythmic, sonorous, pun-filled language—satisfies adult tastes; but the fears of vulnerability they allay are as ageless as human life.

We reasonably infer from the number of references to screamers or roarers that outlandish boasting was frequently heard in the taverns or gathering spots along the Mississippi River or in backwoods areas. In Georgia, according to Longstreet, the boast was inverted: "I'm *a leetle* the best. . . ."[15] But frontier humor suggests that such boasting was a standard feature of backwoods life throughout the lower South during the years of its settlement.

When writers sketch boasting characters ironically or satirically, they obviously shape more realistic stories. Only when the roarer is allowed to talk without a narrator's undercutting him do we have pure American fantasy. And surprisingly few examples exist of such fantasy undiluted by irony or distancing literary form. The number of roarers mentioned, ironically or not, however, suggests the enduring appeal to readers of such flights of fantasy and exuberant language as roarers emitted. In fact, the roarer reappears at least once in 1975, as John Sayles' mysterious trucker, who boasts on his CB transmitter:

> I'm Ryder P. Moses and I can outhaul, outhonk, outclutch any leadfoot this side of trucker's heaven. I'm half Mack, half Peterbilt, and half Sherman don't tread-on-me tank. I drink fifty gallons of propane for breakfast and fart pure poison, I got steel mesh teeth, a chrome-plated nose, and three feet of stick on the floor. I'm the Paul mother-loving Bunyan of the Interstate system and I don't care who knows it. I'm Ryder P. Moses and all you people are driving on *my* goddamn road.[16]

By asserting his invulnerability, his undauntable survival power in places which are alternately deadly dull and full of deadly surprises, the roarer, whether confronting forest threats or highway conspiracies, has delighted American readers. He asserts in his flights of rhythmic rhetoric that he can, and habitually does, overcome and conquer. He, then and now, fulfills a need to believe that humans can fashion everyday triumphs in unpromising places, with a minimum of elitist skills. He leaves a reader reassured that "everyman" living in "anyplace" can win his personal kingdom. When an audience both needs and is willing to entertain this reassurance, such stories are popular.

A good example of a frontier roarer story which functions as fairy tale is the familiar sketch, "The Big Bear of Arkansas." The roarer here has recently felt "neglected, rejected, degraded"[17] in New Orleans, from which city he is returning home on a steamboat. He crows loudly to attract the audience his battered ego needs, and his prospective auditors immediately identify him as a "horse" or "screamer."[18] Thereafter the "Big Bar" can rely for dignity only on his language, his character, and his lifestyle. Thus he magnifies each, discarding fact for hyperbole. He describes an enchanted homeland which produces forty-pound turkeys so fat they drop when shot to spread tallow all over the ground. He locates his virtue, as fairy-tale heroes do, in his simplest qualities and possessions—the air, soil and mosquitoes of his state, his dog, gun, cabin, bear-skin mattress, and his reputation as bear-hunter. As in a fairy tale, this roarer is both uniquely individual and also commonplace, a frontier everyman who speaks for all Arkansans. As his story unfolds, he endures the usual three-part trials of fairy tales. In the process of hunting a great bear he finds that his horse, then his gun, then his ammunition supply fail him. Thereafter he loses his pup, his energy, and his reputation in the neighborhood.

The bear itself, more a creature of enchantment than of nature, can apparently change sexes like the Devil and can outrun any pursuers. But when the hunter is so frustrated that he begins to waste away and to contemplate running to Texas, the magic animal, the "creation bear," comes to his aid. The animal, who can walk a fence or loom like black mist, presents himself to the hunter to be killed. The hunter's conclusion, however, is that "that bear was an *unhuntable bear, and died when his time come.*"[19]

The Arkansan, like many simpletons in Grimm, willingly undergoes the ordeals necessary to prove himself but triumphs only after being seasoned by failure. After identifying himself with simple, natural things—in this case, the need to defecate, which leaves him with his pants down and therefore totally vulnerable[20]—he is aided by a magic animal who sacrifices himself for the preservation of human life. "The Big Bear of Arkansas" seems rather straightforwardly to do what a fairy tale should: assure its audience that "everyman" can conquer heroically in an inauspicious place.

While such frontier humor as "The Big Bear of Arkansas" appears to fall without conscious design into a fairy tale pattern, *The Robber Bridegroom* includes fairy tale events which Welty uses deliberately and self-consciously. She describes her story, in fact, as a "Fairy Tale of the Natchez Trace." Welty mentions as sources for her work two Grimm's fairy tales, "The Robber Bridegroom" and "The Fisherman and His Wife," as well as the Cupid and Psyche story (which Bettelheim also treats as a fairy tale). Upon pursuing her fairy tale sources further, we notice that Welty's central female character also resembles Rapunzel (in being occasionally locked up by her wicked guardian, in having long golden hair, and in singing songs which attract a lover). Rosamond further resembles a large number of fairy tale heroines who own magic tokens (here, a locket which protects her from extravagant harms), who receive messages from magic animals (here, a raven), who marry ominous husbands (here, a berry-stained robber), and who drop symbols which characterize them (in this case, lies) from their mouths when they speak. In many ways Welty's novella serves as a digest of standard motifs in Grimm's fairy tales, for as she explained long ago, the story grew from "a lifetime of fairy-tale reading."[21]

When we look at Welty's fairy tale with Bettelheim's analyses of her sources in mind, however, we are in for some surprises. For Welty's rambunctious story is anything but straightforward. Bettelheim suggests that "The Robber Bridegroom" of Grimm deals with an adolescent girl's suspicion that the groom her father has chosen will rob her of her "life" as she understands it. Bettelheim identifies in the Cupid and Psyche story a young male's need to escape being "known" by the female he sleeps with. And Bettelheim relates the disguised groom stories to the female's ambivalence about sexual pleasure: she consequently finds her lover's "animal nature" disgusting during the day, however satisfactorily human her lover becomes in bed at night.

One is struck by the extent to which Welty has reversed the implications of those older plots. In writing for adults she not only discards what Bettelheim has labelled childish or adolescent anxieties; but she also signals her readers of what she is up to. As she stated in 1975, when she used the word "innocent" to describe her planter Clement Musgrove in the first sentence, she expected the word to shine "like a cautionary blinker to what lies on the road ahead."[22]

Welty's father figure here is not concerned with finding a proper heir for his kingdom, but rather with the nuisance value of building a kingdom at all. The wicked stepmother who has replaced his beloved first wife, he comes to suspect, might be his first wife after all, whom he now perceives as a demanding usurper because he has grown tired of her. His beautiful daughter, far from being pure and innocent, survives by habitually lying. Her concern is not about losing her virginity but about finding somebody to give it to. Her robber "gets" her because she goes out to find him. And having "had" her, the robber disguised with berry stains suits her vastly better than the dandy Jamie Lockhart, whom her father introduces as a prospective husband. When Rosamond cleans Jamie's face while he sleeps, identifies him correctly only to lose him, and pursues him until she finds him again, she can settle down to affluence in New Orleans only because Jamie's business as merchant so nearly resembles his former profession of robber. Jamie therefore preserves his antisocial impulses while becoming respectable. And in adding to Mike Fink's traditional boast, "I'm a lover of the women like you'll never see again," Welty supplies the twentieth-century, adult ingredient to her roarer's speech which is pointedly missing in nineteenth-century versions.

Fairy tales please us, Bettelheim says, not because they inculcate moral lessons like fables, or teach painful wisdom like myths, but because they deal with our common predicaments and desires, and then promise that we can win psychologically satisfactory solutions for them. He does not claim that the need for such reassurance is limited to children or adolescents but merely that the amoral folk stories we label fairy tales usually deal with the anxieties of early life.

What the boastful stories of frontier humor do, and what Eudora Welty does in *The Robber Bridegroom*, is reassure adults that the crises which typify adult life can turn out satisfactorily. Roarer stories counteract feelings of physical vulnerability and inadequacy, of personal insignificance or remoteness from "important issues," whereas Welty's fairy tale pays more attention to the distressing ambiguities of simple facts and to the drawbacks of socially imposed roles and sexual relationships.

According to Bettelheim, fairy tales are important to us not in times when we feel secure but in times when we feel profoundly threatened. Perhaps the revival of scholarly interest in frontier humor during the last decade and the recent revival of "The Robber Bridegroom" as a Broadway musical may say something about the times in which we live. But whether our recurring interest in such fairy tales tells anything about our historical times or not, the stories still allow us to re-experience a buried part of ourselves which continually relishes its splendid triumphs—killing with one shot every wild animal (or ferocious colleague?), stepping safely through hordes of sleeping Indians (or faculty meetings?), avoiding the bungles of dense but well-meaning fathers (or university presidents?), outwitting the malicious designs of jealous stepmothers (or college deans?). At the end of the stories we emerge, our vices as well as our virtues intact, to live happily, if not forever, at least for a long, long time.

NOTES

[1]Eudora Welty, *Fairy Tale of the Natchez Trace* (Jackson: Mississippi Historical Society, 1975), p. 13.

[2]*Ibid.*, p. 11.

[3]*Ibid.*, p. 10.

[4]*Ibid.*, p. 7. The presence of these ingredients has been previously noted by Ruth Vande Kieft, *Eudora Welty* (New Haven: Twayne, 1962), p. 172, and Alfred Appel, Jr., *Season of Dreams* (Baton Rouge: Louisiana State University Press, 1965), pp. 36, 72, 182.

[5]The detail is included in an account of an early journey down the Ohio River written by Thomas Ashe and quoted by Robert M. Coates, *The Outlaw Years* (New York: Macaulay, 1930), p. 46.

[6]Coates, p. 111.

[7]*Ibid.*, p. 112.

[8]*Ibid.*, p. 89ff. In her speech to the Mississippi Historical Society, Welty identifies this detail with Samuel Mason, who was like her Jamie Lockhart in conning a passport but not, as she says, in using berry stains.

[9]Samuel Mason, who used Cave-in-Rock as a hideaway, also secured a passport from a gullible fellow traveler. Coates, p. 124.

[10]Welty says in her Mississippi speech that Little Harp is correctly identified as possessing the head of Big Harp (Welty drops the final *e* of the names). Big Harpe's head was severed and posted in a tree fork on the Trace (as was Little Harpe's, eventually). Big Harpe's head also eventually disappeared. The head Little Harpe had in his possession when apprehended, however, was Mason's, according to Coates. The passage of thirty-two years may have slightly blurred Welty's memory of several historical details.

[11]Bruno Bettelheim, *The Uses of Enchantment* (New York: Knopf, 1975), p. 155.

[12]*Ibid.*, p. 6.

[13]*Ibid.*, p. 24.

[14]*Ibid.*

[15]Augustus Baldwin Longstreet, "The Horse Swap," *Humor of the Old Southwest*. Cohen and Dillingham, eds. (Boston: Houghton Mifflin, 1964), p. 30.

[16]John Sayles, "I-80 Nebraska M.490-M.205," *Great Action Stories*, Kittredge and Krauser, eds. (New York: New American Library, 1977), p. 234. The story originally appeared in *The Atlantic* in May 1975.

[17]Bettelheim, p. 58.

[18]Cohen and Dillingham, p. 269.

[19]*Ibid.*, 279.

[20]James Cox has recently emphasized the salacious joke at the end of the "Big Bear." "Humor of the Old Southwest," *The Comic Imagination in American Literature*, Louis D. Rubin, Jr., ed. (New Brunswick: Rutgers University Press, 1973), pp. 101-112.

[21]R. Van Gelder, "An Interview with Eudora Welty," quoted in Vande Kieft, p. 166.

[22]Welty, p. 9.

From *Studies in American Humor* 3 (October 1976): 96-102.

Eudora Welty's Dance with Darkness: *The Robber Bridegroom*[*]

Barbara Harrell Carson

The nature and purpose of the relationship between fairy tale and reality in Eudora Welty's *The Robber Bridegroom* has been discussed since the earliest reviews.[1] In what is probably the most perceptive long critical analysis of the work, Michael Kreyling has seen in the mixture of fairy tale and history an expression of the tension between pastoral dream and capitalistic reality in America.[2] It is possible, however, to view the work in a larger metaphysical

[1]See, for example, "Briefly Noted Fiction," *The New Yorker*, XVIII (October 24, 1942): 82; Alfred Kazin, "An Enchanted World in America," *New York Herald Tribune Books*, October 25, 1942: 19; Nathan Rothman, "The Lost Realm," *The Saturday Review of Literature*, XXV (November 14, 1942): 16; Lionel Trilling, "American Fairy Tale," *The Nation*, CLV (December 19, 1942): 686-687; Katherine Gauss Jackson, "In Brief: Fiction," *Harper's Magazine*, CLXXXVI (December, 1942): n.p.

[2]Michael Kreyling, *Eudora Welty's Achievement of Order* (Baton Rouge: Louisiana State University Press, 1980): 32-51. Cf. Eunice Glenn, "Fantasy in the Fiction of Eudora Welty," *A Southern Vanguard*, ed. Allen Tate (New York: Prentice-Hall, Inc., 1947): 78-91. Glenn sees in the "dualistic nature" of Jamie Lockhart "the conflict between idealism and realism, the neuroses that result from modern man's inability to attain his ideals . . . . The convincing force of the story is in the juxtaposition of the rough-and-tumble and grotesque life in the wilderness with the conventional, the real; and the harmonizing of the two." For other discussions of the theme of doubleness in *The Robber Bridegroom*, see Joseph Allen Bryant, Jr., *Eudora Welty* (Minneapolis: University of Minnesota Press, 1968): 18-20. Warren French, "All Things Are Double: Eudora Welty as a Civilized Writer," *Eudora Welty: Critical Essays*, ed. Peggy Whitman Prenshaw (Jackson: University Press of Mississippi, 1979): 178-188; Gordon E. Slethaugh, "Initiation in Eudora Welty's *The Robber Bridegroom*," *Southern Humanities Review*, 7 (Winter, 1973): 77-87.

[*]A slightly different form of this essay appears as chapter IV in Professor Carson's full-length study of Welty's holistic vision, *Eudora Welty: Two Pictures at Once in Her Frame* (Troy, New York: The Whitston Publishing Company, 1992).

scheme—one which suggests that the moral weight of the tale comes down on the side of recognizing and accepting the unity of contraries in life, not in choosing one pole of a pair of opposites (such as pastoralism over capitalism) at the expense of the other. In this reading, we can see in the collision of fairy tale and history the tension between the human impulse to simplify life, on the one hand, and, on the other, life's insistent complexity.

Indeed, the folk fairy tale that Welty incorporated into her story is grounded on the child's need for simplicity. As Bruno Bettelheim writes:

> The figures in fairy tales are not ambivalent—not good and bad at the same time, as we are in reality. But since polarization dominates the child's mind, it also dominates fairy tales. A person is either good or bad, nothing in between. One brother is stupid, the other is clever. One sister is virtuous and industrious . . . [etc.].[3]

The child cannot handle the grandmother's crabby moments, so she sees the mean grandmother as the wolf, the nice one as the object of Red Riding-hood's charitable visit. She avoids direct confrontation with her own double nature in stories such as "Sister and Brother," in which her undisciplined self, projected as her brother-companion, is turned into a fawn.[4] In *The Robber Bridegroom*, the characters attempt to sustain the child's simple vision of human nature, while life works inexorably to introduce them to its doubleness. In this way, Welty's novel is about the lesson needed to move us from the child's world to the adult's, from a fairy tale vision of life to a philosophically, psychologically, and historically corrected outlook.[5]

The ontology of this corrected vision is based on the old principles of *concordia discors* and *coincidentia oppositorum*. Reality is not an either/or matter, but is created by the dynamic tension of co-existing opposites. The challenge of life is thus not choosing between opposites—joy or sorrow, true or false, beginnings or endings, life or death—but coming to see a whole in

[3]Bettelheim, *The Uses of Enchantment: The Meaning and Importance of Fairy Tales* (Harmondsworth, England: Penguin books, 1978): 9.

[4]Bettelheim, *The Uses of Enchantment*: 6, 78-83.

[5]In its exploration of life's complexity, Welty's story is closer to the literary fairy tale (Kunstmärchen) than to the Grimms' Volkmärchen. Lawrence O. Frye has pointed out in "making a Märchen: The Trying Test of Romantic Art, Magic, and Imagination" that Kunstmärchen tend to attribute a dualistic structure to the world (Frye uses "dualistic" to refer to a state of coexisting opposites; "polar" would more accurately express this idea), not only because of "a double perspective of how and where things happen" (the story belongs both to everyday reality and to a magical one), but also because characters in literary märchen, unlike those in folk märchen, are allowed to change, and even their heroes may be less than perfect. The Kunstmärchen present "an ambiguous universe within a single narrative" with the result of "more relativity and uncertainty." As Frye says, " . . . life is harder in Kunstmärchen, for it often takes more than wishing or a magic object to work magic" (in *Fairy Tales as Ways of Knowing: Essays on Märchen in Psychology, Society, and Literature*, ed. Michael M. Metzger and Katharina Mommsen [Bern: Peter Lang]: 138-9).

which both poles are as inseparably united, as interdependent as the two poles of a magnet.[6]

In Welty's *The Robber Bridegroom* Clement Musgrove's journey from his blissful home in Kentucky into the Mississippi wilderness is itself a trip from fairy tale to reality. Anthony Steven's analysis of the expulsion from the Garden of Eden applies to Clement's move: the loss of paradise, Steven says, is "a parable of the emergence of ego-consciousness, and the replacement of harmonious unity with the conflicts born of awareness of opposing categories of experience (e.g., good and evil, love and hate, pleasure and pain)."[7] However, Welty's characters will learn a lesson opposite Adam and Eve's. While life in Eden was possible only in the presence of one of the paired opposites (good, love, pleasure) and while Judeo-Christian teachings urge a similar either/or morality in life outside of Eden, in the world Welty presents life can only be lived fully with the acknowledgement of the harmony to be found in the co-existence of the contraries.

In *The Robber Bridegroom* nature itself bears witness to the cosmic reality of *concordia discors*, contrasting vividly with the human desire to see everything in either/or terms. When Jamie Lockhart (the gallant who is also the robber) leaves Clement Musgrove's house after he has failed to recognize in Clement's daughter Rosamond the girl who attracted him in the woods, he enters a natural world whose complexity adumbrates the reality that the avoids. He rides "in the confusion of the moonlight, under the twining branches of trees . . . ."[8] The next day when Rosamond, who has likewise failed to recognize in Jamie the bandit she found so charming, sets out to find her highwayman, she enters the same forest, that old literary symbol for a mind on the threshold of self-knowledge—and, hence,

[6]Alan Watts clarified the distinction between dualism and polarity in his work *The Two Hands of God: The Myths of Polarity*. The dualist, he writes, insists on choosing between opposites, while the principle of polarity acknowledges "the inner unity of opposites"; "For to say that Opposties are *polar* is to say much more than that they are related and joined—that they are the terms, ends, or extremities of a single whole. Polar opposites are therefore *inseparable* opposites, like the poles of the earth or of a magnet, or the ends of a stick or the faces of a coin" (New York: Collier books, 1963: 41, 45). Jose Ferrater Mora has a similar concept in mind in what he calls an Integrationist philosophy: "What is real is only what exists, lives, and moves 'between polarities,' without ever being transformed into any of them, that is, without ever being petrified, so to speak, into absolutes" (*Being and Death: An Outline of Integrationist Philosophy* [Berkeley: University of California Press, 1965]: 6-7).

[7]Anthony Stevens, *Archetype: A Natural History of the Self* (London: Routledge & Kegan Paul, 1982): 94.

[8]*The Robber Bridegroom* (New York: Atheneum, 1973; 1st edition, 1942): 75. Hereafter, references to this edition will be given in the text.

knowledge of the reality into which the self fits.[9] Although she does not realize it at the time, the perceptual confusion she experiences as she penetrates the forest (mistaking the gentle for the cruel, the animal for the human, the predator for the defenseless) hints of the overlapping and intertwining nature of reality:

> On and on she went, deeper and deeper into the forest, and its sound was all around. She heard something behind her, but it was only a woodpecker pecking with his ivory bill. She thought there was a savage there, but it was a deer which was looking so hard at her. Once she thought she heard a baby crying, but it was a wildcat down in the cane. (p. 77)

By the end of the tale she will have learned that other categories that she had also thought to be mutually exclusive are, after all, not so clearcut.

Jamie Lockhart experiences a similar illumination. He is *The Robber Bridegroom's* best exemplar both of the impulse to simplify one's sense of self and one's responses to others, as well as of the need to move toward acceptance of the self's polar reality. Jamie's first conversations with Clement reveal his desire for a life without complications. When Clement confesses his own perpetual guilt before his second wife Salome, Jamie replies: "Guilt is a burdensome thing to carry about in the heart . . . . I would never bother with it." To this Clement replies: "Then you are a man of action, ... a man of the times, a pioneer and a free agent. There is no one to come to you saying 'I want' what you do not want" (p. 27). Things will change for Jamie in the course of Welty's story. But at its start, he has tried neatly to partition his life, seeing himself as alternately the bandit or the gentleman, never admitting that his reality includes simultaneously both identities. When, at their first formal meeting, he fails to recognize Rosamond as the same beautiful girl he met in the woods, it is not only because she in now ragged and dirty, but also because "it was either love or business that traveled on his mind, never both at once, and this night it was business" (p. 69). However, when Clement offers his daughter as a reward if Jamie captures the bandit who stole her clothes, Jamie is repulsed—in spite of the attraction of the dowry that is an unspoken part of the deal—because this "man of enterprise" actually incarnates (without being aware of it) human *concordia discors*, combining within self the contradic-

[9]On the *silva* image, Bruno Bettelheim writes: "Finding oneself in a dark, impenetrable forest is an ancient literary image for man in need of gaining self-knowledge. Dante evoked it at the beginning of the *Divine Comedy*, but long before him, it served as image of man in search of himself, of man caught in a moral crises, of man having to meet a developmental impasse as he wishes to move from a lower to a higher level of self-consciousness" (in *Fairy Tales as Ways of Knowing*: 14-15).

tory qualities of the romantic and the materialist. Welty writes that "in his heart" Jamie "carried nothing less than a dream of true love—something of gossamer and roses, though on this topic he never held conversation with himself, or let the information pass to a soul . . ." (p. 74). Later, when his robber band chides him for staying with Rosamond during the daytime (he had always before confined romance to night and devoted the day to banditry), he halfway draws his dirk in self-defensive protest: "For he thought he had it all divisioned off into time and place, and that many things were for later and for further away, and that now the world had just begun" (p. 87).

Jamie's challenge is to bring into conversation the two sides of himself, accepting his complex reality. Ironically, the innocent Clement voices most clearly the truth of this polarity, when Rosamond visits him after her "marriage" to Jamie. He says:

> 'If being a bandit were his breadth and scope, I should find him and kill him for sure . . . . But since in addition he loves my daughter, he must be not the one man, but two, and I should be afraid of killing the second. For all things are double, and this should keep us from taking liberties with the outside world, and acting too quickly to finish things off.' (p. 126)

It is strangely appropriate in a world where apparent opposites meet that kind-hearted Clement shares this awareness of doubleness with the villains of the piece. In fact, while the innocent planter has only abstract insight into the mingled identity of Rosamond's robber lover, the evil Salome and the Little Harp have specific evidence that Jamie Lockhart and the outlaw are one. At their first meeting, Salome sees the berry stains behind Jamie Lockhart's ear (p. 75); Little Harp sees Jamie with only a partially stained face after Jamie, interrupted as he began to disguise himself, runs to aid Goat's sister, whom Little Harp had decided to kill instead of marry. Little Harp gloats: "Aha, but I know who you are too. . . . Your name is Jamie Lockhart and you are the bandit in the woods, for you have your two faces on together and I see you both" (p. 112).

Salome and Little Harp on the one hand and Clement on the other demonstrate two responses to an awareness of human complexity. Clement shows that an appreciation of the full instead of the partial human being can lead to compassion and to patience with life's unfolding. He shows, too, that understanding of the doubleness of others can illuminate dark areas of one's own life. His speech about Jamie's doubleness includes this startling bit of self-examination:

> 'All things are divided in half—night and day, the soul and body, and sorrow and joy and youth and age, and sometimes I wonder if even my own wife has not been the one person all the time, and I loved her beauty so at the beginning that it is only now that the ugliness has struck through to beset me like a madness.' (p. 126)

The trick in human relationships that Clement has not applied to his own wife and that Jamie and Rosamond must discover is to see the different "sides" of personalities simultaneously and not sequentially.

For Salome and Little Harp, however, knowledge of Jamie's dual self leads neither to compassion nor to self-knowledge. For them it is the basis for their powerplay over Rosamond and Jamie. Salome's and Little Harp's relations to others have their own kind of simplicity: they use them. That Rosamond and Jamie—both of whom deny one side of their identity—are such easy victims implies the vulnerability that accompanies attempted retreats to a simple identity. Paradoxically, however, that very vulnerability contains the seeds for human growth: only when they are forced to confront their duplex identities can Rosamond and Jamie experience life's fullness of sorrow and joy.

On the other hand, Salome and Little Harp illustrate the self-destruction that accompanies inviolate one-sidedness. If Clement is right that Salome is really the other side of his first wife Amalie (their names are practically anagrams), ugly now and hardened since the murder of their son by Indians, Salome has denied so totally the gentle, loving side of her self that she has become stonelike. At one point Welty writes: ". . . Rosamond did not think the trickery went so deep in her stepmother that it did not come to an end, but made her solid like an image of stone in the garden . . ." (p. 123).[10] Salome's singlemindedness leads to her capture by the Indians: ". . . her eye, from thinking of golden glitter, had possibly gotten too bright to see the dark that was close around her now" (pp. 144-5). Her coldly determined self-sufficiency leads to her destruction. When Goat, who has come to free her from the Indians, asks why she is crying, she screams: "I am not crying! . . . . Be gone! I need no one!" (p. 152). And so he leaves her. Brought before the Indians, she claims the power to command the sun. "Shaking both fists in the smoky air," she proclaims, "No one is to have power over me! . . . No man, and none of the elements. I am by myself in

[10]Welty continually emphasizes the idea that Salome in her inflexibility and rigidity has ceased to be human. During his first conversation with Jamie about Salome, Clement remembers "how in her times of love Salome was immeasurably calculating and just so, almost clocklike, in the way of the great Spanish automaton in the iron skirt in the New Orleans bazaar, which could play and beat a man at chess" (26-7). Her end is also described with an appropriate metaphor: she falls over "stone dead" (163).

the world!" (pp. 160-1). And she dances to her death, alone, ordering the sun to retire.

Little Harp also demonstrates that nothing is potentially so destructive as single vision—viewing self or other through a single lens. Having reduced himself merely to the violent outlaw—the shadow self of Jamie Lockhart's bandit persona—Little Harp dies when he declares the death of both Big Harp and the bandit Jamie Lockhart. (His plan was to keep the reward offered for Big Harp's head when it was mistaken for Jamie's). Little Harp, like Salome, asserts that he alone is in control: ". . . the Little Harp rules now. And for the proof of everything, I'm killing you now with my own two hands" (p. 157). Instead, of course, Jamie kills him. Only in death does Little Harp reveal the other, feeling side of himself he had denied in life: "The Little Harp, with a wound in his heart, heaved a deep sigh and a tear came out of his eye, for he hated to give up his life as badly as the deer in the woods" (p. 158).

However, while Little Harp's death, like Salome's, implies the deadness even in life of those who develop and recognize only one part of the self, the central significance of Little Harp's murder seems to lie in its symbolizing the death of Jamie's bandit self. Yet even this is not as simple as it first appears. We recognize as clearly as Jamie did that Little Harp represents the violent, outlaw side of Rosamond's handsome lover. While we, like Rosamond, actually see in action only the dashing Lochinvar/Robin Hood side of Jamie, Welty is careful to remind us of the more somber business of his profession. The first intimation takes the comic form of Mike Fink's obvious fear of Jamie (p. 12): whoever can bring a tremor to that he-bull, he-rattlesnake, he-alligator of a flatboatman must be some sort of a he-terror himself. When Mike Fink's ominously croaking raven sits easily on Jamie's finger "as though there it belonged" (p. 19), we assume Jamie is at home, too, with Mike Fink's grimmer activities. (Fink has, after all, just had a hearty go at beating Jamie and Clement to death with a floorboard.) Less laughter accompanies the next clue to the reality of Jamie's life as an outlaw, one he himself furnishes when he broadly hints to Clement—almost as if he wished to give himself away—about the parallels between the Indians robbing Clement and Jamie's own banditry (p. 22). Further inside the nested boxes of *The Robber Bridegroom* are even darker reminders of the non-fairytale quality of robbers' lives. When Jamie first encounters Little Harp and tries to kill him, he instinctively recognizes their shared identity. Welty writes:

> He half pulled out his little dirk to kill the Little Harp then and there. But his little dirk, not unstained with blood, held back and would not touch the feeble creature. Something

seemed to speak to Jamie that said, 'This is to be your burden, and so you might as well take it.' (p. 112)

So the Little Harp moves into Jamie's hideout, raping and killing the Indian girl in the same house where Jamie lives with Rosamond, whom he had abducted, too (though, in a fairy tale layer of the story, with her loving compliance). In the death of the Indian girl we are about as far as we can get from lighthearted innocence and from gay, soaring dreams without nightmares.[11] And Jamie's character is here revealed as far from the fairy tale Prince Charming. To Jamie's outlaw band, Little Harp declares, ". . . your chief belongs to me! . . . He is bound over to me body and soul . . ." (p. 130). Although Jamie throws him out, he knows that "he'll be back with me tomorrow" (p. 133). Even Rosamond comes close to acknowledging the real life of her lover when she admits to Salome that Jamie still brings home to her fine dresses and petticoats—obviously from other women he has accosted and possibly raped (p. 118).

As the book moves away from its dark center, Jamie resolves comically the problems that have been generated by his keeping the two parts of his self in isolation. However, the solution is not actually the death of his robber side, as the death of Little Harp may seem at first to imply. To think that the robber in Jamie dies completely is to miss the whole point of the theme of doubleness, of the necessary and valuable reality of human psychological polarity. It is also to miss a good joke. Jamie becomes a rich merchant, the perfect way to be both a gentleman and a highwayman. As Welty tells us: ". . . the outward transfer from bandit to merchant had been almost too easy to count it a change at all, and he was enjoying all the same success he had ever had" (p. 148). Thus the death of Little Harp signals, not the death of Jamie's robber self, but his acceptance of integration of the two poles of self into one whole. New Orleans is the perfect setting for this integration, since it too brings into concord apparent opposites: "Beauty and vice and every delight possible to the soul and body stood hospitably, and usually together, in every doorway and beneath every palmetto by day and lighted torch by night. A shutter opened and a flower bloomed" (p. 182). Here, Jamie—now a man of feeling as well as a man of action, and no longer quite so free of the wants of others—lives the wisdom he has come to, his heroic vision: "But now in his heart Jamie knew that he was a hero and had always been one, only with the power to look both ways and to see a thing from all

[11]*The New Yorker* review included this evaluation: "If this *is* a dream it is one of the gay, soaring kind, without a breath of nightmare . . ." ("Briefly Noted Fiction," 82).

sides" (p. 185). In Welty's moral scheme the willingness to take this Janus-like perspective is itself heroic.

Jamie is not the only character with two faces in *The Robber Bridegroom*. Almost everyone has either a double identity or a personality made up of contradictory elements, making it difficult for us easily to pass judgment on or finish anyone off.[12] The "evil" characters seem evil precisely because—and to the extent that—they refuse to acknowledge their complexity, a refusal that reduces them to one-dimensional fairy tale villains in their evaluations of themselves and in their relationship to others. But Welty insists that the reader see virtue even in the villains. So the Little Harp turns out in his death to have human feelings; so Salome and Amalie are two halves of an unrecognized whole. The loud-mouthed, murderous Mike Fink of the first part of the tale is also the timorous, ghost-bedeviled mail rider of the conclusion (and even in the opening scene he has such a queasy stomach that he covers his eyes and feels rather than looks at the ruin he thinks he has brought Clement and Jamie, a comic introduction to Welty's idea that all people are double). Later, we see the stupid Goat moved to tears by Rosamond's song and the pitiless Indians feeling pity for Clement. We end up feeling strangely ambivalent even about Salome, whose defiance of all in heaven or on earth demands a kind of admiration as well as scorn.

However, next to Jamie, the character whose doubleness is most fully developed is Rosamond. She is both the spoiled daughter of a rich planter and the self-sacrificing lover of the bandit of the woods. While she has the fairy tale attributes of Gretel, Cinderella, and Snow White (her name, Rose of the World, is close to the generic naming of fairy tales[13]), she is unlike them in being far from the one-sided, virtuous, long-suffering, passive maiden of fairy tales. She is "a great liar" (p. 38) from whose mouth lies fall as naturally as jewels from the lips of fairy princesses (p. 38). She is also as sexually awakened as Snow White is innocent of all conscious sexuality. Rosamond has had fantasies of abduction and is coolly self-possessed when she is accosted by the outlaw Jamie (". . . Rosamond . . . had sometimes imagined such a thing happening, and knew what to say" [p. 48]). In fact, it seems to be Rosamond who entices Jamie in their first encounter. "Well, then I suppose I must give you the dress . . . but not a thing further" (p. 47). When Jamie takes even her petticoats, she spends no

[12]In her essay on the novel, Welty underlined the importance of this motif to her narrative: "There's doubleness in respect to identity that runs in a strong thread through all wild happenings—indeed, this thread is their connection and everything that happens hangs upon it" ("Fairy Tale of the Natchez Trace" in *The Eye of the Story: Selected Essays and Reviews* [New York: Random House, 1979]: 310).

[13]Her story will remind us that the world is not all fairy tale rosey—another possible ironic implication of her name.

time worrying abut the precarious state of her virtue, but instead wonders "how ever she might look without a stitch on her" (p. 50). And when Jamie offers her a choice between being killed and going home naked, she shows no stupid fairy tale preference for honor over life, asserting, "Why, sir, life is sweet . . . and before I would die on the point of your sword, I would go home naked any day" (p. 50). Returned home, she acquiesces in Salome's orders that she work like a scullery maid, finding in her subservience freedom from others' pleasures and plans for her—a neat instance of *coincidentia oppositorum* in personal relations. The next day, she returns to the forest of her own free will, giving Jamie the opportunity to take what he had left her the day before—a step that will lead to the very unfairytale-like predicament of her pregnancy.

After she begins to live with her robber lover, her psychological state also bears witness to the real-life adult's need for the state of tension created by the simultaneity of apparent contraries. In the robber's cottage, she is perfectly happy, we are told, except that "she had never seen her lover's face. But then the heart cannot live without something to sorrow and be curious over" (p. 88). So even the happiness of love is incomplete without sorrow which passes in the world of the simple as totally alien to love.

Rosamond's doubleness is even more complexly present in her difference from and similarity to Salome. At first the two seem absolute opposites. An early description establishes their contrast: "For if Rosamond was as beautiful as the day, Salome was as ugly as the night . . ." (p. 33). But as in the case of the yin-yang principle, Salome and Rosamond share points of contact and dynamic exchange. Like so many opposites in Welty's fiction, these two begin to reveal their similarities, especially after Rosamond is initiated into love, that business so likely to introduce us to life's complicated reality. It is probably not so much ironic as appropriate in a world where opposites meet that the place where Jamie first made love to Rosamond is the same place where Clement had married Salome: ". . . there under the meeting trees at the edge" (p. 105). When Rosamond tells her father and stepmother of her marriage to the bandit, Salome senses her kinship with Rosamond: ". . . at that moment the stepmother gave Rosamond a look of true friendship, as if Rosamond too had got her man by unholy means" (p. 122). And when Salome voices the doubts that Rosamond feels about her lover's identity: "Salome drew so close to Rosamond that they could look down the well and see one shadow, and whispered in her ear . . ." (p. 123). She is as surely Rosamond's shadow self as the Little Harp is Jamie's. Thus it is fitting that Salome die when Rosamond moves toward integration of the parts of her self, just as Little Harp does when Jamie starts on a similar path.

The attitude toward life conveyed by *The Robber Bridegroom* is as double as Jamie's and Rosamond's identities are. It parallels the splicing of the fairy tale tone to the real horrors of murder, rape, and other savage doings that fill the story. In *The Robber Bridegroom* Welty has given us a story about which we could write precisely what she wrote about Chekhov's stories:

> Yet—Chekhov goes on to say—'Life is terrible and marvelous, and so, however terrible a story you tell in Russia, however you embroider it with nests of robbers, long knives and such marvels, it always finds an echo of reality in the soul of the listener . . . . [Real life] was of itself so marvelous and terrible that the fantastic stories of legend and fairy tale were pale and blended with life.'[14]

Terrible and marvelous—that is the estimation of life Welty gives us in *The Robber Bridegroom.* ("Life is sweet," Rosamond has said, even as she is being robbed; her name, "Rose of the world," implies in the old image of flower and thorns both the beauty and pain of life.) It is a perspective very like the Buddhist outlook described by Joseph Campbell in *Myths to Live By*:

> 'All life,' said the Buddha, 'is sorrowful'; and so, indeed, it is. Life consuming life: that is the essence of its being, which is forever a becoming. 'The world,' said the buddha, 'is an ever-burning fire.' And so it is. And that is what one has to affirm, with a yea! a dance! a knowing, solemn, stately dance of the mystic bliss beyond pain that is at the heart of every mythic rite.[15]

The Robber Bridegroom is one of Welty's dances, acknowledging this insight—not stately so much as spritely, a laugh and a hurrah in the face of horror. And the horror is very much acknowledged, even in this tale so widely read as light-hearted entertainment. The undertone of horror accompanying the wonder of life is introduced early in the story. The first paragraph ends with the declaration, "the way home through the wilderness was beset with dangers," creating a sense of the threats that surround and (if we remember the symbolism of the wilderness) live within the human psyche. The theme of human cruelty to other humans is introduced in the first chapter. The first two innkeepers Clement encounters have lost ears for horse stealing and cock-fighting. While their cropped ears seem funny at the outset, deeper inside the tale we realize that the mutilation of the criminals is but a societally sanctioned version of the mutilation of the Indian girl by Little Harp. Then, after the slapstick attempt by Mike Fink to kill Clement and Jamie, we are chilled with the almost sickening tale of the treatment of

[14]"Reality in Chekhov's Stories" in *The Eye of the Story*: 62.

[15]Joseph Campbell, *Myths to Live By* (London: Souvenir Press, Ltd., 1973): 103.

Clement's party by their Indian captors. Humiliation, torture, murder have left Clement with "less than nothing" (p. 23). Not a funny story, it is hard for readers to bear because we know that every act of cruelty detailed by Clement has been perpetrated by one human on another, again and again, around the world, throughout history.[16]

Indeed, for all the rolicking gaiety of its surface, *The Robber Bridegroom* presents one of Welty's darkest visions of reality, a darkness intensified by Clement's perception of a cosmic horror in which humans appear as "little mice" in a life seen as "a maze without end" (pp. 23, 103). Psychological forces are as mysterious as the powers of nature. Clement cannot even remember why he came into the wilderness; all he knows is that "there was a great tug at the whole world, to go down over the edge, . . . and our hearts and our own lonely will may have had nothing to do with it" (p. 21). Just as frightening as the mystery of causality is the uncontrollable domino effect of human actions (yet another expression of the tangled nature of reality). Jamie determines to rescue Rosamond, saying, ". . . when I went off and left her, I had no idea what a big thing would come of it" (p. 164). In spite of this recognition, however, human will is ineffectual in fighting life's horror. It is not Jamie who rescues Rosamond, but the stupid Goat. And when Clement, uncharacteristically moved from passivity, determines to rescue his daughter himself, he ends up wrestling all night with a monster that turns out to be a willow tree. If this were not a comedy, protected by its fairy tale wrappings, a character like Clement would surely be driven mad by the cruel, senseless, and overpowering forces of life that assail him. Hearing that the gentleman he trusted to rescue his daughter is the bandit who stole her clothes, her honor, and her heart, he forgets his own wisdom about life's doubleness and retreats into the forest (the appropriate place for encounters with horrors within and without), demanding exactness from a world that will not furnish it:

> 'What exactly is this now? . . . Wrath and love burn only like campfires. And even the appearance of a hero is no longer a single and majestic event like that of a star in the heavens, but a wandering fire soon lost. A journey is forever lonely and parallel to death, but the two watch each other, the traveler and the bandit, through the trees. Like will-o-wisps the little blazes burn on the rafts all night, unsteady beside the shore. Where are they even so soon as tomorrow? Massacre is hard to tell from the perfor-

[16]This is a significant contrast to fairy tales. Even a child knows that on the literal level the fairy tale is not true and cannot possibly be true: there are no witches; people do not chop off bits of their feet, even to fit them into glass slippers; dead horse heads do not talk, even as a response to murder and usurpation. See Linda Dégh, "Grimm's *Household Tales* and Its Place in the Household: The Social Revelance of a Controversial Classic" in *Fairy Tales as Ways of Knowing*: 39.

mance of other rites, in the great silence where the wanderer is coming. Murder is as soundless as a spout of blood, as regular and rhythmic as sleep. Many find a skull and a little branching of bones between two floors of leaves. In the sky is the perpetual wheel of buzzards. A circle of bandits counts out the gold, with bending shoulders more slaves mount the block and go down, a planter makes a gesture of abundance with his riding whip, a flatboatman falls back from the tavern door to the river below with scarcely time for a splash, a rope descends from a tree and curls into a noose. And all around again are the Indians.

'Yet no one can laugh or cry so savagely in this wilderness as to be heard by the nearest traveler or remembered next year. A fiddle played in a finished hut in a clearing is as vagrant as the swamp breeze. What will the seasons be, when we are lost and dead? The dreadful heat and cold—no more than the shooting star.' (pp. 141, 143-44)

Love and wrath, massacres and mysteries, bandits and slaveowners, music and a swamp breeze—all become equal in insignificance before the rolling seasons, and the only solace seems to be a recognition of the transcience and insignificance of everything. Clement could be the prophet of Ecclesiastes crying out on the vanity of life. As he watches Salome going to her death, he looks at the faces of surrounding Indians and thinks: "The savages have only come the sooner to their end; we will come to ours too. Why have I built my house, and added to it? The planter will go after the hunter, and the merchant after the planter, all having their day" (p. 161).

The monstrous, self-devouring quality of life is captured in Clement's musings, but clearly this is only the dark center of Welty's tale. For while Clement's thoughts imply the question, "If this is what life is like, why go on?", go on he does. And he can go on, and Rosamond and Jamie can too, because they glimpse something of the whole of Welty's insight. Her story unites a confrontation with the monstrousness of life with a recognition of its wonder, a vision that transforms wandering in a maze into a dance. This evaluation of life is very similar to that reflected in the Hindu legend about the God Shiva. Confronted by a demon demanding that Shiva hand over his wife, the world-goddess Parvati, Shiva hit the earth with lightning and created a new demon which he commanded to eat the first. The first demon threw himself on Shiva's mercy and was forgiven. Bound by the god's original order, the second demon asked, "What shall I eat now?" To which Shiva replied, "Well, let's see: why not eat yourself." And so the demon began, eating its own feet, belly, chest, neck. Joseph Campbell, who tells the story charmingly, continues:

And the god, thereupon, was enchanted. For here at last was a perfect image of the monstrous thing that is life, which lives on itself. And to that sunlike mask, which was now all that was left of that lionlike vision of hunger, Shiva said, exulting, 'I shall call you Face of Glory, Kirttimukha, and you shall shine above the doors to all my temples. No one who refuses to honor and worship you will come ever to knowledge of me.'

The obvious lesson of all of which is that the first step to the knowledge of the highest divine symbol of the wonder and mystery of life and its glory in that character: the realization that this is just how it is and that it cannot and will not be changed . . . . So if you really want to help this world, what you will have to teach is how to live in it. And that no one can do who has not himself learned how to live in it the joyful sorrow and sorrowful joy of the knowledge of life as it is.[17]

It is in the teaching of how to live in such a world that Welty's tale offers help for travellers in life's wilderness, alive as it is with Indians, outlaws, and wild animals. She has no secret to make the threats go away, but she knows what will help us live with the horrors surrounding us. Surely part of her "program" is the recognition of the doubleness of life that the book reveals, an awareness of its marvelous as well as its terrible side.

The second part of Welty's strategy for survival is the old one: to have someone to love may make the world seem less terrifying, even if it does nothing to change objective reality. Clement suggests the power of love when he laments: "My wife will build a tower to overlook the boundaries of her land, while I ride its woods and know it to be a maze without end, because my love is lost in it" (p. 103). It is the lost love that makes the world seem a maze.

However, Welty makes clear that the mere physical presence of the loved one is not enough for sustained solace. Even though Rosamond lies by Jamie's side, "she would look out the window and see a cloud put up a mask over the secret face of the moon, and she would hear the pitiful cries of the night creatures. Then it was enough to make her afraid, as if the whole world were circled by a band of Indian savages . . ." (p. 85). And her fear all wells from the fact that in spite of her study of Jamie's face "she did not know the language it was written in" (p. 85). For love to alleviate the night terrors of existence, it must be love of a whole self by a whole self. That full achievement of this lies beyond human achievement is life's eternal tragedy. However, the closer we approach it, the more effective will be love's protection. Rosamond and Jamie have consummated their love, but each recognizes only half of the other's identity. It is this that makes theirs a false marriage, not just the drunken priest who performed the ceremony.

The desire to push beyond the view of life as *simplex*, into knowledge of its real multiplicity Welty identified as the motivation behind the plot in *The Robber Bridegroom.* The truth in the story, she wrote, lies in the need "to find out what we all wish to find out, exactly who we are, and who the

[17]Joseph Campbell, *Myths to Live by*: 103-4.

other fellow is, and what we are doing here all together."[18] Yet, oddly enough, in the same essay Welty says that in washing off Jamie's disguise Rosamond is making "the classic mistake."[19] So which is it? Is the desire to know others a way to mitigate the pain of life or is it an unforgivable trespass? To an extent, Welty's answer is a perverse Yes—it is both.

More precisely, the novel suggests that there are right and wrong reasons for trying to fathom another's identity. The story opens with the wrong one. Mike Fink threatens to reveal the other part of Jamie's identity in order to have power over him. In silencing Mike Fink, Jamie makes an important distinction: "Say who I am forever, but dare to say *what* I am, and that will be the last breath of any man" (p. 13). Later Clement asks Jamie's name so he can express his gratitude, but he does not ask "*what* you may be" (p. 16). The problem with having handy names or labels for the multiple parts of a human identity is that they can fool us into thinking that we have psychological understanding or "control" of the other person, that we have reduced the mystery of his or her full selfhood.[20]

While it is natural to want protection from the reduction of self symbolized by the threats of Mike Fink and Little Harp to reveal what Jamie is, Welty reiterates in her essays and stories the view that the most pitiful life is one that has been made invulnerable.[21] Certainly the outcome of *The Robber Bridegroom* seems to justify Rosamond's attempt to discover Jamie's identity. As a consequence of her act, Jamie's dual selves are integrated, and he and Rosamond are truly married. However, the initial consequence of Rosamond's penetration of Jamie's disguise is the rupture of their relationship, because she has asked for a label, not for an introduction to Jamie's fuller self.

The cause of Rosamond's growing need to know Jamie's identity is significant. As long as their life together is blissful (that is, as long as it has fairy tale perfection), she can accept the mystery. However, with the arrival of Little Harp in their cabin and the death of the Indian girl, the simple happiness she and Jamie shared is threatened. The threat comes from the insidious invasion of her own awareness of Jamie's shadow self—a self she

[18]"Fairy Tale of the Natchez Trace" in *The Eye of the Story*: 311.

[19]"Fairy Tale of the Natchez Trace" in *The Eye of the Story*: 308.

[20]Later Mike Fink tries to protect himself in a fashion similar to Jamie's, refusing at the end of the story to give his name to Rosamond, who rejoins, "Too much of this secrecy goes on in the world for my happiness . . ." (174). She makes him tell her his real name so that she knows whom to thank (178-9), parallelling Clement's request for Jamie's name so that he can express his gratitude.

[21]Welty speaks of the perils involved in "the courting of imperviousness" in "Writing and Analyzing a Story" in *The Eye of the Story*: 113.

cannot accept and that she, in the form of the psychologically projected Indian maiden, finds terrifying:

> . . . she was torn as she had never been before with an anguish to know his name and his true appearance. For the coming of death and danger had only driven her into her own heart, and it was no matter what he had told her, she could wait no longer to learn the identity of her true love. (p. 134)

Multiplex reality has displaced fairy tale simplicity; Rosamond has entered the world we inhabit. Unfortunately, her reaction to her discovery that her bandit is also Jamie Lockhart does not lead her immediately away from isolation into union with another. Instead of seeing and accepting the sad and joyous human mystery, she retreats to simplistic labelling, and Jamie responds in kind:

> 'You are Jamie Lockhart!' she said.
> 'And you are Clement Musgrove's silly daughter!' said he.
> 'Good-by,' he said. 'For you did not trust me, and did not love me, for you wanted only to know who I am. Now I cannot stay in the house with you.' (p. 134)

We recall that Jamie was willing for Mike Fink to declare *who* he was, but not *what* he was. By seeking merely his name, Rosamond has chosen the least important part of Jamie's identity (one available even to his enemies), condemning herself to superficial knowledge of Jamie.

And yet Rosamond's impulse is not entirely wrong. Jamie, in hiding part of himself from the one who loves him, is endangering their love. Rosamond sounds at least partially right when she cries, after Jamie has left her:

> 'My husband was a robber and not a bridegroom . . . . He brought me his love under a mask, and kept all the truth hidden from me, and never called anything by its true name, even his name or mine, and what I would have given him he liked better to steal.' (p. 146)

What she learns, however, is that "names were nothing and untied no knots" (p. 150). She has to move past the stage where she can assert: ". . . I already know everything and can learn nothing new" (p. 137). Goat's reply to that declaration ("Do not be so sad as all that . . .") is not the *non-sequitur* it seems. Few states are sadder than thinking we have figured out all life's mysteries—especially the mysteries about other people. To get beyond the labels of "Jamie Lockhart" or "robber" or "Clement's silly daughter"—to appreciate the complex humanity on the other side of the name—that is when the universal search for "who we are and who the other fellow is" might pay off.

In Welty's story as in folk fairy tales, the woman is the one who pushes for integration. The message that Rosamond sends Jamie "out of the future"—from their twins to be born next week (p. 177)—makes very real the power of the female suasion to unification. Rosamond's role is much like that ascribed by Bettelheim to the women in other tales who suspect they are married to beastly bridegrooms:

> . . . one very significant feature of the animal-groom cycle . . . [is that] the groom is absent during the night; he is believed to be animal during the day and to become human only in bed; in short, he keeps his day and night existences separate from each other: . . . he wishes to keep his sex life separated from all else he is doing. The female . . . is unwilling to accept the separation and isolation of purely sexual aspects of life from the rest of it. She tries to force their unification. But once Psyche embarks on trying to wed the aspects of sex, love, and life into a unity, she does not falter, and in the end she wins.[22]

Like Psyche, Rosamond does not falter. She does her penance for asking the wrong questions about her lover's identity. Following Jamie's path along the tangled wilderness of the Natchez Trace, she is "tattered and torn, and tired from sleeping in hollow trees and keeping awake in the woods" (pp. 168-9). The imagery here implies both enlightenment and acceptance of the unity of apparent opposites (in this case, the human unity with the natural world).

In the last chapter we feel the book's emerging from its dark inner core (where we watched the death of the Indian girl, the robber band, Little Harp, and Salome), its returning to the realm of fairy tale. Mike Fink joins Rosamond now as he did Jamie in the beginning. (But even he is chastened and improved, shaken from his blustering self-importance by his encounters with what he takes to be Jamie's ghost.) The idyllic life Jamie and Rosamond establish in New Orleans is our best hint that a fairy tale version of reality dominates as the novella ends. Yet even in this conclusion Welty reminds us of the doubleness of reality that Rosamond and Jamie fail to see—in spite of their personal integration (or, perhaps, because of the protection it offers from life's darker side). Describing their life to her father, Rosamond sketches a happy-ever-after world, complete with beautiful twins, a stately house, a boat, servants, and rich friends. For the moment their eyes are not on the wilderness that still surrounds them or the Indians that inhabit it. And yet Welty's concluding references to Rosamond and Jamie's "hundred slaves" and to the pirates' galleons they sail out to watch, as well as to Clement's return to the wilderness, remind us that evil is closer

[22]Bettelheim, *The Uses of Enchantment*: 294.

than they may be aware—"with us, within us," as Welty has declared.[23] Thus, while Jamie and Rosamond have returned to life in a fairy tale, the reader carries away the corrected vision of a reality in which darkness and light, hope and despair, joy and sorrow, beginnings and endings are dynamically united in the terrible and marvelous cosmic dance.

[23]"Henry Green: Novelist of the Imagination" in *The Eye of the Story*: 21.

From *The Southern Literary Journal* 20.2 (Spring 1988): 51-68.

The Wide Net and Other Stories 1943

Fiction in Review

Diana Trilling

In her latest collection of short stories, *The Wide Net*, Eudora Welty has developed her technical virtuosity to the point where it outweighs the uses to which it is put, and her vision of horror to the point of nightmare. Of course even in her earlier work Miss Welty had a strong tendency toward stylism and "fine" writing; she liked to move toward the mythical, and she had a heart for decay and an eye for the Gothic in detail. But she also had a reliable and healthy wit, her dialogue could be as normally reportorial of its world as the dialogue of Ring Lardner, and for the most part she knew how to keep performance subservient to communication; she told her story instead of dancing it, and when she saw horror it could be the clear day-to-day horror of actual life, not only the horror of dreams. There was plenty of surrealist paraphernalia, if you will, in a story like "The Petrified Man"—the falling hair of the customer, the presence of the three-year-old boy amid the bobbie-pins and sexual confidences of the beauty parlor, the twins in a bottle at the freak show, or even the petrified man himself. But compare to "The Petrified Man" the story Asphodel from Miss Welty's current volume, with its Doric columns and floating muslins, its pomegranate stains and blackberry cordial and its "old goats and young," and you will recognize the fancy road up which Miss Welty has turned her great talents.

The title story of Miss Welty's new volume is its best story but not typical. An account of a river-dragging party which starts out to recover the body of a supposed suicide but forgets its mission in the joys of the occasion. "The Wide Net" has its share of the elements of a tour de force, but it has more communicated meaning than the rest of the stories in the book, and it best fuses content and method. Of the six other stories "Livvie" is the only one which I like at all, and the only story, in addition to "The Wide Net," which I feel I understood. Yet the volume as a whole has tremendous emotional impact, despite its obscurity. However, this seems to me to be beside the point, for the fear that a story or a picture engenders is likely to be in inverse proportion to its rational content: witness the drawings of children or psychotics, or most of surrealist art; and Miss Welty employs to good effect the whole manual of ghostliness—wind and storm, ruined buildings, cloaks, horses' hooves on a lonely highway, fire and moonlight and people who live and ride alone. But the evocation of the mood of horror or of a dreamlike atmosphere has become an end in itself, and if, for each story, there is a point of departure in narrative, so that I can report, for instance, that "First Love" is about a deaf-and-dumb boy who falls in love with Aaron Burr, or that Asphodel is about a tyrannical half-mad Southern gentlewoman, or that "A Still Moment" is a legend of Audubon, still the stories themselves stay with their narrative no more than a dance, say, stays with its argument. This, indeed, is the nature of "The Wide Net": it is a book of ballets, not of stories; even the title piece is a *pastorale macabre*.

Now I happen to think that to make a ballet out of words is a perversion of their best function, and I dislike—because it breeds exhibitionism and insincerity—the attitude toward narrative which allows an author to sacrifice the precise meaning of language to its rhythms and patterns. The word sincerity has lost caste in the criticism of serious writing, I know. But this seems to me unfortunate. We live in a very crafty literary period in which what aims to be art but is only artful is too often mistaken for the real thing. When an author says "Look at me" instead of "Look at it," there is insincerity, as I see it. The test of sincerity is wasted in the sphere of popular art, where criticism has sent it; most popular art is nothing if not sincere, and where it is not, it is usually because it is aping the manners of its betters. In these new stories Miss Welty's prose constantly calls attention to herself and away from her object. When she writes, ". . . Jenny sat there . . . in the posture of a child who is appalled at the stillness and unsurrender of the still and unsurrendering world," or "He walked alone, slowly through the silence, with the sturdy and yet dreamlike walk of the orphan," she is not only being falsely poetic, she is being untrue. How does the walk of an orphan differ in its sturdiness and in its dream quality from the walk of a child with two parents? How would you even explain "unsurrender" to a child, and wouldn't a child be appalled precisely by the *surrender* of the world, if the concept could reach him? This is the sin of pride—this self-conscious contriving—endemic to a whole generation of writers since Katherine Mansfield and most especially to the women of that generation.

Somewhere between Chekhov and Katherine Mansfield the short story certainly went off its trolley. I think it is Miss Mansfield who must be held responsible for the extreme infusion of subjectivism and private sensibility into the short fiction of our day. In Miss Welty's case the subjectivism takes the form, as I say, of calling attention to herself by fine writing; in stories for a magazine like the *New Yorker*, which happily has no taste for fine writing, the form it takes is rather more subtle—the calling of attention to oneself for one's fine moral perceptions. This is a point I shall develop next week in discussing several other current collections of short stories, including those of Sylvia Townsend Warner.

I have spoken of the ballet quality of Miss Welty's stories: in this connection I am reminded of the painter Dali and—via Dali—of the relationship between the chic modern department store and much of modern fiction. (One day I should like, in fact, to trace what I see to be the direct line of descent from Miss Mansfield to Bonwit Teller.) Although the suspicion intrudes itself that Dali works with his tongue in his cheek, Miss Welty's dedication is of course unquestionable: this should be said at once. Still, the resemblance in performance and the subtle cultural kinship between the two is striking. Both Dali and Miss Welty are mythologists and creators of legend, both take their metaphor from dreams, and yet both are devoted naturalists; and each has a mother-country—Dali, Spain; Miss Welty, the Natchez country—whose atmosphere and superstition permeate his work and whose confines are determining beyond the power of travel or maturer experience to enlarge them. Rather more suggestive, however, than these similarities is their common service to what amounts to a myth of modern femininity.

For if it seemed a strange day for both art and commercialism when Bonwit Teller engaged Dali to do its windows, actually it was not so revolutionary as it looked. In the making of modern myths, the American department store has been at least abreast of the American artist. The chic department store mannequin is surely one of the great metaphors of our time; the displays of merchandise one of the great abstractions, based upon naturalism, of our art. But more fundamental, we recall the slogan created a few years ago by Bonwit Teller, "Have you that cherished look?" and we realize that it was the department store which stated most unmistakably (so unmistakably, indeed, that the slogan was dropped) the modern woman's dream of herself. Here in all its economic nakedness is the narcissism which is so widely supported in current female writing, including Miss Welty's. This mythologizing of the feminine self, whether by means of clothes or prose, is as far from femininity as from feminism.

There is now running in the magazines an advertisement for a Schiaparelli product, "Shocking Radiance," the illustration painted by Dali. "Shocking Radiance," it appears, is four oils—for the body, the face, the eyelids, and the lips—and to promote its sale Dali has painted a Venus rising from her shell, attended by a trio of sprites, one of whom pours a libation on her breast, while another holds before her the mirror of her self-regard. Even at the risk of satirizing Miss Welty's stories, I suggest a study of this Schiaparelli-Dali advertisement to see the *reductio ad absurdum* of the elements in Miss Welty's latest work which have no place in such a serious and greatly endowed writer.

From *The Nation* 157 (2 October 1943): 386-87.

Consolations of Poetry

Issac Rosenfield

The Wide Net, a collection of eight stories, urges comparison with Eudora Welty's earlier work. *A Curtain of Green*, forecasting her present development, showed a taste for the mildly fantastic, an eye, more than an ear, for an objective poetry of mood and the symbols of mood, and a considerable ease and variety in her treatment of the short-story form. She had many styles at her command: ironic reportage, a still-life intensity, a humor fond of the neuroses and degeneracies in Southern life. She held these styles impersonally and loosely, unsure of her ultimate intentions, sure only of her talent, which she employed with an artiness that gave her gropings an air of finality.

Beginning with *The Robber Bridegroom* (full-fledged in the present volume) her artiness becomes estheticism. *The Wide Net* strikes you at once with its silence. Except in the title story, her characters are largely engaged in flashbacks and in reveries; words are written down, not spoken. She now ignores the resources of Southern speech—in "First Love" even selecting the point of view of a deaf boy where she misses, in addition to sound, all the dramatic possibilities inherent in Aaron Burr's trial and escape from Natchez— in order to ring in a poetry of her own, off beat, in any rhythm, with the swing of actual talk. It is a poetry of textures that are never felt, of glass leaves and glass birds; and what remains of her prose is given over to the creation of characters, soliloquizing in the manner of minor Elizabethan dramatists. This is not to suggest that a departure from naturalism is necessarily a loss. What she has lost is a clear, engaging quality of immediate presence and appeal, sacrificed to an esthetic of presentation.

Nevertheless, one of her new stories, "A Still Moment," is perfectly successful, achieving its tense beauty even while it is so painfully bent on creating a genre for itself. It tells of Audubon, the naturalist, out wandering through Natchez country where he comes upon a murderer and an itinerant preacher viewing a sunset. The preacher is a madman of God, of wild love in the Divine Presence. The murderer is a master of his trade, an artist with a cynical flair in his knowledge of the meaning of murder. Audubon draws a bead on the bird, killing it in its beauty in order to advance his studies. This deed is revelatory. The romantic artist (it is in this capacity rather than as naturalist that Audubon enters the story) is shown preëmpting the impulses of less perfect men to unite love and death in his art.

This may not be Eudora Welty's first dissertation of the nature of the artist—the composite symbolism of *The Robber Bridegroom* makes a nod in that direction—but it is, definitely, her most conscious "problem-story" that takes the activity of the artist as its scope. The theme alone is significant of the development she is undergoing, a development which represents a growth of artistic self-consciousness to the point of an exclusive preoccupation. An esthetic involution takes place. The world is no longer the source and central point of her art (a position it retains even in the fantasies of Kafka) but has become an incidental background related to her writing only by the beauty it may occasionally share with her prose. Imagination grows too careful, too tight and exact; invention becomes too much of a burden and sensation is easier to sustain. But sensation comes without feeling. The latter is available only through the provisions of a formal pattern, which means that emotion grows cold waiting, entering art only by condescension. The formalities must be observed. So art passes into a desperate, dead-end estheticism; writers become the creatures of their own activity, losing not so much of naturalism as of nature.

But there is a motive to such writing. It does not spring of itself, straight from the head. Even the purest esthetic, whatever it may gloss over in psychological content, is shot through with anxiety. For the writer who exchanges centers with the world, focusing his attention on artistry, runs a great risk. There is the risk of incommunicability; the risk of the trivial; the risk of losing emotional reference, that human closeness which gives good writing the feeling of standing on the brink of great discoveries. This anxiety is implicit in Eudora Welty's work; fearing she may have lost the heart of her experience, she forces a compensatory poetry upon her prose.

From *The New Republic* 109 (18 October 1943): 525-26.

Persephone in Eudora Welty's "Livvie"

Peggy W. Prenshaw

Eudora Welty's "Livvie," the story of a young woman who is "carried away" from home and family by an aged husband to a remote house on the sunken Natchez Trace, calls to mind at once the myth of Persephone's abduction by Hades.[1] Although many critics have examined Welty's use of mythic material in this and other stories, no one has explored the elaborate and insistent pattern of details identifying Livvie and the characters surrounding her with the Persephone myth.[2] Perhaps what is most extraordinary about this story, and largely overlooked, is Welty's fusing of a realistic story set in the Mississippi countryside not only with the well-known episode involving Persephone, but with a motif of death and regeneration drawn from the related myths of Demeter and Dionysus, specifically, from the Eleusinian Mysteries.

A brief analysis of some of the main details of the story shows how explicitly Livvie is identified with Persephone. She is sixteen when she marries Solomon, "an only girl." The ambiguous words of the omniscient narrator suggest the youth and uniqueness associated with Persephone, often known as the Kore, Demeter's only daughter. Unlike Persephone, Livvie goes willingly with Solomon, but we are told "she had not thought she could not get back." Further, "where she came from people said an old man did not want anybody in the world to ever find his wife, for fear they would steal her back from him" (p. 153).

In the Homeric Hymn to Demeter, Persephone remains hidden from her mother for nine days when at last the Sun reveals her whereabouts. Livvie

[1]"Livvie" in *The Wide Net and Other Stories* (New York: Harcourt, Brace, 1943). Subsequent page references are to *Selected Stories of Eudora Welty* (New York: Modern Library, 1954).

[2]See especially Neil Isaacs, *Eudora Welty* (Austin: Steck-Vaughn, 1969), p. 4.

has lived with Solomon for nine years, he growing older, she still young, when she is finally discovered. Her loneliness and barrenness are imaged in the stillness of the house and the dirt yard, which she herself keeps free of grass. But a potential fertility, submerged only temporarily, is as unmistakable as that of Persephone, whose recovery brought new life to earth. Livvie's single, treasured possession is the picture of a baby she had once tended, and near the steps of her house are rose bushes with "tiny blood-red roses" that come, like ovulation, every month.

In many respects Solomon parallels Hades. He bears a kingly manner, and he imprisons his wife in an isolated house that the Natchez Trace, like the River Styx, separates from the world. Once, when Livvie ventures down the Trace, she feels as if she is wading a river; dead leaves reach as high as her knees. She climbs the high banks only to find a graveyard and trees enclosed in caterpillar nets that seem in the sun to burn like flames. Around the trees, which remind her of a torch-lit entrance to the Underworld, stretches a desolate scene accompanied by the sound of a mourning dove.

Solomon himself epitomizes death, ceasing to eat and sleeping day and night in a bed that is "like a throne." He seems to Livvie a "strict man"; he has a "strict mouth" and "strong eyes with second sight." Of course, Hades is typically portrayed as a grim and mournful character; H.J. Rose describes him as "severely just" and "inexorable in the carrying out of his, or Fate's, decrees."[3] Furthermore, the name "Solomon," associated in the Old Testament with wisdom, calls to mind a similar feature of Hades, who was sometimes known as Eubuleus, meaning "Wise in Counsel." Another of Hades' names, Pluton or Plutos, designating "the Rich" or "Wealth," suggests another parallel to Solomon, who is a well-to-do owner of his own house and land. Finally, Solomon, like Hades, cuts a regal figure: he shines forth in a youthful picture that shows "a fan of hair . . . like a king's crown" (p. 160).

What emerges in the story as Solomon's most remarkable activity, however, is not his accumulation of wealth but his effort to keep spirits from entering his house through the magic of bottle trees, which he has carefully wrought during the nine-year marriage. The trees line the approach to the house—bare crepe myrtles that sprout no leaves but green and blue bottles. Also in the yard, near the red roses, are peach and pomegranate trees, the latter of course important in the vegetation myth associated with the Hades-Persephone story. Persephone, having eaten the pomegranate, is eternally infected with death. Although Demeter wins her reinstatement to the land of

[3]*A Handbook of Greek Mythology* (New York: Dutton, 1959), p. 78.

the living, she cannot abrogate the death penalty which strikes her daughter for part of each year.

The character who finds Livvie seems at first an unlikely Demeter figure. Miss Baby Marie arrives suddenly outside Livvie's door in a little car "steaming like a kettle." She is coarse, intrusive, and insistent on selling the cosmetics she brings. But further details of her appearance and behavior do indeed parallel a mythical being who rescues the maiden and returns her to home and life. For example, she is immune to limits of time and space. At first she appears as young, then old, to Livvie. She is "more than middle-sized" and wears a big hat, but she manages to enter the house through a door barely cracked open. An air of "triumph and secrecy" surrounds her. The lipstick she hands to Livvie is purple, a color specifically associated with Demeter. It "opens like magic," and its fragrance—"Chinaberry flowers," says Livvie—instantly transports the young woman home. She imagines her mother holding up an apron heavy with ripe figs and her father "holding a fish-pole over the pond, . . . the little clear fishes swimming up to the brim" (pp. 165-66). This image of fertility—fecund and phallic—anticipates the next stage that awaits the imprisoned Livvie, the stage that brings release from bondage and the promise of ever-renewing life.

Aside from her name several details suggest a Madonna figure in the characterization of Baby Marie. In Welty's comic but nonetheless deliberate description, the woman has a face that "draws the light" and otherwise reminds us of traditional portraits of Mary. As she leaves Livvie, "in the air and all around like a bright halo around the white lady's nodding head, it was a true spring day" (p. 168). The Biblical overtone seems less a confusion or doubling of myths than a subtle reinforcement of what is essentially the Persephone-Demeter story. Mary is invoked as simply another face of the goddess of earthly life. Baby Marie, who journeys to find Livvie, parallels the awesome mother, who holds sovereignty over nature's life and death. Baby Marie's reply, when Livvie tries to pay for the lipstick with eggs, "No, I have plenty of eggs—plenty," gives further evidence of an infinitude of life enclosed within this mother figure. When she leaves, she does not take Livvie with her, but she gives her a vision of home and, with the painted lips, a renewed, pulsing sense of life. After her visit, Solomon's hold on Livvie is surely broken.

A final characteristic of Baby Marie that invites attention is her witch-like aspect. The intense red and white coloring of her face, the tousled red hair and, especially, the wavering, flame-like image reflected in the mirror, all suggest an evil stepmother or witch, plotting the doom of an innocent maid. The relationship between the witch and the Demeter figure is, however, not at all incongruous or inconsistent. In his detailed study of

Kore, Carl Kerényi shows that Hecate, the Mistress of Spirits, is an essential figure in the Demeter-Persephone cult. In some accounts of the myth Hecate, Demeter's ally, helps in the search for Persephone. In the archetype of the divine mother she is a second Demeter, a double, who retains a certain motherliness as a fertility goddess closely related to the moon. Frequently represented as bearing a torch, she appears as a light-bringer. Kerényi notes that in one version of the myth, it is Hecate rather than Demeter who is led to the Underworld in search of Persephone. He concludes in his study of the archetype that Hecate, Demeter, and Persephone are embodiments of a single mythological idea.[4] Basic to the identification is the essence of each goddess: destruction, mourning, and rebirth, inseparable in any account of man's earthly experience.

In the popular myth the beneficent Demeter restores the earth's vegetation after she recovers Persephone. In Welty's story Baby Marie initiates only the beginning of Livvie's movement from barrenness to fertility. Her release from Solomon is accomplished finally in the union with Cash, a young field hand portrayed in the story as a Dionysian figure. Like the god of the vine, Cash appears suddenly on a spring day; his coat is "leaf-green"; and an "emerald green" feather adorns his plum-colored hat. Cash's manner suggests an animal, perhaps a bull or a goat, the familiar avatars of Dionysus;[5] or a Pan-like satyr, part man, part goat. He "flings" his head, and in a miraculous gesture "wags" it against the sky. He stamps and plunges zigzag up the front steps. Entering Solomon's room, he makes "a noise like a hoof pawing the floor."

In his work on Dionysus, Walter Otto tells us that the god's arrival transforms the earth, shattering the well-ordered world in a "frenzied, all-engulfing torrent of life." With his coming, "everything that has been locked up is released. The alien and hostile unite in miraculous harmony. Age-old laws . . . suddenly [lose] their power, and even the dimensions of time and space are no longer valid."[6] Ultimately, the presence of the god produces an irrepressible desire to dance.

This description mirrors Cash exactly. He dazzles Livvie with the prospect of passion and menace, walking as he does with a phallic "guinea pig in his pocket," and "kicking the flowers as if he could break through everything in the way and destroy anything in the world" (p. 170). He sails a stone into Solomon's bottle trees, releasing them, and immediately after the old man's

[4]"Kore" in C.G. Jung and C. Kerényi, *Essays on a Science of Mythology*, trans. R.F.C. Hull (1949; rpt. New York: Harper Torchbooks, 1963), pp. 109-113.

[5]See J.G. Frazer, *The Golden Bough* (New York: Macmillan, 1930), p. 390.

[6]*Dionysus*, trans. Robert B. Palmer (Bloomington: Indiana University Press, 1965), p. 95.

death, he seizes Livvie, whirling her in a furious dance, until she, oblivious to time and death, drops the treasured silver watch that had been Solomon's final gift to her.

Further identifying Cash with Dionysus is a description of the field hands whom Livvie notices just as she feels the arrival of spring. Like a band of Dionysian celebrants anticipating the arrival of the god, they seem to be "going to some place on a journey" and to be awaiting a sign when "they would all start at once shouting, hollering, cajoling, calling and answering back, running, being leaped on and breaking away, flinging to earth with a shout and lying motionless in the trance of twelve o'clock" (p. 161).

Such mythic parallels persist throughout the story; I have noted only those most explicitly put forward in the text, least susceptible to the charge of a too-ingenious reading. Clearly Welty takes some liberties with the myths, changing and fusing mythic characters and episodes in ways that intensify and universalize what is foremost, Livvie's vivid and realistic story. What I find most remarkable, however, is precisely the linking of the Persephone and Dionysus motifs. This association ties the story of Livvie's return to the two most important Greek cults celebrating fertility. In the great Eleusinian Mysteries the Greeks worshipped Demeter and Persephone, who assured the regeneration of earth and the human species. Dionysian cults, similarly, honored a god who died and was reborn and thus gave evidence that vine and man alike must take on a kind of death to be assured rebirth. In fact, in accounts of the Eleusinian Mysteries there occurs an essential third figure, Iakchos, who is frequently identified as Dionysus, or variously as a son of Demeter or Persephone (Zagreus), a husband of Demeter, or even the son of Dionysus.[7] Kerényi writes of the divine triad that presided over the merry women's mysteries in December and over the Dionysian festival at Eleusis: "Its members are Demeter, Kore [Persephone], and Dionysus, who belong inseparably together."[8] The basic theme in all the rituals associated with these gods is the eternal coming of life from death.

In Welty's story Solomon, like Hades, takes a young wife whose very name, Livvie, points to her role as ever-renewing life. She is rescued from sterility when her husband, the god of the dead, becomes the dying god, making way for the appearance of a new king of the woods, or, more emphatically, for his own reincarnation in the figure of the youthful Dionysus. Solomon's bottle trees, images of an enforced sterility, protect

[7] Rose, pp. 95-96.

[8] *Eleusis: Archetypal Image of Mother and Daughter*, trans. Ralph Manheim, Bollingen Series 65, No. 4 (New York: Pantheon Books, 1976), p. 140.

Solomon—like a sacred grove—as long as they remain intact. When Cash hurls the rock into the trees, Solomon's death is imminent.

The experience of dying, crucial in the archetype of regeneration, is thus furnished in the story by the aged man, a waning Dionysus. As a young man Solomon had produced abundant harvests, cultivated orchards, but in his last years he is a maker of bottle trees. According to an Orphic hymn Dionysus sleeps in the house of Persephone until he returns.[9] It is not surprising to find that he who sleeps with Persephone is a god with two faces, Hades and Dionysus, who are identified by ancient and modern students of myth as one and the same.[10] These are two essential forms of a god who vanishes and reappears, one who dies and is reborn.

Interpretations of the Welty story have generally viewed the Solomon-Cash opposition as an Apollonian-Dionysian conflict, in which the organic life principle takes precedence over individual accomplishment. Thus the story is read as a sort of tragi-comic reversal of the "Sailing to Byzantium" theme; here the young in one another's arms outlast the artistry of golden birds—or bottle trees. The interpretation is reasonable but does not account, I think, for the similarities between Solomon and Cash nor for the tone of celebration which infuses the story.

The original title of the story, "Livvie Is Back,"[11] seems a rather explicit reference to the Persephone myth of renewal. But Livvie is back precisely because one consort dies and another appears. Solomon's death, his loss to Cash, is not simply regrettable; it is necessary. Dionysus, inciting procreation and creativity, dies and thus assures a renewal of desire—sexual and artistic.

Many details suggest that Solomon's dying is very much like a birth. Livvie begins eating for two, consuming the meal that Solomon refuses. She is said to feel the "stir of spring," as "present in the house as a young man would be." The outside scene reflects a similar intertwining of death and life. The moon is in the last quarter as the distant field hands turn the sod, planting peas and beans. Inside, in his bed, Solomon looks like a "different and smaller man," like "someone kin to himself," with a face "like new . . . smooth and clear." It seems to Livvie that "the quiet she kept was for a sleeping baby, and that she had a baby and was its mother." Solomon embodies death, lying wrapped in a quilt "as if it were winter still." But he, like Phoenix, the old black woman of Welty's "A Worn Path," also

[9] Otto, p. 197.

[10] See Otto, pp. 115-16; Kerényi, *Eleusis*, p. 40. Kerényi cites Heraclitus as one who reaches the same conclusion.

[11] *Atlantic Monthly*, 170 (November 1942), 57-64.

incarnates life in death. Beneath his quilt, we are told, Solomon might have been "a bird, an Egyptian, . . . or a swaddled baby, about to smile and brush all away" (p. 174).

Throughout the story the Phoenix, or regeneration, principle is elaborated through parallels to the Greek version of the archetype. We see as a central element in the Persephone and Dionysus myths the figures of a dying god. The tragic elements of "Livvie" do not grow so much from the Apollonian-Dionysian conflict in society as from the inevitability of death for the separate self. The Greeks gave civilization a heightened consciousness of the individual, who, separated from organic life, living *in time*, fully perceived the abyss of his mortality. But in the Eleusianian Mysteries they maintained a complementary vision of the self recovered from isolation and death, returned to life through the promise of procreation and, more mystically, through faith in a god of the earth who vanished and reappeared.

Livvie, like Persephone, and Solomon and Cash, like Dionysus, contain an infinitude of lives and deaths. Cash, whom Solomon knew "all the time"—and who is appropriately named as a son, or double, of Plutos (Wealth)—appears miraculously at the bleak, tragic moment of death. Like a bridegroom or a returning god he walks with Livvie down the Trace, the "white irises shining like candles." The resurrection of Livvie and life is joyously celebrated at the conclusion in sexual images of flying birds and brilliant sunlight that fills the bottles. In the dying Solomon we see the assertion of the self that is a losing battle. "Life" wins out; ultimately, as in Faulkner's *Light in August*, a comedy serenely enfolds the tragic moment.

Livvie, a late version of the ancient Persephone, lives on like the reappearing grain. Like the myth, Welty's story shows the struggle between life and self, or nature and art, to be less a battle than an old dependency. Finally, "Livvie" gives a classical vision of an enduring earthly pattern.

From *Studies in Short Fiction* 17.2 (Spring 1980): 149-55.

Delta Wedding
1946

Eudora Welty

Mary Alice Bookhart

It is not surprising to learn that the local book dealers have found it necessary to order and re-order shipments of Eudora Welty's novel, "Delta Wedding," since it came off the press the middle of April. It is not enough to borrow a copy from the lending library, read and return, for even without the distinction of bearing the author's autograph, this first full-length novel by Jackson's own Miss Welty is a book to own, to read and re-read.

Written with the same fluent, exquisite prose which characterized her earlier work, but lacking the grimness of some of her short stories and the fantasy of her short novel, "The Robber Bridegroom," "Delta Wedding" is an important contribution to American literature. Not only is it the memorable story of an unforgettable family, but it is a record of a certain era, a certain way of life in a part of this country which is a nation within a nation.

Acclaimed as one of the country's outstanding short story writers, Miss Welty has followed the pattern of the short story in her first novel. With her usual economy of words—each with a purpose—Miss Welty presents to her readers a section of life at Shellmound, plantation home of the Fairchild family. There is no detailed background for introduction to the scene, time and characters; instead, the reader, with nine-year-old Laura McRaven (whose mother was a Fairchild), who rode the Yellow Dog up from Jackson, is dropped squarely in the middle of the delta town on a hot September afternoon in 1923, when the family is gathering for the wedding of Dabney Fairchild to Troy Flavin, the overseer. With Laura, the reader is swept along into the excitement of those seven days, meeting the members of the family and initiated into the circle, which is a strong and unbroken one.

In presenting this one section of the life of a gay, extravagant and charming family, Miss Welty follows her custom of writing honestly, without prejudice and authoratively. It is as if she spotlights a portion of a wide canvas, bringing it into sharp relief for concentrated interest. The rest of the picture is in shadow, bit it is there in the reader's consciousness, forming a backdrop against which the illuminated scene stands out in bright focus.

"Delta Wedding" is not for those who demand that their novels start with a bang, end with a flourish and are peopled with characters forever becoming involved in situations so desperate that they can only be extricated by coincidence or hokum. For Miss Welty is not so much concerned with plot as she is in creating a mood, which is sustained throughout the story she has to tell. Indeed, there is a dream-like hypnotic quality about her work, which, however, never interferes with its clarity. Her observations, through the eyes of a child, for instance, are so remarkably presented, with emphasis on the most minute detail that the reader recalls with surprise and nostalgic delight similar incidents or memories almost forgotten with the passing of time.

One critic writes that Miss Welty writes of the unusual in terms of the usual. We disagree: Eudora Welty writes of the usual in terms of the unusual. The Victrola at one end of the room, for instance, "stood like a big morning glory." Or, the two aunts, "in their pinks and blues looked like two plump hydrangea bushes side by side." Or, Brunswick-town, where . . . . "the old women had it shady, secret, lazy, and cool. A devious, invisible vine of talk seemed to grow from shady porch to shady porch, though all of the ole women were hidden."

When more "picturesque speech" is spoken and better metaphors are turned, it will be Miss Welty who does both.

From *The Clarion-Ledger* 28 April 1946: 8.

Fiction in Review

Diana Trilling

I find it difficult to determine how much of my distaste for Eudora Welty's new book, "Delta Wedding," is dislike of its literary manner and how much is resistance to the culture out of which it grows and which it describes so fondly. But actually, I think, Miss Welty's style and her cultural attitude are not to be separated. It is impossible for me to conceive of a Northern or Western or, for that matter, a European or an Australian or an African scene that could provoke an exacerbation of poeticism to equal Miss Welty's in this novel. Compared to Miss Welty's sensibility, the sensibility of a Katherine Mansfield, a Sylvia Townsend Warner, a Christina Stead, or an Edita Morris—to name some of the writers, all of them women, notable in our time for the delicacy of their intensities—presents itself as a crude, corporeal thing indeed. Dolls' houses, birds, moonlight, snow, the minutiae of vulnerable young life and the sudden revelations of nature may have their distressingly persistent way of agitating the modern female literary psyche in whatever climate or social context; but it seems tome that only on a Southern plantation could the chance remark of a gardener to the effect that he wished there "wouldn't be a rose in de world" set the lady of the house to "trembling . . . as at some impudence."

It is out of tremulousnesses like this, as a matter of fact, that the whole of Miss Welty's novel is built. Dramatically speaking, nothing happens in "Delta Wedding." Miss Welty is telling the story of seven days in the life of the Fairchild family of Mississippi: it is the week in which Dabney, the seventeen-year-old daughter of the house, is being married to her father's overseer. Relatives pay calls and are called upon; meals are eaten; gifts arrive; people dance; servants rally in the established plantation fashion. Domestic bustle and a spattering of family reminiscences are all the narrative structure Miss Welty needs to house her treasures of sensibility.

And yet one suspects that, for all its tenuousness, "Delta Wedding" says precisely what it intends to say. Among evocative novelists Miss Welty is extraordinarily gifted; and if one finishes her book with a strong sense of confusion as to Miss Welty's own judgment upon certain aspects of Delta life, one has no reason to feel that it is because Miss Welty lacks the ability to communicate any content she wants to. For instance, in common with most of our talented Southern writers, Miss Welty is frank to acknowledge the possible blemishes on the surface of the society she so much adores: she specifies snobbery, xenophobia, "mindlessness"—the kindly euphemism, we gather, for idiocy or insanity—and others of the distractions and sorrows that we have so often been told are part of the price the South pays for its heritage of pride. Yet this much honest revelation of Southern fact can in no way be interpreted as an adverse criticism of the Fairchild way of life. Quite the contrary, it must rather be interpreted as a test of Miss Welty's love for it—a love so strong that it can not only admit these failings but even cherish them. For just as the Fairchild women have always loved the large indolences which they see as the other side of the coin of the large generosities of their men, so Miss Welty would seem to love the Fairchild meannesses and arrogances and weaknesses as the inevitable other side of the coin of their aristocratic grace and charm. She leaves her honest cultural observations in rosy poetic solution exactly because she does not wish to precipitate them as moral judgment.

Now obviously in asking for moral judgment I am asking only for moral discrimination, and not for what usually passes for it—moralizing hostility; even more than other forms of growth, art flourishes in affection. And I would not wish to dismiss as without worth or good meaning all the elements in the Fairchild culture that Miss Welty finds so beguiling. Certainly the careless abundance of Fairchild life—the abundance of children, of visitors, of fondness, of hams, beaten biscuit, iced lemonade, coconut layer cakes, even of indulgence of a daughter's wilfulness when she selects a socially undesirable husband—is something to be cherished; and I for one would not wish to replace it with the brittle and meager domestic ideal of much of our "progressive" Northern literature. As I say, it is where "Delta Wedding" implies—and the implication is pervasive—that the parochialism and snobbery of the Fairchild clan is the condition of the Fairchild kind of relaxation and charm, or that the Fairchild grace has a necessary source in a life of embattled pride, that I must deeply oppose its values.

In writing about Miss Welty's last book, "The Wide Net," I spoke of the self-consciousness of her developing style, of the narcissistic dream quality of the stories in that volume as compared to their earlier work. In the light of her present novel one begins to see the connection between this style and Miss Welty's relation to traditional Southern culture. For in the best of her stories, and they were the earliest ones, Miss Welty gave us what was really a new view of the South, indeed a new kind of realism about the South; and for this she used, not a dance prose, but a prose that walked on its feet in the world of reality. But increasingly Miss Welty has turned away from the lower-middle-class milieu of, say, The Petrified Man, to that part of the Southern scene which is most available to myth and celebrative legend and, in general, to the narcissistic Southern fantasy; and for this her prose has risen more and more on tiptoe. As a result, one of our most promising young writers gives signs of becoming, instead of the trenchant and objective commentator we hoped she would be, just another if more ingenious dreamer on the Southern past.

From *The Nation* 162 (11 May 1946): 578.

Look Away, Look Away, Look Away

Hamilton Basso

Although the South has had enough of a literary going over to satisfy even the most demanding student of the subject, a trio of novels about the territory have recently appeared to prove that the going over is still going on. The chorus of enthusiasm that has greeted the publication of Eudora Welty's new novel, "Delta Wedding," the first of these three books, made me wary of it at first, but now I'm doubting after having reread the book, so much did I like it, whether the chorus was loud enough. I'm equally uncertain that it has been praised for the right reasons. Miss Welty, generally speaking, is most frequently praised because she can write. There's no doubt about that. She can do things with the English language that have all the unpredictable wonder and surprise of a ball of mercury rolling about in the palm of one's hand. But the point, it seems to me, is not whether Miss Welty can write but what she has done with her writing. For my part, she has done enough to produce as fine a novel as any contemporary American author has turned up with in recent years.

Miss Welty's novel is one in which, as the saying goes, nothing happens. There have been several novels of such a nature recently, but, unlike most of them, Miss Welty's book is not a prolonged exercise in arty ineptitude. Although nothing "happens" in "Delta Wedding" (a little girl comes to visit her relatives for the wedding of her cousin, she is caught up in the swirling life of the family, and the wedding takes place), *everything* happens. I am sure that Miss Welty didn't write her book to prove the truism that character is action just as much as action is character, but that, along with plenty of other things, is what she has done. Risking a guess, I'd say that Miss Welty has spent a great deal of time reading Henry James; risking a flat statement, I'd say that she has looked as intelligently into the workings of human beings as any modern writer who has come along since that unpleasant snob but great writer mastered the lessons that Stendhal set down. Miss Welty's South is not Caldwell's South, or Faulkner's (I think, however, that she has read him, too, more than she has read Katherine Mansfield and Virginia Woolf, as is so often said), or anybody else's but hers. The portrait she gives us of a large Southern family is nothing short of wonderful, and the way she gets hold of the particular quality of Southern speech, with its nuances, obliquities, and special kind of humor, is a minor triumph. Nor do I know of any writer, with the possible exception of Faulkner and of Marjorie Kinnan Rawlings, who works a different sector, so deeply sensitive to the Southern landscape. The emphasis I have placed on locale may make it sound like a regional book, which is just what I intended. It is regional in the same way as Gogol's "Dead Souls" is regional. I'm not even hinting that Miss Welty is a writer of Gogol's stature, but her book has some of that same universal quality, and should be read as happily in Moscow and Oslo as in Passaic, San Francisco, and Des Moines.

From *The New Yorker* 22 (11 May 1946): 89.

The Problem of Time in Welty's *Delta Wedding*

Douglas Messerli

Perhaps more than any other of Eudora Welty's novels *Delta Wedding*, published in 1946, most clearly presents her preoccupation with time. However, the characters central to this novel, especially those who are blood members of the Fairchild clan, seem to be oblivious to time and its effects. As Louis Rubin notes of characters in all of Welty's works, "they do not contend with time; instead they pretend that it does not exist."[1] But this pretense is misleading, for the Welty characters who are "intruders" in the Delta home of the Fairchilds are very much aware of the problem of time and even within the pretense the Fairchilds, in their moments of separate awareness, relate differently to time.

As a group, however, the Fairchilds resist time and, for that matter, anything outside of themselves. Like the Renfros of *Losing Battles*, the Fairchilds are one of those large Mississippi families of Welty's fiction whose love is boundless to those within the family structure, but who simultaneously use that active love as a shield to protect themselves from the world at large. The Fairchilds of *Delta Wedding* have almost succeeded in realizing Sutpen's dream in Faulkner's *Absalom, Absalom!* of creating a cosmos peopled by sons, daughters, uncles, aunts and other relatives who in their similarity of appearance, ideology, and emotional temper repeat one another over and over again, insuring in that repetition—in that complete oneness—a sort of immortality for each member of the clan. In their insularity death is not observed. In the homes at Shellmound and the Grove, portraits of the Fairchild great-grandparents, the Delta settlers, hang imposingly, seeming as alive for Laura McRaven and Robbie Reid as is all the past for the Fairchild Aunt Shannon, who in her dialogues with the dead confuses past names and events with present, and for whom "boys and men, girls and ladies all, the old and the young of the Delta kin even the dead and the living . . .—were alike—no gap opened between them."[2]

But the Fairchilds are not primarily a family which remembers the past for that would entail the recognition of change and of difference, and would destroy the type of immortality made possible by the uniformity of the family and its descendants. For the most part the Fairchilds live without a past or a future. They are a people caught up in present action to such a degree that the flux of time seems to stand still. As Laura, the newly motherless cousin who comes to live with them, observes:

> They were never too busy for anything, they were generously and almost seriously of the moment: the past (even Laura's arrival today was past now) was a private, dull matter that would be forgotten except by aunts.
>
> Laura from her earliest memory had heard how they "never seemed to change at all" (p. 15).

However, as Laura suspects, the Delta family is not free in its actions ("Laura was certain that they were *compelled*—their favorite word" [p. 15]), and for a young girl whose journey from Jackson up to the Delta plantation presages the journey she must make mentally to partake of the insular Fairchild love, this compulsion to act, this uncontrollable whirl of quick and instant fluctuations which in its obliviousness to time seems to exclude her, is rather frightening. Her ties are not yet severed with the past. As Welty suggests, unlike the Fairchilds, "Laura remembered everything" (p. 7). As an outsider Laura is very much aware of time and the separation from loved ones that time can cause, a heavy burden of awareness for a nine year old. As she arrives at the Fairchild home, she vomits, demonstrating her fears of the awesome struggle to re-enter a would where she is loved. To Laura that love is still unconditional, a love that she innately understands in the act of her mother's creation of her doll Marmion. Late in the novel, she recalls that upon returning home from a summer vacation she had asked for a doll and her mother had made it, racing against an approaching storm (pp. 230-33). The creation was an immediate, unquestioned act of love which, because it was not dependent upon time "this time was the most inconvenient that she could have chosen" [p. 231]), temporarily defeated time and the separation it causes (the doll was finished before the first raindrop). Laura recognizes "that the reason she felt so superior was that she had gotten Marmion the minute she wished for him—it wasn't either too soon for her wish or too late" (p. 233).[3] But while her mother sewed the doll, her father wound the clock:

"I always like to know what time it is," he said, to which her mother laughed. The loud ticks and the hours striking to catch up responded to him and rose to the upper floor (p. 231).

Time has inevitably won and separated Laura from love; her mother has died. Laura's dilemma is at the outset of the novel, then, very similar to the dilemma Welty poses in her story "A Still Moment": "How to explain Time and Separateness back to God, Who had never thought of them. . . ."[4] In order for Laura to see herself as accepted into the Fairchild family, in order for her to re-enter the loved state, she instinctively recognizes that the Fairchilds must be made to understand time and separateness as she does. Without that understanding, the Fairchilds—who live a "life not stopping for a moment in deference to children going to sleep" (pp. 8-9), a life which is attuned to the throb of the compress that never stops (p. 17), a life in which when the hall clock strikes two it means that it is eight—cannot give Laura the acceptance she needs; they can only pity her, joke with her and forgive her for her differences. Even as she rides the train to the Fairchild home she knows that "when she got there, 'Poor Laura, little motherless girl,' they would all run out and say . . ." (p. 3). And when upon Laura's arrival, Battle, father to the Fairchild clan, puts a gizzard on her dinner plate and calls to her "Now eat it all!" she realizes "it was a joke, his giving her the gizzard, for it was her mother that loved it and she could not stand that piece of turkey" (p. 12). Battle cannot resist teasing Laura for being separate from her mother. Laura must find a way to make the Fairchilds aware of her presence as a individual desirous of love; she must find a way to break through that Fairchild "solid wall of too much love" in order to share the love from the inside.

Laura's dilemma is similar to the problem that faces another intruder, Robbie Reid, who has married Battle's brother George who, next to the dead brother, Denis, is the favorite of the Fairchild clan. However, Robbie's solution is to draw George away from the intense family love so that she and he may share in a relationship free from family. She adamantly responds to the suggestion that it is a difficult process marrying into the Fairchilds, "I didn't marry *into them*! I married George!" (p. 141). Unlike Laura, who thinks that "it was the boys and the men that defined that family always" (p. 14), Robbie believes that it is the Fairchild women who "rule the roost" (p. 144), and accordingly it seems to her that all the Fairchild women wear a "pleading" mask, demanding of their men "small sacrifice by small sacrifice" (p. 146). Her desire is to free her husband from that demanding family love and replace it with

> a love that could be simply beside him—her love. Only she could hold him against that grasp, that separating thrust of Fairchild love that would go on and on persuading him, comparing him, begging him, crowing over him, slighting him, proving to him, sparing him, comforting him, deceiving him, confessing and yielding to him, tormenting him . . . those smiling and not really mysterious ways of the Fairchilds (pp. 148-49).

Before the action of the novel begins, Robbie has left George and her Memphis home because George has given in once again to those Fairchild demands. The incident which has caused this reaction is central to the whole novel. Briefly, George, Robbie, and most of Battle's children are returning to Shellmound from a Sunday morning of fishing. When they approach a trestle all except Robbie decide to walk on it rather than cross under through a creek dried up for the summer. Robbie, dressed in high heels, protests by sitting down and refusing to go any further. But the rest continue without her. Suddenly a train appears moving toward them. All of the children jump except Maureen, a mentally retarded cousin who lives with the Fairchilds, who has caught her foot between the railroad ties. George stays to free her, and together they fall off the trestle moments before the train successfully stops. Robbie cries out, "George Fairchild, you didn't do this for me!" (p. 61).

To Robbie it appears that George has endangered his life unnecessarily only to affirm his irrevocable commitment to family. Robbie is not selfish or even jealous as much as she, like the Fairchilds, simply is unable to accept separateness in love. But unlike the Fairchilds, she is acutely aware of that separateness because she recognizes the past; she is aware of past time. Later in the novel she recalls her poverty-stricken youth, the time *before* George, when she worked for the Fairchilds in the local general store where she "spent all of her life hearing Fairchild, Fairchild, Fairchild" (p. 149). The Fairchild name in her past has instilled within her an awareness of her own difference. Thus she sees the Fairchild love as a "separating thrust" which makes George's act on the trestle once again something that pulls him from her. Her leaving George is in her mind only a playing out of what has already occurred.

But the Fairchilds, unwilling to recognize separateness, cannot comprehend; they cannot explain Robbie's departure. For the Fairchilds such as Tempe Summers, Battle's sister who lives in Innverness, Robbie's act is simply a "mortification," an event that reasserts Tempe's opposition to "outsiders." When Ellen, mother to the Shellmound Fairchilds, suggests that Robbie be given "just a little more time!" Tempe asks characteristically "Whose side are you on?" (p. 106). Indeed, because the Fairchilds are always ready to protect the love which binds them, everyone must do battle. If Laura must battle her way into the Fairchild hearts, and Robbie must battle to bring George out of the grasp of their love, the Fairchild children must undergo their own struggles to become individuals distinct from their family name.

Laura almost immediately perceives that the uniformity and unchangeableness of the Fairchilds is only a fiction created by the family as a group:

> Laura could see that they changed every moment. The outside did not change but the inside did; an iridescent life was busy within and under each alikeness (p. 15).

It is this inner individuality and the process of coming to terms with it that is really the subject of *Delta Wedding*. Despite Battle's inability to accept time and separateness, despite his inability to accept change or "anything alone" (p. 18), his family is growing and changing. The event around which the novel is centered, the event which brings together all of the family and the intruders is the wedding of his second eldest daughter, Dabney.

Dabney understands that her upcoming marriage to the Fairchild overseer, Troy Flavin, hyperbolically speaking is "killing" her father, but she does not perceive that in the breaking down of the family unity she may be literally killing him as well because she is threatening the concept of immortality based upon unchanging motion of the family in time and place. Dabney's marriage preparations represent the beginning of a new time, a time of discovery in which she looks forward into the future, a time which often is represented in Welty's fiction as the time of the dream because it is a time which includes the real and the imagined world, being and becoming and the present and the future all in the same moment; grounded in daily action it is, nonetheless, a time touched with magic; it is the time of "double vision" where one sees a new self growing out of the old.[5] As Welty writes,

> Sometimes, Dabney was not so sure she was a Fairchild—sometimes she did not care, that was it. There were moments of life when it did not matter who she was—even where. Something, happiness—with Troy, but not necessarily, even the happiness of a fine day—seemed to leap away from identity as if it were an old skin, and that she was one of the Fairchilds was of no more need to her than the locust shells hanging to the trees everywhere were to the singing locusts. What she felt, nobody knew! (p. 33).

It is no wonder that Battle, Tempe and Aunt Shannon view the whole affair as an impending disaster. Aunt Shannon expresses that reaction best, again confusing generations but not events: "Duncan dearie, there's a scrap of nuisance around here ought to be shot. . . . You'll see him. Pinck Summers, he calls himself. Coming courting her" (p. 119).

Dabney's vision, however, is no more complete, for in devaluing her Fairchild identity she devalues all of the past. Even if they do not recognize it, the Fairchilds obviously do have a past, but it is evident that Dabney may be no more sensitive to it in her own marriage than her father has been in his. This is most clearly demonstrated by her treatment of the night light given to her as a wedding gift by her aunts, Jim Allen and Primrose, who inhabit the house at the Grove, a few miles from Shellmound. The night light also presents a "double vision"; on its surface is the outward world of "trees, towers, people, windowed houses, a bridge, and a sky full of clouds and stars and moon and sun" which, when the candle inside is lit, glows red as if "all on fire, even to the motion of fire which came from the flame drawing" (p. 46). It is a perfect gift, for the light, like Laura's observation of all the Fairchilds, has two aspects: on the surface it never changes, yet "an iridescent life" exists within it. It combines the real and the imagined world, the present and the future as Dabney does in her new happiness. But most importantly the light should suggest to Dabney something which she is missing, the past. As Aunt Primrose says of the light, "it's company. That's what it is. That little light, it was company as early as I can remember—when Papa and Mama died." "As early as *I* can remember," adds Jim Allen, her older sister (pp. 44-45). The light symbolizes a completeness of vision that the Fairchild family is missing, for with the joining of the past, present, and future, the closed family love would be joined with all of time, with the world at large. Since Dabney, through her love of someone outside of the family circle, has come already to a "double vision" of present and future, the potentiality for this transcendent vision is within her. She need only come to recognize the importance of the past for giving meaning to the present which shapes her future. But that requires that she come to terms with pain, loss, and death as well, and that is something that few of the Shellmound Fairchilds have been prepared to do. For Dabney, as for most young people just beginning a new life, the past seems to have little to do with her. When she returns home with the gift, she drops the night light upon seeing Troy, breaking it into pieces, and runs into the house. Only India, her younger sister, observing the destruction of the light, begins to cry uncontrollably, comprehending what the act signifies. Dabney will not fulfill her potential for a more complete vision of life. Like Miranda in Katherine Anne Porter's "Old Mortality," who, assuming that at the very least she can find the truth about what happens to her, leaves home in "her hopefulness, her ignorance,"[6] Dabney goes forward blindly and proudly, "her eyes shut against what was too bright" (p. 34).[7]

Dabney, however, is not the only one of the Fairchild children to make new realizations. Shelley, Dabney's older sister, seriously questions the family perspective. Through her diary one discovers her struggling, like Laura and Robbie, with the problem of her family's "solid wall of too much love":

> We never wanted to be smart, one by one, but all together we have a wall, we are self-sufficient against people that come knocking, we are solid to the outside. Does the world suspect that we are all very private people? I think one by one we're all more lonely than private and more lonely than self-sufficient (p. 84).

Shelley comes to perceive what few in her family can, namely that their wall of family identity does not truly protect them, that imposing group action upon the world does not prevent the world from acting upon each member of the family; and she understands the need for accepting separateness, the necessity for recognizing time which causes separation:

> we can be got at, hurt, killed—loved the same way—as things get to us. All the more us poor people to be cherished. I feel we should all be cherished but not all together in one bunch—separately, but not one to go unloved for the other loved (p. 84).

But Shelley's comprehension includes more than Dabney's mere acceptance of a modality of time different from her family's presentism. Shelley intimates that she comprehends *how* time affects people. She appears to understand, for example, the connection between the past and the present, the way to which one affects the other. Writing of her Uncle George's "trouble" with Robbie, Shelley suggests that Troy, Dabney's fiancé, sees that George has something on his mind because Troy is the type of person who

> gets the smell of someone studying, as if it were one of the animals in trouble. Trouble acts up—he puts it down. But I know, trouble is not something fresh you never saw before that is coming just the one time, but is old, and your great-aunts not old enough to die yet remember little hurts for sixty years . . . (p. 85).

Shelley recognizes that the past is not completed, finished, dead, but is something living and forceful because it shapes the present, defines it. In that awareness, Shelley, like Dabney, has a "double vision," but she too has difficulty accepting the whole of reality.

Shelley's vulnerability lies not in the past, but in the future. She is hurt by having her sister "walk into something" that she [Shelley] dreads. She dreads the future because, unlike Dabney, she is not blind to it, and she is troubled by the contradictions that she sees in it. The problem she is faced with is at the heart of the problem that Welty poses concerning time. If the past affects the present, if a past hurt gives pain to people in the present, then one must define people as *in time*. However, time separates people from one another; time brings back individual pain and brings about loss and death. How, then, can people love one another knowing separateness in time? How can love occur between people separated by the gulf of time, each with different pasts and, therefore, with different presents? Shelley cannot conceive of a love which would not "fight the world," that would not fight against time by creating its own time-present to stand opposed to the flowing time of the world, as her own family has done. But she sees that she must then ask who is loving or being loved? For without a past the individual is undefinable and non-existent and there is no one to stop the world from entering, just as Troy has entered Shellmound, to lead the loved one away. Shelley's fears only bring her back to where she has begun, locked in family love. It is no wonder that she resists the idea of future love and marriage. She claims that she will "never" marry, and certainly she may not unless she solves the problem of time and separateness, unless she finds the "key to the clock" for which she is seen searching early in the novel (p. 29).

Of the Fairchild children it is perhaps only India who intuitively resolves the contradictions that trouble Shelley. For India, who at nine is the same age as Laura, is still able to partake of the amazing childhood consciousness wherein the family and the outside world exist as one. As Ellen says of this daughter: "I can't imagine how India finds out things. . . . It's just like magic" (p. 105). And clearly India's world, like her name, is magical.[8] India emotionally comprehends the meaning of the night light, and she imposes that meaning upon physical space by making a "circle" with her fingers and "imagining" that she holds the little lamp "filled with the mysterious and flowing air of night" (p. 49). The key words here are "circle" and "imagination," for in her childhood vision India is able to break through the separateness between people and make of the world a circle in the imagination; by creatively acting and perceiving, she is able to transcend the barriers of time and is able to connect the past, present, and future in a "magical" moment wherein all of Shellmound is joined with the world, wherein each man and woman is linked with one another. India "finds things out" because through her imagination she is able to join the world around her and experience its joys and sorrows. In the imagination time is not at all a severing force. As India says to Laura upon seeing her for the first time in a year, "We never did unjoin" (p. 10). However, India is yet a child surrounded by love in the present. She has not yet known separateness.

The Fairchilds are as threatened as Robbie by George's act of saving Maureen on the railroad track for it represents another act of separateness.

George has risked his life to save the daughter who, as the child of Denis and his now-insane wife, is a living symbol of the danger of interaction with the world outside the family: that fact astounds them. In his willingness to sacrifice his life for hers George has asserted an individuality separate from family love which endangers the whole Fairchild concept of life. Because they recognize this, the Fairchilds attempt to nullify George's act by repeating it, by embodying it in family history, by turning it into something at which they can laugh. Throughout the novel the incident is repeated and referred to again and again (pp. 58-61). Mr. Doolittle, the train's conductor, Maureen, and George all become figures in a tall tale instead of people involved in a dangerous series of events. Indeed, the Fairchilds purposely refuse to recognize the happening on the trestle as a series of events because events occur in time, but a tale is "not answerable to time," as Welty writes of children's tales in "Some Notes on Time in Fiction." "The tale is about wishes, and thus grants a wish itself."[9] The wish of the Fairchild tale is simply that George's individual act be converted into a comedic family story which stands against difference, change, and time.[10] George simply took the "path of least resistance," beams Battle. "Path George's taken all of his life" (p. 60). Even George himself scoffs at Robbie's fear: "Mr. Doolittle wasn't going to hit me!" (p. 148). But Robbie "knew all the time that George was sure Mr. Doolittle was." And Shelley perceives that it is only the fact that the engine came to a stop, it is only the "tumbling denouement" that permits her family to laugh (p. 87). Later, when the wedding photographer mentions that the train has hit and killed the young girl seen near Shellmound, one is made to see just how absurd is that family laughter. Shelley knows this, and she sees that in risking death George has manifested his respect for individuality. "I think Uncle George takes us one by one," writes Shelley. "That is love—I think" (p. 85). But Shelley's perception of George's love, because of her vision of time, is incomplete. She recognizes in his risking death that George loves members of the family individually, that George loves and is devoted to the family which he has known from birth and which, therefore, represents his past, but she cannot understand George's connection with the world outside the family, with a time outside what is already known; again Shelley cannot make sense of the future. She is at a loss to explain *why* George "wants" Robbie Reid. It is, understandably, Dabney who feels sympathetic to this future aspect of George's love.

Dabney remembers another incident which involves George from which she first learned that her uncle loves people individually. She recalls a childhood occurrence in which George broke up a fight between two Negroes only to ask their names and release them. Again, George had dangerously taken a chance with his life in wrestling a knife away from one of the Blacks. Dabney realizes that her cry had been uttered because the act revealed to her that George was separate, that George was not just a Fairchild, that "all of the Fairchild in her had screamed at his interfering—at his taking part—caring about anything in the world but them" (p. 36). Now, thinking back upon that incident, Dabney comes to understand that George, like herself, loves not just the Fairchilds, that his love of family is just the surface:

> Sweetness then could be the visible surface of profound depths—the surface of all the darkness that might frighten her. . . . George loved the world, something told her suddenly. Not them! Not them in particular (p. 36).

But Dabney does not comprehend what loving the world requires. She loves not the world, but Troy, a representative of the world, and in looking ahead to her marriage with Troy she does not foresee a separation that would wrench her from family love. Troy is brought into the Fairchild world, she is not brought into his. Troy invites only one person to the wedding, Robbie Reid, who has been hiding out from George at the general store. And, other than himself, the only representatives of his identity at the affair are the dozen patch-work quilts that his mother has sent down as a wedding gift from the mountains. In other words, Dabney has no reason to associate love outside the family with pain, loss, or death. Separateness to Dabney merely means selfhood, albeit a new selfhood. When Troy reports that, having sent them all her quilts, his mother will "freeze all winter," Dabney responds (referring to a note attached to the quilts), "Your pretty bride. . . . How did she know I was pretty?" (p. 113). Dabney has simply passed over what is perhaps the key to time which Shelley seeks, the full meaning of George's act, the secret by which George has come to be able to love the Fairchilds and the world simultaneously.

Just before the wedding rehearsal, with the whole family and the outside participants gathered together, George reveals that secret of his love. To Robbie, who has just returned, George speaks quietly across the room:

> I don't think it matters what *happens* to a person, or what comes. . . . To me. I speak for myself. . . . Something is always coming, you know that. . . . I don't think it matters so much in the world what. Only. . . . I'm damned if I wasn't going to stand on that track if I wanted to! Or will again (p. 187).

Robbie's reaction—"But you're everything on earth to me"—is so plainly limited that even Tempe realizes that "Robbie was leaving out every other thing in the world with that thing she said. The *vulgar* thing she said!" (p. 187). For, George's words make clear that his love takes in everything in all of time, and that includes death—his own death. Because he recognizes his own death, recognizes that "something is always coming," George is made free to live, to devalue his own life enough that he can risk and sacrifice it and give his love in action to the world. Because he accepts exactly what everyone else in the family so fears, George is able to bridge the gulf between himself and the world; he is able to resolve the conflict between man and time. Finally, with that gulf bridged, George is able to reintegrate himself with all of mankind and find true immortality. His immortality lies not in the specific but in the universal family which includes everyone in all of time.

Ellen alone perceives the full "miraculousness" of George's act; only she comprehends just how amazing is George's resolution of love and time. But then Ellen is an extraordinary character. Even after raising the Fairchild family she is still considered by Tempe to be an "outsider," is still Battle's bride from Mitchem Corners, Virginia. But Ellen has borne, nurtured, and loved the Fairchild clan, and if she is an "outsider" one is convinced that there is really no inside to this Fairchild front. Ellen loves the world also, and in this novel of family yarns, the tale which tells of this love shows her to be George's spiritual mate. After the wedding, Ellen tells her own tale of the time her mother came from Virginia to stay with her while she was pregnant with Shelley. When Ellen had pains the day before the birth, her mother sent for the doctor. But when the doctor arrived he sneered at her and insisted that Ellen had "all the time in the world." The mother decided to cook the doctor such a fine breakfast that "he wouldn't dare go," and, being from Virginia, she cooked him a Virginia breakfast which meant "everything in creation from batter bread on." Inevitably, the doctor became ill from eating; when the time came for the birth he was incapacitated, and when he was finally roused by the mother, he ended up putting himself out with gas instead of the patient. Ellen told her mother to leave the room and had the baby herself (pp. 215-16).

Here again is a story of risk and sacrifice, of a love of living and people that transcends the fears of pain, loss, and possible death. Ellen, like George, is able to laugh with the Fairchilds:

> They laughed till the tears stood in their eyes at the foolishness, the long-vanquished pain, the absurd prostrations, the birth that wouldn't wait, and the flouting of all in the end. All so handsomely ridiculed by the delightful now! (p. 216).

But like George, she is able to see beyond that ridicule, beyond the "delightful now" and recognize that pain, loss and death are not just in a tale, or even just in the past, but are also in the future; she knows that since they are inevitable, risk and sacrifice must always be a part of living and loving as well. Even Robbie comes finally to see that "things almost never happened, almost never could be, for only time only! They went back . . . started over . . . " (p. 244). Love, then, is a process, not a static thing. Despite the Fairchild assertion, despite their pretense there can be no "solid wall of too much love" for even "too much love" exists in a larger context, in time.

Laura comes finally to discern this. Despite her loss in the past, Laura is brought into the Fairchild present and is caught up in its action by being made a member of the wedding party when Tempe's daughter, Lady Clare, comes down with chicken pox. Just before the wedding, with her cousin Roy, Laura has a vision of the future as George and Ellen perceive it. Together the children explore Marmion, the decaying mansion across the Yazoo River in which Dabney will soon begin her married life, and which through inheritance will someday belong to Laura. The children soon discover that the future which Marmion holds is far more portentous than Dabney foresees. The mansion is "a green rank world instead of a play house" (p. 177). Inside, Aunt Studney, an old black woman, stands Pandora-like over a bag which Roy believes to contain his mother's future babies, and for which Aunt Studney appears to be "not on the lookout for things to put in, but was watching to keep things from getting out" (p. 177). The Pandora metaphor is extremely suggestive for in the next moment Roy climbs to the top floor of the house where he sees "the whole creation," a vision which is purchased by pain: upon descending, Roy stoically announces to Laura that he has been stung by a bee. Laura, meanwhile, has suspected that the bees have escaped from Aunt Studney's bag. The connection is evident; the bees are symbolic of the escaped evils of the world. The vision of creation requires that one accept pain. Intuiting that the bee sting is connected with the vision, Laura suddenly wishes that she had also been stung. But she soon achieves a similar vision as she finds a "treasure" (Ellen's lost jewelled rose pin), and she discovers that she must accept worse evils for the vision which her "treasure" symbolizes when, while rowing back to Shellmound, Roy throws her into the Yazoo (the "River of Death") where she loses the pin. Laura has thus been baptized into a new awareness that there are frightening aspects of the future, that the future holds not just the sublime "happiness" that Dabney anticipates. Together Roy and Laura have metaphorically experienced pain, loss, and death in their visions of the world. Moreover, in glimpsing the vision, the children have also seen why the future is worth the risk and sacrifice. What they have seen is the world in triplicity. As Roy shouts down to Laura from his point of observation atop Marmion, he shares a view of the world in three modalities of time:

I see Troy! I see the grove—I see Aunt Primrose back in her flowers! I see *Papa*! I see the whole creation (p. 176).

He sees Troy, the representative of the outside world and his future brother-in-law, he sees Aunt Primrose, a closer blood relative who by her age connects him with the past, and he sees his father with whom he naturally identifies himself in his present existence, all in three successive moments which permit him to see "the whole creation."[11] When the family, self, and the outside world come together with the past, present and future, a vision occurs which transcends all, which presents the individual's connection with all the universe in all of time which is as magical as India's imaginary light.

Now that Laura has been shown the vision she must repeat the process by which she can come to the vision herself. Since she still seeks love and acceptance from the Fairchilds, she must act out that newly discovered process of risk and sacrifice. She risks stealing George's pipe and presents it to him as a sacrifice after he has missed it for a time. That gift bridges for Laura the separation she has previously felt. In that act she perceives herself as finally joined to the Fairchilds and the world outside her father and past. Had she India's imagination, Laura would have known that she had been loved from the start. Early in the novel Ellen observes that Laura's wish to be "taken into their hearts" is "steadier than her vision and that itself kept her from knowing" (p. 77). Perhaps it is because, as Ellen suggests, Laura's father—so bound by clock time—has "no imagination" (p. 227) that Laura has not previously had the opportunity to develop her imaginative powers. But by the end of the novel, when Laura is asked to stay on permanently at Shellmound, and Laura and India join arms around each other's waist, one sees that imagination and action have been conjoined, and together they have broken down that Fairchild wall, letting that love spill out into the world around it, into the "radiant night" (p. 247).

From George and Ellen, then, it is clear that at least some of the Fairchild children (perhaps all) have learned to participate in that awareness of time which connects them with the universe; it is clear that, unlike their father, they will live a life attuned to the present but not exclusively of the present, that they will accept the flux of time and will partake of the legacy of the past, of the future's hope.

NOTES

[1]Louis D. Rubin, Jr. "The Golden Apples of the Sun," in *The Faraway Country* (Seattle: Univ. of Washington Press, 1963), pp. 131-32.

[2]Eudora Welty, *Delta Wedding* (New York: Harcourt, Brace, 1946), p. 14. All further references are to this edition.

[3]I am indebted to Robert Penn Warren's "The Love and the Separateness in Miss Welty," *KR*, 6 (1944), 246-59, for this reading.

[4]Eudora Welty, "A Still Moment," in *The Wide Net and Other Stories*, as reprinted in *Selected Stories of Eudora Welty* (New York: Modern Library, 1954), p. 93.

[5]Simultaneously, Dabney's marriage signifies the beginning of a new place. After the honeymoon she will live in Marmion, the decayed mansion across the Yazoo River.

[6]Katherine Anne Porter, "Old Mortality," in her *The Collected Stories of Katherine Anne Porter* (New York: Harcourt, Brace, 1985), p. 221.

[7]For a variant but excellent discussion of the same metaphor of the night light, see Ruth M. Vande Kieft's *Eudora Welty* (New York: Twayne, 1962).

[8]One may conjecture that Welty, in the naming of India, was thinking of E.M. Forster's *A Passage to India*; in that novel, Forster, a writer whom Welty greatly admires, is concerned with just this magical ability of some people to transcend human barriers.

[9]Eudora Welty, "Some Notes on Time in Fiction," *MISSQ*, 26 (1973), 484.

[10]Welty is concerned with this same process to a greater degree in her *Losing Battles*.

[11]I have attempted to draw these same parallels between these characters and time elsewhere in this essay. It should be evident that Troy represents for the Fairchilds that threatening future; Aunt Primrose, along with Aunt Jim, it should be remembered, gave Dabney the night light which symbolizes the past; Battle is clearly at the heart of the Fairchild's present-time orientation.

From *Studies in American Fiction* 5 (1977): 227-40.

The Golden Apples
1949

Main Street in Dixie

Lee E. Cannon

In the small imaginary town of Morgana, Miss. (and one hopes it is), life teems with suppressed desires and frustrations. The mysterious wanderings and appearances of Mr. King MacLain, whose story runs in and out through the narrative, symbolize the search for the golden apples of dreams and happiness, so often an illusion, perhaps the Fata Morgana. Many other inhabitants are also under this spell. With deft artistry Miss Welty has probed into the lives of these people and has woven a colorful tapestry of their inner and other experiences, for in Morgana it is difficult to distinguish between reality and actuality, and at times the dead alone seem living and the living alone seem dead, while over all seems to hang an aura of decadence—a decadence which is a kind of blight in the work of a number of our contemporary southern writers.

Out of this collection of short stories emerges gradually a feeling of design, a realization that the various units blend symmetrically into a pattern that seeks to interpret the life and atmosphere of a small community. Thus we have another in the ever growing group of novels portraying the village in American literature. For, in a Pickwickian sense, this is a novel.

In the realm of actuality there are little lifelike sketches of the doings, superstitions, talk and appearance of dwellers in small southern towns, cleverly put down and easily recognizable. The descriptions of the June recital of the music class, the summer camp for orphans and, as a climax, the funeral of Mrs. Rainey communicate an air of kindly humor and gentle disillusionment and throw light on folk manners and morals.

The inner, real life is revealed through use of the stream of consciousness, through the inferences of eavesdroppers, frequently children, and sometimes through the reproduction of the inner life itself. The actions of grownups form a world into which the child mind penetrates with astonishing flashes of insight and deduction.

With her skill in developing characters and her knack of suggestive phrasing, Miss Welty seems to give her creations a philosophical significance which perhaps isn't there. At least, these stories have a pleasing freshness in their elaboration of a old, old theme.

From *The Christian Century* 66 (7 September 1949): 1039-40.

Notes by the Way

Margaret Marshall

The device of "our town" and the tone of reminiscence are almost sure to enlist the reader's sympathy in advance. The American reader is particularly susceptible to this approach, for no one can be more sentimental about the old home town than the rootless American who, for better or worse, wouldn't go back where he came from for anything in the world but enjoys his daydream about going home.

This device and this tone are a great temptation to the writer of fiction: they not only serve to establish an immediate bond with the reader but also seem to save him the labor of creating characters and a world—since these are already given, to a point, once he has conjured up "our town." But the advantages of this artistic short cut, as of any other, are more apparent than real, while the disadvantage can be fatal. The disadvantage is that the writer, relying on the device and the tone, neglects to animate his characters except as "characters" in "our town" and tends to luxuriate in evocations for their own sake of atmosphere and landscape.

At least these are the two great flaws in Eudora Welty's latest book, "The Golden Apples," which is composed of a series of sketches having to do with life in a small Mississippi town called Morgana and a group of characters who are ordinary folk but who comprise the town's "main families."

Miss Welty is a talented writer, and she has shown her capacity, in her earlier stories, for creating character and for involving the reader in the fate of even so unlikely a character as a "petrified man." The persons and events in this book are likely enough, but its impact on the reader is not that of participating in the experience of more or less autonomous human beings related to us all but of watching forms of life as through glass—which is transparent but not a very good conductor of primary emotions. Meanwhile, our sense of the reality of Morgana and its inhabitants is diminished, not increased, by the piling up of details of observation and sensibility which are often good in themselves but serve no dynamic function.

The reviewers have spoken in praise of the trance-like atmosphere of the book, and of the exquisite writing to be found in its pages. I should say that the atmosphere is that of a daydream, which soon becomes claustrophobic, and that Miss Welty, caught in her own spell, has indulged herself in finespun writing that becomes wearing.

In the piece called "Moon Lake" she does come very close to actuality than anything else in the book. It deals with the relations between the daughters of Morgana's main families and a group of orphans who are thrown together for a week's camping on Moon Lake. Miss Welty sets the scene with humor and perception. She also creates suspense and seems to be building toward a climax that will resolve or at least dramatize the situation she has posed. There is a climax, to be sure, when the orphan Easter is tipped into the water by a small colored boy and is resuscitated only after the prolonged life-saving ministrations of the boy, Loch Morrison, who has been dragooned into acting as the lifeguard for the party. But the meaning of this climax in relation to the rest of the story escapes me, and I must assume that it is just another reminiscence.

The basic trouble, I suspect, is that Miss Welty was somehow led to write, on this occasion, of characters and situations that did not really engage her own primary emotions or her creative energy. As a result they never seem quite real to the reader—and the convention of "our town" combined with the reminiscent tone makes them seem all the more like figures in a remote landscape.

The book does, I suppose, convey the quality of life among the main families of Morgana, but this is its only accomplishment, and the quality of life among the main families of Morgana is, to speak rudely, not worth 244 pages. Even so, one is left wondering if this is really the way it is. Morgana is a small town in the deep South. Yet, reading "The Golden Apples," one is scarcely ever made aware of the mixed racial background which must surely affect the quality of life even of the main families of small towns in the deep South. I don't mean at all to suggest that Miss Welty should have given us stories of race conflict. I only find it curious that a basic and dramatic circumstance of life in the South should count for so little in her picture of Morgana.

From *The Nation* 169 (10 September 1949): 256.

Five Southerners*

Louis D. Rubin, Jr.

. . . . Faulkner's characters are usually vivid and intense. They are, however, only moderately deep. Somehow, we are always looking at them, not into them and with them. A less lauded Mississippian, Eudora Welty, is Faulkner's master in this respect. The characters in *The Golden Apples* are superb creatures of fiction. Miss Welty is excelled by none in her ability, in these stories, to express the universal human experience in the particularized Southern environment. Without losing verisimilitude as human beings, her people seem almost to take on a mythlike aura.

Particularly is this so, I felt, in "Sir Rabbit," the one story in the collection that Hamilton Basso, in his review in *The New Yorker* for September 3, 1949, found something less than perfect. "Sir Rabbit" concerns a meeting in the forest between a wanderer of a man named King MacLain, and a young countrywoman, Mattie Will Hollifield. Mattie Will's husband, Junior Hollifield, is along, and he and King engage in a whimsical duel of wits, the advantage lying all with King. Finally King fires a shot in Junior's direction, causing him to fall down and knock himself cold. Then King and Mattie Will embrace with an inevitability both poignant and intense, after which King vanishes into the nearby woods while Mattie Will, throbbing with the ecstasy of the episode, can think only of a little song that runs through her mind,

*Note—The author writes as follows: "The review from which this excerpt is taken was the very first attempt of mine to write about literature in terms of the South. It was written in 1949, and its incomprehension of William Faulkner's fiction (based on having read *Knight's Gambit* and a few short stories) is obviously monumental. L.D.R., 12/29/91."

In the night time,
At the right time,
So, I've understood,
'Tis the habit of Sir Rabbit
To dance in the wood—

This completely appropriate song at once epiphanizes King MacLain and the entire fantastic-realistic occurrence; indeed, at the instant of the song's introduction the story seemed to take on the glow of enchantment.

Mr. Basso, however, finds the device whereby Miss Welty got rid of Mattie Will's husband contrived. On the contrary, it seems to me to be so very subordinate to the structure and texture of this beautiful story as to be beneath notice.

With Miss Welty, plot is subordinate to character, serving only to develop her people. Her regional flavoring is infused so well into her people and her narrative that it is quite impossible to separate any one ingredient. More so than Faulkner's, more so than anyone else's I have ever read with the exception of the creatures of Thomas Wolfe's North Carolina mountains, these people of hers are Southern. It is possible to conceive of an episode similar to "Sir Rabbit" taking place in some other region, but the particulars would have to be so changed, and the reactions of the characters so different, that it would not be the same story at all. This is prime regional literature. Excepting only some of the work of the more turbulent and wild (but often less integrated) Wolfe, I agree with Mr. Basso's statement that "I doubt that a better book about 'the South'—one that more completely gets the feel of the particular texture of Southern life, and its special tone and pattern—has ever been written."

Best of all of the five writers under examination here [Scott Hart, Barbara Avirett, Ben Lucien, William Faulkner, Eudora Welty], Miss Welty has accomplished the aim of our regional writer: she has presented valid Southern characters in a valid situation, and afforded us a clear glimpse of a region and its people.

From *Hopkins Review* 3 (Spring 1950): 44-45.

The Thematic Unity of Welty's *The Golden Apples*

Wendell V. Harris

Though each of the seven stories of Eudora Welty's *The Golden Apples*[1] was published separately, the plots combine to provide a survey of life in the small Southern town of Morgana over the period of a generation, the themes to provide a commentary on human life over the centuries. The structural devices through which the volume's recurrent themes are expressed and unified make it probably the most technically fascinating of Miss Welty's works, yet it has received relatively little appreciative commentary. Even the very helpful critical analyses devoted to the volume by H.C. Morris and Ruth M. Vande Kieft[2] fail to do full justice to its technical complexity: the art with which the linked series of stories is constructed becomes clear only when it is recognized that the three central thematic elements are generated by three distinct techniques.

The most explicit of these themes is the insistence upon the enforced changes visited by time upon each person, the ironic fate which awaits both seeming stability and hopeful promise. The marriage of the charming Snowdie Hudson to the desirable and gallant King MacLain is merely the prelude to the long years through which King will live as an exile and Snowdie as an object of pity. Similarly, Miss Eckhart, the music teacher who had seemed an institution in the life of Morgana, becomes an outcast who will return at last as a miserable, mad old woman. Much of the symbolism of the early stories is employed in deepening this theme of individual failure. For instance, in "June Recital" the adolescent Cassie

[1]New York: Harcourt, Brace and Co., 1949. Page references inserted in the text are to this edition.

[2]Morris, "Zeus and the Golden Apples: Eudora Welty," *Perspective* V, No. 4 (Autumn, 1952), 190-199; Vande Kieft, *Eudora Welty* (New York: Twayne, 1962).

recalls the manner in which Miss Eckhart had worshipped her metronome; as a symbol of musical rather than existential time the metronome thus sums up an aspect of Miss Eckhart which is apparent from Cassie's other recollections: the music teacher's tragedy is that she was never truly part of the life of the town; she had existence only within her profession.

Such dismal instances of unromantic tragedy are regarded by the younger generation merely as the background against which they discern the gleam of their own bright future. This divergence of attitudes toward time and experience is symbolically conveyed in the central episode of "June Recital," Miss Eckhart's attempt to burn down the old MacLain house in which she formerly had her studio. While Loch Morrison, still a young boy in this story, watches what is happening in the neighboring house, his sister Cassie, intent on dyeing a scarf for a hayride, is aware only of the sounds of the piano next door which call up a whole system of past events. To Miss Eckhart the house is a thing to be destroyed as an emblem of the past she wishes to forget. To Cassie the vision of the past evoked by the old house is full of mysteries; she is old enough to feel the necessity to search for meaning in the little past she knows, to try to understand the way lives unfold and fate works itself out. The boy Loch sees the house romantically: to his inexperience, each incident is a portent of exciting future events.

In the second system of thematic significances, this hope with which the young regard that future which will fulfill all their desires is symbolized by a series of allusions to the golden apples of myth. The allusions are two-edged. The golden apples of the Hesperides, representing life-fulfillment, stand for the ultimate goal sought by each of the inhabitants of Morgana, while the golden apple of discord which led to the Trojan War and the golden apples which distracted Atalanta are the false apples which lead all astray. For example, there are two allusions to the golden apples in "June Recital." The first occurs as Loch looks longingly at the fig trees which he intends to visit as soon as the golden fruit is ripe. Here the promise of an enjoyment of the sensuous offerings of life is sufficient for the young boy; at his present age he is able to find a meaningful life in the natural enjoyment of nature. The second allusion, more oblique, is suggested by the fragment of Yeats's "The Song of the Wandering Aengus" which runs through Cassie's head:

> Though I am old with wandering
> Through hollow lands and hilly lands,
> I will find out where she has gone. . . .

The closing lines of the poem concern "the silver apples of the moon" and the "golden apples of the sun" as symbols of sexual and spiritual fulfillment, the fulfillment which Cassie is unconsciously desiring as she brokenly recalls the poem. The difficulty of finding one's way to the goal has already begun to suggest itself—she is vaguely puzzled though not yet dismayed.

The third moment of the thematic complex is provided by the numerous mythological analogues which exist side by side with the motif of the golden apples and the explicit theme of time's burden of disillusionment. In each case these analogues serve to emphasize the futility of the path chosen by a specific character. The comparison of Miss Eckhart's hair to that of Circe in a print of Circe feeding the swine is an ironic comment on her role in the life of Morgana. The multiple parallels between Ulysses' travels and Eugene MacLain's day in "Music from Spain" represent another ironic commentary on an unsuccessful attempt to break the bonds of a monotonous life. Eugene does not emerge from the day's incidents victoriously, and he does not return with the hard-won glory and wisdom of a Ulysses. In addition, the manner in which the unimaginative Emma has awaited him is in equally ironic contrast to the faithfulness of Penelope. Similarly, Artemis is the obvious mythological parallel for Virgie Rainey, an identification implied both by her first name (in itself ironic) and the sympathy which she feels with nature, especially with the moon. But Virgie, despite her assertion of independence and her eschewal of marriage, is not an immortal Artemis—the parallel is as mocking as the others. Her life cannot rival the carefree immortality of a goddess; Eugene MacLain can never attain the stature of a Greek hero; Miss Eckhart can never wield Circe's powers.

Each of the stories of the volume is centered about one moment of the triune theme. As we have seen, "June Recital" establishes the theme of the search for the golden apples, and "Music from Spain" uses mythological analogues to deepen its portrayal of an unsuccessful search for fulfillment. As a third example, "Sir Rabbit" is focused on the inevitable and irreversible changes wrought by time. In that story Mattie Will feels just prior to her loss of virginity "as though a little boat was going out on a lake, never to come back." (p. 87) More explicit is her later recollection of the romp with the MacLain twins in which she recalls them as "mysterious and sweet—gamboling now she knew not where." (p. 98) But Ran and Eugene are no longer gamboling. Eugene is living his monotonous life in San Francisco; Ran, as we discover in "The Whole World Knows," has so unsuccessfully handled an affair with a country girl that she has committed suicide.

The final story, "The Wanderers," brings the lives of all the major characters up to date as it describes the death of Katie Rainey, the narrator of the first story. The older generation are "still watching and waiting for something they didn't really know about any longer, wouldn't recognize to see it coming in the road." (p. 205) The incident of Ran MacLain's affair "showed" on Ran, and had been valuable when he ran for office. Nina Carmichael is married, and is no longer the sensitive girl of the camping trip at Moon Lake. The Morrison's house is cut up now for boarders in the way Snowdie's had been years before, and Cassie is still unmarried, unfulfilled. Eugene has been buried in Morgana; nothing is known in the town of his life in San Francisco. King MacLain has returned to Snowdie and is reputed to be over a hundred—although now feeble and in some ways pathetic, he is still untamed and self-willed. Virgie, for whom had been predicted an exciting and romantic life, has applied her musical talent to the piano in the movie theater and subjugated her taste for adventure to the duty of caring for her aged mother.

Of the major characters in these stories, only Virgie and King MacLain seem to rise above a mundane and meaningless participation in the life of Morgana. All the other characters who are presented in any completeness fail in the search for fulfillment, and by the implications of the final story, the minor characters, if their lives were fully told, would fare no better. The victory achieved by Virgie and King is the assertion of their own individuality—both live by their own codes—but there is no final victory. In the closing paragraphs of this last story Virgie remembers one of the prints in Miss Eckhart's studio, the picture of Perseus with the head of Medusa. "Cutting off the Medusa's head was the heroic act, perhaps, that made visible a horror in life that was at once the horror in love, Virgie thought—the separateness." "Endless the Medusa, and Perseus endless." (p. 243) The function of this last allusion to the mythological undercurrent is to suggest the separateness of each individual's pursuit of happiness and fulfillment, and the eternally repeated struggle of the human situation which allows one to aspire toward, but never reach, the golden apples. In this image of the human tragicomedy the three thematic elements merge.

From *Texas Studies in Literature and Language* 6 (1964): 92-95.

The Ponder Heart
1954

Bossy Edna Earle Had a Word for Everything

V.S. Pritchett

In some ways the novelists of the American South have the independent force of the writers of the Irish revival; in other ways, to an English critic, they recall the rich and ineradicable pockets of Scottish and Welsh regionalism; in their more decorative and ironical phases, the neo-peasant writers like T.F. Powys. In any case, they are all brilliant deviationists from a main tradition. They are a protest by old communities, enriched by wounds, against the success of mass, or polyglot, culture. They make a pawky local bid against the strong hand of the centralized society we live in.

This individuality has its dangers. Sometimes the regional writer becomes the professional topographer of local oddity. With one sophisticated foot outside his territory, he sets out to make his folk quaint or freakish (the abnormal becomes a matter of local pride), and he can be said to condescend to and even exploit them. He may even go so far as to suggest that people are not real until they are eccentric and decorative and then we have the disastrous impression that the author is philandering with his characters. (This was a great vice in James Barrie's comic Scots.) Of course isolated provincial societies *do* live a sort of family life, all rough and tumble but fundamentally closeknit, where mild lunatics, simples, notorious public nuisances, gossips and embarrassing relations have a great importance as personalities.

Indeed it is an awkward fact that there is more personality in the small worlds than in the big ones. All the critic can do is to warn against accepting the more endearing clichés of this expanded family reminiscence.

As Eudora Welty's new *nouvelle* shows, it all depends on depth and technical skill; and in Miss Welty's case on a sardonic comic brio. She has written some excellent short stories in the last ten years and an especially brilliant first volume, so that she comes to her subject with a good deal of experience. She has had the art to place her Uncle Dan in a complex position in the narrative. He is embedded in the mind of a bustling, hoydenish, bossy niece, a girl of fierce practical capacity, snooty manners and possessive temperament, who will scornfully defend the old idiot partly because she passionately loves him, partly to keep her head up among the neighbors. She is the soul of small-town pugnacity and self-conceit and has an endless tongue.

It is part of the beauty of the telling that this young limb, Edna Earle, runs a small hotel (the setting is unmistakably Miss Welty's native Mississippi) and is forcing a traveling salesman to listen to her. She is really a more considerable character than Uncle Dan and it is her apparent normality which sets off his idiocy perfectly. The underlying suggestion that she may be as dotty as he is adds to the pleasure.

Uncle Dan is an amiable freak with a low I.Q. He has one dominant passion: he loves everybody with childish ingenuity. His love takes the delicate form of an irresistible desire to give everything away. He sheds property as a tree sheds leaves. He is a saint of the compulsion to distribute, and in the course of the tale even distributes himself twice in marriage. Edna Earle keeps a prim, head-tossing silence about what went on in these marriages—one of them he described as a "trial"; certainly his wives left him in time, though without rancor. The bother about people who are not all there is that one can never be quite sure of the nature of what is there: it is likely to be unnerving. Once or twice it was thought that Uncle Dan ought to be put away, but uncle had a sort of somnambulistic instinct for last-minute success. When his father took him to the asylum, it was father, not the son, who found himself consigned.

Edna Earle's narrative is remarkable for its headlong garrulity and also for its preposterous silences and changes of subject at the crises of the tale. She is a respectable young scold with a long tradition in English sentimental comedy. If it was a shade tricky and arch of Miss Welty to make her tell the tale, she has the advantage of being able to bring a whole town to life in her throwaway lines and she has the scolds of Scott, Stevenson and Katherine Mansfield behind her in the world of feminine tongue rattling. Her breathless, backhanded, first person singular has been caught, word by awful word, in all its affectionate self-importance, by a writer with a wonderful ear. "The Ponder Heart" is one of Miss Welty's lighter works, but there is not a mistake in it.

From *The New York Times Book Review* 10 January 1954: 5.

Witless on the Delta

John Chapman

The Ponder Heart is the pumping organ thought to be characteristic of a family named Ponder who lived in Mississippi. The heart of this tribe was not sufficiently distinguished, however, for one to be quite sure of the aptness of the title. In the case of one member, the organ failed at a very appropriate time, while in the case of the two others the heart seems to have led only to some rather eccentric behavior.

♦

The hero of this story—it is perhaps better not to apply the term "novel," which has connotations that might mislead the reader—is a mentally deficient Ponder known locally as Uncle Daniel. And it is chiefly about his rather remarkable heart—not an organ, but a feeling now—that Eudora Welty has chosen to write. The manifestations of cardiac activity, so far as Uncle Daniel was concerned, consisted of explosive generosity. It was his pleasure to dress in the grand manner and to go about giving away not only whatever he happened to have in his pockets, but also anything else about the place that happened to be loose.

Only by reason of Uncle Daniel's remarkable largesse and the standing of the Ponder family in the community was he permitted to remain at large. For somewhat the same reasons, in spite of his clouded wit he was permitted to get married—not once, but twice. Neither marriage was exactly successful, but it was the second—to Bonnie Dee, a dainty scrap of po' white trash—that led to his trial for murder.

"The Ponder Heart," as narrated by Edna Earle, Uncle Daniel's niece, suffers from a somewhat overlong introduction. If one grants that the style is amusing and that some background is necessary to understanding, it remains true that the real reason for the whole story is the remarkable and truly comic courtroom scene.

♦

It is perhaps worth remarking that while Faulkner has dealt with the malignant aspects of mental deficiency and John Steinbeck with its pathos, Eudora Welty works it for its comedy. There are probably no profound conclusions to be drawn from the fact that these three writers have chosen to deal with fools, nor is it particularly important that Shakespeare knew his fools better. What may have some meaning, however, is the fact that writers, like contemporary painters, find it technically advantageous to produce deliberate distortion. This is not to suggest that all art is not a distortion from life; it would be incredibly dull if it were not. But, as in painting, if the distortion doesn't seem to come naturally, one gets the feeling that perhaps the aim is for effect rather than communication of experience or thought.

From *Dallas Morning News* 10 January 1954, sec. VI, p. 15.

Edna Earle Ponder's Good Country People

John L. Idol, Jr.

Despite a contrary promotional claim in the blurb printed on the back cover of the Dell Book edition of Eudora Welty's *The Ponder Heart*, the novel was not unanimously praised. For example, a critic for the *Hudson Review*, Robert Adams, faulted Welty's characterizations on the grounds that her principal characters "exhibit all the squeaky energy and self-conscious buffoonery of television comedians. They strain, they caper, they make free with the time-honored stage props, they wallow in idiom; and, my, aren't they *nice* folks? . . . . Surely Miss Welty knows better than this."[1] Another faultfinder, Gilbert Highet, objected to the narrator. "Edna Earle . . . is a ferocious bore."[2]

Like Adams and Highet, Kingsley Amis disapproved of Welty's characterization and narrator. His review mocks the narrator and scoffs at Welty's use of Southern idioms. "You-all really must see the way the story (if you-all can *call* it that) gets told, just the cosy little friendly way I'm *talking* to you-all right now, hush my mouth. It can be hushed at any time, fortunately, by simply closing the covers. . . ."[3] From the standpoint of those readers who kept the covers open, the judgment of Amis's countryman V. S. Pritchett comes much closer to the truth: "'The Ponder Heart' is one of Miss Welty's lighter works, but there is not a mistake in it."[4] Pritchett clearly saw the novel's technical mastery and found an explanation for what he calls Edna Earle's "headlong garrulity."[5] Out of her love for him, she rushes breathlessly on in her tale of Uncle Daniel because "he is embedded in the mind of a bustling, hoydenish, bossy niece, a girl of fierce practical capacity, snooty manners, and possessive temperament. . . . She is the soul of small-town pugnacity and self-conceit and she has an endless tongue."[6]

It is Edna Earle's small-town pugnacity and self-conceit, her image of herself as a member of the landed gentry now absorbed into the life of a small Southern town, that I wish to examine. Such an undertaking brings me, in my arguments and conclusions, into direct opposition with Cleanth Brooks, no mean foe, who has offered this advice: "Let no one object that Edna Earle isn't really one of the folk since she has deserted the countryside and become a townie, subject to some of the corruptions of a citified existence."[7]

While it is true that Edna Earle learned from her grandfather, a country gentleman, that "everybody in general" had to measure up to the standards of "the old school,"[8] Edna Earle has learned even more from her fifteen years in town, as the manager of the Beulah Hotel, about sizing people up. More importantly, she has developed a strong civic pride in Clay, a pride which emboldens her to defend Clay when others would corrupt its old and cherished ways, as in her sardonic comment that the leading citizens of Clay, not knowing how to deal with the money Uncle Daniel lavished on them at the end of his trial, talked of building a monument—"an arch to straddle the highway with the words in lights. 'Clay, If You Lived Here You'd Be Home Now.'" Edna Earle says, "I spot that as a Sistrunk idea" (p. 155). For all the pugnacity underlying this cutting remark and ones similar to it, the most obvious evidence that Edna Earle is no longer simply a country girl is her comments on the Peacock family and Dorris R. Gladney, county attorney. In her self-conceit, she is partially a "townie," a solid, cultured Presbyterian lady who because of love and tolerance and the absence of "an ounce of revenge" (p. 122) in her body never speaks as harshly of country folk as she might.[9] But in such bits of portraiture as her degrading description of Mrs. Peacock as a woman as "big and fat as a row of pigs" (p. 76) and of Mr. Peacock's face as matching a turkey's in redness, while she continually describes Uncle Daniel as a man "as good as gold" (p. 124), Edna Earle, through these folk similes, clearly shows where her sympathies lie. She could, however, look upon the ways of the country folk—their rusticity, fecundity, and shiftlessness—gaze upon their uncouth tastes and gullibility, and not bear malice. She could also acknowledge their sagacity, loyalty, and ability to endure without venting some sentimental claptrap about unspoiled native primitives.

Her sizing up of the country folk from Polk and elsewhere stands at the heart of much that is fine and admirable in the character of Edna Earle. Given traits other than those she has, she might well have disdained country folk as much as Hulga (Joy) Hopewell does in Flannery O'Connor's story entitled "Good Country People." Unlike Hulga, she would not even think of trying to show Manley Pointer, who is "from out in the country around Willohobie, not even from a place, just from near a place,"[10] how meanly hypocritical he is. In fact, there is nothing unfair or vulgarly prejudiced about Edna Earle. She could have been trusted with the narration of the characters of *Losing Battles*, reporting each of them to be, as Brooks said, "as genuine as a handmade hickory kitchen chair, not in the least common or trashy."[11] But she would likely have lost her charity with Fay McKelva and some of the Chisoms. In short, Edna Earle's account of country people includes both their warts and wings. Yet the warts would probably not have stuck out so prominently if Edna Earle had been a daughter of Polk and not an adopted daughter of Clay.

As a townie from Clay, she notices the spot within the Peacock graveyard where the Peacocks preferred to be buried, "where you could look out and see the Clay Courthouse dome like a star in the distance" (p. 78). She also remarks that Polk no longer is on a main road, that neither Polk nor the Peacocks got up and followed the road, "up until Bonnie Dee" (p. 79). The fact that Bonnie Dee did see that courthouse dome and, in Edna Earle's word, did "traipse" into Clay to pursue her dream of a better life than Polk could give her forms the occasion for Edna Earle's renewed acquaintance with country folk and helps to underscore just how far she has come to accept Clay and its more highfalutin standards as her own. But she will not be so snooty as Judge Clanahan, so much of a mossback, or so intolerant to become bothered when Uncle Daniel looks beneath his class in agreeing to a trial marriage with Bonnie Dee. She will not join Clay's leading citizens in their snobbishness, but she can be easily rankled by country people when she confronts their shiftlessness, unbridled fecundity, uncouth behavior, corrupted dreams of a better life, penchant for violence, and unchecked, self-serving ambition.

On the subject of shiftlessness, she caustically remarks that "the most they [the Peacocks] probably hoped for was that somebody'd come find oil in the front yard and fly in the house and tell them about it" (p. 29). A more amusing example of the shiftlessness of the Peacocks, this one characterized by Edna Earle as "they didn't mind hearing how lazy they were" (p. 96), occurs when Narciss tells the court of pushing a sofa, with Bonnie Dee sprawled upon it, away from a window when lightning threatened the old Ponder house. Edna Earle pointedly remarks that the Peacocks laughed to hear how indolent one of their own could be. But Edna Earle has to admit that Bonnie Dee had not married simply to retreat to the country and do nothing at Ponder Hill except play with dogs, cats, and "one little frizzly hen." Such a life was "not her dream" (p. 49). Whether that life she dreamed of would have been fulfilled by masterly English essays written for Mr. Cody, recitals given on the piano after one easy lesson, or conversation based on a reading of Balzac's novels, we are never told. All we know is that Bonnie Dee judged her trial marriage a failure and ended her reconciliation with Uncle Daniel by sending him off to the refuge of the Beulah Hotel in Clay. Edna Earle can feel the sadness of Bonnie Dee's predicament and would not blame her, "with her origins" (p. 49), for spitting like a cat around Uncle Daniel. Even though she cannot blame her, she "could just beat her on the head, that's all" (p. 49).

From Bonnie Dee's actions and from Edna Earle's assessment of her uncle's seventeen-year-old bride, we gather that the simple rusticity of Polk will not suffice. Bonnie Dee will aspire to the height of fashion shown at Woolworth's, by the kewpie dolls at country fairs, in advertisements in *True Love Story*, *Movie Mirror*, and later in the *Commercial Appeal* from Memphis. Even with her coon eyes, her dreams, and her perpetual childishness, Bonnie Dee is not Fay McKelva. She remains far too much of the uncouth daughter of the unsophisticated Peacocks to evoke anyone's deep or lasting wrath. It is hard to imagine a Fay McKelva being tickled to death by a tassle from someone's antimacassar. Bonnie Dee, in short, has not yet been Snopes-bitten. She is displaying some sagacity in agreeing to a trial marriage and is certainly more than patient in living for years without an allowance for personal and household expenses.

However much her frail heart yearns after life's better things, Bonnie Dee does not rise above the country woman's practice of keeping the electric washing machine on the front porch, in the path of the front door. Such countrified behavior would never have been condoned in Clay. It would have been less scoffed at than unbridled fecundity, but ridiculed nonetheless.

During her trip to Polk for Bonnie Dee's funeral, Edna Earle noticed how numerous the Peacocks seemed to be. It is at the trial, however, that their numbers become oppressive.

> They came in a body. I didn't count either time, but I think there were more Peacocks if possible at the trial than at the funeral. . . .
>
> The immediate Peacock family had paraded into town in Uncle Daniel's pick-up truck that he'd sent them, as pretty as you please. To see them in Polk was bad enough, but you ought to see them in Clay! Country! . . .
>
> We saw them come in; I turned right around and looked. Old lady Peacock wagged in first, big as a house, in new bedroom slippers this time, with pompons on the toes. She had all of them behind her—girls going down in stairsteps looking funnier and funnier in Bonnie Dee's parceled-out clothes, and boys all ages and sizes and the grown ones with wives and children. . . .
>
> *They're* not dying out. Took up the first two rows, with some sitting on laps. (pp. 86-87)

The note of irony in that last sentence is one of the saddest realizations Edna Earle must face: she and Uncle Daniel are the last of the Ponder line. The numerous but none too meek Peacocks will one day inherit the earth but not before Edna Earle protects Uncle Daniel and herself from their destined take-over. If a lie must postpone the inevitable, then so be it—lie she will, or at least not tell the whole truth about how one of the Peacocks died, tickled to death by a tassel on one of Grandma Ponder's antimacassars. Yet, Edna Earle refuses to be too much chagrined by the prolificacy or interchangeability of the Peacocks. When all is said and done, she can genuinely feel Bonnie Dee's loss: "ordinary as she was and trial as she was to put up with—she's the kind of person you do miss. I don't know why—deliver me from giving you the *reason*. You could look and find her like anywhere" (p. 156).

Bonnie Dee's kind, raw country girls finding their models in pulp magazines, popular movie stars, and over made-up junior misses in catalogues, often develop as little more than empty-headed kewpie dolls. As far as Edna Earle's narration allows us to understand her more than five-year association with Bonnie Dee, she intentionally takes the uncouth girl under her wing and advises her what clothes to buy and when to wear them. "I bought her something ladylike to put on her back. I couldn't just leave her the way she was!" (p. 49). Edna Earle thus tries to cure the worst of Bonnie Dee's taste in clothes. These town-bred hints do not prove a great help when Bonnie Dee orders clothes. Later, we learn that Bonnie Dee's dress-buying spree filled the house with clothes—"evening dresses and street dresses and hostess dresses and brunch dresses—dresses in boxes and hanging up. Think of something to wear. Bonnie Dee had it" (p. 67). Only she didn't know when to wear what she bought. When the telephone man came to install a phone, Bonnie Dee came out in the yard to watch him "in a hunter's green velveteen two-piece dress with a stand-up collar" (p. 69). Sophisticated clothes for a very unsophisticated lady.

But her lack of sophistication by now was not so blatant as her mother's grossness when she laid out her daughter for burial.

> They had her in a Sunday-go-to-meeting dress, old-timey looking and too big for her—never washed or worn, just saved: white. She wouldn't have known herself in it. And a sash so new and blue and shiny it looked like it would break, right out of Polk general merchandise. . . . (p. 77)

Mrs. Peacock's crassness appears everywhere—in flowers placed in pie pans "along the front porch. And the mirror on the front of the house" (p. 76). Most obvious, however, are the tennis shoes she wore to Bonnie Dee's funeral.

If she could not dress to match Clay's standards at funerals, Mrs. Peacock was not likely to know how to act in the Clay courthouse. As Edna Earle snappishly remarks of Mrs. Peacock's talking at every opportunity throughout the trial, at one point asking whether anyone in the courtroom could tell her what to do about swollen fingers, "she wasn't spending the day in a doctor's waiting room" (p. 106). Even as she talks, Mr. Peacock interrupts to ask someone the time of day, and Peacock children run in and out for water while one breathes in air with a harmonica in his mouth.

Boorish as these good country people are, proud as they can be of their ability to make their way in life without charity—Uncle Daniel's gift of a pick-up truck was not charity but an act of love from a man who wanted a watermelon when they hauled a load of them into Clay—and overjoyed as they are to see Johnnie Ree protect the family's honor from DeYancey's attempt to besmirch Bonnie Dee's good name and give her fingers "three little scrapes" to show that DeYancey should be ashamed, the Peacocks are not ready to be embraced by Clay or its citizens. Two events support this contention, the first being the gathering of the Peacock clan on the Courthouse stile to eat their jelly sandwiches, biscuits and molasses, and sweet milk from a tin bucket, and four watermelons "left lying on the courthouse grass for the world to see and pick up" (p. 121). The second event occurs when, unlike the townsfolk, the Magees, Clanahans, and Sistrunks, the Peacocks waste no time in spending the money gathered in at the trial by the clan, except that eaten by one of the babies, without a qualm, in Polk. By contrast, the citizens of Clay cannot think of what to do with their share of Uncle Daniel's grandest gesture of liberality. Most of the townies just sit there holding theirs while the ever-progressive Sistrunks think of suggesting a civic project, a sign straddling the highway entering Clay. At this point Edna Earle is distinctly not on the side of the townies, for to her the idea of a sign is obviously distasteful. Here she chooses boorishness over gaudy boosterism.

She can brook both of these more readily than she can the transparent ambition of another bumpkin, Dorris R. Gladney, county attorney, and "no friend of the Ponders" (p. 80), a sort of kinsman to Faulkner's Flem Snopes who told the Peacocks what they could do to Uncle Daniel, bring him to trial for the murder of their beloved Bonnie Dee. Perhaps thinking that a victory over the Ponders in Clay might put him on the road to the governor's mansion in Jackson, Gladney, a redneck parading as the champion of other rednecks, provokes Edna Earle to anger, especially in his rustic labelling of Edna Earle as "Mizriz." "That's what he calls me—Mizriz. He likes to act country, but he don't have all that far to go—he *is* country" (p. 116). By intimating that he has been peppered by buckshot several times in his career, Edna Earle links him to such violent country folk as Williebelle Kilmichael, who "empties a load of birdshot into her husband's britches, every so often" (pp. 116-117). Gladney not only crosses

Edna Earle because he intentionally plays the countryfolk against the townspeople but also because he seemed to be living proof of one of Grandma Ponder's generalizations—"'Show me a man wears a diamond ring, and I'll show you a wife beater.' There he was." (p. 116). The less truck she can have with Gladney, thinks Edna Earle, the better, for it sometimes seems to her that Gladney urged the Peacocks to lodge a murder charge "for lack of something to do, out of his evil mind" (p. 153). She is glad to see him jump "in his Ford and hit the highway" (p. 152). Clay does not need the likes of him.

That Edna Earle has cast her lot with the townies is not altogether shown by her small-town pugnacity or her lightly satiric description and narration of the boorish ways of Bonnie Dee and the other Peacocks.[12] Yet another sign that she sees herself one of the citizens of Clay is the hurt she feels when her neighbors, and even her preacher, prove standoffish after Uncle Daniel's "money has come between the Ponders and everybody else in town" (p. 155). No one has called, not even Eva Sistrunk, but Clay's cold shoulders are not enough to drive Edna Earle back to Ponder Hill. The Peppers, tenants on the farm, like good country folk, will remain on the place, even if no landed gentry remains to give direction to their work and lives. Meanwhile, Edna Earle will live with the hope that other guests and then the townfolk will come to the Beulah Hotel. She has this hope because, once when she had to lock up the Beulah and watch over Uncle Daniel at Ponder Hill, where there was no electricity, she later reported, "I missed my city lights" (p. 54). And city lights will hold her there, as long as she can keep the Sistrunks and their kind from bringing too great a glare upon it. Edna Earle has thus adopted Clay as her own even if some if its oldest citizens feel a little uncomfortable with her and Uncle Daniel just at the moment. Clay, in time, will see that it must have the likes of Edna Earle, Bonnie Dee, and other country folk if it is not to go the way of Polk.

Most likely, then, it is from this place, from the Beulah Hotel in Clay, that Edna Earle will continue to make her vivid but loquacious comments on country people, both the good and the bad, implicitly lamenting as she does the passage not only of Southern landed aristocracy but also the kind of poor whites, who, like the Renfros, loved the soil and took great pride in their families and family traditions. The light by which Edna Earle sees the world is now largely energized by the forces generated by Clay and its society. Landed gentry has come to town and there wants to survive. This optimistic daughter of the Ponders sees, in the end, a continuing need for good country people as well as the urgency of upholding the best features of life in a small town as she has come to know them in Clay.

Welty, who said during a symposium at Millsaps College that Edna Earle's vision of other characters was her aim, went on to acknowledge: "I did everything through her, including my own ideas, of course."[13] In *The Ponder Heart*, as elsewhere in her work, Welty accepts a social, political, and cultural order based on patterns existing in her area of the South. Her prime concern is manners, with cultural traits, not political or social doctrine.[14]

Like her creator, Edna Earle is also a keen student of manners. To the mode of life she has known for years as the granddaughter of one of the last of the landed gentry, she has added something of the code of Clay's best citizens, not the Bodkins or others on their way down the social ladder. She now stands presently as a lonely, but far from silent, defender of what she sees as good and worth keeping.

The questions we are left to weigh at the end of the novel are whether one of the best of the uncouth good country people, Narciss, will overcome her town-bred loneliness and remain at the Beulah and what will Uncle Daniel and Edna Earle do now that their wealth is gone. Will a sprightly pugnacity and buoyant self-conceit enable Edna Earle to survive? Just how long will good country people be more like Bonnie Dee than Fay Mckelva? Such questions cast shadows on the sunniness of the novel.

NOTES

[1]Robert M. Adams. "Formulas and Fiction." *Hudson Review*, 7 (Spring 1954), 145.

[2]Gilbert Highet, Review of *The Ponder Heart*, *Harper's Magazine*, Feb. 1954, p. 97.

[3]Kingsley Amis, Review of *The Ponder Heart*, *The Spectator*, 29 Oct. 1954, p. 534.

[4]V. S. Pritchett, "Bossy Edna Earle Had a Word for Everything," *New York Times Book Review*, 10 Jan. 1954, p. 5.

[5]Pritchett, p. 5.

[6]Pritchett, p. 5.

[7]Cleanth Brooks, "Eudora Welty and the Southern Idiom," in *Eudora Welty: A Form of Thanks*, ed. Louis Dollarhide and Ann J. Abadie (Jackson: Univ. Press of Mississippi, 1979), p. 14.

[8]Eudora Welty, *The Ponder Heart* (New York: Harcourt, Brace, 1954), p. 8. All subsequent references to the novel will appear parenthetically in the text.

[9]See Alfred Appel, Jr., *A Season of Dreams* (Baton Rouge: Louisana State Univ. Press, 1965), p. 57.

[10]Flannery O'Connor, *The Complete Stories of Flannery O'Connor*, ed. Robert Giroux (New York: Farrar, Straus and Giroux, 1971), p. 279.

[11]Brooks, p. 8.

[12]Michael Kreyling sees Edna Earle as "the voice and walking embodiment of Clay," a judgment I only partially accept. See *Eudora Welty's Achievement of Order* (Baton Rouge: Louisiana State Univ. Press, 1979), p. 111.

[13]"Symposium: The Artist and the Critic," *The Stylus* (Spring 1960), 23.

[14]See Eudora Welty, "Must the Novelist Crusade?" in *The Eye of the Story: Selected Essays and Reviews* (New York: Random House, 1978).

From *The Southern Quarterly* 20.3 (Spring 1982): 66-75.

Ponder Heart
Now out in Dramatic Version

Frank Hains

Miss Eudora Welty would be the first to say, I expect, that the story line of *The Ponder Heart* is rather slim; that her delightful book is not a novel of plot but one of character and atmosphere. As such, it is a gem and there's no debating that point.

It would seem immediately dangerous, then, to strip the story to its bones for the purposes of dramatic presentation. That Messrs. Chodorov and Fields should have been able to do so and still retain as much as they did of the book's flavor seems commendable if not entirely satisfying to those who were charmed by Uncle Daniel in the novel.

Miss Welty's particular genius imparted to him in the original a complete credibility; an individuality which makes him unique in any fiction that I know. In the play, however, I fear he tends toward an occasional Elwood P. Dowdishness; he seems sometimes unhappily near silliness.

I'm sure that the artistry of Mr. David Wayne succeeds in returning to Uncle Daniel some of his individuality and believability; indeed he must, to account for the success which the play is enjoying and for critical reviews and comments which I have heard from those who have seen it.

In reading the script, it's evident that the almost unanimous critical verdict concerning the first two acts is accurate; the play does not really come alive and Uncle Daniel does not really hit his stride until the courtroom scene in the third act. Certainly it is—as has been elsewhere noted—more than enough to compensate for the lags in the first two rather lethargic acts.

There would appear to be little doubt that the play is a labor of love on the part of the authors; that they were as charmed by Miss Welty's drolleries as were we all. I think that they have done as faithful a job of presenting them, within the obvious limitations imposed by their medium, as might have been done.

Whatever its shortcomings, *The Ponder Heart* is as fresh and unusual as any Broadway offering of recent years; it has much to offer in the way of joy and warmth. It is, unfortunately but unavoidably, overshadowed by the work on which it is based.

The Jackson Little Theatre, it is reported, is considering the presentation of the play here in the event that it should be released to amateur groups. It will surely be met by a receptive audience and will just as surely leave that audience delighted with the charm which it indeed possesses.

From *The Clarion-Ledger* 27 May 1956, sec. IV, p. 6.

Eudora Welty's *The Ponder Heart* Gets Rave Notices at Broadway

Bette E. Barber

NEW YORK CITY (Special)—At the Music Box Theatre in the heart of Broadway Thursday night the Mississippi characters portraying Eudora Welty's delightful first play, "The Ponder Heart," opened to the unrestrained delight of first nighters and tough drama critics sang as sweetly about it as did the mockingbird the star, David Wayne, talked about!

After being almost the exclusive property of the intellectual reader for many years, Miss Welty got to the heart of creative genius as her work was revealed to and relished by the general theatre-going audience, and therefrom we predict a following she has long deserved.

From the literary heights where she has always been successfully perched, she has swooped down with all sorts of delightful humor and excitement to set before chuckling audiences a delightful comedy peopled with first-rate actors telling a tale about the Deep South.

Jackson Girl in Cast

Jacksonians in the audience, while busting with pride over Miss Welty's triumph got a double delight as they watched a local lass, pretty Jeanne Shelly, daughter of Mr. and Mrs. James E. Smith, bring down the house in the trial scene as she described a trip to the movies in Memphis.

Herald-Tribune

Walter Kerr of The New York Herald Tribune went all-out for the show, saying in part:

"And 'The Ponder Heart,' as a play, is as errant and wispy and filled with the wanderlust as its principal character. Adapted by Joseph Fields and Jerome Chodorov from a celebrated Eudora Welty short-story, it plays hob with quite a few conventions. Its mood is almost a shrug: its most serious passages have a ripple of cracker-barrel shiftlessness and corner-store humor about them; though the time is the present, the stage insists on looking as much as possible like something left over from Currier and Ives.

Continuous Chuckle

"No one is quite serious about the folk habits of the South, even if the plot does call for a lightningbolt that rips through a doorway and shatters a few lives. Nor are we committed to farce, even if a new bride keeps her shoes in the icebox and drops to her knees to play jacks with the family maid. A gentle, wry, unpredictable chuckle is what the authors seem to be after and they got an almost uninterrupted one from me.

"The images are fresh: a spate of children crawling all over a small-town witness stand, a defendant congratulating his prosecutor on his prowess, a delighted witness insisting on telling the plot of "Quo Vadis" to her stunned interrogators. (Jeanne Shelley of Jackson was the witness who did the "Que Vadis" scene.) Let the action ramble, let the plotting climb trees, let some of the scenes go on too long for their own good—the impudent grin that shines through the nonsense is still remarkably winning."

New York Times

This comedy of rural manners was characterized by the distinguished critic of the *New York Times*, Brooks Atkinson as "original, charming and funny." Among other things, he had this to say:

"But the play does not hold the characters up to ridicule. It respects their loyalty to the town and each other. Although they are temperamental, they are neighbors. Although the courtroom scene is uproarious, it is enchanting, also. Will Geer's homely histrionics as the prosecuting attorney, Don Hanmer's anxiety as Uncle Daniel's sorely tried attorney, John McGovern's comic vexation as the judge, Ruth White's rebelliousness as a witness whose dignity as a social leader has been affronted, Juanita Hall's anger as one of the witnesses and John Marriott's invincible taciturnity as another—all contribute to the comic shambles of the scene.

But the acting is excellent all the way through. As the timed, colorness, backward bride, Sarah Marshall's shiftlessness and innocence compose a full-length portrait. Miss Merkel and Mr. Wayne are the actors whose taste and daintness give the comedy its distinctiveness and keep it on the level of a comedy of rural manners—absurd but admirable also. They do not go after easy laughs. They respect the characters they are playing. What is absurd in the parts they forgive because it derives from goodness. It's funny and delightful. It also includes some forgiving truth about unpretentious people."

N. Y. Daily News

John Chapman of the *New York Daily* said in part:

"Uncle Daniel Ponder is a Confederate twin of Denver's Elwood P. Dowd—a warmly friendly fellow who wants everybody to have as pleasant a time as he is having, and who isn't even irritated when somebody wants to put him in the crazy-house just because he is easy going. Uncle Daniel's play, "The Ponder Heart," was produced by the Playwrights' Company at the Music Box last evening, and in its gentle southern way it is as screwy a play as Elwood Dowd's "Harvey" was.

At the beginning, Uncle Daniel Ponder, a rich and middling-aged resident of a small town not far from Mississippi, is coming up for trial on the charge of having murdered his bride. Nobody has bothered to put him in jail because everybody knows he wouldn't hurt anybody. His bride, it soon becomes known, was a girl named Bonnie Dee Peacock—a barefoot lass whom the old rake trapped into marriage by getting her drunk on pistachio ice cream and giving her a solid gold wedding ring from a Box of Crackerjack. She was, we are informed, the kind of girl who could spend hours trying to figure out how the tail of the C gets through the L on the Coca-Cola sign.

At this point, being an addict of daffiness, I decided to settle back [in] my Music Box chair last evening and enjoy whatever came my way. A great deal came my way, and almost all of it was gently and beautifully funny."

Glamour of Opening Night

Adding to the glamour of an opening night were Mr. and Mrs. David Rockefeller, Herbert Marshall, the actor, whose daughter, Sarah Marshall, played the part of the bride Bonnie Dee Ponder, and other celebrities.

Miss Welty's party included Mr. and Mrs. William Maxwell of "The New Yorker Magazine", Mr. and Mrs. Diarmuid Russell, Charlotte Capers, Rosa Wells, Ruth Forbes, and Mary Lou Aswell, one of the editors of "The Readers Digest" who has visited in Jackson. . . .

From *The Clarion-Ledger* 19 Feb. 1956, sec. I, p. 6.

The Bride of the Innisfallen and Other Stories
1955

The Bride of the Innisfallen

Fred Bornhauser

Let the commentator consider, as a starting point, the two titles side by side. "The Bride of the Innisfallen," though it may be a characteristic story, even a thematically crucial story, can lend to the collection of which it is a part no more than a nominal clue that it is (at best) the key to the rest, or that it is the longest (which it is not), or that it is the author's favorite, or that in the publisher's mind it wraps up a more saleable commodity. "A Good Man Is Hard to Find," on the other hand, suggests boldly at the outset the major idea which permeates all the stories collected with it, and indeed makes the inherent point in that collection as collection. It is of course merely an accident, but a happy, convenient one, that one of Miss O'Connor's stories should bear a name so suitable for the book; and an accident that none of Miss Welty's (unless it be by an awkward stretch "No Place for You, My Love") do. But, barring the lucky accident, a reader might with justification often be annoyed by meaningless titles for volumes of shorter fiction, and wish for a mere Collected or Selected or New or even Volumes 1 and 2. . . .

While more than half of Flannery O'Connor's stories are based on what could very well be out of or for public prints, none of Eudora Welty's are. This is not to suggest that the one writer is journalistic and the other not, but to attempt the charting of a public world in fiction as distinguished from a private world in fiction. For a more personal, subjective world is certainly what Miss Welty has created. Amazingly enough, it is this smaller world which is presented on the larger stage. Of the seven stories comprising the present volume, two are concerned with Americans travelling in or to Europe, one with the retelling of a classical legend, one with an episode of the Civil War, one with sophisticated Yankees in modern New Orleans, and two with Mississippi situations best called, in the highest sense of the term, sentimental comedies. Therefore *The Bride of the Innisfallen* lacks the total coherence of *A Good Man Is Hard to Find*.

The question may be asked whether a collection of short stories should be expected to hang together so absolutely, to which the answer is no, but there cannot but be a different, more diffuse effect if they don't. In reviewing Miss Welty's second collection of stories, *The Wide Net*, in *The Kenyon Review* in 1944, Robert Penn Warren took note of the fact that since her first, *A Curtain of Green*, Miss Welty had distilled her fiction through an alembic that produced greater unity with regard to both theme and style, leaving behind much of her earlier experiment and variety. The question now is whether she is attempting whole new domains in the seemingly disparate works in *The Bride of the Innisfallen*, or whether in the mature mastery of her art she now leaves upon them a more subtly unifying stamp.

In the same review Mr. Warren also expressed his understanding that despite this later concentration the two books did show some common preoccupation with the themes of isolation and alienation, which in time were by inspissation to become the more significant theme of Innocence and Experience, or what he called "terms of contrast: . . . the dream and the world, idea and nature, individuality and the life-flux"—all resting upon a passage from "A Still Moment" involving the polarities Love and Separateness.

I believe that the major thematic idea analyzed by Mr. Warren is still present in *The Bride of the Innisfallen*. The aching desire for knowledge of reality, the need for recognition of the meaning of love after separateness and of separateness after love, the sense that experience is understood only in terms of contrast and memory, the loneliness that is all mystery in the very presence of fulfillment, the very end of despair at the moment despair is desired—these are the realizations gained at all the summits of this magnificent range of stories.

> Then the melons and the arch of the gate, the grandmother's folding of the fan and Mama's tears, the volcano of early morning, and even the long, dangerous voyage behind her—all seemed caught up and held in something: the golden moment of touch, just given, just taken, in saying good-by.
>
> —"Going to Naples"

> In the future would the light, that had jumped like the man from Connemara into the world, be a memory, like that of a meeting, or must there be mere faith that it had been like that?
>
> —"The Bride of the Innisfallen"

> The mirror's cloudy bottom sent up minnows of light to the brim . . . quivering, leaping to life, fighting, aping old things . . . sometimes what men had done to Miss Theo and

Miss Myra and the peacocks and to slaves, and sometimes what a slave had done and what anybody now could do to anybody. Under the flicker of the sun's licks. . . . like an act of mercy gone . . . the mirror felled her flat.

—"No Place for You, My Love"

. . . he remembered for the first time in years when he was young and brash, a student in New York, and the shriek and horror and unholy smother of the subway had its original meaning for him as the lilt and expectation of love.

—"No Place for You, My Love"

I stood on my rock and wished for grief. It would not come. . . . I am sure now grief is a ghost—only a ghost in Hades, where ungrateful Odysseus is going—waiting on him.

—"Circe"

If anything, the theme of Separateness and Love can be said to be even more particularized in this new book. It is now presented almost entirely in terms of the Stranger. Interesting coincidence, after what we have attempted to say about the stranger in the world of Flannery O'Connor. But we quickly see that the idea of the stranger is here treated quite differently. Instead of having a connection with perverseness, it is associated with subjective loneliness, with the sensitive, reflective personality, the personality wondering about reality. We have moved, basically, from the active to the contemplative.

"No Place for You, My Love," story of a strange interlude, begins, "They were strangers to each other, both fairly well strangers to the place," and ends with the two people still strangers who "had ridden down into a strange land together and were getting safely back." In "The Burning" the delicate, aristocratic ladies are strangers to their time and situation, at last strangers in a familiar town. The American girl in "The Bride of the Innisfallen" sits estranged from her husband in a train among strangers, is "no lonelier than that little bride" whose groom is "taken for granted," finally tears up a message for her husband and walks "into the lovely room full of strangers." It is Circe who asks to be remembered as one who died of love, as Ulysses departs with all his "beautiful strangers." Dicey Hastings, narrator of "Kin," cheerfully received as "long-lost cousin" into the bosom of her family, is still a stranger, a visitor chiefly remembering the past. And despite her screaming vivaciousness, Gabriella in "Going to Naples" is dealing in her way with the problem of strangeness. Why go to Naples when she was happy in Buffalo? or, reflecting by the ship's rail: "Was now the time to look forward to the doom of parting, and stop looking back at the doom of meeting? . . . . Gabriella would only have to say 'Good-by, Aldo,' and while she was saying the words, time would be flying by."

There is always the stranger. "Whatever people liked to think, situations (if not scenes) were usually three-way—there was somebody else always. The one who didn't—couldn't—understand the two made the formidable third."

The way the theme of the stranger is treated accounts, of course, for the manner, at times almost impressionistic—the oblique style, the warmth and delicacy and profusion of the rhetoric. Miss Welty proves here that if she is mainly deepening and enriching what she has plotted before, she has in the process become master of a most highly distinguished and, it now seems to me, thoroughly controlled style. Surely pages 34-5, in this volume, to indicate a passage almost at random, can be matched only by great writers. If a story like "Ladies in Spring" seems at her ebb-point, one like "Kin," with its own kinship to *The Ponder Heart*—essential demonstration of Miss Welty's greatest (but not by any means only), gift, the noble Comic Spirit—places her among the unquestioned masters.

Miss Welty stabilizes a tragic world, resolves it with vivid imagination, clean control of language, and her comic gift. It emerges a world of sensibility, subtle psychological play, "nuance and scruple"—seen from behind the mask of order. Sentimentality, when it appears, is well-shaped, and it is good.

Miss Welty is more directly in the tradition of the story-teller than is Miss O'Connor, who generally conceives in terse dramatic scenes. There is greater fluency and ease in Miss Welty's work, as distinguished from the architectonic thrust of detail in Miss O'Connor's. If in Flannery O'Connor we are more conscious of a distant view of a whole world and given the impression of stories written on subjects which lend themselves to that view, we are in Eudora Welty conscious of a singular personality lendings its wholeness to a fragmentary world and putting its own impress on each story.

But when all is said and done, what is a story? "A thing is incredible, if ever, only after it is told—returned to the world it come out of." ("No Place for You, My Love") "For whom is a story enough? For wanderers who will tell it—it's where they must find their strange felicity." ("Circe")

From *Shenandoah* 7 (Autumn 1955): 71, 77-78.

Miss Welty Magnificent in Newest Short Pieces

Frank Hains

This is Eudora Welty's seventh volume and it contains seven stories. But that's coincident. It would have been her sixth and it would have contained eight had not "THE PONDER HEART" assumed such proportions and such significance that her publishers dissuaded her from including it in this book.

It's fortunate that they did, for the separately published story of the Ponders won Miss Welty the coveted William Dean Howells award of the American Academy of Arts and Letters.

Even more important is the fact that now these other seven magnificent short pieces can stand on their own and out of the Ponder shadow.

Miss Welty regrets that there is no truly, as she puts it, "funny story" in this collection—that was to have been "THE PONDER HEART."

It doesn't need it.

There are in these stories warmth and tenderness and humor—along with the terrible underthreads which weave their occasional dark designs into Miss Welty's work.

Each creates its own particular mood; each is, in effect, a mood.

Miss Welty's every line is characterized by an awareness, an insight, that never reports as much as it reveals.

She says herself that she considers plot secondary to feeling.

Her work is singular in the overallness of its effect; lines taken out of context seldom carry much impact. but there is a remarkable unity in each piece that slips over the reader's perception—rather like a tea cozy.

In "No Place for You, My Love," the first story in the collection, it's impossible not to feel the sultry oppression of a summer Sunday evening on the gulf coast; not to be permeated by the heat and steaminess, not to be contained in the humid, angry frustration.

"The Burning," a ghastly little side-swipe of Sherman's march is sheer horror in its understatement. Tiny details stand out crystal clear in a stress so great that it dulls the night to the magnitude of the scene.

The title story is concerned with a train trip. The people are secondary to the feeling of the trip. There comes to mind no other writing which conveys so completely the personal loss of identity, the excursion into a limbo that train travel brings.

"Ladies in Spring" is a strange little story which hints at more than it says.

It is concerned with a small boy's reaction to the feverishness of spring (which is not at all the same thing as spring fever). His sense of the mystery of the season and consequently of life itself, focuses on the ladies who represent mystery to him. There's a wet, rainy, growing mood to the story that is not just spring but its epitome.

"Circe," Miss Welty calls "a little bit of fun." It many not seem greatly funny for, as so often, Miss Welty's surface humor covers very unhumorous undercurrents.

In this, she says she wondered what it would be like to be Circe—to have no feelings—to have only magic. So she tells the familiar legend from the Odyssey in Circe's words. Again, feeling is all important; here, of the brassy sun-and-windswept Mediterranean Island. Circe no longer is the villain of the piece but becomes a woman frustrated by her magic and longing for mundane emotions.

Environment is all important in every one of Miss Welty's stories. She sees always the characters caught in the context of their surroundings and subordinated to them.

There is no other writer with the nearmagic power of conveying these feelings. Even Faulkner, whose greatest honor is perhaps the esteem in which Miss Welty holds him, cannot compare with her in the evocation of a mood.

What makes Miss Welty tick? It's doubtful if she knows herself. She admits that she doesn't always consciously put in all the things which individual readers get out of her work.

But she's pleased with whatever interpretation her work receives.

At the moment, she has many writings in mind but hasn't had time to put them on paper. Her recent time been occupied by critical work done on a Guggenheim fellowship.

From *The Clarion-Ledger* 10 April 1955, sec. IV, p. 6.

"The Sharp Edge of Experiment": The Poetics of "No Place for You, My Love"

Albert J. Devlin

A few years ago, I helped to advise a Welty film project designed for the American Masters series on PBS. "No Place for You, My Love" was one of the three stories chosen for dramatization to mark the progress of Eudora Welty's fine career. Suffice it to say, we advisors were no Civil War, and the National Endowment for the Humanities denied our request for a production grant. My consolation was to think that the masterful language of the report may have concealed a fairly simple objection: perhaps a Welty film that eschewed such standbys as "A Worn Path" and "Petrified Man" and seemed to prefer the dynamics of the career itself was not very Weltian after all. Our choice of "Lily Daw," "June Recital," and "No Place for You, My Love" was not eccentric, but it certainly did confirm the daring nature of Welty's career.

In choosing "No Place for You, My Love," I felt that I was heeding Welty's own strong signals about this intriguing story. They are recorded in her essay "How I Write," printed first in 1955 and then revised extensively and retitled for *The Eye of the Story: Selected Essays and Reviews* (1978). In part, Welty writes to correct bogus notions of creativity that overdetermine the writer's art. "'Sweet Analytics, 'tis thou has ravish'd me!'", she mocks, in her well-known critique of "upside down" explication (HIW 244). But Welty's deeper intention is to reveal her artistic identity and acts, in a way that was rather exceptional for her in 1955, and thereafter as well. That her own attempt to tell "the story of a story" would echo those of the master is not surprising in light of Welty's modernist principles and the highly authorized status of the Jamesian preface itself.

"How I Write" has much the same accent as the famous prefaces that Henry James wrote for the New York Edition of his works. James's "sheer moral delight of solving a technical difficulty or securing a complicated effect" (in R.P. Blackmur's words) is precisely the form that Welty's self-revelation takes. "As first written," she explains, "the story told, from the inside, of a girl in a claustrophobic predicament: she was caught fast in the over-familiar, monotonous life of her small [southern] town, and immobilized further by a hopeless and inarticulate love." Welty realizes in retrospect that the story "had gone on too long" in its first drafting, and that its protagonist was known "too well" by the writer (HIW 246-247). It was "a pleasant holiday" trip south of New Orleans that taught Welty how to revise, in particular "where the real point of view belonged." With this discovery of the story's true center, Welty's balky subject was at last "out in the open" and ready for treatment. "I saved the story," Welty exults, paying tribute to the "extravagance" of the imagination, as Henry James would describe its freedom (HIW 247-248).

Welty's "preface" bespeaks at every point her "love [of] hard things to write" (*Conversations* 60). This posture of exposure, of writing dangerously "on the sharp edge of experiment" (HIW 246), is the essence of her self-disclosure; and Eudora Welty has not revealed anything more intimate about herself in later autobiographical writing. In planning the aforementioned film, I hoped that the keyed-up experimentation of "No Place for You, My Love" would convey this daring identity and momentarily displace other stories that are perhaps known "too well." I hoped also that Reynolds Price, Miss Welty's on-camera interlocutor, could be persuaded to ask if she would qualify her statement that "neither version" of the story had "any personal connection" (HIW 246) with the author. I wanted to test a special application of the term "personal," which I think pertinent to Welty's self-disclosure.

In "How I Write," Eudora Welty described the "predicament" of a girl "caught fast" in her small southern town and blocked by a "hopeless" love. Recast as a midwesterner and given leave to travel, this woman who was known "too well" by the writer has been "extracted" (HIW 246) from nothing other than Welty's prototypical story of the "buried life": her essential literary plot which culminates in *The Golden Apples* of 1949. Has Eudora Welty not described in effect a double escape of author and character from their respective "cultures," one literary, the other social and psychological; and does not their freeing in "No Place for You, My Love" constitute a fable of creativity? Welty has said that "the vain courting of imperviousness in the face of exposure is this little story's plot" (HIW 249). The impulsive trip of an unnamed man and woman, strangers who meet by chance in New Orleans, does not greatly alter Welty's aesthetic, but its elaboration in "No Place for You, My Love" is unusually risky and daring, and it may well bespeak a special ferment in her career. This, at least, is what I took to be the strong "personal" signal of Welty's astute preface and story.

In "No Place for You, My Love," the shock of the world is measured by its illimitable force and presence. The highway leading out of the "maze" of New Orleans hurries "south of South," where hordes of mosquitoes and gnats play "idiot games" and there is a downpouring of summer heat and light and a steady probing by the wind. When the man and woman cross the Mississippi from east to west, they touch "the nerve" of heat, whose effect is hypnotic: "Dead snakes stretched across the concrete like markers—inlaid mosaic bands, dry as feathers, which their tires licked at intervals that began to seem clocklike." Welty's comic timing leads her to break this portentous clicking, and so her male traveler, solely a product of revision, plays the banal tourist: "'It's never anything like this in Syracuse,' he said." "'Or in Toledo, either,' she replied with dry lips" (CS 471-472).

As the car continues south, the land becomes more nearly "amphibious," and when it reaches the "sparse" turn-around "settlement" of Venice, the shell road lapses into "broad . . . moving water that stretched to reach the horizon and looked like an arm of the sea" (CS 473). Inside "Baba's Place," a "beer shack," the man and the woman eat, they dance to a "raging juke box," and leave just as the festive locals arrive for a "Shrimp Dance" (CS 476-477). The return trip follows the west bank of the river, pushes through "the same loneliness" of heat, dust, and mosquitoes, includes a stop for a kiss, then merges with other traffic "turned cityward" (CS 479-480). Their good-bye at the woman's hotel seems no more special than the chance meeting earlier that day at Galatoire's. As "she disappeared through the revolving door," the woman seems to resume her identity "with a gesture of smoothing her hair." The middle-aged man recalls in turn a youthful "expectation of love" in still another city, New York (CS 480-481).

One thing only is certain about this foray "south of South": the woman's "panic" question after crossing the river is a rephrasing of Welty's own artistic extremity: "Just how far below questions and answers, concealment and revelation, they were running now—that was still a new question, with a power of its own, waiting. How dear—how costly—could this ride be?" (CS 472). The danger, as Welty had come to understand, waited precisely in the "new question" posed by the woman's adventure. For her, this is a time of waiting, and perhaps of recoil from some intensity, whose metonymical "bruise" (CS 477) is marked on her temple. Rather closely in this regard does she resemble the wives of William Wallace and George Fairchild, antecedent figures in "The Wide Net" and *Delta Wedding*, or the mysterious traveler in "The Bride of the Innisfallen," who hide or run away to ponder some transforming disclosure; but in "No Place for You, My

Love" Welty more avidly enters this gap to hypothesize its curious substrate of emotion. Presumably, Welty's own trip determined her to send the woman into the same hypnotic country where she might "play at danger" (HIW 249) and further savor her unspeakable desire. The "inimical world" of the delta might be trusted in turn to foment what "merely could, or almost could" (HIW 248) happen in this provocative land. Once her imagination had seized this design, Welty realized that both the world and the hidden self must be shielded from the usual blunt tools of analysis. In part her technique is intended to meet this retrograde need.

The stranger's function is two-fold: he gives Welty the outside point of view that she required; and with his map, watch, guiding hands, and over-determined language, he often plays the comic husband beset by foul circumstance. Insects "blind" the windshield of his rented convertible, prevailing winds tatter the map, and the elements overwhelm even his masterful kiss: "The heat came inside the car and wrapped them still, and the mosquitoes had begun to coat their arms and even their eyelids" (CS 479). In exposing itself, the world reveals only a supremely indifferent architecture; and at Venice, "the end of the road," it was "all water" to any rationalizing eye. To preserve the delta as a mysterious signifier whose oppositional force is nearly demonic aptly describes Welty's technique. The kind of countervailing force that it would require set her to reject anything resembling "an easy or . . . tempting sympathy" (HIW 249) between the strangers. More precisely, it led her to bracket, and to mark with special instructions, certain familiar enactments of the quest narrative itself.

A tethered alligator is a focus of merriment on the ferry that crosses the river. Rather ponderously does the man find in these antics "the last worldly evidence of some old heroic horror of the dragon." The woman covets instead the gator's thick hide. In disembarking, she looks back twice at the tethered creature, "waddling like a child to school," and thinks how "merciful" such protection would be (CS 470-471). Shortly thereafter, the man calls "Time out" as he turns abruptly from the main road:

> They bolted over a cattle guard, where some rayed and crested purple flowers burst out of the vines in the ditch, and rolled onto a long, narrow, green, mowed clearing: a churchyard. A paved track ran between two short rows of raised tombs, . . . [which] he passed between . . . in the manner of a feat. (CS 472)

When the woman asks, "'What is your wife like?'", the "right hand" of her companion "came up and spread—iron, wooden, manicured," to deflect this untimely question. "Then he lit a cigaret, and the portrait, and the right-hand testimonial it made, were blown away. She smiled," Welty adds, "herself as unaffected as by some stage performance." "[S]uddently the rays of the sun" strike near the base of the priest's house, and a figure appears on the porch, "in his underwear," on cue as it were, to fetch a cassock for Vespers. Summoned, the ghost of Tiresias "stared at the car [for] a moment as if he wondered what time it was" (CS 473).

Welty's descent into Hades is a highly stylized conflation of heroic narratives, as her glancing allusion to Odysseus, Orpheus, Perseus and their attending women make clear. Somewhat less clear is the reader's path through this near-comic maze. The man designates the episode "Time out" in a story whose larger action is also "time out," so that we witness in effect the "performance" of a play within a play. The core text is the "buried life" of trapped women, as the implied stories of Penelope, Persephone, and Eurydice convey; or punishment and revenge, as Perseus and the Medusa. Welty titled an early draft of the story "The Gorgon's Head," and then cancelled it, one thinks, because it stated too boldly a covert, and deliberately fragile, mythological substructure. In any event, the woman's question is untimely and disruptive, and it may also imply resistance to the violence and abuse of these stories, a trace element of the woman's own rescue from both unpromising fictional origins and her present intensity, whatever its Hyacinthine "bruise" may portend. I doubt, however, that Welty's primary intention is to subvert, reconstitute, or even critically examine these quest narratives, at least in the present rendition. Rather she intends to bracket them, as the signal "Time out" indicates. The trip begins impulsively as a "play at danger," and the present episode is governed by that same stage metaphor. Classical roles are tried on like props, as the man, and Welty, too, one thinks, improvises upon these quintessential "boy-girl" stories; but they lack definitive power beyond the present moment and cannot confer identity. For all their timeless appeal, these narratives go up in smoke. This I take to be Welty's primary defense against a too "easy" understanding especially of the woman's dilemma. Neither words, memory, nor story itself, paradoxically, can presume to rationalize her secret emotion.

Welty said in 1972 that she "wanted the characters [in her novel *Losing Battles*] to be down to bedrock—no money, no education, no nothing, except themselves—the rest all being cleared away" (*Conversations* 67). Welty's technique in "No Place for You, My Love" seeks "bedrock" as well, or at least a watery variant of that figure, with no past, no future, no cosmology, no authorized quest narratives, and no rational psychology either, as the woman's question may seem to invite. Essentially, such radical clearing left Eudora Welty with a ghost story of sorts governed by the irreducible mystery of place. What happens in the course of the trip, Welty says, is this:

> . . . there'd come to be a sort of third character present—an identity, rather: the relationship between the two and between the two and the world. . . . It was what grew up between them meeting as strangers, went on the trip with them, nodded back and forth from one to the other—listening, watching, persuading or denying them. . . . Its role was that of hypnosis—it was what a relationship *does*. . . . I wanted to suggest that its being took shape as the strange, compulsive journey itself, was palpable as its climate and mood, the heat of the day—but was its spirit too, a spirit that held territory. (HIW 247-248)

"Relationship," Welty concludes," *is* a pervading and changing mystery . . . . Brutal or lovely, the mystery waits for people wherever they go, whatever extreme they run to" (HIW 250).

Henry James said that his own so-called ghost stories, including "The Jolly Corner," would "never have existed but for that love of 'a story as a story' which had from far back beset and beguiled their author." The inimical specter of place in James's story of Spencer Brydon is suggestive of Welty's "third character," and so more generally is James's beguilement by pure technique reflected in Welty's own subtle practise in "No Place for You, My Love." But somewhat more precise and personal prods to composition are revealed in the story itself and in statements of intention in "How I Write." Of the purifying effect of revision, Welty says that "you never dream the essentials can be simple again, within one story. . . . I was writing of exposure, and the shock of the world; in the end I tried to make the story's inside outside and then throw away the shell" (HIW 247, 248). Reduced to essentials by Welty's scrupulous narrative, the mystery of relationship takes near palpable form and "merge[s]," in her words, "the abstract with the concrete" (HIW 250). On the return trip to New Orleans, the woman's "deep sleep" (CS 480) signals her repose in this mysterious unity; and more specifically her silent exposure to the heart's innate desire for relationship. This is her unique freedom as well, and Welty has revealed it to be a moment devoid of social, sexual, and historical causality, and of story as well, the familiar determinants of her theme of the "buried life." So avid is Welty to evoke pure inwardness that she gives autonomy to the mysterious eye of the country itself, wishing it somehow to be "more real, more essential, than the characters were or had any cause to be" (HIW 247). The man in particular resists this anonymity with an elaborate metaphor, but his projection of a "face" (CS 479-480) upon the landscape serves only to measure the gap between language itself and the woman's mysterious possession of an otherness that is known silently, unspeakably, to be within.

In revising "How I Write," Welty added only one important statement to the 1955 version; she realized, "in retrospect," that texts were likely to be interactive, that stories may "repeat themselves in shadowy ways, that they have returned and many return in future too—in variations—to certain themes" (ES 108), and all this without any flouting of her deeply ingrained formalism. Only briefly can I stress again the parallel dangers, aesthetic and psychic, faced by Welty and the woman in their venturing "south of South," and indicate how Welty may have laid special claim to her own freedom in "No Place for You, My Love." Her urge to clear away, "to make the story's inside outside and then throw away the shell," comes at the end of two decades of writing which culminate in the highly rationalized societies of Shellmound and Morgana—each a mausoleum of desire. If any image can be said to encompass this writing, to hold in true balance its nearly equal measures of aspiration and defeat, it is that of Virgie Rainey at the end of "The Wanderers." In the course of *The Golden Apples* (1949), she has lost or rejected the familiar sources of identity—family, community, lovers, her artistic vocation—to become another "bedrock" case. A further clearing occurs, I believe, as she and a black companion, sitting on the public stile, hear a "percussion" (CS 461) of mythological sounds that anticipates a similar conflation in "No Place for You, My Love." In each case, not so much intimacy as a certain distance seems to mark the relation between the observer and the implied performers of a legendary past. The image of Virgie on the stile had been "treated," I would guess, along with the frustrated girl of the first draft, to Welty's liberating "ride" (HIW 246) south of New Orleans. Further, the very suggestiveness and amplitude of this image would seem to have found an answering image in Welty's new design. In revising "No Place for You, My Love," has Welty not dramatized precisely the "magnitude" (CS 460) into which Virgie stares, silently; and has she not fulfilled her secret desire to be justified anew by the "pervading" mystery of relationship? The freedom that Welty claimed lay only in following the rather dangerous dictates of her own artistic will. Whatever inertia may have formed as the culture of her career took shape in the 1940s was daringly redirected in "No Place for You, My Love." This special ferment, as much as anything else, I had hoped the Welty film would capture and hold for a moment.

BIBLIOGRAPHICAL NOTE

Only recently, after delivering a briefer version of this paper in May 1991, did I learn that the NEH had approved a revised film proposal. "No Place for You, My Love" does not, however, remain in the new script, and the emphasis falls squarely upon dramatization of "June Recital." In part the effect of such concentration is to diminish the sense of Eudora Welty responding to the inherent risks of an evolving career. Regrettably, the status of the project is still uncertain, for the NEH grant is a matching one and requires considerable additional support to begin production.

"No Place for You, My Love" was printed first in the *New Yorker*, 20 September 1952. It was the lead story in the collection *The Bride of the Innisfallen and Other Stories* (New York: Harcourt, Brace, 1955), and, of course, it appears in *The Collected Stories of Eudora Welty* (New York: Harcourt Brace Jovanovich, 1980). My citations follow the text of *The Collected Stories* and are noted above parenthetically. Welty's extensive revision of "How I Write" may be followed in part by consulting Pearl McHaney's useful compilation of textual variants in the *Eudora Welty Newsletter* 15 (1991): 1-9. Because my remarks focus upon a particular compositional moment in Welty's career, the first version of this essay is the preferred text. Noel Polk cites Welty's provisional title—"The Gorgon's Head"—in his thoughtful essay "Water, Wanderers, and Weddings: Love in Eudora Welty," *Eudora Welty: A Form of Thanks*, ed. Louis Dollarhide and Ann J. Abadie (Jackson UP of Mississippi, 1979). Suzanne Marrs has also described this early typescript in her invaluable compilation entitled *The Welty Collection: A Guide to the Eudora Welty Manuscripts and Documents at the Mississippi Department of Archives and History* (Jackson: UP of Mississippi, 1988) 36. In all likelihood, Welty found the first edition of *Louisiana: A Guide to the State*, American Guide Series (New York: Hastings House, 1941) to be a useful source in revising "No Place for You, My Love." See in particular Tours 1A, 8, and 11 for a guide to Welty's itinerary.

WORKS CITED

Welty, Eudora. *Collected Stories*. New York: Harcourt Brace Jovanovich, 1980.

___. *Conversations with Eudora Welty*. Ed. Peggy Whitman Prenshaw. Jackson: UP of Mississippi, 1984.

___. *The Eye of the Story: Selected Essays and Reviews*. New York: Random House, 1978.

___. "How I Write." *Virginia Quarterly Review* 31 (1955): 240-251.

General Criticism
1955-1969

Name and Symbol in the Prose of Eudora Welty

William M. Jones

Although most critics tend to classify Eudora Welty as only a good regional writer, a careful look at her yet unexplained symbols will, perhaps, make it clear that she has something more in mind than regional atmosphere. The tortuous path she sets for her reader leads through a forest of symbol, but there is a path and there is a reward at its end. From her earliest published work to her latest collection of stories Miss Welty has drawn heavily upon the worlds of myth and folklore[1] and, while handling many of the same motifs again and again, has consistently absorbed them more and more fully into her own meaning, so that in her most successful work it is impossible to say that here is Cassiopeia and here Andromeda. The reader can only be aware that these legendary figures, along with similar ones from Germanic, Celtic, Sanskrit, and numerous other folk sources, are suggested by the characters that Miss Welty is drawing.

Miss Welty, although never alluding directly to her own method of writing, has occasionally made statements that would seem to justify her use of folk material as source: "And of course the great stories of the world are the ones that seem new to their readers on and on, always new because they keep their power of revealing something."[2] According to this quotation, she might feel justified in presenting a story firmly based in antiquity in terms familiar to her own generation. Thus, her seemingly new stories might draw upon the great stories of all time for their "power of revealing something."

[1]Although I agree with the distinction between myth, legend and fairytale made by Susanne K. Langer, *Philosophy in a New Key* (New York, 1955), p. 144, such careful differentiation is not necessary for the purpose of this paper.

[2]"The Reading and Writing of Short Stories," *Atlantic Monthly*, CLXXXIII (February, 1949), p. 54.

The something revealed in these old stories would seem to be, according to Miss Welty's selection from them, true characters, whose validity has been proved in folk stories of many cultures and many ages. Quite consciously Miss Welty has taken the characters common to several mythological systems and translated them into present-day Mississippians. Although a faintly fantastic element remains in her stories, her characters and her atmosphere are too thoroughly Southern to be mistaken for those of Siegfried's Germany or Perseus's Greece. So typically Southern are they, in fact, that many critics damn her for her provincial approach to life.[3]

By patterning her characters closely after folk heroes Miss Welty has avoided exactly such a strictly regional approach as that for which she has been blamed. Since her first published story she has been working toward a fusion of the universal mythic elements embodied in various culture-heroes with the regional world that she knows first-hand. The effect of this attempt on her work and her degree of success with it may be followed throughout her work.

The most obvious advantage to such an approach to fiction may be seen in the stories of her first collection, *A Curtain of Green* (1941). The last story in this collection, "A Worn Path," may appear at first to be a sweet story of an old Negro woman who makes periodic trips into Natchez for medicine for her grandson. But sweet stories are readily available in women's magazines everywhere. Miss Welty has added depth to this one by building closely upon a legend that was told first about an embodiment of the Egyptian sun-god and retold later by medieval Christians to glorify the resurrection of Christ. The Old Negro woman, Phoenix Jackson, like the original Phoenix, is definitely golden: "Her skin had . . . a golden color . . . , and the two knobs of her cheeks were illuminated by a yellow burning under the dark . . . her hair . . . with an odor of copper."[4] Just as the Egyptian Phoenix is guided back to its home every five hundred years to renew itself by being consumed in fire, so the modern Phoenix sees, at the end of her journey, a gold seal in a gold frame, "which matched the dream that was hung up in her head." Then "there came a flicker and then a flame," after which "Phoenix rose carefully." With this Mississippi Phoenix it is love that renews and love that will lead the ancient and eternally young one back down the worn path.

[3]Granville Hicks quotes several such critics in "Eudora Welty," *English Journal*, XLI (November, 1952).

[4]All quotations from Miss Welty are from the first editions of the novels and of the collections of stories.

In other stories in this collection Miss Welty also makes use of a specific name from folk knowledge as a point of departure for the story itself.[5] In such a story as "Clytie" Miss Welty presents a Southern spinster with a very appropriate name, but it also happens to be the name of a jealous girl in Ovid's *Metamorphoses* who, having pined away because of her unrequited love for the sun-god, eventually became a sunflower. Miss Welty's very description of Clytie gives a suggestion of just such a huge sunflower: "On her head was one of the straw hats from the furnishing store, with an old black satin ribbon pinned to it to make it a better hat, and tied under the chin. Now under the force of the rain, while the ladies watched, the hat slowly began to sag down on each side until it looked even more absurd and done for." Not only does Miss Welty know her Ovid; she also knows sunflowers in the rain.

The rest of the story even more explicitly carries out the myth idea: "With this small, peaceful face still in her mind, rosy like these flames, like an inspiration which drives all other thoughts away, Clytie had forgotten herself and had been obliged to stand where she was in the middle of the road." Just so, Ovid's Clytie "never stirred from the ground; all she did was to gaze on the face of the sungod. . . ." To support the idea of the dependence on Greek myth even more, Miss Welty introduces another name, Lethe. It is old Lethy, a Negro woman, who finds Clytie drowned in the rain barrel. What promise for Clytie's soul that she is discovered by the river of forgetfulness! And yet also, what an appropriate name for a Southern Negro!

In these first stories the myth from which Miss Welty has drawn her material is easily recognized. Once the first hint in the story is found, the source material can easily be observed throughout the rest of the story, hidden certainly under Southern trappings but observably present, nevertheless. At first Miss Welty seems to have thought of a myth, then thought of ways in which to modernize and southernize it. The stories constructed in this manner are not as transparently derivative as might be expected, since Miss Welty from the beginning of her career has been a marvelously skilled and careful craftsman. Even in stories where only one myth is used the Southern veneer is so thick that the basic material is hardy recognizable. Yet, satisfactorily enough, its unrecognized presence still gives a weight to the story that it might not otherwise have had. Miss Welty, at least, was aware of the myth used, and even if the reader misses its presence, its availability may well be felt.

[5]Uranus appears in a story about a titanic Negro pianist, "Powerhouse"; the shadow of Hercules, the famous archer of antiquity, hovers over R. J. Bowman in "Death of a Traveling Salesman."

In her next work, *The Robber Bridegroom* (1942), Miss Welty reveals her folk sources more clearly and at the same time goes a step further toward combining various myths and legends in order to avoid the one to one equating which she had practiced in *A Curtain of Green*. The title and basic plot, as well as the main characters, are almost direct borrowings from "Der Rauberbräutigam," one of the stories in Grimm's collection.[6] In both stories the bridegroom lives far out in the dark forest. In Grimm a raven warns "Kehr um, kehr um, du junge Braut, / du bist in einem Mörderhaus." Miss Welty changes this warning only slightly: "Turn again, my bonny, / Turn away home." Miss Welty's robbers, like those in Grimm, kill a young girl. In Grimm she is cut to pieces. In *The Robber Bridegroom* she is an Indian girl who is first raped.

But perhaps the most significant similarity in the two stories is the cutting off of a finger. In both stories the dead girl's finger is cut off, in Grimm because that was the easiest way of obtaining the ring on it. In Miss Welty's story, however, "none of them saw where the finger went or hunted for it, for it had no ring on it." This direct echo of the Grimm story suggests that here Miss Welty fully expects that her readers be aware of her sources. Otherwise, much of the significance of the retelling of the story is lost. Any careful reader should have curiosity enough to wonder why an author would give such a negative piece of information as the absence of a ring from a finger.

Many more parallels between the two stories could be pointed out, but they are easily observable once the basic similarity has been established. To this story Miss Welty has added many other legendary features: the wicked step-mother, a box with a talking head inside, a Salome who dances, casting off one "petticoat" after another. And to these general folklore characters she adds an important one from Mississippi folklore, an old acquaintance of Davy Crockett himself, Mike Fink, the last of the keelboatmen.[7] Fink serves an essential function in the novel. At the beginning of the story he introduces the heroine's father to the robber bridegroom, and at the end he serves to reunite the two lovers. To this fantastic[8] conglomeration of legends Miss Welty adds her own serious comments on the struggle of good and evil

[6]In his previously cited article in the *English Journal*, p. 465, Granville Hicks says that the plot is "as implausible as anything in Grimm." Apparently he did not check his Grimm to discover that the same thing was really there.

[7]For a thorough treatment of Fink see Walter Blair and Franklin J. Meine, *Half Horse Half Alligator* (Chicago, 1956).

[8]Miss Eunice Glenn, "Fantasy in the Fiction of Eudora Welty," *A Southern Vanguard* (New York, 1947), seems completely unaware of any of Miss Welty's "fantastic" sources.

within the individual human spirit and, possibly most important of all, the power of love to remake a personality and overcome all obstacles.

In *The Robber Bridegroom* Miss Welty is clearly reaching for a more complex use of folk material than that of *A Curtain of Green*. This complicating, fusing process continued in her next group of stories, *The Wide Net* (1943). As she absorbs more and more folk elements into her work it becomes increasingly difficult to recognize any one specific source. The stories themselves take on more of the general characteristics of the folk tale and thus become less obviously stories that draw on folk material.

The introduction of almost inhuman cruelty into such a story as "At the Landing" recalls stories from Grimm in which girls are cut into pieces and salted. This story concludes with the mass rape of the leading character, Jenny, by fishermen who go in to her where she is imprisoned in a chicken house, while outside the younger boys "took their turns throwing knives with a dull *pit* at the tree." Such cruelty as this would be almost unbearable except for another folk-tale characteristic, the remoteness of the characters. In spite of numerous realistic details they remain in this collection rather aloof, neither purely symbolic nor purely human, only distant from the present-day world. They seem more like Rapunzel than like Liza of Lambeth.

Part of their remoteness may be attributed to still other folk-tale characteristics. In the title story, "The Wide Net," the sudden action and lack of thoughtful motivation show close kinship to folk tales. While walking in the woods, the hero, without reason, "ran at a rabbit and caught it in his hands." A king of snakes suddenly rises from the Pearl River; a man begins dancing with a catfish at his belt; another man drinks water from his mother-in-law's well. All these seemingly unmotivated actions are direct echoes from mythology[9] and, according to Erich Fromm,[10] become meaningful if viewed on a symbolic level.

Miss Welty seems still to have been experimenting with the stories in "The Wide Net," for along side these stories that add something of the form of folk tales to the material derived from them, there are others that, while also based on legend, are more obviously Southern like her first ones. In "Asphodel" the name of the immortal plant is the only really legendary feature of the story. The discovery by three old maids on a picnic of the lusty Do McInnis, "naked as an old goat," and their escape from "billy-goats, and nanny-goats, old goats and young, a whole thriving herd," is all good Southern humor. But, with the aid of vague classical hints and all those

[9]Cf. subject index to Angelo de Guernatis, *Zoological Mythology* (London, 1872), 2 vols.
[10]*The Forgotten Language* (New York, 1951), p. 195.

goats, the reader gets the impression that one of the three old maids may someday dance with the satyrs or worship at Bacchus' shrine: "But Phoebe laughed aloud as they made the curve. Her voice was soft, and she seemed to be still in a tender dream and an unconscious celebration—as though the picnic were not already set rudely in the past, but were the enduring and intoxicating present, still the phenomenon, the golden day."

In her next work, *Delta Wedding* (1946), Miss Welty seems to have doubts no longer about what to do with her sources. She has almost completely obscured them under a wealth of Southern atmosphere. As in her earlier work there are key names,[11] but the majority of them have nothing to do with the plot and do not come directly from folklore. The key names are there, however, and as usual they point the way to an understanding of Miss Welty's form and purpose.

On the surface the story is only one of a Southern family, concerned because their daughter is about to marry a common overseer. A more careful examination reveals two devices that Miss Wetly has used before. These devices give meaning to what otherwise might have been only a somewhat rambling, atmospheric, overly detailed story of Southern plantation life in the 1920's.

First, the reader notices that Mr. Rondo, who appeared in "Why I Live at the P.O.,"[12] is now a minister who is to marry the daughter and the overseer. It is to him that the story of Uncle George's saving the feeble-minded child Maureen from the train is first told. The story, thus set up, returns again and again in its rondo-like movement to the original statement: George stands on a trestle holding Maureen, who has caught her foot. The oncoming train, the Yellow Dog, stops in time to avoid an accident, but George's wife resents George's action. She cries, "George Fairchild, you didn't do this for *me*!"

Once Mr. Rondo has heard this tale, he disappears until the wedding. Before the final treatment of the train theme, however, Mr. Rondo appears again. This time he rides with the Fairchilds and Laura McRaven when the Yellow Dog stops again to let them by. He is then put out at the church

[11]An old Negro woman who wanders through the story with a sack over her shoulder has the name Partheny, a suggestion of the virgin goddess Minerva and the Parthenon.

[12]In "Why I Live at the P.O." (*A Curtain of Green*) two of the central characters are Uncle Rondo and Stella-Rondo. These names suggest musically the form in which a central theme is stated again and again with subordinate material interwoven between statements. *The Oxford Companion to Music* describes the form A-B-A-C-A-D-A. This circular motion of a static situation accounts for part of the humor in the story. Stella-Rondo's return home on July 4, sets up the situation. Stella-Rondo has stolen the narrator's suitor. Now she returns to steal the narrator's place in the affections of one member of the family after another. The story moves rhythmically along in this manner. There is a summary of this rondo movement before the last figure: "So that made Mama, Papa-Daddy and the baby all on Stella-Rondo's side. Next Uncle Rondo."

stile, where he is last seen taking out his watch, "which . . . seemed to have stopped." Then, with a sudden shift, the next scene begins, "'Poor Ellen,' said Tempe, clasping her softly, her delicate fragrant face large and serious. . . ." And Aunt Tempe (tempi) takes over to bring the times of the Fairchilds to a close.

There is little doubt that Aunt Tempe sets the time in the novel just as Mr. Rondo sets the form. On Aunt Tempe's first appearance Miss Welty emphasized the idea of time: "Aunt Tempe, in a batik dress and a vibratingly large hat, entered (keeping time) and kissed all the jumping children." And in the background of Aunt Tempe's conversation the reader is always aware of music from a distant piano. She it is who regrets the children's not taking piano lessons; she it is who sometimes speeds up the action, sometimes slows it down. But her function is never obvious, nor is Mr. Rondo's. They are first of all real characters in a real world.

The second device which Miss Welty has used before is the piling up of names from the same source. Any one of these names in itself might not have special meaning, but their combined weight leads to an interesting source discovery. The names Battle, Lady Clare, Ellen, Inverness, Marmion, plus three excerpts from Scottish songs on one page, leave no doubt that Miss Welty was thinking of Scott's *Marmion* when she wrote *Delta Wedding*.

Any attempt, however, to compare the plot or theme of the two works fails. Miss Welty's Marmion is a house which rightfully belongs to Laura, but which is given instead to Dabney, the girl about to marry the overseer. Scott's Marmion is a villainous knight who forsakes Lady Clare, wife of a man he has supposedly killed, and who finally dies in battle at Flodden Field. It is definitely not the plot here that Miss Welty uses. But the names, the songs, and the fact that Scott's poem ends on September 9 and Miss Welty begins *Delta Wedding* on September 10 may suggest that she is taking up where Scott left off. Scott's introductory "Advertisement" says something very similar to what Miss Welty might have said, but did not: "Any historical narrative, far more an attempt at epic composition, exceeded his [the author's] plan of a romantic tale; yet he may be permitted to hope, from the popularity of 'The Lay of the Last Minstrel,' that an attempt to paint the manners of the feudal times, upon a broader scale, and in the course of a more interesting story, will not be unacceptable to the public."

In other words, Miss Welty's second long work, like Scott's second long narrative poem, deals more with description than with the narrative elements which dominated their first works, is more simply a romantic tale to please the public. This interpretation might be developed with the idea also that Miss Welty is analyzing "manners of feudal times" as they exist in the

South. And the two who rise above these regional and outmoded manners, Uncle George and Laura, both have a universality that causes the Yellow Dog, a local train, to stop out of respect for them.

It almost seems that Miss Welty's mind dwelt on *Marmion* even after the completion of *Delta Wedding*. Although she might easily have got her information from any other source of Arthurian legend, the earlier argument for Marmion suggests that when she decided to name the town Morgana in her next group of short stories, *The Golden Apples* (1949), she was thinking of the introduction to the first canto of *Marmion*:

> But thou, my friend, cans't fitly tell,
> (For few have read romance so well,)
> How still the legendary lay
> O'er poet's bosom holds its sway;
> How on the ancient minstrel strain
> Time lays his palsied hand in vain;
> And how our hearts at doughy deeds,
> By warriors wrought in steely weeds,
> Still throb for fear and pity's sake;
> As when the Champion of the Lake
> Entered Morgana's fated house. . . .

This quotation, which ends with the name that became Miss Welty's imaginary Mississippi town in *The Golden Apples*, expresses her own idea of literature. She herself has supported the idea that the good stories, the true stories, are not dulled by time. Nowhere does she better illustrate the truth of this idea than in *The Golden Apples*. Here, for the first time in the short story, she succeeds in fusing a number of legends so completely that her Southerners take on the basic attributes of these legendary characters, engage in the same general sort of activity.

The entire series of stories seems to deal in a general way with the Perseus legend.[13] In the first story, "Shower of Gold," Jove's visit to Danaë in the form of a shower of gold is suggested in Mrs. Fate Rainey's description of her first view of Snowdie MacLain after Snowdie had met King MacLain in Morgan's Woods, probably the woods of King Arthur's half-sister Morgan la Feé: "Me and Lady May both had to just stop and look at her. She looked like more than only the news of her pregnancy had come over her. It was like a shower of something had struck her, like she'd been caught out in something bright. It was more than the day. . . . I

[13]For the most thorough treatment of all variations of the Perseus Legend see E. Sidney Hartland, *The Legend of Perseus* (London, 1894), 3 vols.

remember it was Easter time and how the pasture was all spotty there behind her little blue skirt in sweet clover. He [King] sold tea and spices, that's what it was."

Already in this quotation it is evident that Miss Welty is fusing elements common to various mythological systems. The Easter reference, the blue skirt, the clover, and the spices add to the pagan myth the idea of the Virgin Mary's own discovery that she was to give birth to a hero. The narrator of the story is all Southern, except her rather significant name; but the tale she tells echoes through ages and ages of myth, Greek, Hebrew, Egyptian, British, Germanic, and Egyptian. What Miss Welty seems to have striven consciously for in her first stories, the fusion of many myths with Southern life, takes place here so frequently and effortlessly as to seem almost unavoidable.

In the second story, "June Recital," the legends become so intermingled that it is impossible to tell if her character Cassie is Cassiopeia, Cassandra, or a combination of numerous other mythical figures. Miss Welty finally seems to have succeeded in finding a successful balance between her Southern atmosphere and the numerous characters from folk knowledge, now thoroughly merged.

In this story, too, Miss Welty creates one of her most effective symbols, built, like the characters, on ages of myth. Miss Eckhart, who is trying to burn down King MacLain's old house where she used to live, "worshiped her metronome." Old Man Moody and Fatty Bowles want to destroy "the obelisk with its little moving part and its door open." "Old Man Moody stumped over and picked it up and held it upon the diagonal, posing, like a fisherman holding a funny-looking fish to have come out of Moon Lake." To those acquainted with folklore, Miss Welty's use of the Egyptian obelisk and the Hindu fish to support her own new phallic symbol is an amazing accomplishment. And, when the two frightened men throw away this symbol, the young man, Loch, retrieves it:

> On his hands he circled the tree and the obelisk waited in the weeds, upright. He stood up and looked at it.
> Its ticker was outside it.
>
> He felt charmed like a bird, for the ticking stick went like a tail, a tongue, a wand . . . .
>
> When he examined it, he saw the beating stick to be a pendulum that instead of hanging down stuck upwards. . . .
>
> He held still for a while, while nothing was ticking. Nothing but the crickets. Nothing but the train going through, ticking its two cars over the Big Black Bridge.

This creation of symbol and expansion to the ticking pounding movement of the rest of life is a good example of how Miss Welty can pour new meaning into old mythic material. And yet Robert Daniel, writing in the *Hopkins Review*, can simply say that the metronome is "a symbol of time" and leave it at that.[14]

Not only does Miss Welty use myth to best advantage for the creation of symbol and character in *The Golden Apples*, she also expresses most clearly here an idea common to folklore which holds a central position in much of her work, the idea that a descent into the depths results in a fuller awareness of life. These descents are numerous both in the work of Miss Welty and in folklore. Loch Morrison,the retriever of the metronome in "June Recital," dives into the depths of Moon Lake in the story "Moon Lake" in order to save one of the girls, Easter; Laura, one of the leading characters in *Delta Wedding*, falls into the Yazoo River; William Wallace in "The Wide Net" dives far below the surface of the Pearl River; and Virgie Rainey, the Virgin figure, who is to feel the fertilizing power of the rain at the end of *The Golden Apples*, had also swum beneath the surface of the river: "Virgie had reached the point where in the next moment she might turn into something without feeling it shock her. She hung suspended in the Big Black River as she would know to hang suspended in felicity."

In each instance some new revelation about life is the result of the descent into depths, just as in folklore the person who eats of the charmed fish or who goes beneath the surface of the water comes up with knowledge that leads him to riches or success.

Although it is in *The Golden Apples* that the descent is most emphasized, it was also treated thoroughly in "The Wide Net," where, partly because of the less thorough fusion of the folk elements, they appear most clearly. William Wallace's River is the Pearl River. Serpents are supposed to hold pearls under their tongues and, on warm days, spit them into the river for a larger serpent to catch. William Wallace holds the eel that is, of course, a fairly common phallic symbol, and for a moment he holds the green plant which he brought up from the river bottom. In myth this plant would have held the semen of the god. Miss Welty even introduces the King of the Snakes into the story. At the end of the story sexual adjustment between William Wallace and his pregnant wife is the riches gained. But at the close of the story she smiles at him, "as if she were smiling down on him." Miss Welty may be suggesting that William Wallace's descent into the depths will

[14]"The World of Eudora Welty," *The Hopkins Review*, VI (Winter, 1963), p. 56.

make his wife the mother of a hero, a not uncommon occurrence in folk stories.[15]

According to Miss Welty, the riches gained form the descent are frequently a fuller understanding of nature. This coming into harmony with nature is often manifested, as with William Wallace, in a more satisfactory sexual adjustment. Just as William Wallace and Loch Morrison gain from their descent, those who do not descend are denied riches. Nina Carmichael and Jenny Love, watching Loch undress after his life-saving expedition into the depths of Moon Lake, feel that they will always be old maids. And after Laura returns from her descent into the Yazoo River she sees the unhappy Dabney, who is wearing "a beautiful floating dress." Dabney will never be able to dive beneath the surface in a floating dress.

In *The Golden Apples*, then, there is this division of the characters into those who can descend and those who cannot, and there is also the reliance in all the stories on the basic idea of the Perseus legend. The other stories in the collection, significant to the legend as they are, can be passed over lightly here since, if they are compared with the Perseus myth and the Grimm story "The Two Brothers," their general significance comes through. "The Whole World Knows" deals with the unsuccessful brother told of in the Grimm story and "Music from Spain" deals with the successful one. In "Music from Spain" the names are significant for both the Perseus story (Aeolian Hall) and the Grimm tale (Bertsinger's Jewelers and fish eggs). These names are added references to butterflies more frequent than any yet seen in Miss Welty's work,[16] a symbolic method based on folklore that emphasizes Eugene's success in the story.

In the final story, "The Wanderers," Miss Welty offers her clearest indication of what she has attempted in *The Golden Apples* and suggests, indirectly, what she has been striving for in everything else that she has written: "It [Miss Eckhart's picture] showed Perseus with the head of the Medusa. 'The same thing as Siegfried and the Dragon,' Miss Eckhart had occasionally said, as if explaining second-best. Around the picture—which sometimes blindly reflected the window by its darkness—was a frame enameled with flowers, which was always self-evident—Miss Eckhart's pride. In that moment Virgie had shorn it of its frame." Clearly, the recurrent Perseus legend, that which is eternally true about mankind, is here

[15]All the folk elements mentioned in this paragraph and those directly preceding are treated in detail in the previously cited *Zoological Mythology*.

[16]There are a woman with a butterfly birthmarks, a Mariposa lily, and a waitress with mascared eyelids "like flopping black butterflies." And finally a Mr. Herring waits with Eugene's wife when he, the successful brother, returns home. Again Miss Welty has put strong emphasis on the phallic symbols of folklore: butterflies and fish.

shorn of the flowery decorations, seen without the blinding reflection of the present. And Virgie at this moment knows the ageless.

In the last two pages of "The Wanderers" Miss Welty explains how myth may be viewed. It may be observed abstractly ("far out and endless, a constellation which the heart could read over many a night"), personally ("Miss Eckhart, whom Virgie had not, after all, hated . . . had hung the picture on the wall for herself."), or socially ("The rain of fall, maybe on the whole South, for all she knew on the everywhere."). And seeing the myth in these three ways, as Miss Welty herself has seen it, "was the damnation—no, only the secret, unhurting because not caring in itself. . . ."

With this clear expression of her attitude toward myth Miss Welty concludes the series of stories in which she achieves the most successful fusion of mythic characters and Southern setting.[17] She has, with her explanation of the Perseus picture, suggested that she is attempting in her stories to give new meaning to the oldest stories of all, not in the manner of Tennyson or O'Neill, who were satisfied with primarily one group of myths, but in her own unique manner of taking for her province the whole world of folk knowledge and compressing it into the modern South.

In all her work Miss Welty is assuming that these stories from ancient sources and the symbols involved in them contain the truth about the inmost nature of man. If she wants to reveal man as he really is and ever shall be, there is no better way then by resorting to these myths. And, in addition, by so doing she comes into contact with the world not visible, the world of imagination and beauty, the world of myth.

This mythic world, which contains an endless Medusa and an endless Perseus, says a great deal. Men may be capable of cruel deeds, but there are heroes among us, men who can dive down into the depths of life, take hold of the eel, strap a catfish to their belts and dance. There are yet those men who, in spite of cruelty around them, have seen butterflies in flight, listened to the echo of the world, or felt the fall of the impregnating rain. And always there will be a Virgie, like the one at the conclusion of "The Wanderers," who will feel the power of the god in the rain and know that she will in her turn be the mother of a hero. Virgie and the old Negro

[17]In Miss Welty's two latest works there are also echoes from ancient sources. Uncle Daniel Ponder of *The Ponder Heart* recalls the Biblical Daniel, who had a habit of pondering things in his heart, which beat, like Uncle Daniel's, under the finest linen garments. And Florabel, the Negro girl of the first version of "The Burning," becomes Delilah when the story appears in the collection *The Bride of the Innisfallen*. A pretty flower thus becomes a woman of another culture whose marriage into the race of the faithful (she had a white man's child) caused much turmoil for all concerned—just as Samson's Deliah did. And Florabel-Delilah finishes the story by wading into the river because "At that time it was only Friday [Venus' day] so it hadn't rained." Even without the fertilizing power of the rain she will become the mother of a hero.

woman can sit together under a Southern tree and hear as great people of all times have heard "through falling rain and the running of the horse and bear, the stroke of the leopard, the dragon's crusty slither, and the glimmer and the trumpet of the swan."

From *Southern Folklore Quarterly* 22 (December 1958): 173-85.

Losing Battles
1970

Eudora Welty Talks about Her New Book, *Losing Battles*

Frank Hains

Publishers always speak of new books by established writers as "long-awaited events." But, on April 13, comes one that indeed is.

It's the first book—save her children's story, *The Shoebird*—in fifteen years by one of America's most important literary figures, Eudora Welty.

It's called *Losing Battles*, is the first long novel in a body of work which has been most distinguished by some of the best short stories ever written in America, and it's already on sale in Jackson in advance of its official publication.

The book will be reviewed here next Sunday by Louis Dollarhide so it is not my purpose to anticipate that today.

But, in the meantime, I went this week to visit Miss Welty at her Jackson home and to talk about her feelings on the eve, as it were, of the book's publication.

It is almost 15 years to the day since my first meeting with Miss Welty and, this time as then, she was waiting on the stoop of her comfortable old English-flavored house on Pinehurst.

That time—at the publication of *The Bride of the Innisfallen*—I was very much in awe of one of America's greatest writers. The intervening years have served, if anything, to deepen the awe—not only of the writer but of the great and kind and warm and witty and thoughtful lady she is.

She is, she said, a bit apprehensive that some of the reviewers may criticize *Losing Battles* because of her apparent lack of concern for the preoccupations of today: where, she fancies them saying, is her awareness of black versus white, the degeneration of the family, all the "relevant" problems?

"I'm aware of what so many reviewers seem to be looking for," Miss Welty said, "but I'm content with the way I wrote it—it's the only way I can and it seems to me just as legitimate to write of people in a family group as in any more 'relevant' grouping.

"Human relationships are the same no matter what the context. It never occurred to me not, to write it as I did, but not that it's about to come out"—she stopped and laughed wryly.

"Well, you DO get jumped on."

Does the serious writer have any obligation to his society?

"To have deep feelings about it—to try to understand it—to be able to reflect on things—to know what's happening and to care.

"But, in a work of fiction, that can only come through in the mind and heart behind the work. One wants it to show through understanding of characters.

"A book should only reflect and present—not lecture people. I haven't got the presumption to feel you should lecture."

Losing Battles takes place in and around and through the recollections of those at a rural Mississippi family reunion. A large clan has gathered on Granny's 90th birthday and the major events surround the return from Parchman of the youth who is the apple of the family eye.

NO LESSON

"I didn't know the title until the book was finished," Miss Welty says. "I never do." It's about all the battles which we always seem to be losing—battles against everything: poverty, disgrace, misunderstanding, and also funny battles I hope; trying to make a go of it, trying to survive. And old age. And the teacher's battle against ignorance.

"Oh, when you say all that it sounds like some kind of social science idea; like I was trying to give a lesson. I certainly wasn't. It's like all of our daily battles—when in an everyday way you feel like you might not make it.

"I hope that it's a comedy of one kind of another—of laughing at people," she hastens to interject. "But I think they're able to laugh."

The title might seem pessimistic?

"I didn't mean it to be. I think life is pretty darn hard and serious but—well, I think somewhere in there they said"—and she picks up the book and leafs through it—"Jack said, after he really loses everything:

'They can't take away what no human can take away. My family, my wife and girl baby and all of 'em at home. And I've got my strength. I may not have all the time I used to have—but I can provide. Don't you ever fear.'

"Oh, it's so darn hard to talk about. I can't express anything about my writing. I never have put it to myself what I was doing while doing it. When you get through, you can say SOMETHING but it really doesn't express it—to me."

ETERNAL DILEMMA

And that seemed to me to express quite well the artist's inevitable and eternal dilemma when asked to talk about his own work—which has always seemed to me an unfair thing to ask anyway. It is not the author's obligation to talk about his work.

Of the questions she's continually being asked, the one that Miss Welty says she "really hates" is "did you mean that to be symbolic?"

"When symbols occur naturally within the content of a story, that's when the author recognizes them; after they spring up, I consider them legitimate because they function in the story. The other kind is pretentious and just in the way."

Her family in *Losing Battles* is not one she's ever known, but "I have travelled all over the state and I have seen places like this. I went to the "W" and worked for the WPA; I've known many families—families as families. I have known what poor families live like.

"The real reason that I used this family setting, and felt that the family should be poor, is that I wanted to reduce my narrative to the simplest denominators. The battles being lost seem so much more important when there is so little left to lose.

"And, I wanted to show everything outwardly if I could; rather than writing about what people were thinking, I wanted to show it in word and action.

"It seemed to me that comedy was best, and it seemed to call for a rural scene, a family scene, and a big day."

The book grew to be much longer than Miss Welty had originally intended. "As it grew, the parts grew," which called for constant rewriting and expanding of scenes; "I work in scenes." Usually Miss Welty says she "tears up as I go," but this time, "I kept thinking 'it really can't be this long': I'll probably go back and use the old one. So when I finally finished, I had a suitcase full of earlier drafts." Some have been given to the state archives, which has all of Miss Welty's manuscripts; some will not be. "I don't want people looking at my mistakes."

THREE IN OFFING

There are three other Welty books in the offing now: perhaps four, depending on whether one long story (which appeared in an entire issue of the *New Yorker* last spring as "The Optimist's Daughter") is brought out by itself or as the lead story in a collection.

The other two are a book of essays and a book of her photographs, for which she is writing brief captions.

While she's naturally interested in what the reception of *Losing Battles* will be, she herself is satisfied with it.

"And some of the people I like have liked it, and that's what matters most."

From *The Clarion-Ledger* 5 April 1970, 6F.

Eudora Welty's *Losing Battles* Is Magnificent Feast

Louis Dollarhide

When I told a writer friend recently the length of Eudora Welty's new novel, *Losing Battles* he commented, "Can you imagine having that much of Eudora Welty between two book covers!"

Now that I have read the book, and only now, can I conceive of it—and every page is part of a magnificent feast, a reunion, if you will, after fifteen years. There are, in fact, so many things to admire and enjoy about this big new book that the reviewer whose best service is to whet appetites, hardly knows where to begin.

IDENTITY APART

Perhaps one should begin where Welty fiction is at its strongest, with its humanity. When Miss Welty's Uncle Daniel Ponder first worked his charming ways on readers back in 1953, many people marvelled at how well she knew their favorite uncle. They didn't know how she knew him, but they were sure she did. Now with the release of *Losing Battles*, others are going to wonder how she ever knew other uncles, aunts, cousins, grandmothers, and maiden school teachers.

The reason for this wonderment, is not that Miss Welty has known an Uncle Daniel or a Granny Vaughn, but that she is able to make her characters so real that readers are quite convinced that they have an identity apart from their created fictional world. *Losing Battles* literally teems with people, who move, act, and above all, talk. And each one is as individual as, perhaps more individual than, the living, breathing Uncle Daniels of earth because in Miss Welty's fiction they are portrayed in essence.

But the word "humanity" means more than the mere head count of characters or individual eccentricities. It also means the breadth of an author's sympathies for these created puppets. In all her writing this sympathy shows. But nowhere does her encompassing feeling for and understanding of this frail creature, man, show mere clearly than in *Losing Battles*. With all his weaknesses, the clogs that weigh him down, he is still worthy of respect; with the world against him, he will not give up.

ETERNAL SPRINGTIME

At the heart of the story are two beautiful young people, Jack and Gloria Renfro, who, one is made to feel, have garnered up in themselves like an eternal springtime the persistent, generative force of life coming down to them from their elders. They tremble and shine with its sentience. In addition to their own presence, its evidence is their fat cherub of a baby, Lady May, and the promise of more children to come. Back of them, of course, is Granny Vaughn, like the source of a river, whose birthday is the occasion for the reunion. At ninety she holds a firm, if tenuous (it must always be tenuous), grip on life. Nothing important escapes her. Throughout the novel the skein of life runs like a bright ribbon from Granny to Lady May.

Only in the sense that it is a projection of the Human Comedy should *Losing Battles* be called a comic novel. It is richly humorous—but one never forgets completely that around this laughter is an encompassing tragic circumference. Man can be the cause of laughter (this fact often saves him), but he is also possessed of mortality. So the novel begins with a reunion and a joyous homecoming. Jack Renfro steps into the pages of the book like life itself, like a whirlwind. The story ends with a funeral. Even as one looks with wonder on the beauty of Jack and Gloria, whose stunning blaze of red hair draws to an essence the vitality they represent, one is aware of the ultimate sadness of it all, of all of life's losing battles.

POKE IN RIBS

Miss Welty's humor is sometimes no more than an unexpected turn of a phrase, which surprises one like an unlooked for poke in the ribs. It can also be broadly farcical, hilariously funny, as the events prove which relate to Judge Moody's misadventures with his Buick and his and his wife's afternoon and evening as guests of the spirited Renfros. Finally it is a humor compounded of many things—of situation and character, of conversation.

Perhaps above all else the source of humor is conversation. No other author writing about the South has a better ear for the cadences of Southern speech that Eudora Welty. No other writer has attended to the idiom of

Southern speech more instructively. One of the wonders of *Losing Battles* is the flow of talk back and forth, character to character, and its endless variety. No two characters talk exactly alike, and their habits of speaking are sustained for the length of the novel. In fact, it would be easy to set the novel up as a play, with a few explanatory paragraphs along the way. Where some characters in fiction (and out) may be said to talk themselves and others to death, Miss Welty's literally talk themselves alive.

FINALLY WROUGHT

Those relatively few paragraphs of exposition, action, or description contain some of Miss Welty's best writing. Any one who cherishes good writing will find sentence after sentence, page after page, to marvel at. The English sentence can be as finely wrought as exquisite jewelry. Miss Welty has mastered its intricacies. I don't suppose dawn has ever risen more beautifully than it does in the opening lines of the novel, light touching here and there like theatrical illumination until the scene is flooded to reveal Granny Vaughn, dressed, seated in her chair on the porch, ready to celebrate her birthday.

"When the rooster crowed, the moon had still not left the world but was going down on flushed cheeks, one day short of the full. A long thin cloud crossed it slowly, drawing itself out like a name being called. . . . The distant point of the ridge, like the tongue of a calf, put its red lick on the sky. . . . Then as if something came sliding out of the sky, the whole tin roof of the house ran with new blue."

The world should take note that the publication of *Losing Battles* is no small event. A major work by a major writer, it will be read and will give pleasure long beyond the life of what may seem to some like more "stylish" writing. For, in the words of another distinguished writer about Miss Welty a few weeks ago, "This girl—well, now she is an artist. No doubt about it."

From *Mississippi Library News* (June 1970): 96-98.

Everything Brought out in the Open: Eudora Welty's *Losing Battles*

Louis D. Rubin, Jr.

I

Miss Welty when last seen, in 1955, published *The Bride of the Innisfallen*, her third collection of short stories (fourth if you count *The Golden Apples*). Thereafter, and for fifteen years, silence, the only exceptions being a little privately-printed essay, *Place in Fiction*, and a few magazine pieces. So it has been a long time between books.

Now comes, in the year 1970, the 61st of the author's age, her longest novel, *Losing Battles*, an affair of some 436 pages all told, being the story of a family reunion in the northeastern Mississippi community of Banner. This particular place in fictional Mississippi is too small even to be a town, and most of what happens does so on a farm up a hillside several miles away from the post-office general store. The elapsed time is something more than 24 hours of a summer day and night in the 1930's. Most of what takes place is talk. The talk begins when Miss Beulah Renfro, grand-daughter of Elvira Jordan Vaughn, "Granny," puts in an appearance on the second page, after some 500 words of place-setting, shouting, "Granny! Up, dressed, and waiting for 'em! All by yourself! Why didn't you holler?" There-after everybody talks, all the time. It ends with a hymn, "Bringing in the Sheaves."

When Eudora Welty's people talk, it is a special kind of talk. They do not talk *to*, they talk *at*. Part of the reason that they talk is to communicate, but part of the reason is to dissemble, to mask, to hide. They converse obliquely, chattering away all the time but never entirely revealing themselves or saying what they think; and the barrier, the mystery that results, lies at the center of the high art of Eudora Welty.

I say high art, because the more I read and think about Miss Welty's fiction, the more I suspect that she is not merely a good writer, one of the very best of the half-a-dozen fine women writers that the South has produced in the past half-century, but a major author, one of the three or four most important writers to come out of twentieth-century America. Her best fiction—*The Golden Apples*, some of the stories, now *Losing Battles*—goes beyond story-telling, beyond people and places, to those truths of the human heart that only the greatest art can reveal. There is only one other Southern writer of her generation in her league: her fellow Mississippian William Faulkner, the greatest of them all.

Eudora Welty does it the hard way, and what is happening and what it means has to sink in, in retrospect, after reading the story. The writer she most resembles, I think, is Thomas Mann. That is to say, she is not technically experimental to any notable degree, and when you read her books you have to let the story pile up, until it is done. Then when you think over what you have read, you begin to perceive the ramifications, the events begin to link up, the people take on their meaning *sub specie aeternitatis* as it were, and the depth, the profundity of what you have seen happen in the story now begins to emerge. It isn't like the searing, tragic art of a Faulkner, for example, which holds you enthralled and breathless as a great elemental drama thunders toward climax and conclusion. The surface of fiction is always deceptively mundane, matter-of-fact, usually funny. The difference between Miss Welty's fiction and that of less gifted authors is that her fiction doesn't lie on the surface, and the surface is anything but superficial yet, paradoxically, everything is contained right there in the surface.

This is the chief difficulty with *Losing Battles*, one that may prevent it from attaining the massive popularity of so many lesser novels by lesser but more flamboyant novelists, and that gets in the way of immediate recognition for its author. What must be overcome, if the wisdom of *Losing Battles* is to be savored in its fullness, is its density of surface. Every line must be read carefully. It cannot be skimmed. *Losing Battles* is not difficult in the way that many novels are difficult. It hasn't an opaque surface that hides the story and the meaning behind a texture of dense language and obscure references. Everything is out on the surface, but the art *is* the surface, and every inch of the surface must be inspected. This means that you have to follow the conversations and note the narrative directions and take in every word, every phrase, holding it all in suspension, letting it accumulate. Many of us don't like to read that way; we haven't the patience to follow every footpath and byway in a novel that takes approximately the same amount of time to read as it does for the events themselves to happen. So we tend to go racing through, and we miss the detail and so the story; and we can, if we want, say that this constitutes a criticism, an adverse judgment, a limitation of the art. Fiction that demands more attention than one is willing to give, we can say, is to that extent unsuccessful art. To which Miss Welty might reply (along with Lawrence Sterne, James Joyce, Thomas Mann and one or two other artists with the same shortcoming), "Oh, but you see, what I have to show you can't be shown in any other way than this, more's the pity, so that you'll have to choose whether *you* want to know what I have to tell you, in which case you'll have to let me show it to you the only way I know it, or whether *you don't* want to know it. For if I tried to show it any other way, *it* wouldn't *be*. You would instead be getting something else, something other. I'll do my best to divert and amuse and please you all along the way, but it must be along *this* way, for there isn't any other."

Of course Eudora Welty wouldn't say that. She would let her art, at whatever risk and at whatever cost, speak for itself, as she has always done. But she might point out, as she has in *Place in Fiction*, that

> . . . the business of writing, and the responsibility of the writer, [is] to disentangle the significant—in character, incident, setting, mood, everything, from the random and meaningless and irrelevant that in real life surround and beset it. It is a matter of his selecting and, by all that implies, of changing, "real" life as he goes. With each word he writes, he acts—as literally and methodically as if he hacked his way through a forest and blazed it for the word that follows. He makes choices at the explicit demand of this one present story; each choice implies, explains, limits the next, and illuminates the one before. No two stories ever go the same way, though in different hands one story might possibly go any one of a thousand ways; and though the woods may look the same from outside, it is a new and different labyrinth each time.

II

Losing Battles begins with the wait for the various grandchildren of Granny Vaughn and their families to arrive at the family residence, now the home of her granddaughter Beulah Beecham Renfro and her husband Ralph, and located way up at the end of a winding road north of the town of Banner. Among the most eager of those who are doing the waiting is a daughter-in-law Gloria Renfro, whose husband Jack has been away at the state penitentiary at Parchman since the day of their wedding. All are certain that Jack will get home for Granny's birthday reunion, however, not only to honor Granny and rejoin his wife but to see his little daughter, Lady May, for the first time. And soon Jack arrives, in good spirits, not at all resentful or embittered at his incarceration. He is overjoyed at seeing Gloria again, delighted with Lady May, and properly attentive to everyone present (though he does find time to get Gloria off by herself and renew relations properly). All the other relatives arrive, too, and everyone is in high spirits, remaining so for the entire occasion.

Unexpected guests at the reunion, and most reluctant to be there, are Judge Oscar Moody and his wife Maud Eva. It was Judge Moody who had sentenced Jack to his two years in prison, for fighting with Curly Stovall, the storekeeper at Banner, but nobody seems to mind that, Jack least of all. The judge and his wife are present because their fancy Buick Automobile has, hilariously and improbably, become lodged against a tree, far up on a hillside, after the Judge swerved off the road to avoid running over Lady May and Gloria. For the ensuing 24 hours the Buick remains there, teetering over the edge, its motor still running, with Aycock Comfort, a friend of Jack's, seated in it to keep it balanced. Not until the next morning, in just about as wild and as comic an episode as Miss Welty has ever created, is the Buick rescued, somewhat the worse for wear, and taken, tied between a school bus and a truck and with a pair of mules harnessed behind to do the braking, down the hill side and into the community of Banner.

At the reunion, people talk, sing, play, gossip. Among the numerous topics discussed are Granny's youth, the family's history, the obscure antecedents of Jack's wife Gloria, and the life, death, and influence upon the men and women of the Banner community of Miss Julia Mortimer, longtime teacher at the Banner school. Miss Julia has just died, at the nearby town of Alliance, but she is to be buried in the Banner cemetery. Gloria had been Miss Julia's protégé, and had married Jack against her wishes.

All the Vaughns and Renfros and Beechams and the related descendants and cousins and kin at the reunion, and all the other townsfolk of Banner community as well, have been Miss Julia Mortimer's pupils, and she has vexed them all. In the mingled rage, guilt and nostalgia with which they speak of her, whether oblique or direct, the nature of their vexation becomes apparent. For in what she was, what she wanted them to do, what she sought to force them to learn about the world and themselves, she was a threat to the entire Banner community. It was her objective to make the people of Banner, her pupils, realize and confront the ultimate consequences of their humanity.

What all these generations of men and women want to do—, indeed, succeed in doing for the most part—is to go about their lives and their family and community doings innocently and unthinkingly, meeting birth, life, love and death as they arise, without the dread and the knowledge of anticipating or asking why. In so doing, they are not only helpless against time and change, but unable to deal with their circumstance. Miss Julia Mortimer had sought to force them to see who they were and what they were doing. As Gloria Renfro, who has come closest to being marked by Miss Julia's imprint, expresses the matter, in a rare moment of confrontation,

> Miss Julia Mortimer didn't want anybody left in the dark, not about anything. She wanted everything brought out in the wide open, to see and be known. She wanted people to spread out their minds and hearts to other people, so they could be read like books.

That statement, uttered by Gloria after the funeral, and as she sees that she may not be able to win her husband Jack away from the family and into a life of their own, amounts to a confession that Gloria has been marked my Miss Julia's determination, even though by marrying Jack she had done her best to escape the mantle placed upon her.

Gloria's statement, I suggest, comes very close to being a statement of Eudora Welty's artistic credo. For in *Place in Fiction*, we find her saying much the same thing. She is writing about the importance of place in grounding fiction in reality. "The good novel," she says, "should be steadily alight, revealing. Before it can hope to be that, it must of course be steadily visible from its outside, presenting a continuous, shapely, pleasing, and finished surface to the eye." For place

> has a good deal to do with making the characters real, that is, themselves, and keeping them so. The reason is simply that, as Tristram Shandy observed, "We are not made of glass, as characters on Mercury might be." Place *can* be transparent, or translucent: not people. In real life, we have to express the things plainest and closest to our minds by the clumsy word and the half-finished gesture; the chances are our most usual behavior makes sense only in a kind of daily way, because it has become familiar to our nearest and dearest, and still demands their constant indulgence and understanding. It is our describable outside that defines us, willy nilly, to others, that may save us, or destroy us, in the world; it may be our shield against chaos, our mask against exposure, but whatever it is, the move we make in the place we live has to signify our intent and meaning.

Thus the novelist, by selecting and defining people in a place—"the more narrowly we can examine a fictional character, the greater he is likely to loom up"—can through his focus provide awareness, discernment, order, clarity, insight—"they are like the attributes of love." The novelist seeks, hopes to write so that "the exactness and concreteness and solidity of the real world achieved in a story correspond to the intensity of feeling in the author's mind and to the very turn of his heart," since "making reality real is art's responsibility."

III

It is from just that kind of searching recognition that people seek diligently and determinedly to hide, and in Eudora Welty's fictional world, families and communities exist to enable their members to hide from reality. For as Gloria Renfro understands and tells her husband Jack, "people don't want to be read like books," whether by others or by themselves. In Miss Welty's work, we sometimes come upon people who realize this. We find characters who shrink from such knowledge, and also a precious few who, like Miss Julia Mortimer, do not thus shrink.

In Miss Welty's first novel, *Delta Wedding*, Laura McRaven travels to Shellmound, the family seat of the Fairchilds in the Delta country. For the Fairchilds (except for one of them, Shelley) everything that happens is gentled, humanized, incorporated into their ordered world. Violence, death, terror—a cyclone, a shooting, a train that runs over and kills a girl—are denied; the Fairchilds pretend that such things never exist, and that the protected, comfortable family world that is Shellmound can go on forever. The community existence, the constant coming and going in company with each other, protects the private loneliness of each participant by being carried on as if such secret knowledge did not exist. In the family, certain things are known, and so those who are in the family can deal with each other in terms of the known, thus avoiding inquiry into private matters. As Shelley Fairchild records in her diary, "we never wanted to be smart, one by one, but all together we have a wall, we are self-sufficient against people that come up knocking, we are solid to the outside. Does the world suspect? that we are all very private people? I think one by one we're all more lonely than private and more lonely than self-sufficient."

Shelley, who knows this but for the time being at least will take part in the pretense, and little cousin Laura McRaven, who is from Jackson and knows things about the outside world that will not fit into Shellmound's version of life, realize what is going on. "My papa has taken me on trips—I know about geography. . . . ," Laura insists. But she goes unheard: ". . . in the great confines of Shellmound, no one listened." Yet Shellmound is doomed, for change is inevitable, and the vague uneasiness that the peaceful, contained version of reality that Shellmound comprises will soon disintegrate is present throughout the book. Only Shelley, and Laura, will not be entirely helpless in its face; for only they, of all the Fairchilds, know that it is bound to happen.

The Golden Apples, published in 1949, is the masterpiece of all the books. In a set of seven closely-related narratives, together comprising forty years of human experience in the town of Morgana, Miss Welty sets forth a profound and hauntingly beautiful account of human beings in time, banded together to screen out the knowledge. The inhabitants of Morgana—King MacLain, far-wanderer, Morgana's favorite fertility symbol; his twin sons Ran and Eugene, marked for life (and for death) by their father's heritage; the Morrison children, Loch, who can leave Morgana, and Cassie, who can stay; Miss Eckhart, the German music teacher who brought "*the* Beethoven" to Morgana and thus left her impress on those able to receive it (or unable to escape it); and, most of all, Virgie Rainey, who duelled with time, place, and Miss Eckhart all the way—these are unforgettable people; and so, to only a lesser degree, are a host of minor characters.

"Time goes like a dream no matter how hard you run, and all the time we heard things from out in the world that we listened to but that still didn't mean we believed them," declares Virgie's mother, Miss Kate Rainey, to a stranger at the outset (and *only* to a stranger, for like Prufrock and Guido, Miss Katie Rainey would dare not say what she did to anyone who might report it in Morgana). It was not that Morgana did not believe the news from the world outside, so much as that its citizens strove not to believe it. King MacLain left town for years—and left his wife Miss Snowdie to raise the twins—but he always came back, usually at key moments, and at the end he attends Miss Kate Rainey's funeral, knowing he will be the next to die. Yet King never "left" Morgana; though separate from the town, he was never separate from its ways. He played by its rules, and operating within them, took what he wanted. Those rules were: never remind us that time, death and art exist, and are not accountable by Morgana's ways of measurement. Do not, in other words, tell us that we do not control our fate.

Poor Miss Eckhart—Lottie Elisabeth Eckhart, who taught Virgie Rainey to play "Für Elise" and to master the Liszt concerto, and who said that "Virgie would be heard from in the world, playing that"—never learned those rules. She set a metronome in front of her piano pupils, let it tick away remorselessly, timelessly, in absolute disdain of Morgana clock-time; Virgie Rainey, outraged, demanded it be put away. When a terrible thing happened to her—attacked, raped—she would not leave town, and take from Morgana the knowledge that desperate things did happen, and that people survived as people even so. When the man she loved so timidly and inchoately was drowned, she nodded her head in helpless rhythm at the graveside, and then sought to throw herself into it—and Morgana could not countenance the evidence that there was grief that terrible or feeling that desperate.

At the end of her story—"June Recital," the heart of the book, Miss Welty's supreme creation—she comes back to Morgana from her place at the county poor farm, goes inside the old MacLain house where she had once lived and taught, and while her erstwhile pupil Virgie Rainey and a sailor boy cavort around and upon a mattress upstairs, sets her metronome to ticking and tries to set fire to the house. She fails at it, as with all she ever attempted; she is led away, back to the poor farm, and when Virgie Rainey, racing out of the still-smoking house, runs past her, they do not say a word or exchange a glance. For they were both, as Cassie Morrison divines, "human beings terribly at large, roaming on the face of the earth. And there were others of them—human beings, roaming, like lost beasts."

But Loch Morrison, too young to understand what was going on, retrieves the metronome, fetches it up to his room, waits to hear it begin ticking of its own volition: "All by itself, of its own accord, it might let fly its little door and start up."

"You'll go away like Loch," Cassie calls out to Virgie many years later, after Virgie's mother's funeral. "A life of your own, away—I'm so glad for people like you and Loch, I am really." Loch has long since departed, but not before, in the story entitled "Moon Lake," he has successfully given artificial respiration to a drowned orphan, tirelessly, rhythmically, with no heed to clocks, the steady in-out, in-out rhythm of elemental life-giving itself—and of generation, of sex, as the scandalized Morganans sense instinctively while they watch him at work. They must bring him down to their size; Jinny Love Stark, already a determined citizen though still a child, will "Tell on him, in Morgana tomorrow. He's the most conceited Boy Scout in the whole troop; and's bowlegged." But Loch Morrison is one of those who will leave, because he cannot pretend that Morgana is the world.

Yet it is Virgie Rainey—the gifted one, who battled Miss Eckhart all the way, sought to deny her own self, took a job playing "You've Got To See Mama Every Night" at the movie house rather than going on with "*the* Beethoven," went away briefly but came right back, sought fulfillment in a succession of lovers—who was most marked by Miss Eckhart. At the close, forty years old, unmarried, alone, ready at last to leave for good, she realizes that like the old music teacher, she too saw things in their time, in the rhythms of art and life and of ultimate human existence. Miss Eckhart had "offered, offered, offered—and when Virgie was young, in the strange wisdom of youth that is accepting of more than is given, she had accepted *the* Beethoven, as with the dragon's blood. That was the gift she had touched with her fingers that had drifted and left her."

So brief a summary, and of only the main plot-relationship at that, can do little justice to what is in *The Golden Apples*. It is, I think, an even more successful work than *Losing Battles*, but perhaps I say this for having known

The Golden Apples for two decades, while *Losing Battles* is still to be lived with. But one recognizes at once, in the new novel, that Miss Julia Mortimer, with greater success, and Miss Lottie Eckhart, with lesser success, fought the same battle, representing for their fellow townsfolk the possibility, and the threat, of a greater and more ultimate discovery and self-revelation, and so were both feared and shunned. And similarly, Virgie Rainey and Gloria Renfro are of the same kind: both have been touched with the dragon's blood, and neither may put aside the legacy, struggle though they do. When the family accepts Gloria that day at the reunion, it is only with suspicion. They want her to become part of their common conspiracy, even down to the way she wears her clothes. As Aunt Beck says to Gloria, "you're just an old married woman, same as the rest of us now. So you won't have to answer to the outside any longer." But they ought not be so sure as that; "some day yet," Gloria tells her husband, "we'll move to ourselves." That is not what Miss Julia Mortimer had in mind for her; but neither is it what the Renfros and Beechams and Vaughns want, either.

Miss Julia Mortimer is dead when the family reunion that constitutes *Losing Battles* takes place, and she never appears as a charter, but increasingly her presence comes to dominate the story. At the last, as the inhabitants of Banner watch the long funeral procession from Alliance and the burial in the Banner cemetery—there are hundreds of persons present, former students from distant states, a governor, a Catholic priest, a judge (for that was what Judge Moody was doing in the neighborhood), dignitaries and plain folk both—we realize that the spinster schoolteacher has been a worthy adversary indeed to the family, and to all that makes human beings seek to flee from themselves and others. She has, in her time, made time run.

All of this is not told, or pointed out, as one goes along; it is realized as the reader begins putting together the experience of the bright, thick-textured surface of people, doings, and talk that constitutes this novel. *Losing Battles* is not, as it moves along its way, a somber book. It is alive in humor and merriment, and especially after we get into it well, filled with almost constant humor and diversion. But there are no shortcuts. It demands that the reader invest time and attention without stint, for as long as it takes it through. What it requires is sentence-by-sentence participation. What it provides, for those willing to take part, is delight ending in wisdom.

From *Hollins Critic* 7.3 (June 1970): 1-12.

Miss Welty's Wide World

Robert Drake

Eudora Welty's long-awaited novel—her first since *The Ponder Heart* (1954)—might well be cited as evidence that most writers of authoritative fiction are often severely limited in the stories they choose—or are forced—to tell. (Ernest Hemingway is possibly the most outstanding recent example of a writer of such limitations—great not in spite of but perhaps because of them.) In any case, *Losing Battles* is in many ways the Welty "mixture as before": the family, the community—the blood ties of heart and home, and the teasing paradoxes they pose for those who can see the least bit around or outside them. Here is again what Robert Penn Warren years ago called the love and the separateness in Miss Welty's work: the individualism, the identity which must be cherished—even fought for—in the face of the pre-emptive and often devouring claims of the group, with all its traditional sanctions. And the tension between these two "pulls"—these twin allegiances which may be likened to the two faces of love itself—has constituted one of Miss Welty's principal thematic concerns.

I might add that in that masterpiece of American comedy, "Why I Live at the P.O.," these claims are made manifest. I mention this particular story—which appeared in 1941 in Miss Welty's first short-story volume, *A Curtain of Green*—because it constitutes something of a sphinx riddle, perhaps even a Procrustean test for those who would like to enter into the fullness of Miss Welty's world. Unfortunately, many readers and critics have "bought" Katherine Anne Porter's absurd observation (made in her introduction to the 1941 volume) that the postmistress-narrator of "Why I Live at the P.O." is a terrifying mental case who suffers from paranoid delusions. Of course "Sister" is nothing but a southern old maid who has had a fuss with her family on "the Fourth of July or the day after" and is now enjoying a good pout in her new abode, the post office, where she is telling her "side" of the story to whoever in the whole wide world of China Grove, Mississippi, will listen. What is so depressing about the ease with which Miss Porter's interpretation has been accepted (and how anybody born in Indian Creek, Texas, ever could have thought up that one remains a mystery to me) is that such acceptance is due partly to a deficiency in many readers' sense of humor (they don't realize how serious the story really is: it passionately affirms, by apparent denial, the paramount claims of family and community) and partly to many readers' ignorance not just of southern culture but of *any* traditional culture where the values of family and community constitute the inhabitants' whole wide world.

I think that this point is worth making not only because Miss Porter's interpretation has done an enormous amount of mischief where this particular story is concerned, but also because the readers who took that comment as delivered gospel are certainly going to have trouble with *Losing Battles*—as indeed some of them have already had with *Delta Wedding* (1946), a Welty book with which this novel will inevitably be compared. In fact, this new novel might well be viewed as some kind of counterpart to the earlier one—with the time changed from the '20s to the '30s, and the locale moved from the delta to the red clay hills of the Banner community in northeast Mississippi. This time the family occasion is the reunion held on the 90th birthday of "Granny" Vaughn; and the outside—or even hostile—forces which threaten the group are represented by Judge and Mrs. Moody, now present literally by accident (the judge had sent Jack Renfro, Granny's great-grandson, to the penal farm at Parchman for "aggravated battery" against Curly Stovall); such new Beecham relatives as Sister Cleo, Uncle Noah Webster Beecham's new wife, to whom the family must be *explained*; and even Gloria, the former Banner school teacher who is now Jack's wife.

The old tensions between families that "can't be too close" and the individuals either within or outside them who must repudiate some of the family claims in order to have a life of their own—thereby maintaining a perilous balance between the two loyalties—appear again here; indeed, this conflict comes close to being Miss Welty's one story. One character, who is heard of only in conversation yet somehow assumes greater importance as the novel progresses, fits significantly into this pattern. She is Miss Julia Mortimer, the devoted teacher who trained Gloria—the orphan girl of uncertain origins who may just possibly have been born a Beecham from the wrong side of the blanket—and despaired of her should she deny what Miss Julia regarded as her true calling: fighting ignorance (a losing battle, naturally, but one with claims almost equal to those of the family). Of course Miss Julia has lost in more ways than one (the novel ends with her burial); yet the perennial battles which every individual must fight remain—always to be lost yet always to be fought because, paradoxically, in the losing the individual gains in wisdom and insight. People such as these—good Baptists, fasola singers, quilt-piecers, tale-tellers or just plain talkers, none of whom confuses indoor plumbing with culture or electricity with the good life—hardly need to be reminded of what literally are *home truths*. Alas, one cannot assume so much for Miss Welty's readers today.

It will be said that this novel has an extremely dense texture, that its many characters and thematic motifs—in all their permutations and combinations—weave in and out in a seamless philosophical and social garment. And so they do, almost to the point of constituting an embarrassment of riches—to say nothing of disproportionate thematic development. One feels somehow disappointed here—perhaps most so during the birthday reunion scenes, where there is a good deal more self-conscious, mannered sentiment (and consequent stylization, even affectation, in the prose) than the narrative can assume and support. There are just too many "blessed sweethearts" and too much family petnaming and verbal cuddling. And it's so sad to see (or rather to hear) Miss Welty's ear succumbing to what often sounds factitious and even—God forbid—quaint and folksy. She's at her best when she remembers her characters'—and perhaps her own—real grounding in the lusty, robust Faulknerian humor of the old southwest, when she lets them all go to it without further ado. "Arty" tendencies have manifested themselves in her earlier fiction—in certain stories in *The Bride of the Innisfallen* (1955) and *The Golden Apples* (1949); and one always hoped that she would suppress them in light of her great gift for the real, the elemental thing. They were held well in check in *Delta Wedding*, where the characters and their social position would admit of more ambitious things. But they are, I believe, out of place here: one sighs for the real authority of voice found in *The Ponder Heart* and some of the earlier stories.

Nevertheless, though I cannot place *Losing Battles* in the front rank of Miss Welty's fiction, I admire the wonder, the reverence, the joy she has once again brought to her great, her inevitable theme. Her style, her art may occasionally have played her false here; but she has never really been false to the truth of the compelling story she has told again and again. She remains one of the most distinguished of 20th century American writers of fiction.

From *The Christian Century* 87 (17 June 1970): 766-67.

Speech and Silence in *Losing Battles*

James Boatwright[1]

"I want to write a novel about Silence [about] the things people don't say."
Virginia Woolf, *The Voyage Out*

"It is for a voyage into solitude that man was created."
E.M. Forster, "A New Novelist"

"God created the world from nothing with words" Paul Goodman reminds us in *Speaking and Language*, and he goes on to list some of the other remarkable properties of speech:

> A prophet's lips touched with a coal of fire create new ethics. If an ordained priest says *"Hoc est Corpus,"* the wheaten bread is transfigured. A man can win salvation by repeating the one right syllable. . . .

Goodman suggests here the "amazing energy" of speech and the persistent belief in its magical powers. Speech may be magic, but it is also a given of the world, one of those obvious phenomena that betray us: they are so obvious that we don't often regard them with the spirit of awe and wonder that they legitimately demand even in their ordinariness. I want to speak of the obvious, to regard speech and its potent opposite or negative, silence, and their role in *Losing Battles*.

Most novels of course contain speech and silence, but *Losing Battles* seems to me a special case, in that it is not only an astonishing *gathering* of

[1]This essay is adapted from a talk given in February 1974 at Hollins College as part of a program honoring Eudora Welty.

voices—dozens of them—shouting, whispering, intoning and preaching thousands of words, thousands of sentences, among them some of the funniest, saddest, hardest and most truthful we are likely to hear anywhere—*Losing Battles* not only *is* the voices, and the silences that sometimes lie between them, ticking like time bombs: it is also *about* speech and silence, about these profoundly curious phenomena. In its unfolding, the novel suggests to us, for the most part obliquely, dramatically, what to make of speech and silence.

That it is about these things seems fairly clear, both from important evidence within the novel, and from what Eudora Welty has herself said about the book. When she was interviewed by the *New York Times Book Review* shortly before the publication of *Losing Battles*, she described her needs and intentions:

> I needed that region, that kind of country family, because I wanted that chorus of voices, everybody talking and carrying on at once. I wanted to try something completely vocal and dramatized. Those people are natural talkers and story-tellers, in a remote place where there was time for that.

She describes what sounds like a technical choice, an experiment in form primarily, "to try something completely vocal and dramatized." At the same time, her desire seems to have been something more than to experiment, as we might have guessed it would be. The formal choice is clearly grounded in character and circumstance: the fact that "those people are natural talkers and story-tellers, in a remote place where there was time for that." I take it that one of the reasons Eudora Welty wanted to write about these natural talkers was the *fact* of their talk itself, the phenomenon itself. We can assume, I think, Eudora Welty's dazed wonder before the phenomenon (assume it, because *our* response is dazed wonder)—wonder at the sheer human energy of all these voices, their infinitely interesting tones and accents, the range of feeling and desire that lies beneath the voices, the seemingly endless surprises they are capable of springing on us.

Our dazed wonder is shared by one of the book's characters. He meditates on the phenomenon, as we are moved to do, and it is a striking passage in the book, because it's the only extended meditation in the whole novel, the only time when the objective surface is broken through and we find out what a character is thinking. In this one instance, we are allowed into the mind of Vaughn Renfro, Jack's young brother. The passage comes at the end of the reunion; everyone has gone home, only the Renfros and Judge and Mr. Moody are left, and they are all in bed. Conversation has finally ceased. Vaughn goes about some last chores (pulling the school bus out of the ditch, for one) and he reflects in wonder on Jack's return; on the whole livelong day. It is one of those poignant and utterly convincing representations, frequent enough in Miss Welty's work but singular in *Losing Battles*, of the growth into knowledge of the human psyche, the psyche's encounter, both stricken and rapturous, with reality, with the nature of things:

> . . . . Riding through the world, the little boy, moonlit, wondered . . . Over and under the tired stepping of Bet, he could hear the night throb. He heard every sound going on, repeating itself, increasing, as if it were being recollected by loud night talking to itself. At times it might have been the rush of water—the Bywy on the rise in spring; or it might have been the rains catching up after them, to mire them in. Or it might have been that the whole wheel of the sky made the sound as it kept letting fall the soft fire of its turning. As long as he listened, sound prevailed. No matter how good at hollering back a boy might grow up to be, hollering back would never make the wheel stop. And he could never outride it. As he plodded on through the racket, it rang behind him and was ahead of him too. It was all-present enough to spill over into voices, as everything, he was ready to believe now, threatened to do, the closer he might come to where something might happen. The night might turn into more and more voices, all telling it—bragging, lying, singing, pretending, protesting, swearing everything into being, swearing everything away—but telling it. Even after people gave up each other's company, said goodbye and went home, if there was only one left, Vaughn Renfro, the world around him was still one huge, soul-defying reunion.

That seems as rich and complex to me as any number of poems, and like a poem, it resists analysis; nevertheless, I'd like to try to get closer to it. The day, crammed with voices, has left its mark: the night, the sounds of the night world, are a continuation of the day and its endless talk. They are in collusion: the wheel of the sky, the racket of the night, the hundred cousins and aunts and uncles, "swearing everything into being, swearing everything away . . . telling it" have one purpose: the thwarting of Vaughn Renfro, this lone boy, trembling on the brink of knowledge, close to "where something might happen." He considers the racket of night *and* day a "soul-defying reunion," the soul balked, brought up short whenever it approaches that place of revelation. Vaughn's conception of voices, human voices and the voices of the world, is at first encounter an unexpected one. "Telling it—bragging, lying, singing, pretending, protesting, swearing everything into being, swearing everything away" is precisely *not* telling it, in some paradoxical way. The voices are instead a threat to his soul, speech a means of denying the soul's hunger for its truth and freedom, silence the means of feeding it.

Which brings us to a general question, provoked by Vaughn's wonder. What do we make of all this talk? Of this speech, and its silences? Unthinkingly, we make light of them, by regarding them reductively, simplistically. Speech is something often called *communication*: silence its pure negative, its absence. In the first chapter of *Speaking and Language*, Goodman leads us to look more closely, with greater discrimination, and he outlines some possibilities:

> . . . . There is the *speech* that names things and reads off sentences of how they are . . . that creates and maintains community bonds; that recognizes the other as a person, asks questions, and exchanges information; that directly touches another by imperatives; that exteriorizes and shares what one is feeling. . . . There is the dumb silence of slumber and apathy; the sober silence that goes with a solemn animal face; the fertile silence of awareness, pasturing the soul, whence emerge new thoughts; the alive silence of alert perception . . . the silence of listening to another speak . . . the noisy silence of resentment and self-recrimination . . . baffled silence; the silence of peaceful accord with other persons or communion with the cosmos. . . .

What Goodman describes analytically and objectively, Eudora Welty dramatizes selectively, and this dramatization takes place waywardly, a muted gesture or insistent whisper, caught by the alert eye and ear, as the novelist pours out her other gifts before us: a gathered multitude, as numerous and colorful as the figures in a painting by Brueghel, the earth solid under their feet, loving arms filled with flowers, the tables groaning with food, dust flying from arriving cars, exploding tires, and wrestling boys, who howl at the loss of a shirt-tail.

What she dramatizes are particular relations between speech and silence, particular kinds of speech and silence, and I use the verb *dramatizes* with some consciousness of its weight. Drama is, after all, *the* art of speech and silence, and *Losing Battles* is like a play, except there is a narrative voice which makes clear to us, through the description of gesture and through assertions of silence, what is happening when there is no speech. We are familiar with the peculiar power of this juxtaposition of speech and silence in Shakespeare, especially in *Lear*. In the first scene, when Cordelia speaks in asides that are the equivalent of silence: "What shall Cordelia speak? Love, and be silent" or says, in answer to Lear's "What can you say to draw a third more opulent than your sisters? Speak" the one word, *Nothing*—in this scene, Shakespeare seems to me to be dealing in speech and silences that are also about speech and silence, and *Losing Battles* and *King Lear* appear to be saying similar things about speech and silence, things Vaughn dimly recognized: that speech can defy the soul and silence can be pasture for the soul's truth.

In Vaughn's reverie we have already encountered some of the kinds of speech that have so overwhelmed him—"telling it—bragging, lying, singing, pretending, protesting, swearing everything into being, swearing everything away." Why and how do they defy the soul? Maybe the best answer might be found in pursuing another question: Why all the telling it? Why all the talk? We can come up with a simple, naturalistic answer: gather such people around and there will be talk. But one's impressions of the novel won't allow that simple an answer: it as a *flood* of talk, this endearing multitude talk as if their lives depended on talk, as if it were responsible for their survival. And perhaps it is.

As in the first scene of *King Lear*, the family is gathered for a reunion, but with different immediate purposes in mind. They are gathered to celebrate Granny's ninetieth birthday, and, not very incidentally, to welcome Jack home from the pen. The reunion is a ritual, a ceremony, to celebrate Granny's endurance: it draws together all of her grandchildren and great-grand-children and celebrates her survival in them and *their* survival. But the mere drawing together is not enough; the ceremony is incomplete without the family's verbal rites: the telling of tales, recounting of ancient and modern history, the initiation of new members, the blessing by Brother Bethune—a wide range of speech, song, and prayer—Vaughn's whole catalogue, in fact. Both those inside the family and the outsiders are at least partly conscious of the purposes of their speech, of what they are up to, and their knowledge is reflected indirectly in their comments. Gloria complains: "They're all up there just sitting and listening to 'emselves talk" and Jack wonders: "Recounting for Granny some tale or another about me?" They are expert critics of narrative, sharp-witted analysts of rhetoric. When Percy Beecham finishes a particularly good bit of mimicry, Aunt Birdie says: "Ain't Percy grand? He gets 'em all down pat. . . . I wish I was married to him. . . . He'd keep me entertained." Even though Cleo is new to the scene, she understands the aesthetic of the heroic brag: Beulah delivers her hymn of praise for Sam Dale Beecham:

> "Handsome! Handsomer than Dolphus ever was, sunnier than Noah Webster, smarter than Percy, more home-loving than Curtis, more quiet-spoken than Nathan, and could let you have a tune quicker and truer than all the rest put together," said Miss Beulah.
> "He sounds like he's dead," said Aunt Cleo.

Or more somberly, closer to the bone, there is Aunt Beck's comment on Beulah's self-deception about the possibilities of Sam's having been Gloria's father: ". . . if the right story comes along at the right time, she'll be like the rest of us and believe what she wants to believe." Beulah is the priestess of these verbal rites, attacking Brother Bethune's performance (he can't hold a candle to Grandpa Vaughn), overseeing the comic and shocking initiation of Gloria ("Say Beecham" the women shout as they stuff watermelon in her mouth: say *Uncle*, they mean, say anything, but *talk*, join the family and talk). Beulah is the arbiter of speech, urgently, sometimes desperately moving forward to deal with the two gravest threats: silence, and speech that wanders off in the wrong direction, speech that goes too far. When Lexie arrives at the terrible center of Miss Julia's story, Beulah chastises her for "giving out talk of death and disgrace around here." And when Cleo's questions finally get too persistent, and she asks of Nathan, after his fainting spell, "Well, what's *he* got to hide," Beulah's passionate defense comes as an open demonstration of faith in the miraculous powers of speech, of rhetoric:

> "Sister Cleo, I don't know what in the world ever guides your tongue into asking the questions it does! . . . By now you ought to know this is a strict, law-abiding, God-fearing close-knit family, and everybody in it has always struggled the best he knew how and we've all just tried to last as long as we can by sticking together."

This brave and defiant speech is spoken by a woman whose brother maimed himself after murdering a man, a woman whose parents abandoned her and all the rest of their children and were killed in their flight, a woman whose son has returned from the penitentiary that very day.

I imagine Goodman might have characterized most of the speech in *Losing Battles* as the speech "that creates and maintains community bonds" but that doesn't seem an adequate description to me. Eudora Welty goes deeper, I think, in suggesting that much speech—speech in community, the speech of family—is at bottom a means of survival, self-preservation. It is a signal of inclusion; it cements the bonds of love, tests loyalty, asserts lastingness, rehearses the heroic act. But most important, it creates a fragile surface that will hold us up. We construct our world through speech. We sing hymns to ward off boogers; we're whistling in the dark, when we talk.

* * * *

The silences of *Losing Battles* are not, certainly, a separate subject. They fill out and complete what is said, as the spaces in a sculpture complete the image. And as with the spaces in a sculpture, they must be carefully attended to. There can be no image without the spaces to define it, and there can be no speech without *its* defining silence, but image and speech assert themselves so strongly that they almost persuade us to ignore their complement. We can notice who the silent ones are in the midst of all these talkers, our attention drawn to their silences, frequently, through mere gestures, mere gestures which many times fairly shout at us if we are acute enough to observe them. When the whole scene becomes quiet and the narrator draws attention to the silence, it is always a pregnant and dramatic moment, full of wonder, or threat, or promised knowledge.

If Beulah is the priestess of these ceremonies, Granny Vaughn is their sibyl, their oracle. Her silences are as potent and weighty as her speech, and as ambiguous. She is granted the freedom of the very old, to say or not say anything, because nothing she says necessarily means what it says: the auditors are free to pick and choose. Likewise, they are free to choose among her silences, which may speak agreement, or rebuke, or mere absence of mind. And yet (and therefore?) she is, for me, the fullest, richest, most touching character in the book: her confusions of silence and speech are something more than confusions: when she mistakes Jack for Sam Dale, calls for her horse, asks for her presents again, or invites Vaughn into her bed she shimmers in our sight as a figure who has transcended time, stripped life down to its core of feeling, as she repeatedly suffers through our sorest, most unrelenting needs.

Of the characters notable for their silence, Judge Moody is the most predictable—after all, he is both an outsider, and an enemy—he sent Jack to the pen. But his silences speak of more than enmity: he is a man of mournful countenance. When Miss Pet Hanks tells Jack, Gloria and the Moodys of Julia Mortimer's death, Gloria breaks into tears, and Judge Moody stands "with his head sunk." It becomes his characteristic gesture: he is like one of those damned but somehow comic figures of Michelangelo's, faced at the last judgment with the enormity of human failings. He sighs, groans, and beats his fist upon the school desk as the family prattle on, talking easily and callously of the suffering in a life he knows far more about than they do.

Nathan's silence also comes from knowing too much, from being privy to some dreadful truth. His is the silence of the exile, who speaks only with signs. He finally does speak, and what moves him to speech is the same powerful presence that causes the Judge's moans, that hovers over the reunion like a stern angel—the schoolteacher Julia Mortimer. We learn that it had been her words which saved Nathan from despair. Nathan is the most troubling and mysterious figure in the tableau: he stands like a man of stone and does not share the feast. He is the image of solitude, the member of the family who never truly joins the circle of blest ties that bind, who challenges the family's solidarity. He seems an anomaly, less than kin. And yet his image is the magnetic pole in what is for me the novel's great summary scene. Night has fallen and all the family has gathered on the porch, in the glare of the dangling light bulb:

> Suddenly the moonlit world was doused, lights hard as pickaxe blows drove down from every ceiling and the roof of the passage, cutting the house and all in it away, leaving them an island now on black earth, afloat in night, and nowhere, with only each other. In that first moment every face, white-lit but with its caves of mouth and eyes opened

> wide, black with the lonesomeness and hilarity of survival, showed its kinship to Uncle Nathan's, the face that floated over theirs. For the first time, all talk was cut off, and no baby offered to cry. Silence came travelling in on solid, man-made light.

For a moment, every face shows its kinship with Nathan's: for a moment, his state,—exile, solitude, silence—is the human norm; for a moment, each is a silent and wounded Nathan.

When we turn to Gloria, her beloved Jack, and her mentor Miss Julia, we reach the passionate vortex of the narrative, where all lines meet, the site of the major battle. It is a battle readers of Miss Welty's work have witnessed before; in her vision, from her perspective, it is the battle of our lives. Ellen says, in *Delta Wedding*, there is a battle "*in* us, already, . . . *in* people on this earth, not between us. . . . It's part of being alive. . . . The fight in you's over things, not over people. . . . Things like the truth, and what you owe people."

The weapons in that battle, as it is fought out in this novel, are speech and silence. By speaking we honor the whole world of duty, of love, of our community with others, our need for them; speech is, in Vaughn's words, "another part of people's getting tangled up with each other," that tragic and glorious tangle of lives at the reunion. In silence we assert our separateness, our joy in the soul's integrity; we pay homage to the perdurable and dangerous truth about our condition—its final solitude. Vaughn dimly recognizes that the voices are soul-defying: Gloria, a comic and pastoral Cordelia, sees the issues with greater clarity and tries not to speak, fights the Beecham women as they attempt to drag her into their world. But Gloria has forgotten some of the lessons Miss Julia taught her: she wants pure freedom *and* pure love, caught in timeless amber, the truce called. She shares the penchant of many in the family for denying facts plain as the nose on your face. When she cries fervently of Miss Julia, "But she changed! I'll never change," Jack's only response is a gesture: "he clasped her."

It is one of many of Jack's silences. He is a great *listener*:

> When he listened to Uncle Homer it was the same as when he listened to all his family—he leaned forward with his clear eyes fixed on the speaker as though what was now being said would never be said again or repeated by anybody else.

We learn only afterwards that he has returned to the house and stood out of sight as Miss Julia's story was being told. He has listened and heard: to hear truly is to comprehend, to understand, the first momentous steps toward something larger—as he signifies when Gloria asks him if he could do better than pity Miss Julia, since he didn't even know her. "I reckon I even love her," said Jack. "I heard her story." He wields with a hero's courage the weapons of speech *and* silence. Like George of *Delta Wedding*, he is an adept of love and truth, a battle-scarred veteran, scarred in his struggle between "things like the truth, and what you owe people." Defending the family honor, he ends up in the pen; but he can be as passionate as the judge in his concern for abstract justice, and refuses with him the promiscuous forgiveness of the family. He describes for Gloria the difficult middle road they will take: "There's room for everything, and time for everybody, if you take your day the way it comes along and try not to be much later than you can help." They are words as brave as his mother's, and possibly as full of pathos, except they are charged with the strength of generous youth, they come form the mouth of a hero who is Hercules, the Prodigal Son, and Samson, all in one.

Miss Julia, that perverse and serious warrior, is the most oddly silent of all. She doesn't seem silent to us at first: she had plagued them all with her harangues when they were young, spurring them on, berating them for their foolish family pride, their self-love. But she is silent, absent; she was always an observer of the soul-defying reunion, and now she lies stone cold in Alliance. Only the heat of her passion speaks, and her written words. The written word is a form of silence in *Losing Battles*. It is radically discontinuous from the spoken work: it proceeds from solitude, from a furious need to say the truth. The aunts know this, and hate books; they find writing and reading most peculiar ways of acting in the world (in the midst of the Judge's reading of Julia's letter, Aunt Birdie says, "I can't understand it when he reads it to us. Can't he just *tell* it?") There is no more painful scene in the novel than Lexie's description of Miss Julia's last days: when Lexie has taken away Miss Julia's pencil and paper, in fierce silence Miss Julia continues to write, using her finger for pencil, the bedsheet for paper. (Lexie had told her: "Listen, Julia, if you've got something this bad to say about human nature . . . why don't you go ahead and send it to the President of the United States?") Earlier, Miss Julia *had* been able to write that letter to Judge Moody, in which she describes all her lost battles with the ignorance of her charges, and then goes on to lament her present state:

> I don't know what it is I've come to. They prattle around me of the nearness of Heaven. Is this Heaven, where you lie wide open to the mercies of others who think they know better than you do what's best—what's true and what isn't?

The company is only too willing to think Miss Julia mad as she nears her end, but it's the same Julia they've always known, as determined as ever to distinguish between "what's true and what isn't," as others "prattle around" her of Heaven and last things. The judge had said that the story of Miss Julia's final days "could make a stone cry," but tears are not enough for

Miss Julia. She grows before our eyes into a queen of tragedy. Recently, Miss Welty has written with great sympathy of Willa Cather, how her characters rebel, not for the sake of rebellion, but for "the sake of something a great deal bigger—that of integrity, of truth." Willa Cather found such rebellion, such heroic hunger for truth, in artists, like Thea of the *Song of the Lark*, and Miss Cather embodied such rebelliousness herself, "not without tragic cost," as Miss Welty observes. In *Losing Battles*, a country schoolteacher gives her life for truth, and she pays the tragic cost.

It's not, I suppose, Miss Julia's story in the end. Her silence and the silence of her grave are crowded out by Jack's singing, for all Banner to hear. "Bringing in the Sheaves," as he and Gloria trudge back toward the farm, to an uncertain harvest, to family, to the whole swarming world of talk, with its sustaining duplicities. But they have had Julia in their lives, and whom, after all, do they have in Vaughn, this wondering boy, who so loves Banner School that the night before he "would have beaten sunup and driven there [then], if the doors had any way of opening for him?" And in the midst of all the prattle, they have listened to—but have they heard?—Brother Bethune preaching to them on the Last Judgment:

> "Why, Banner Cemetery is going to be throwed open like a hill of potatoes!" Brother Bethune cried. "All those loving kin who have gone before, there they'll all be—waiting for you and me! How will you start behaving *then*, precious friends? I'll tell you! You'll all be left without words. Without words! Can you believe it? Think about that!"

From *Shenandoah* 25.3 (Spring 1974): 3-14.

The Optimist's Daughter
1972

The Continuity of Love

James Boatwright

Admirers of Eudora Welty's work have had a busy time of it since their *first* sight of *The Optimist's Daughter*. It was published in *The New Yorker* in the spring of 1969. At that time I was putting together an issue of *Shenandoah* as a tribute to Miss Welty, to which Reynolds Price contributed a detailed reading of the story, calling it her "strongest, richest work"—which was saying a lot but not, in my opinion, too much.

But that was before the publication, in April 1970, of the comic and epic *Losing Battles*, a long novel overflowing with both youthful energy a serene, impartial wisdom. It was a book that a writing career and a body of work even as distinguished as Miss Welty's had hardly prepared us for. With the exception of *Delta Wedding*, her work had been essentially miniaturist: much in little, the perfectly controlled and executed novella and short story. As John Aldridge noted in his review, *Losing Battles* challenged Faulkner on his home ground, in ambitiousness and scope.

Then Random House published last year Miss Welty's photograph album of her Mississippi neighbors in the 1930s, *One Time, One Place*. An object lesson in the proprieties of photographing other human beings, it showed us definitively that the documentary camera is not necessarily a savage or a sentimentally condescending eye but can have the complexity and truthfulness of vision of a gifted novelist. The preface, written over 30 years after the taking of the pictures, tells the reader as much about Miss Welty and her fiction—but indirectly, obliquely—as it does about the photographs.

Now, to further complicate our responses, to disarm our complacent notions about what the proper limits of energy and invention are, *The Optimist's Daughter* appears in book form, with deceptively understated information that it "appeared originally in *The New Yorker* in a shorter and different form." To be specific, she has added 10,000 words to the original

30,000, has changed names, altered the order of some scenes, subtly modified some of the characters, added much to our knowledge of the protagonist's past and present. She has re-written and re-thought the book, so that it is both essentially the same and almost everywhere slightly different. To compare the two versions is another object lesson: we can observe the evolution, the accretion of a work of art as it is shaped by a master of narrative.

The story is stark and simple in its outline, a depiction of the trauma we suffer in witnessing the death of parents, in burying them. It's the order of nature: it occurs when most of us are middle-aged, when we have learned, we think, what we are going to learn. An old dog learns new tricks. When before *have* we grown up? With our first job, with marriage, with the first child? Maybe, but they are not the same kind of event as this odd, painful liberation, which pulls the mind inward to a contemplation of our own lives as we witness the end of and make some final judgment on the lives of our parents, as we step free of them toward our own death.

The story told her, of course, is much more than its outline, as any story is. Laurel McKelva Hand flies hurriedly from Chicago to New Orleans, where her father is to undergo an operation. It is apparently successful, but Judge McKelva doesn't respond as he should and slowly drifts into death. Laurel and Fay, the Judge's young second wife, accompany the body back to the small Mississippi town where Laurel grew up and where her father still lived. The rest of the novel deals with the funeral, the gathering around of her friends and her father's friends, and Laurel's straightening out her affairs before she returns a few days later to her job in Chicago.

The abrasive conflict at the center of the novel is between Laurel and Fay. The usurping step-mother is younger than her step-daughter; she is not from the right sort of people, she's mean-spirited, totally self-absorbed. A blur of gold buttons and cheap costume jewelry, she bewails missing Mardi Gras, the judge is thoughtless enough to die on her birthday. But the real problem is not, I think, Fay's being unsuitable or unworthy, her entrance into Laurel's father's life is menacing in some as yet unspecified way, a deep wound, the desecration of holy ground, as Laurel makes explicit to Fay toward the end of the narrative. What is further involved here is a brooding on the nature of family and relationship itself.

It is only well into the story that we learn that Laurel is a widow, has been a widow for perhaps 20 or 25 years: her husband was lost at sea in World War II. She now presumably lives alone in Chicago, devoted wholly to her work as a fabric designer. It shouldn't surprise the reader then to learn that it was "still incredible to Laurel that her father, at nearly seventy, should have let anyone new, a beginner, walk in on his life, that he had even agreed to pardon such a thing." No beginner has walked into Laurel's life to replace her beloved Philip. Why? We aren't allowed much into Laurel's consciousness until the narrative begins to draw to a close, but we do learn that "her marriage had been of magical ease, of *ease*—of brevity and conclusion and all belonging to Chicago and not here," and that with Phil lost, "love was sealed away into its perfection and had remained there." *Ease, brevity, conclusion, perfection*: hardly the words to attach to the other relationships in the novel.

Instead, we are confronted with images of voracious need and hunger, love that is burdensome, endless, inconclusive, imperfect. At the hospital, Judge McKelva shares his room with crazy old Mr. Dalzell, who thinks the judge is his long lost son Archie Lee. Down the hall, the rest of the Dalzell clan, including the returned prodigal son, keeps its vigil. They are hilariously comic but something else too: steadfast, tenacious as snapping turtles. The Dalzells, gathered together in a lunatic confusion of loving gestures and burlesque pratfalls, are the first variation on the theme which builds throughout the narrative.

Fay has told Laurel that her family is dead, gone, every one of them: "Grandpa . . . that sweet old man, he died in my arms." But on the day of the funeral, a truckload of her family shows up: Fay's mother, a brother, a sister, a nephew—and finally Grandpa himself. In the midst of this long scene—which is, to my mind, brilliant beyond praise, a miraculous balancing of face and the gravest pathos—Laurel recognizes what makes Fay's family seem familiar:

> They might have come out of that night in the hospital waiting room—out of all times of trouble, past or future—the great interrelated family of those who never know the meaning of what has happened to them.

Why don't they know? Because hunger, need and love are blind? (Literal eye trouble sends the judge to the hospital; Laurel's mother, Becky, had become blind and embittered in her long dying.) Toward the end of the book, as Laurel recalls her childhood vacations "up home" in West Virginia with her mother and grandmother, one particularly striking image stands out: the appearance of her grandmother's pigeons:

> . . . Laurel had kept the pigeons under eye in their pigeon house and had already seen a pair of them sticking their beaks down each other's throats, gagging each other, eating out of each other's craws, swallowing down all over again what had been swallowed before: they were taking turns. . . . They convinced her that they could not escape each other and could not themselves be escaped form. So when the pigeons flew down, she

> tried to position herself behind her grandmother's skirt . . . but her grandmother said again, "They're just hungry, like we are."

What the grandmother accepts, acquiesces in, Laurel hides from in terror. I think the implication is clear enough: Laurel has borne this image of relation, dependency, need through her life, and it has in part determined her vision, her demand for freedom, flight, escape—for clarity, for the knowledge of what has happened to you. She *did* marry, but the brevity, the unreal perfection of the marriage stand in contrast to what the nature of dependence actually is.

The strongest and most mysterious scene in the book is the account of Laurel's last night at home. When she enters the front door, a chimney-sweep loose in the house drives her into her parents' room, where she spends the night plunging into memory, following out affectionately but remorselessly what her parents' lives were: the high promises of their beginning, the eventual decline into sickness of Laurel's mother, the terrible failure of love to prevent pain and loss, love's betrayal. But Laurel's settling of accounts, seeing clearly the inescapable doom awaiting any hope of contingency, ends in a surprising way, a melting of resolve—"She lay there with all that was adamant in her yielding to this night, yielding at last. Now all she had found had found her."—ends with the resurrection of her dead husband.

> He looked at her out of eyes wild with the craving for his unlived life, with mouth open like a funnel's. . . . What would have been their end, then? Suppose their marriage had ended like her father and mother's? Or like her mother's father and mother's? Like—

And it would have, wouldn't it? Their life would have ended in a blind blundering, the price paid for a lived life.

Fay's role in this painfully acquired knowledge of Laurel's is not a simple one, but I think it's something like this: Fay is Laurel's deepest fear, a figure of absolute isolation, totally incapable of love, in panicky flight from blood ties and the wounds of mortality, a grotesque parody of Laurel's own worst possibilities. In the showdown between Fay and Laurel in the novel's final scene, Fay is the instrument as Laurel affirms the shape of the lives of her parents, *lets go* of them, no longer tries to protect them—they don't need her protection, don't ask for it, they stand in memory in their complex and temporal imperfection, in their final dignity. Laurel returns to Chicago to what kind of life? No answer is given, but she has met a great fear and overcome it, "the deepest spring in her heart had uncovered itself, and it began to flow again." Or, as Laurel learns again, in her dream of Philip

following his ghostly appearance to her—and what Fay does not know, cannot learn—life is meaningful and whole only in "the continuity of love."

From *New Republic* 166 (10 June 1972): 24-25.

The Past Reexamined: *The Optimist's Daughter*

Cleanth Brooks

Eudora Welty's *The Optimist's Daughter*[1] has the power and authority of a small masterpiece. Line by line, her writing has never been better. This short novel is filled with descriptive passages such as these: (of an old man's arm) "its skin soft and gathered, like a woman's sleeve" (p. 33); (of Judge McKelva's aging secretary) "She came in with her nonchalant, twenties stalk on her high heels" (p. 64); (of a gull over Lake Pontchartrain seen through a train window) "a seagull was hanging with wings fixed, like a stopped clock on a wall" (p. 45). The conversation is just as memorable: (a country woman reminiscing about how badly patients are treated in hospitals) "'He shot hisself or somebody shot him, one. He begged for water. The hospital wouldn't give him none. Honey, he died wanting water'" (p. 39); (of Mrs. Verna Longmeier who sewed for a living) "If even a crooked piece of stitching were pointed out to her, she was apt to return: 'Let him who is without sin cast the first stone'" (p. 72); (of old Mrs. Pease on the unexpected arrival of the Chisom family at Judge McKelva's funeral): "'You can't curb a Baptist, Mrs. Pease said. 'Let them in and you can't keep 'em down, when somebody dies'" (pp. 108-9).

Yet *The Optimist's Daughter* is much more than a tapestry of brilliantly evoked scenes from small-town life and dialogue in the Southern idiom; it is a novel with a very definite shape. As a fictional structure it shows a surprising complication of development and a rich exfoliation of themes.

Laurel McKelva Iland, a widow in her early forties, has been summoned from Chicago, where she now lives, because of the illness of her father, Judge McKelva. Laurel's mother had died some ten years earlier. Her

[1](New York: Random House, 1972).

father, now in his early seventies, had, a year and a half before, married a woman much younger than he, Wanda Fay Chisom, a shallow little vulgarian. As the story begins, we obviously do not know very much about Laurel, but we can sense her feelings as she listens to the conversation and witnesses the conduct of her father's second wife. Wanda Fay comes of the plain people; some would use a harsher phrase: common white trash. She is cheap, self-centered, aggressive, and completely unmannerly. Her tactlessness all too clearly manifests her lack of understanding and concern for other people.

Fay's conduct at the hospital before and after Judge McKelva's death is so outrageous that a reader not well acquainted with Miss Welty's work might be tempted to attribute her treatment of Wanda Fay to a contemptuous dislike for the Southern poor white, but he would be badly mistaken. Eudora Welty knows the poor white inside out—knows his faults and his lacks, but his virtues too. In her stories and novels she has treated him in all sorts of modes: with considerate understanding as in that beautiful story, "A Piece of News"; with gusto and good humor in *The Ponder Heart*; with a loving admiration for the heroic dignity of the characters whom she depicts in *Losing Battles*. Her intimate knowledge of the way in which the Southern countryman (whether sturdy yeoman or down-at-heels subsistence farmer) thinks and talks—indeed of the very cadences of his speech—bespeaks a fascination with, and a loving attention to, the rural whites of the South. She never degrades and dehumanizes them by reducing them to a stereotype: in Eudora Welty's fiction they are always individuals. Her depiction of the conduct of Fay McKelva—and Fay's conduct is perfectly awful—is not to be taken as a snobbish slap at the Southern poor white. Miss Welty has intimated this point quietly but effectively by bringing into the hospital scene the Dalzells, a sizable clan of poor whites, who have come to wait out the operation of old Mr. Dalzell. The Dalzells are primitive, unlettered, and earthy in their thought and speech, but they are not sleazily cheap; they are not on the make; they have not cut their connections with the land; they are family-minded. Mrs. Dalzell has nothing of the utter self-absorption of Fay.

When the Judge's young widow and his daughter return from the hospital in New Orleans to Mount Salus, Mississippi, with his corpse, we move into—on one level at least—social comedy. We are aware of Laurel's feelings at the funeral, which takes place in the McKelva house, but Miss Welty does not subdue the scene to the tone of Laurel's grief. She expects her reader to attend to the social types and personalities, and there is a considerable human variety among Laurel's own friends.

Major Bullock, the father of one of the bridesmaids at Laurel's wedding, is not very bright, indeed something of a numbskull. Later it becomes plain enough that the Major has been making a number of trips to the sideboard to solace his grief. Mrs. Bullock ("Miss Tennyson") is no numbskull, but she has her eccentricities. So it goes, through a series that includes the Judge's secretary, the Presbyterian minister who is to preach the funeral sermon, his wife, crotchety old Mrs. Pease, and many another friend and, not to be left out of account, the very efficient undertaker with his "Baptist face" (p. 62). To complete the range of social types, there come into the house, at the last minute, and to Laurel's shocked surprise, Fay's family—she had earlier denied having any family left at all—including her mother, brother, sister, her grandfather, old Mr. Chisom, and several children. Fay's nephew, little Wendell, wearing a cowboy suit, is not too much overawed by his first funeral; Wendell can't wait to peer into the face of the corpse lying in the open casket.

Laurel had tried to prevent her father's body being put on display, but her objections are overborne, not merely by Wanda Fay and her unmannerly clan, but, rather disconcertingly, by some of Laurel's own friends. Miss Tennyson protests: "'But honey, your father's a Mount Salus man. He is a McKelva. A public figure. You can't deprive the public, can you? Oh, he's lovely'" (p. 63).

The scene is a set piece of the sort that Miss Welty always does so well, but she has not created the scene simply because she does this sort of thing well, or to exploit regional folk ways; it has its function in the story to be told. The funeral is in the most profound sense a social occasion. A closely knit community is here gathered around the bier of one of its more prominent members, not so much to mourn him as to celebrate—and with genuine affection—his achievements. The community means to do him honor, but as the Judge's friends, talking together before the funeral begins, exchange reminiscences about him, Laurel is shocked to find how many things about her father they have got quite wrong. They have described—apparently in good faith—virtues that she knows he simply never had, and they have failed to mention what she regards as his truly admirable qualities. In spite of the presence of life-long friends and the company of her six bridesmaids, she feels that she is now really alone—driven back upon herself. She even tells herself that the community hadn't deserved her father any more than Fay had deserved him (p. 120).

If Laurel is critical of the community's lack of any deep understanding of her father, this does not mean that she is completely comfortable at dismissing the community's implied censure of her. Though that censure is implied rather than stated, and given jokingly rather than seriously, some of Laurel's friends make it plain that if she had come home after her husband's death and stayed with her father, he would not have fallen a victim to

Wanda Fay. Why, old Mrs. Pease asks, did she, in the first place, have to go away to Chicago and marry a boy from the great world outside? (p. 115). Why, now that her father is dead and her inheritance leaves her well off, does she want to return to her job in Chicago? Why not stay here with her friends? (p. 112).

Yet, though Laurel cannot accept the notion that she was personally responsible for what happened to her father, the question as to why he married Fay obviously troubles her. Fay violates—in her cheapness, her lack of feeling, her hard aggressiveness—every concept of womanly behavior that the Judge reverenced. We, as readers, witnessing Fay's violent behavior—attempting to pull her dying husband out of his hospital bed, and later, hysterically embracing him as he lies in his coffin—are made thoroughly sympathetic with Laurel's bepuzzlement. How could Judge McKelva have chosen this creature for his second wife? Neither the usual explanation offered—a lonely, old man, flattered by youth and what he takes to be beauty—nor the reason given by the Judge's servant: "'He mightily enjoyed having him somebody to spoil'" (p. 59), satisfies the daughter. Not even the more charitable remark by Miss Adele, Laurel's first-grade teacher: "'She gave a lonely old man something to live for'" (p. 116), really explains his choice.

Laurel has been more than shocked and puzzled by her father's strange second marriage: all her feelings about her father and mother and what their married life was have been terribly disturbed. She will not allow herself to ask: Did my father truly love my mother. Instead she says out loud to her friends: "'He loved my mother.'" But in the context of the story, her assertion before the world protests almost too much. We gradually come to understand that Laurel is a far more troubled woman than the opening pages had revealed. The novel thus moves from fairly broad satire and social comedy into Laurel's reexamination of the past. Bereft and alone, her review of her early life becomes urgent and almost compulsive: "In her need . . . Laurel would have been willing to wish her mother and father dragged back to any torment of living . . . . She wanted them with her to share her grief . . ." (p. 150).

Laurel's dark night of the soul is literally that. Miss Welty has very skillfully cleared the stage for her retreat into the past and into herself. The pickup truck from Texas which had brought Fay's family to the funeral is returning to Texas that same evening, and Fay, on impulse, decides to ride back with her family for a short visit, planning to return on the day on which Laurel will leave for Chicago.

With Fay's departure, Laurel has the family house (which now belongs legally to Fay) to herself for the last time. As she wanders through it, she cannot help noticing the little changes in decoration, the tell-tale rearrangements of furniture and objects, that speak of the new wife and of the Judge's closing years. His desk is empty—emptied not only of his legal papers but of all the letters that her mother had written to him. But Laurel soon recalls that the destruction of the letters is not to be attributed to Fay. Her father never had kept her mother's letters; it was his habit to answer *any* letter promptly and drop it into the waste basket. There was nothing in his desk of her mother for Laurel to "retrieve." But her father's letters to her mother have been preserved: Laurel finds them in her mother's little secretary which had been shunted away into the sewing room.

Laurel makes the discovery on the last evening that she is to be in her old home. She has had dinner with friends, and Major Bullock has escorted her home on this rainy night of early spring. Closing the door on the night, she enters the house and finds that a chimney swift—Laurel had acquired an irrational horror of swifts in her childhood—has got down the chimney and is now frantically flying about in the darkened house. She is terrified by the swoops and dartings of the bird, and finally, in desperation, shuts herself away from it in the little sewing room where she had sometimes slept as a child. Here she finds her mother's secretary and the letters that her mother had preserved—presumably all the letters she had received from her husband and from her own mother. Laurel spends the night reading those letters and at last falls asleep in a chair. Next day, with the return of morning light and of the old family servant, Missouri, who had known and loved her mother and father, Laurel manages to capture the bird and release it into the sunshine.

Does the bird merely represent the vague terrors of the night that beset Laurel? Or does the sooty bird, soiling with its meaningless lunges the curtains that Missouri had washed so carefully the day before, betoken the alien presence of Wanda Fay in the house, troubling its old inhabitants, putting a smudge on everything? Or is the bird, so eager to get out of this strange labyrinth into which it has fallen, Laurel herself, trapped in the past that has suddenly become to her strange and problematical? Perhaps all these suggestions apply, yet the author has wisely not directly hinted at any of them. Whatever we want to make of the bird episode, or even if we dismiss from it any symbolic import, we will almost certainly feel that the incident is beautifully placed and answers perfectly to Laurel's emotional situation: her sense of a disturbing element in the house on this gusty night of spring, one that creates in her mind anxieties and vague fears—for what troubles her, of course, is not the literal darkness, but the darkness of her past, which she now realizes she does not understand.

One of the most brilliant aspects of this novel is the way in which Laurel's mother, Becky, is made to rise up as a vivid presence out of her notebooks, school books, recipes, the letters her own mother had written to her from West Virginia, and the letters written to her by her husband. Becky was evidently a tremendously intense person. She was brave, as Laurel believes her father, for all his other virtues, was not. Becky was demanding—perhaps she demanded too much of her loved ones. She was hard on the Judge—in her own special way, as hard on him as Fay. Laurel remembers the last months of her mother's life, her failing eyesight, her pain in her last illness, and her reproaches to her husband. Becky actually called him a coward, presumably because he would not face the tragic possibilities of life, the tragic "irremediable things," as George Santayana has termed them. Judge McKelva, in his more "optimistic" view of the world, could not grant that anything was truly irremediable.

Laurel's commiserative understanding almost extends to Fay herself. At the funeral, Laurel, looking at Wendell as he begins to cry, thinks: "He was like a young, undriven, unfalsifying, unvindictive Fay. So Fay might have appeared, just at the beginning, to her aging father, with his slipping eyesight" (p. 76). And now on this night of self-examination and casting up of accounts, Laurel realizes that "Both times [her father] chose [a wife], he had suffered . . . . He died worn out with both wives . . ." (p. 151). Laurel realizes further that whatever rivalry there was between her mother and Fay, it was not "between the living and the dead, between the old wife and the new; [it was] between too much love and too little" (p. 152).

Laurel is not trying here to justify Fay, but to understand her father and to realize that though her father did love her mother, the relation between them had never been an easy one. How could it have been in view of their polar opposition in outlook? Her mother, for example, had always been passionately attached to her mountain home in West Virginia, and in her last illness, when she mentioned the wild strawberries that she used to gather there, her husband had cried out: "'I'll take you back to your mountains, Becky.'" To which Becky replied: "'Lucifer! Liar!,'" (p. 149-50). And Laurel remembers that in her last illness her mother had irrationally reproached her too: "'You could have saved your mother's life. But you stood by and wouldn't intervene. I despair for you'" (p. 151). After her father's death, Laurel had thought: "I [do] not any longer believe that anyone [can] be saved, anyone at all. Not from others" (p. 144).

Yet in the deeper understanding achieved on this night—even in gaining some comprehension of why her father might have turned to Wanda Fay—Laurel never for a moment comes to doubt the significance and the importance of the relationship that existed between her mother and her father. If there was any element of torment in that relationship, and it is now plain to Laurel that there was, "that torment was something they had known together, through each other" (p. 150). Even when her mother "despaired" of her father and demanded of him "'Why is it necessary to punish me like this and not tell me why?'" she "still . . . held fast to [his hand and] to Laurel's too. Her cry was not complaint: it was anger at wanting to know and being denied knowledge; it was love's deep anger" (p. 148). Such a relation, if full of pain, is nevertheless profoundly human, and therefore infinitely valuable. Laurel has at last come to recognize and accept the relationship between her father and mother, and her numbed heart at last comes to life. "A flood of feeling descended on Laurel. . . . [She] wept in grief for love and for the dead. She lay there with all that was adamant in her yielding to this night, yielding at last. Now all she had found had found her. The deepest spring in her heart had uncovered itself, and it began to flow again" (p. 154). Throughout the first third of the book the reader could scarcely have guessed how badly hurt Laurel had been and how frozen had been her heart. Now, looking back from the vantage point of this crucial moment, all becomes apparent, and many of the earlier events in the novel fall into proper perspective.

This summoning back into vivid life of her parents and their long and, at the very end, difficult relationship, serves to recall Laurel's own brief and, as she remembers it, perfect love affair with her own husband. (He had been killed aboard a naval vessel in the Pacific in the Second World War.) "[Laurel] had gone on living with the old perfection undisturbed and undisturbing. Now, by her own hands, the past had been raised up, and *he* looked at her, Phil himself—here waiting, all the time, Lazarus. He looked at her out of eyes wild with the craving for his unlived life, with mouth open like a funnel's" (p. 154). The revivification of her parents' fulfilled, though sometimes tormented life, makes her realize with new poignance the fact that her own life with Phil was not, and never can be, fulfilled.

> What [she asked herself] would have been their end, then?
> Suppose their marriage had ended like her father and mother's?
> Or like her mother's father and mother's? Like—
> "Laurel! Laurel! Laurel!" Phil's voice cried.
> She wept for what happened to life. (pp. 154-55)

Yet even if Laurel's night of memories and explorations of the inner self ends with the "deepest spring in her heart [having begun] to flow again," Laurel has not yet resolved all her problems, for she is not yet quite done with Fay. Fay returns a little earlier than she had been expected, and there is a final encounter between Judge McKelva's daughter and his second wife.

Earlier on that morning, before Fay had turned up, Laurel had burnt every scrap of her mother's papers—the recipes, including one for "My Best Bread," the school notebooks, the letters written to her by her husband and those written to her by her own mother, Laurel's grandmother—everything, so that the slate is now wiped clean—or almost clean. She can now turn the house over to its legal owner without regret: "There was nothing she was leaving in the whole shining and quiet house now to show for her mother's life and her mother's happiness and suffering, and nothing to show for Fay's harm; her father's turning between them, holding on to them both, then letting them go, was without any sign" (p. 170). But when, looking into a kitchen pantry, she finds the breadboard so lovingly made by Phil for her mother and always kept clean and polished by Becky for her breadmaking—when she finds that board scarred and gouged (Fay had used it to crack black walnuts on)—it is almost too much. She burst out to Fay, "'You desecrated this house'" (p. 173).

At last she puts a question about the scene in the hospital room on the night of her father's death, the question that hitherto she had suppressed. She asks, "'What were you trying to scare Father into—when you struck him?'" Fay's answer is simple and, according to her lights, sufficient: "'I was trying to scare him into living! . . . I wanted him to get up out of there, and start him paying a little attention to *me*, for a change'" (p. 175). Then Laurel tries to tell Fay about the breadboard—why it matters—but none of her explanations can make any impression on this woman. All bread "'tastes alike, don't it?'" Fay asks. And as for Phil's labor of love in making the board for Becky, Fay asks in perfect good conscience: "'What has *he* got to do with it? He's dead, isn't he?'" (p. 177). Fay goes on to tell Laurel that the "'past isn't a thing to me. I belong to the future, didn't you know that?'" (p. 179). Fay's estimate of herself is profoundly true and this, of course, is why she is not fully human. People to whom the past means nothing cannot be fully human. In this matter Fay resembles Faulkner's Flem Snopes and Jason Compson. They all lack the pieties that bind one generation back to another, the loyalties and the imaginative sympathies which affirm that all men are of one race and, further, that the living and the dead are of one race too.[2]

[2]Fay's statement that she belongs to the future has a further significance. Though *The Optimist's Daughter* is not designed to be a tract for the times, it is, nevertheless, a document of our times. Fay represents a human type to which the future may indeed belong: the rootless, finally amoral, individual whose insistence on self-aggrandizement is not countered by any claim of family or clan or country. The true significance of Fay's ethos is not a reflection of a particular class or section; she might just as well have been born in the Bronx or the Bay region of San Francisco.

After her experience of the night before, however, Laurel is at no loss to handle the situation. She is aware that the past is nothing to Fay, but what she says to Fay is: "'I know you aren't anything to the past . . . . You can't do anything to it now'" (p. 179). Nor can Laurel, as she now well knows, do anything to the past either. She does not speak this aloud to Fay, but she does say to herself: "The past is no more open to help or hurt than was Father in his coffin. The past is like him, impervious, and can never be awakened. It is memory that is the somnambulist. It will come back in its wounds from across the world, like Phil, calling us by our names and demanding its rightful tears. It will never be impervious. The memory can be hurt, time and again—but in that may lie its final mercy. As long as it's vulnerable to the living moment, it lives for us, and while it lives, and while we are able, we can give it up its due" (p. 179).

Other writers, of course, have come to this insight. Wordsworth, for example, wrote:

Thanks to the human heart by which we live,
Thanks to its tenderness, its joys, and fears,
To me the meanest flower that blows can give
Thoughts that do often lie too deep for tears.

The discovery is made over and over again, and is dramatized—through flower or breadboard—by each successive writer in his own appropriate fashion.

So Laurel can now put her mother's scarred breadboard "down on the table where it belonged," forgoing the quixotic gesture of taking it along with her. All that she leaves behind—family home, furnishings and all—is impervious to Fay and the future. What for her is precious in it is past any harm that can be done to it by anyone. She is now ready to take her plane back to Chicago and her job.

From *The Mississippi Quarterly* 26 (Fall 1973): 577-87.

"The Freed Hands": The Power of Images in Eudora Welty's *The Optimist's Daughter*

Kim Martin Long

Locating the central image or controlling pattern of Eudora Welty's *The Optimist's Daughter* can prove frustrating because of the complex series of recurring motifs throughout the book. Early in the novel, certain images or patterns begin to appear repeatedly—images of nature, like flowers and birds; references to time and clocks; images of the body, like hands and eyesight; even references to pattern itself. As expected with Eudora Welty's fiction, nothing is without meaning. Reading Welty continually gives readers reason to feel anticipation and even perplexity. Her carefully written fiction with its subtle descriptions and richly connotative language rewards the careful reader. Consequently, finding that connective link between the flowers, the hands, and the clocks enhances the setting, characterization, and plot and even helps unravel more complex issues. Many critics have noticed, not surprisingly, the wealth of imagery in the novel.[1] As Gail Mortimer says in "Image and Myth in Eudora Welty's *The Optimist's Daughter*," Welty "generates a particularly intricate network of meanings in which no single image stands alone, for each is modified by the simultaneous presence of others."[2] Examining these images in more detail provides needed insight into Welty's richly suggestive art and helps us understand more fully Laurel's moment of recognition in the novel when she truly becomes the "optimist's daughter."

Flowers provide one of these repeating elements, not only giving the novel a nice backdrop and enhancing the description of the characters, but also providing a symbol for Laurel's mood. Even her name stands for the state flower of West Virginia, the place of her mother's birth. The novel first mentions her mother, Becky McKelva, in reference to her hearty climbing roses which would "hardly take a setback."[3] In the first few pages, Fay, the judge's new wife, claims the judge's eye injury has been caused by a rose bush scratch. Even this early repetition of roses begins to suggest that the flower references in the novel contribute more than simply elements of the setting. We find out later that part of the judge's problems with his spiritual vision has resulted from his first wife and their relationship; therefore, associating her with roses seems to intensify her continued effect on his present life. Thus, Fay's words take on more meaning: "'He just took a scratch from an old rose briar! He would have got over that, it would all be forgotten now! Nature would have tended to it'" (41).

Other flower images appear in the novel in references to the Hibiscus Hotel; garden descriptions; references to the old Garden Club; Laura being handed a "double-handful of daffodils, the nodding, gray-white kind with the square cup" like those her mother had raised; the description of the camellia on her mother's grave "big as a pony, saddled with unplucked bloom living and dead, standing on a faded carpet of its own flowers" (90); and others. So many casual mentionings of flowers appear in the novel written in Welty's rich language that they at least provide a consistent setting for springtime in the South and at most give clues to a much larger pattern in the novel, related to the relationships among the McKelva family.

Pattern itself serves as a unifying image in *The Optimist's Daughter*. Early in the novel Laurel notices the hospital tile: she "had never noticed the design in the tiling before, like some clue she would need to follow to get to the right place" (31). Indeed, in this hospital lies her father, the man in whom she now finds her identity. Thinking of her past, Laurel remembers sitting on the sewing room floor, putting

> together the fallen scraps of cloth into stars, flowers, birds, people or whatever she liked to call them, lining them up, spacing them out, making them into patterns, . . . with the shine of fire-light, or the summer light, moving over mother and child and what they both were making. (133-4)

As John Desmond observes,

> Throughout her fiction Welty has frequently presented the life struggle in terms of a dynamic, rhythmic battle between order and spontaneity, between the human need to pattern experience and the vital, erupting forces which, for better or worse, shatter the human design.[4]

Memories of Laurel's husband, Phillip Hand, remind her of trying to find a pattern to her existence. Because he was an architect, he had "taught her to draw, to work toward and into her pattern, not to sketch periferies" (161). Like her memories of her mother and her parents' relationship, her memories of her husband also fit nicely into Laurel's patterned existence.

Hands themselves work significantly into the pattern of the novel as they relate to the idea of manipulating a structure or maintaining control. The Judge says at the beginning of *The Optimist's Daughter* that he places himself in Nate's hands, Laurel pays close attention to the hands of the little Chisom boy Wendell, Fay sleeps with her hands clinched tightly in angry fists, and the last words of the novel describe what Laurel sees after her revelation: "The last thing Laurel saw, before they whirled into speed, was the twinkling of their hands, the many small and unknown hands, wishing her good-bye" (180). Other minor allusions to hands, such as Miss Adele's constant use of her hands in communicating with Laurel and the discussion of the pigeons eating out of Laurel's hand "if she'll let them," draw our attention to the importance of hands—personal, creative, and capable of molding things—in the overall theme of the novel. Even the fact that Laurel's vocation involves designing fabrics suggests her desire to make sense out of life, to have its control in her hands. The most obvious reference, however, to hands and patterns occurs in the scene of Laurel's moment of understanding, not unlike a Joycean epiphany when, after Fay and her presence shatters every pattern that Laurel had so carefully guarded, Laurel reaches a conclusion: "Memory lived not in initial possession but in the free hands, pardoned and freed, and in the heart that can empty but fill again, in the patterns restored by dreams" (179). Welty says of her own childhood that the sewing woman who came to her house was a stabilizing influence: "Her hands steadied me like claws as she stumped on her knees around me, tacking me together."[5] The sewing woman, who also talked continuously as she worked, could work with free hands as she weaved her tales, teaching Eudora Welty what it means to listen and then to pass on stories. The hands in the novel likewise represent this kind of possibility: Laurel learns that while they manipulate and limit, they also wave, give, and love.

Time provides another recurrent idea through the novel, with numerous references to clocks and the passage of time. The first question asked by the Judge when he resumes consciousness is "What's the time, Fay?" As Laurel sits in the hospital room, she sees out the window a seagull "hanging with wings fixed, like a stopped clock on a wall." When she wakes after a short nap, "the seagull became the hands on the clock in the courthouse dome lit up in the night above Mount Salus trees" (45). Asleep in her own childhood home after the funeral, Laurel "listened for . . . the striking of the mantle clock downstairs in the parlor. It never came" (58). These early references to time draw the reader's attention to time so that later we are ready for more significant implications of time's importance:

> Laurel looked over their heads to where the chinese prints brought home by an earlier generation of missionary McKelvas hung in their changeless grouping around the mantel clock. And she saw that the clock had stopped; it had not been wound, she supposed, since the last time her father had done duty by it, and its hands pointed to some remote three o'clock, as motionless as the time in the chinese prints. (73)

As Keats' urn does, these pictures perpetually display a changeless past that Laurel desires, and in this scene she wants to find the key and set the clock—that object that gives time a pattern—and remembers her father had "counted the minutes and the hours to make his life go by" (73). Now she stands by his coffin as she had stood beside his hospital bed passing the time with him.

Another reference to time helps to characterize Fay, who lives totally in the present:

> "When you coming back?" asked Major Bullock, swaying a little.
> "When I get ready."
> The clock struck half-past twelve.
> "Oh, how I hate that old striking clock!" cried Fay. "It's the first thing I'm going to get rid of." (100)

Toward the end of the novel, Laurel thinks that "Protection, like self-protection, fell away from her like all one garment, some anachronism foolishly saved from childhood" (161). She comes to some new understandings about her parents' relationship and her relationship to her husband, putting these things into the context of time. She describes her final realization about her mother and Fay, also in terms of time:

> Experience did, finally, get set into its right order, which is not always the order of other people's time . . . . What Becky had felt, and had been afraid of, might have existed right here in the house all the time, for her. Past and future might have changed places, in some convulsion of mind, but that could do nothing to impugn the truth of the heart. Fay could have walked in early as well as late, she could have come at any time at all. She was coming. (174)

Although Welty says that in her own house "we grew up to the striking of clocks," and that "we all of us have been time-minded all our lives,"[6] Laurel ultimately acknowledges that life cannot always fit into a pattern or follow a time schedule, and Laurel must be about the business of living, regardless of the sense she can make out of it all: "The past is no more open to help or hurt than was father in his coffin. The past is like him, impervious, and can never be awakened" (179). Time, on the other hand, is what Welty calls "the continuous thread of revelation"; it remains ever changing and leads to new discovery.[7]

Distorted vision, blindness, the confusion between illusion and reality—these also contribute to the pattern of significant images in the novel. The judge suffers from "dislocated vision" (14-15) caused by a slipped retina. By the end of the book, we suspect the dislocated vision involves more than physical visual impairment, having chosen Fay as a wife, such a different person from his first wife Becky and obviously out of place in the Judge's home with her selfish whining and backward ways.[8] Other characters in the book make incorrect judgments because of their unsuccessful vision. Grandfather Chisom at first thinks Laurel is Fay, giving her the pecans and a big kiss. Laurel herself thinks that Fay's sister is fat, then recognizes that she is pregnant. The fact that Tom Farris, the blind man is described as "so happy" (78) seems to indicate the bliss connected with not seeing, with remaining in a condition of distorted vision. In the scene at the beginning with Laurel in the hospital room, she at first "did not realize she could see the bridge—it stood out there so dull in the distance, its function hardly evident. . . . The river was not visible" (14). Several times in the novel Laurel misinterprets what her eyes tell her. Once again in the hospital room she sees "inside the room's darkness a watery constellation . . . throbbing and near." She then perceives that she is "looking straight out at the whole Mississippi River Bridge in lights" (33). Once Laurel misidentifies the bridge because of its dullness; later she does not recognize it because of its brightness. In either case, she has trouble making a connection between her eyes and her brain. Remembering a train trip with her husband Phil she recalls seeing a beech tree, appearing "to travel along with their train, gliding at a magic speed through the cypress they left behind. It was her own reflection in the windowpane—the beech tree was her head. Now it was gone" (45). Interestingly, once Laurel makes a positive identification of something, she lets it go just as she does in the novel's climax when she makes the connection between her past and her present.

Of all the repeating motifs and devices Eudora Welty uses to bring her character to this reconciliation, none produces an effect as complete as that of the birds. Like the flowers, many times they seem to provide only an element of setting necessary to a story taking place in the spring, such as when red cardinals feed at the feet of the ladies gossiping in the garden. Another time, however, Laurel sees a seagull but thinks of time; the seagull merely serves to help her make a connection to something else. The incessant song of the mockingbirds throughout the scene of the gossiping ladies lends an irony to their judgmental conversation and serves as a reminder of their hypocritical actions. Miss Tennyson Bullock compares Fay to a sparrow, her high-pitched laugh having been described earlier "as derisive as a jay's" (5). At the cemetery the birds suggest the tone of the funeral to Laurel:

> As they proceeded there, black wings threaded in sudden unison, and a flock of birds flew up as they might from a ploughed field, still shaped like it, like an old map that still served new territory, and wrinkled away in the air. (91)

After the funeral, in the "wake of their footsteps, the birds settled again. Down on the ground, they were starlings, all on the waddle, pushing with the yellow bills of spring" (93). Here the birds combine with the idea of distorted vision as Laurel sees one thing before the funeral and another thing afterwards. The trapping of the chimney swift toward the end of the novel, however, does more than add characterization, enhance setting, or reveal tone. Laurel fears the bird with the same irrational terror with which she seems to view her past:

> "It'll get in every room in the house if you let it," Laurel said, controlling herself from putting her hands over her hair.
>
> "It ain't tryin' to get in. Trying to get out," said Mr. Cheek. (165)

Laurel views her past—her parents' relationship as well as her own marriage to Phil—with the same kind of fear, but based on denial. Just as she has tried to lock the bird out of her room, she has tried to lock the truth out of the present. Once the chimney swift is out it looks "small and unbearably flat to the ground, like a child's shoe without a foot inside it" (168); consequently, once she acknowledges the imperfections of her past, they cease to frighten her, just as the image of the beech tree had disappeared once she correctly identified it. Missouri prophetically calls from the porch, "'All birds got to fly, even them no-count dirty ones'" (169). Even the bad memories deserve to be remembered.

The most important and obviously symbolic use of birds involves pigeons, a unifying and revealing image from Laurel's past and present. Based on an incident taken from Welty's own biography, Laurel's grandmother had mistakenly thought Laurel enjoyed feeding the pigeons and even suggested sending her one for her birthday once:

> But Laurel had kept them under her eye in their pigeon house and had already seen a pair of them sticking their beaks down each other's throats, gagging each other, eating out of each other's craws, swallowing down all over again what had been swallowed before: they were taking turns. (140)

Laurel's association of her mother with the pigeons helps her to begin to understand the mutually destructive relationship her mother and father had shared and Laurel's own role in it: she "battled against them both, each for the other's sake . . . " (145). More importantly, however, it is through the images of the pigeons that Laurel reconciles her feelings for her dead husband; when Phil's image comes to her, it is with "his mouth open like a funnel's" (154), suggestive of the pigeons who gag themselves. Had Phil lived, they too might have destroyed each other; however, just as she had not allowed the pigeons to eat from her hand, she does not allow Phil's memory to exact some unwilling emotion: "But Phil was lost. Nothing of their life together remained except in her own memory; love was sealed away into its perfection and had remained there" (154).

One bird image draws several of Welty's themes together. Laurel describes the view of the merging Ohio and Mississippi Rivers on the train trip she had taken with Phil on the way to Mount Salus to be married:

> They were looking down from a great elevation and all they saw was at the point of coming together, the bare trees marching in from the horizon, the rivers moving into one, and as he touched her arm she looked up with him and saw the long, ragged, pencil-faint line of birds within the crystal of the zenith, flying in a V of their own, following the same course down. All they could see was sky, water, birds, light and confluence. It was the whole morning world. (159-160)

Here Laurel sees the birds flying in a V—mirroring the merging of the rivers, symbolizing her union with Phil, at least in her memory. As she later says,

> It is memory that is the somnambulist. It will come back in its wounds from across the world, like Phil, calling us by our names and demanding its rightful tears. It will never be impervious. The memory can be hurt, time and time again—but in that may lie its final mercy. As long as it's vulnerable to the living moment, it lives for us, and while it lives, and while we are able, we can give it up its due. (179)

Laurel finally faces her past squarely and acknowledges that the present controls our memory, which remains malleable and vulnerable. Just as she lets the bird out and witnesses its ineffectiveness, she faces the pain of her past and finds that it cannot hurt her.

Welty brings Laurel to this point of understanding by way of some plot—her father's death, the conflicts with Fay, the encounters at the funeral, the discovery of her mother's desk, and the parting with her past; however, flowers, clocks, patterns, hands, eyes, and birds take us along with her in a way no mere story line ever could. Another Mississippian, William Faulkner, says in *Light in August* that "Memory believes before knowing remembers. Believes longer than recollects, longer than knowing even wonders."[9] Faulkner makes a distinction between the conscious act of remembering and the unconscious and powerful act of the memory, which is beyond our control. As Welty herself put it, "to the memory nothing is ever really lost."[10] She seems in *The Optimist's Daughter* to be drawing on this idea that Laurel's own memory has had her in its control; it has bound her in its pattern and stability. But memory, as Welty shows, is the "somnambulist." It can change. It is "vulnerable to the living moment." As Welty says of her own fiction, "Greater than scene, I came to see, is situation. Greater than situation is implication. Greater than all of these is a single, entire human being, who will never be confined in any frame."[11] Laurel, after the chimney bird escapes and after she lets the bread board down, is ready to let the present shape her memory of her parents and even herself. She has, in fact, learned a little from Fay, the child of the future. Laurel is ready now to go back to her present life, waving good-bye to all the little hands of Miss Adele's children.

Welty herself says that the true subject in all her work is human relationships, that an important part of her stories is "vision, dream, illusion, hallucination, obsession, and that most wonderful interior vision which is memory."[12] In *The Optimist's Daughter*, she brings many of these elements together in the character and interior journey of Laurel Hand. Despite all the critics' efforts to unify satisfactorily the images of the novel, they ultimately refuse to fit perfectly into any one scheme just as Laurel's memories resist her control but continue to exist independent of her will. Welty says in *One Writer's Beginnings* that it

> is our inward journey that leads us through time—toward or back, seldom in a straight line, most often spiraling. Each of us moving, changing, with respect to others. As we discover, we remember; remembering, we discover; and most intensely do we experience this when our separate journeys converge. Our living experience at those meeting points is one of the charged dramatic fields of fiction. (102)

She then speaks of one her favorite words, *confluence*, which Welty claims "exists as a reality and symbol in one," and quotes from the last pages of *The Optimist's Daughter* where Laurel remembers the train trip with Phil:

> And they themselves were part of the confluence. Their own joint act of faith had brought them here at the very moment and matched its occurrence, and proceeded as it proceeded. Direction itself was made beautiful, momentous. . . . Left bodiless and graveless of a death made of water and fire in a year long gone, Phil could still tell her of her life. For her life, any life, she had to believe, was nothing but the continuity of its love.

She believed it just as she believed that the confluence of the waters was still happening at Cairo. . . .

Welty comments on the passage, explaining that

Of course the greatest confluence of all is that which makes up the human memory—the individual human memory. . . . The memory is a living thing—it too is in transit. But during its moment, all that is remembered joins, and lives—the old and the young, the past and the present, the living and the dead.[13]

Since memory comes in images, in *The Optimist's Daughter* Welty chronicles the living memory of Laurel Hand, using the effective images of both nature (flowers and birds) and man (clocks and patterns), using the images of vision and memory to bring them together in the confluence of her imagination.

All the image motifs of the book—birds, clocks, flowers, hands, patterns, water, vision—contribute to this journey of the soul captured in *The Optimist's Daughter*. As Gail Mortimer says, "our imaginations roam among the network of meanings implied by [Welty's] linked motifs" (627). The clocks and the hands represent the constricting power of the past. The birds and the flowers, contrasting these images, show that memory can continue to live and change. Vision can be distorted by our focusing on the wrong things. The patterns can provide stability or sterility, depending into whose hands they are entrusted. All the images in this novel converge and separate in Laurel's memory and cause her moment of understanding and reconciliation. After being her mother's, the pessimist's, daughter throughout the book by refusing to allow the present to take the place of the past, Laurel finally becomes the title character in this last scene, allowing the images to form a new pattern in her imagination, one of hope and renewal: "She waved. So did the children. The last thing Laurel saw, before they whirled into speed, was the twinkling of their hands, the many small and unknown hands, wishing her goodbye" (180).

NOTES

[1]In "Image and Myth in Eudora Welty's *The Optimist's Daughter*," Mortimer cites numerous critics who have dealt in some way with the images in the novel. Among those she mentions are Marilyn Arnold, "Images of Memory in Eudora Welty's *The Optimist's Daughter*," *Southern Literary Journal* 14 (Spring 1982): 28-38; John F. Desmond, *Still Moment: Essays on the Art of Eudora Welty*, Metuchen, NJ: Scarecrow P, 1978; Reynolds Price, "The Onlooker Smiling: An Early Reading of *The Optimist's Daughter*," from *Eudora Welty*, Ed. Harold Bloom, Modern Critical Views, (New York: Chelsea House, 1986), 75-88; and William Jay Smith, "Precision and Reticence: Eudora Welty's Poetic Vision," from *Eudora Welty: A Form of Thanks*, Ed. Louis Dollarhide and Ann J. Abadie, (Jackson: UP of Mississippi, 1979), 78-94. Mortimer states that while all these works touch in some way upon the images and patterns in the novel, none makes the images fit together in a satisfactory way. In Mortimer's own essay she attempts to give the

images a unity related to myth and word etymologies; while convincing in some places, the essay, in this writer's opinion, fails to do what the others likewise fail to do.

[2]Mortimer 618.

[3]*The Optimist's Daughter* by Eudora Welty, (New York: Random House, 1972), 5. Subsequent references to this edition will appear in the text.

[4]See John Desmond, "Pattern and Vision in Eudora Welty's *The Optimist's Daughter*," from *A Still Moment: Essays on the Art of Eudora Welty*, Ed. John Desmond, (Metuchen, NJ: Scarecrow P, 1979), 118.

[5]*One Writer's Beginnings* by Eudora Welty (Cambridge: Harvard UP, 1984), 14.

[6]*One Writer's Beginnings*, 3.

[7]*One Writer's Beginnings*, 69.

[8]Gail Mortimer notices that while Fay may serve as a "foil for the passivity and apparent aloofness of Laurel in the early parts of the novel," her "persistent self-centeredness and insensitivity make a favorable reading of her difficult to sustain." 619n.

[9]William Faulkner, *Light in August*, (New York: Random House/Vintage Books, 1972), 111.

[10]*One Writer's Beginnings*, 90.

[11]*One Writer's Beginnings*, 90.

[12]*One Writer's Beginnings*, 89.

[13]Quoted from *One Writer's Beginnings*, 103-04.

WORKS CITED

Desmond, John F. "Pattern and Vision in *The Optimist's Daughter*." *A Still Moment: Essays on the Art of Eudora Welty*. Ed. John Desmond. Metuchen, NJ: The Scarecrow Press, 1978. 118-38.

Faulkner, William. *Light in August*. New York: Random House/Vintage Books, 1972.

Mortimer, Gail. "Image and Myth in Eudora Welty's *The Optimist's Daughter*." *American Literature* 62 (December 1990): 617-33.

Welty, Eudora. *One Writer's Beginnings*. Cambridge: Harvard UP, 1984.

____. *The Optimist's Daughter*. New York: Random House, 1972.

General Criticism 1972-1979

Eudora Welty and the Use of Place in Southern Fiction

Elmo Howell

In an essay published in the *South Atlantic Quarterly* in 1956, Eudora Welty declared that place in fiction is just as important as character and plot. This statement, a few generations ago, would have been meaningless, since no novelist would have thought of telling a story without reference to location. But with the general uprooting of life in the village and on the farm and with a growing subjectivity in art where characters in fiction are more likely to talk than act, Miss Welty's statement comes as a wholesome reminder of an elemental fact. Southern writers, however, have never been deficient in this respect, even the most modern ones. If anything, they have suffered from too much place. The peculiar history of the South has made the Southerner place-conscious—he may like it or dislike it, but he can seldom leave it alone—so that with him place becomes almost an extra dimension and sometimes to the disadvantage of his art. The great writers have taken it for granted, or almost done so, like Mark Twain and William Faulkner and at best, I think, Miss Welty.

Like many of her generation, Eudora Welty learned from Faulkner the advantage of hanging on to what is near and familiar. She is more deliberate than Faulkner in her use of the regionally distinct and perhaps lays a greater burden on the reader from the outside; but with her devotion to the small and inconsequential in daily life, she is in some respects even closer to the heartbeat of her region, in a sense, his feminine counterpart. Faulkner is concerned with men and ideas and the course of history; she is most at home in a domestic situation where people talk about seemingly unimportant things, while at the same time revealing a whole pattern of life. As soon as man stopped wandering around and stood still in a particular place, she says, "he found a god in that place; and from then on that was where the god abided and spoke from."[1]

Miss Welty's "god" speaks from Mississippi, in a clear, unabashed accent. She is proud of him, as almost any page of her work will show. At the end of *Delta Wedding*, the mistress of a plantation has a casual conversation with the gardener:

> "Now those dahlias can just come up out of there," she said, pausing again. "They have no reason for being in there at all, that I can see . . ." She wanted to separate the bulbs again too, and spread the Roman hyacinths out a little under the trees—they grew so thick now they could hardly bloom last spring. "Howard, don't you think breath-of-spring leans over too much to look pretty?"
>
> "Yes, *ma'am.*"
>
> "Howard, look at my roses! Oh, what all you'll have to do to them."
>
> "I wish there wasn't no such thing as roses," said Howard. "If I had my way, wouldn't be a rose in de world. Catch your shirt and stick you and prick you and grab you. Got thorns."
>
> "Why, Howard. You hush!" Ellen looked back over her shoulder at him for a minute, indignant. "You don't want any roses in the world?"
>
> "Wish dey was out of de world, Miss Ellen," said Howard persistently.
>
> "Well, just hush, then."[2]

The scene serves no purpose except to show, in the wake of the wedding with all its bustle, how the garden has been neglected. To some readers it might suggest racial tension, though Miss Welty has nothing of the sort in mind. "You hush" is only a teasing rebuke of the boy, who sets out first to tease his mistress by saying an outlandish thing about her favorite flower. In spite of the surface discord (to the eye perhaps but not to the ear—Miss Welty's soft intonations give up their full meaning only when her speech is heard), the scene suggests only mutual love. It is racial only incidentally. The lady protests, only in half earnest, against male indifference to beauty, while Howard rebukes her, in an accepted way, for feminine extravagance, at the same time he takes pleasure in serving her. Their conversation is simple, even banal—until it suddenly comes alive with intimations of a whole culture.

[1]Eudora Welty, "Place in Fiction," *South Atlantic Quarterly*, 55 (January 1956), 63. (Subsequent references to this work will appear in the text in parenthesis.)

[2]Eudora Welty, *Delta Wedding* (New York: Harcourt, Brace & Co., 1946), p. 226.

II

Eudora Welty is completely at home with her material, which only occasionally reaches beyond the country of her birth. There are novelists, however, who write about place for its own sake, to give a surface excitement to what Miss Welty calls "the Isle of Capri novel." The South has had more than its share of this type, not only the literary "drifters" who specialize in out-of-the-way places, but native writers who suddenly realize the marketability of the home material. In some cases, writers of small talent make a reputation by presenting their region in a light favorable to the national audience at a particular time, without strict regard to accuracy; but even the most scrupulous are tempted by a popular vogue to introduce place when it is quite irrelevant. Place to the Southern writer in particular can be a curse as well as a blessing and the way he uses it a true measure of his stature as an artist.

Miss Welty writes out of what she calls "saturation of place," by which she means not only the outward visible country of her origin but the ways of thinking and feeling that lie too deep for the casual observer. For place has its own freemasonry, which puts the outsider at a disadvantage; he is never quite sure of the signals, in spite of research or even long residence, unless that residence means putting down roots. Marjorie Kinnan Rawlings lived for more than twenty years in north Florida and wrote entertaining stories about the local people without ever fully understanding them. Once she tried to hire an old man "in the uncivilized Cracker interior" to accompany her and her guests on a Sunday fishing trip. He refused the offer. "I don't fish on Sundays. . . . I wa'n't raised up that-a-way."[3] She was amused at what she considered the old man's pious cant, since he made his living in illegal trapping and bootleg liquor. Actually, what she had struck was a deep vein of piety. In the old Cracker's county, Sabbath observance is a cultural pattern based on divine law, which has nothing to do with man's law. "Fishing?" cries an old colored nurse in William Faulkner's last novel. "On Sunday? If his paw could hear that. . . ."[4]

But Southern writers born and bred have written falsely about their region. In the generation following the Civil War, Joel Chandler Harris, Thomas Nelson Page, and a score of lady novelists built up the romantic legend of the Old South, in part at least to correct the version publicized by Mrs. Stowe. Their own people loved it, and now that the war was over and slavery a dead issue, the North was willing to relax and weep a little over

[3]Marjorie Kinnan Rawlings, "Cracker Chidlings," *Scribner's Magazine*, 89 (February 1931), 133.
[4]William Faulkner, *The Reivers* (New York: Random House, 1962), p. 63.

"Marse Chan." as Henry Ward Beecher, the celebrated ex-Abolitionist brother of Mrs. Stowe, is supposed to have done. By the turn of the century, Ellen Glasgow, a young Virginia novelist, declared that the Southern novel was not in a state of health and that she was going to do something about it by writing "of the harsher realities beneath . . . the romantic nostalgia of the present."[5] She was no revolutionary, however, like her contemporary George Washington Cable of Louisiana, who moved North and campaigned against the traditional South on the platform as well as in the press. She stayed at home, wrote twenty novels, and lived on into the generation of Faulkner and Erskine Caldwell, whose crass realism she was never able to understand, even though she prepared the way for it. After all, she was a genteel lady herself, who never dreamt that her mild irony would devolve in other hands into a lurid exploitation to satisfy a vulgar audience, most of it beyond the South. *Sanctuary*, says Faulkner in his celebrated preface, was "a cheap idea, deliberately conceived to make money." It is more than that, of course; but after publishing some of his best work, including *The Sound and the Fury*, with little public notice, he decided to apply the Southern formula which never fails—decadence, perversion, and an all-important lynching. Thus *Sanctuary* (in surface appeal at least), along with the best sellers of Erskine Caldwell, is an escape novel like the romantic fiction of the nineteenth century, in that it is based on a distortion of reality. Nobody reads Page today nor even Uncle Remus, at least in the original, but much of the fiction that has come out of the South in the last generation coursing with the blood and irony that Miss Glasgow sponsored is marred in the same way. It lacks fidelity to place.

Whatever artificial formula Faulkner applied to fiction, at the actual moment of creation he gave himself wholly and honestly to it. *Sanctuary*, along with *Sartoris*, the first of the Mississippi novels, is one of the richest in delineating the Yoknapatawpha landscape on which the best of his work is based. He is, says Miss Welty, "the triumphant example in America today of the mastery of place in fiction" (p. 66). How different is the world of Caldwell, who came on the scene about the same time as Faulkner with, superficially at least, the same raw interest in Southern life. *Tobacco Road* and *As I Lay Dying* are about the agricultural morons of Georgia and Mississippi—gross, funny, and improbable; yet such is the devotion of Faulkner to place that his Bundrens have the immediacy of life. It is all a matter of commitment. Caldwell's approach is cerebral; his intention is to show humanity in a brutalized condition as the result of the prevailing social order. "Caldwell has learned to hate," says Deming Brown in his study of

[5]Ellen Glasgow, *The Woman Within* (New York: Harcourt, Brace, 1954), p. 98.

Soviet attitudes towards American authors, and "he knows *what* he hates: the rapacious capitalistic system."[6] With no interest in place beyond the needs of thesis, he is not always dependable as a reporter. "He says things which are not so," says Caroline Gordon. In one scene, she points out, he has hound dogs in a well, while men sit around talking and not trying to get them out. "That just couldn't happen. Simply couldn't happen. You can't trust him on detail."[7]

Faulkner's Bundrens are more than a phenomenon to be eradicated by social planning. Shut off on their wretched hill farms in the backwash of Southern history, they gaze out on the world with tragic and sometimes comic futility, suggestive of the South in the aftermath of war and Reconstruction.

> Slow as sheep they moved, tranquil, impassable, filling the passages, contemplating the fretful hurrying of those in urban shirts and collars with the large, mild inscrutability of cattle or of gods, functioning outside of time, having left time lying upon the slow and imponderable land green with corn and cotton in the yellow afternoon.[8]

Young novelists have turned up all across the South trying to write like Faulkner and sometimes succeeding, at least in the surface excitement of their prose. Faulkner once admonished a young, fellow Mississippian, Shelby Foote, to strive less to be like Faulkner and more like himself.[9] Mr. Foote, a distinguished historian as well as novelist, turned out four books in quick succession from 1948 to 1952, in which he attempts to create in the Mississippi Delta the counterpart of Yoknapatawpha county. Bristol in Jordan County is the home of a planter aristocracy, while poor whites live in Issawamba County to the south, roughly paralleling Faulkner's Jefferson and Frenchman's Bend. Mr. Foote must have had a map and genealogical charts beside him as he wrote; the knowledge of his country, where his family has lived for generations, he carried in his head. It was a good start, but even Mr. Foote's superb talent could not bring it off. He bet everything on place, as Faulkner did, but without reckoning the importance of his attitude towards it. For the most part, he is clinically fair and only occasionally reveals an animus against the sentimentalists. "I used to plan to climb that shaft someday," says one of his characters concerning the

[6] Deming Brown, *Soviet Attitudes Toward American Writing* (Princeton University Press, 1962), p. 123.

[7] *Recent Southern Fiction: A Panel Discussion*, Wesleyan College, October 28, 1960 (Macon, Ga.: Wesleyan College, 1960), p. 6.

[8] William Faulkner, *Sanctuary* (New York: J. Cape & H. Smith, 1931), p. 132.

[9] *Faulkner in the University*, ed. Frederick L. Gwynn and Joseph L. Blotner (Charlottesville: University of Virginia, 1959), p. 50.

Confederate monument, "just to whisper in his ear he'd lost the war."[10] His Civil War stories *Shiloh* and "Pillar of Fire" are as empty of partisan feeling as Stephen Crane's *The Red Badge of Courage*, a work he much admired. But this is not enough. "The exactness and concreteness and solidity of the real world achieved in a story," says Miss Welty, "correspond to the intensity of feeling in the author's mind and to the very turn of his heart" (p. 67). Foote set for himself the difficult task of exploiting place while disclaiming all attachment to it.

Many Southern writers since the 1920s, perhaps a majority of them, have been led into what Robert Drake calls "deracination from home country and heart territory." Writing of Carson McCullers, he says she left her native Georgia only to fall among "the thieves and vultures of the New York literary salon scene," where the stereotyped Southern fare never fails.[11] Her last novel is little else: race, sexual perversion, and a harebrained scheme to revitalize Confederate money. Tennessee Williams has used the same formula on the stage, while Hollywood carries it on with a mock drawl that turns on millions in a formulated response. The young novelist can hardly resist. It is too simple and the rewards are too great. Put money in thy purse, the very times cry out, as if it were a moral injunction. Miss Welty has made her position clear concerning social reform: that is not the artist's territory. "The zeal to reform . . . has never done fiction much good. . . . There is absolutely everything in great fiction but a clear answer." Whatever his view, if the artist crusades he is bound to narrow his vision. The large perspective gives way to the short one, in which place is a mere pawn in the game.[12]

III

Flannery O'Connor once remarked that writers like herself who were stuck with the South had a very good thing to be stuck with. That has been a general opinion in the last generation, since Faulkner in particular; but awareness of place does not contribute to its wholesome use in fiction. *Pilgrim's Progress* is rich in the details of peasant life in a Midland county of seventeenth-century England, which John Bunyan employs without the least deliberation. Since this was the only country he knew, he was unaware of the treasure he possessed or of the part it played in projecting his spiritual

[10]Shelby Foote, *Follow Me Down* (New York: Dial Press, 1950), p. 53.

[11]Robert Drake, "The Lonely Heart of Carson McCullers," *Christian Century*, 85 (January 10, 1968), 51.

[12]Eudora Welty, "Must the Novelist Crusade?" *Atlantic Monthly*, 216 (October 1965), 105.

vision. The Southern writer of the twentieth century is not so innocent and all too often brings in the local matter when it has no business in his story.

Even Miss Welty sometimes seems too conscious of the theory she has formulated concerning place and too intent on being a Mississippian. With so much wealth of folk material lying about her, she sometimes goes too far and drowns her story in folksiness, as she does in her most recent novel, *Losing Battles*. One comes away from the Beecham family reunion with the feeling that Miss Welty set out not to write a novel about a particular family so much as to communicate the texture of life in the hill country of North Mississippi. This, of course, she does superbly, but she is more fortunate when with a single stroke, a gesture or turn of phrase, she sums up the life of her people in the process of narration. In "A Worn Path," an old Negro woman stops a white woman on the streets of Natchez and asks her to tie her shoe. The white woman lays down her Christmas bundles on the pavement and ties the old woman's shoe, an act which says a great deal about race relations in a particular time and place. To the casual observer, the scene is startling. Mr. John Edward Hardy says the white woman is too proud to refuse the request and that the Negro has learned how "to take subtle revenge" on white people by exploiting their pride in this way.[13] Miss Welty does not see her region in such divisive terms. Both women know what is their due and their responsibility from a long contractual relationship of the two races, even though they have never seen each other before. In isolation, the scene is meaningless, grotesque. In the context of place, it takes on the quality of poetry.

"The family of Dashwood had been long settled in Sussex": from this first sentence, Jane Austen's novel is so comfortably fixed that, to paraphrase Miss Welty, the idea of lifting it from the English countryside brings rude havoc to the mind. The Southern writer, however, has a problem that Jane Austen did not have in that the abortive history of his country places on him the burden of self-consciousness. He may go too far in identification with place, in the belief that his region has a special value in the fictional market. But at least he has solid ground to stand on. He writes from a land whose natural aspect as well as its history and social forms strike him in a vivid, almost tactile way. If he loves it, as Miss Welty does, his fidelity to place can add an important dimension to his art. It is the writer's duty, she says, "not to disown any part of our heritage," but to accept it all as uniquely our own and to build on and use it (p. 72).

[13]John Edward Hardy, "Eudora Welty's Negroes," *Images of the Negro in American Literature*, ed. Seymour L. Gross and John Edward Hardy (Chicago: University of Chicago Press, 1966), pp. 227-28.

From *Arizona Quarterly* 28 (Autumn 1972): 248-56.

Eudora Welty: The Three Moments

John A. Allen

The characters in Eudora Welty's fiction are fortunate indeed, for they are conceived in kindness, justice and compassion by the imagination that creates them. In Miss Welty's work, the strong and the weak, the magnanimous and the mean alike, in every circumstance retain their human dignity. "I don't have an ounce of revenge in my body," Edna Earle Ponder assures her auditor, and the words may aptly be applied to the author of "The Ponder Heart." The reader, too, enjoys Miss Welty's even-handed bounty. On every page she tacitly gives him credit for being adequately prepared to face the shock of truth, sufficiently enamored of the real to relish its unexpected faces, rational enough to know that reason yields in the end to mystery. Her view of life is not idealized, nor is it tough in the sense of denying mortal existence its proper and inalienable graces. We are safe, in reading a Welty novel, from being dinned at, scolded, hoodwinked, lectured, flattered or condescended to. Secure from malice, anger or contempt, we enjoy a vision of the world depicted with an objectivity which is enriched by warmth and charity. If Eudora Welty has a bias, it springs from affection for the human race.

Three of Miss Welty's novels—"Delta Wedding," "The Ponder Heart" and "The Optimist's Daughter"—unfold through the consciousness of female characters. And these women are also fair-minded and humane. Of course, they present a feminine point of view; but this, in Miss Welty's work, is a matter of perspective which does not involve distortion. For Eudora Welty, showing the action of a novel through a woman's eyes is not an act of aggression but of illumination.

To be sure, Miss Welty delights her readers with the heroic antics of certain male characters: Uncle Daniel, Mike Fink, Jamie Lockhart, Jack Renfro, Curly Stovall, Major Bullock. However, as we will try to show, the suggestion here is not that male heroes are inherently ridiculous but that these characters are not, at least initially, true heroes at all. Criteria for genuine heroism as Miss Welty sees it can be found obliquely conveyed throughout her fiction. The work of demolition—to call it that—which she performs upon the conventional image of the male hero has the effect not of attacking the male sex and its image of itself but of clearing the way for a conception of heroic action which does fuller justice to the actual potentialities for heroism in men and women alike.

II

The tendency of Eudora Welty's fiction is indeed antiheroic; that is, it makes legitimate fun of the posturing male hero-adventurer whose main objective, to paraphrase Uncle Curtis in "Losing Battles," is to butt the world like a billy goat and make it pay him heed. An appropriate emblem of this species of hero is the Perseus of Greek myth; appropriate, that is, when Perseus' heroics are taken at face value: he averts his eyes, swings the magic sword, and lo!, with upraised arm he displays his trophy—the snaky severed head of the Medusa. Thereafter, he can use the Medusa-power as his own, striking his pose again and again with the gory trophy held on high to turn his enemies to stone.

A survey of Miss Welty's heroes shows at once that their achievements in the public eye bear only a marginal resemblance to those of conquering Perseus. George Fairchild, as Ellen Fairchild correctly observes, is not "a challenger, a proud defier," although his family does conspire to place him in that false position. On the other hand, Jack Renfro, loser of battles, egged on by his adoring family, challenges and defies to such disastrous effect that his father, surveying the damages, can only say in wonder, "You couldn't bring something like that to pass just by trying." The most flamboyant vaunting hero is the legendary Mike Fink of "The Robber Bridegroom." He drinks and brawls superbly but finds himself demoted from king of the river boats to carrier of the territorial mails. He has been put down with shocking ease by brainy Jamie Lockhart, a bandit who also takes his lumps before he settles down with charming Rosamond to fatherhood and domesticity.

The female hero in Miss Welty's fiction may not be recognized at all as such by the unwary reader. Rosamond regularly faints in critical moments. Ellen Fairchild, from the outside, is simply a preoccupied mother of eight. And when Laurel McKelva in "The Optimist's Daughter" raises a weapon over her adversary's head, she does not complete the blow but arrests it in mid-air. Even that most staunch and pertinacious of heroes, Miss Julia Mortimer of "Losing Battles," proves no match for her particular dragon;

and Miss Beulah Renfro says of her with some justice, "Taking over more'n her territory, that was her downfall."

III

The interpretation of the Perseus myth in "The Golden Apples" is put forward by Miss Welty through the thoughts of that book's hero, Virgie Rainey. She appears in "June Recital" as by far the most talented piano pupil of Miss Lotte Elisabeth Eckhart; then we lose sight of her for 25 years before, on the occasion of her mother's death, she re-enters the story in "The Wanderers." On the morning after the funeral, Virgie has pulled up stakes and is about to leave Morgana for good. She is sitting on the stile in front of the courthouse in MacLain, enjoying the light rain and the solitude. Her thoughts turn back to Miss Eckhart and to a picture that had hung on one of her walls—Perseus with the head of Medusa. "The vaunting was what she remembered, that uplifted arm." Yet it is not the image of the hero triumphant that has become a permanent part of her mind but the stroke of the sword he wielded. "Cutting off the Medusa's head," she thinks,

> was the heroic act, perhaps, that made visible a horror in life, that was at once the horror in love . . .—the separateness.

The stroke of Perseus is not, in itself, a triumph of any kind. So far from ridding the world of a horror, it reveals one. It is not an act of liberation, not even an assertion of the sovereign will. The important thing, for Virgie, is not what Perseus has done to Medusa; it is what the deed, like a stroke of fate, has done to him.

The hero Virgie has in mind is not Perseus alone but a composite being, Perseus-Medusa, seen as one. Identification of the hero with the victim is essential to this conception of the heroic act:

> Because Virgie saw things in their time, like hearing them—and perhaps because she must believe in the Medusa equally with Perseus—she saw the stroke of the sword in three moments, not one.

Realizing long after the fact that Miss Eckhart has taught her far more than how to play the piano, Virgie recalls the teacher herself as both hero and victim. All of Miss Welty's teachers, and above all Miss Julia Mortimer, play this double role. Gloria Renfro remembers Miss Julia's saying, "If it's going to be a case of Saint George and the Dragon, I might as well battle it left, right, front, back, center and sideways." As Gloria points out, "She was Saint George. . . . And Ignorance was the dragon." Unhappily, the dragon weathers this contest better than Saint George. Virgie's Miss Eckhart, isolated from the beginning in Morgana by her foreign origin and ways, had also fought a losing battle and had also died in misery. She had seemed to fail even with Virgie, who had done no more with her talent than play background music at the Morgana picture show, who thought she hated Miss Eckhart and had refused to greet the mad old lady when they met for the last time on the streets of Morgana. Now we discover that

> Miss Eckhart, whom Virgie had not, after all, hated— . . . , for she had taken Miss Eckhart's hate, and then her love, extracted them, the thorn and then the overflow—had hung the picture [of Perseus] on the wall for herself. She had absorbed the hero and the victim and then, stoutly, could sit down to the piano with all Beethoven ahead of her.

In the first moment of the heroic stroke, the hero wields the sword; in the second moment, he becomes the victim of that stroke. In the third moment, he achieves some measure of gain in understanding which leads on to self-renewal. Having herself "absorbed the hero and the victim," Virgie had been able to accept Miss Eckhart's gift of Beethoven—not Miss Eckhart's Beethoven but her own.

As hero, Virgie has seen the horror in life and love, vicariously through Miss Eckhart and her mother's life and death. She herself has felt the separateness which can cripple and kill, and it has not destroyed her. On the evening of her mother's death, "alone, untouched now, she felt like dancing; knowing herself not really, in her essence, yet hurt; and thus happy."

Although, in the eyes of the world, Virgie Rainey has achieved nothing noteworthy, she is, in her context in "The Golden Apples," a type of the true hero. Her heroism does not derive from what is usually thought of as heroic action but from her capacity to feel and, through feeling, to know. Like a virgin goddess, an Artemis, she is self-sufficient and inviolable. The harmonious accord which she has reached exists between herself and natural things—the Big Black River, the moon—and within herself, where the eternal pair of mother and daughter, woman and child, continues to exist in peaceful oneness. Mother and daughter are the complementary elements of a whole feminine personality, a whole self. This is beautifully suggested by Miss Welty in the waking vision which comes to Virgie late at night after her mother's funeral:

> She knew that now at the river, where she had been before on moonlit nights in autumn, drunken and sleepless, mist lay on the water and filled the trees, and from the eyes to the moon would be a cone, a long silent horn, of white light. It was a connection, visible as the hair is in air, between the self and the moon, to make the self feel the child, a daughter far, far back.

Virgie's uniqueness, the child in herself as the source of her renewal, is sometimes lost for a while, but it will always be returned. The mother, mistress of the cycles of natural things in time, will include her always, wherever and for however long she may remain a wanderer.

IV

"Delta Wedding" provides us with the counterpart of Virgie Rainey, a type of the male hero. The subject of heroism is explored and developed in fugue-like fashion in almost every corner of the book, in relation to every major character and even some of the minor ones. The main focus, however, is upon George Fairchild and Ellen Fairchild, his sister-in-law. The two characters are closely interrelated because there is a bond of feeling between them and because we see George mainly through the eyes and thoughts of Ellen.

The emblematic heroic act which is recalled and recounted again and again in "Delta Wedding" concerns George as hero. The essentials of the incident are these: a group of Fairchilds find themselves on a railway trestle when the train, the Yellow Dog, approaches them. All but two of the group quickly jump to safety from the trestle to the dry creek bed below. But Maureen, a child of nine who is mentally afflicted, has caught her shoe on the track and George is still trying to free her as the train bears down. At the last possible moment, Mr. Doolittle, the train's engineer, brings the train to a stop; and, by this simple miracle of fact, potential tragedy becomes the subject of anecdote, a tale to be told as one more bizarre incident in the Fairchild family history.

Throughout "Delta Wedding" it is George Fairchild who serves to set off in the mind of the other characters reflections upon the association of feeling with knowing, and of both of these with acute perception of the outside world. For example, the thoughts of Shelley, the eldest Fairchild daughter, turn at one point on her memory of a tiny incident at a picnic, when a butterfly crossed the gaze of her Uncle George:

> She had then known something he knew all along, it seemed then—that when you felt, touched, heard, looked at things in the world, and found their fragrances, they themselves made a sort of house within you, which filled with life to hold them, filled with knowledge all by itself, and all else, the other ways to know, seemed calculation and tyranny.

It is because George possesses the faculty which Shelley describes and because his very presence inspires in others the recognition and exercise of that faculty in themselves that one can say he is, so to speak, a full-time hero of the sort which Miss Welty celebrates.

In the mind of Ellen Fairchild, toward the end of "Delta Wedding," George's intensity of feeling is brought together with his public heroic act on the railway trestle. At that moment the heroic act emerges clearly as an occasion when a quality of life in an individual meets and responds to a challenge from fate. Ellen notices the disparity between the way in which she is coming to perceive the meaning of the trestle incident and the meaning of it for others in the Fairchild family:

> . . . the family would forever see the stopping of the Yellow Dog . . . as a preposterous diversion of their walk . . . , for with the fatal chance removed the serious went with it forever, and only the romantic and absurd abided. They would have nothing of the heroic, or the tragic now, thought Ellen, as though now she yielded up a heart's treasure.

Here we have a valuable clue to the heart's treasure of Miss Welty's fiction itself: the combination, in a kind of double vision, of surface events which are preposterous, romantic and absurd with the inner perception and effect of those events, which emerges as the essence of what is tragic and heroic in human life.

George, Ellen goes on to reflect, "saw death on its way, if [the others] did not." Like the bird in the house in both "Delta Wedding" and "The Optimist's Daughter," like Laura McRaven whose loss of her mother makes her, for the Fairchilds, "Insistently a little messenger or reminder of death," the Yellow dog superimposes death on heedless and self-regarding life and sets the stage for the moment of heroism. Seeking in her mind the true nature of George's heroism, Ellen finds that it springs from "a quality of his heart's intensity and his mind's." George regarded some things,

> just things, in the outside world—with a passion which held him so still that it resembled indifference . . . But . . . shock, physical danger . . . roused something in him that was immense contemplation, motionless pity, indifference.

The heroic moment for George, as for other Welty characters, combines vaunting—"I'm damned if I wasn't going to stand on that track if I wanted to!"—with acceptance of danger, the threat of change and its necessity. Further, it combines both of these things, paradoxically, with the capacity for strength in love. "He was capable," Ellen thought,

> —taking no more prerogative than a kind of grace . . .—of meeting a fate whose dealing out to him he would not contest . . . And . . . the darker instinct of a woman was satisfied that he was capable of the same kind of love. . . .

George carries within himself the reconciliation of life and death, of indifference and passion, which is the essence of the third moment of the heroic act and which sums in itself Virgie Rainey's understanding of the stroke of Perseus.

V

The emphasis, in Miss Welty's conception of the hero, upon feeling and knowing applies to male and female alike. However, this kind of experience seems to come more easily to women than to men. Unlike George Fairchild as Ellen sees him, male heroes on the conventional Perseus model are likely to be preoccupied, up to a point, with a reckless reliance on physical force like that of Jack Renfro's unfortunate father, Ralph, who cripples himself with dynamite just before his marriage to Miss Beulah and, some 20 years later, still looks to dynamite for the solution to hard problems:

> "He'll shortly blow up something else. He won't learn, he's a man," said Miss Lexie.
>
> "Yes sir, your touch is pure destruction!" Miss Beulah told him.

Because, for all their own liability to error, women know man-foolishness when they see it, they are often, in Miss Welty's work, the teachers of their unwilling lovers and husbands. In that capacity they are unflaggingly persistent in their efforts to save their consorts from untimely ends brought on by their extravagant behavior:

> "The system you're trying won't work," Gloria said. "I wouldn't need to bring you down to earth if I wasn't your wife . . . it's up to your wife to pit her common sense against you, Jack. . . ."

To be sure, it is Gloria's love and not her common sense that works for Jack in the long run, but it would be futile to deny that Miss Welty's women have her men beaten easily when it comes to keeping their feet planted firmly on the ground.

Rosamond, the charming ingénue in "The Robber Bridegroom," is called upon not only to bring Jamie Lockhart down to earth but also, having accomplished that, to find the man beneath the disguise of lawlessness he wears. Fortunately, Rosamond's love, like Gloria's, never falters while she suffers one adversity after another at her lover's hands. When she first meets him, Jamie is a typically opportunistic male hero, his worser self always "out for a devilment of some kind." By day he is a respectable merchant but by night, having stained his face with berry juice, he becomes the notorious Bandit of the Woods. What is worse, like other male heroes where women are concerned, he combines a theoretical high romanticism with an efficient bent for sexual brigandage. As romanticist, "in his heart Jamie carried nothing less than a dream of true love—something of gossamer and roses. . . ." For this reason, he had been collecting clothes and jewels "that would deck a queen," but "as for finding his dream on earth, that Jamie was saving until the last. . . ." One result of Jamie's romantic attitude is that when he first comes upon Rosamond in fancy dress, he strips the poor girl naked and ravishes away not the girl but her clothes. At next encounter, however, he is all brigand and makes off with the maiden herself—not to become his dream on earth but to serve perforce as housekeeper and bedmate for his robbers' den.

Rosamond's heroic act, her stripping away of Jamie's disguise, together with the consequences of her boldness, unfolds before us by degrees in an amusingly exact sequence of three moments. The prelude to the first moment begins when Rosamond, hiding behind a barrel in the robbers' den, witnesses the rape and murder of an Indian girl, the victim of Jamie's alter ego, a homicidal maniac named Little Harp. Though she remains concealed while the deed is done, Rosamond had heard the robbers swear to Little Harp that the Indian girl was none other than herself, and she "was almost ready to believe that she stood out in the room under the robbers' eyes and was not hiding down behind the barrel." Rosamond's curious intuition is, in fact, essentially correct. What she sees enacted before her eyes is her own plight as captive of the bandit king. Being ravished away by an attractive stranger, however delightful it may be at first, is not without its penalty. Ignorance of her lover's name, as Rosamond begins to find, deprives her of her own, and such a loss is rape of individuality, a threat of murder to her own identity. As she puts it subsequently,

> My husband was a robber and not a bridegroom. . . . He brought me his love under a mask, and kept all the truth hidden from me . . . , and what I would have given him he liked better to steal.

Now, in order to satisfy her longing for the secret truth, she takes her courage in both hands and wipes the berry stains from Jamie's face while he is sleeping.

The consequences of doing the necessary and forbidden act, as always, are immediately disastrous. She recognizes the King of the Bandits as Jamie Lockhart; and at the same instant he recognizes her, alas, as "Clement Musgrove's silly daughter." Charging angrily that Rosamond did not trust him but only wanted to know who he was, Jamie disappears through the window, and Rosamond, intent on following him, falls in the dust. Then, just before losing consciousness, "She felt the stirring within her that sent her a fresh piece of news." The primary event of this first moment of the heroic act is, of course, Rosamond's successful bravery or foolishness in finding the reality hidden behind her lover's disguise. To find him is to lose him, for she can never be the bandit's property again. But a hint of the fruit of her continuing love, to arrive in due course, simultaneously appears.

Not long after Rosamond regains consciousness, she is presented with her second moment—another grisly tableau. This time the vision consists of a severed male head, held up in Perseus fashion "at arm's length so it turned round like a bird cage on a string. . . ." This, it is clear, is Jamie Lockhart's head by another name. It has a price on it, and it will soon be displayed over Jamie's name on a post in Rodney Square. Gazing upon it, Rosamond can hardly fail to be aware of the horror which she has made visible in her life and love. It is more than she is prepared to cope with at that moment, and she swoons again. This marks the end of the second moment, one in which Rosamond identifies herself with the victim of her own heroic act. Of course, if Rosamond only knew it, her desolation would be eased by the fact that as there are two Jamies there are also two heads; and one of them, that of the respectable merchant, is still fixed securely to the neck of its owner. But Rosamond is unaware of this, and her sense of irredeemable loss is unassuaged.

The third and final moment begins when Rosamond, having recently awakened from her second swoon, is captured by the Indians. These are a people who, being themselves marked for early extinction, bear an aura of death about them. Their camp in the Devil's Punch Bowl is a Land of Shadows. Finding herself the prisoner of these savages, Rosamond not unexpectedly swoons once more, and she is borne away to the Indian camp to be sacrificed in revenge for the slaughtered Indian maiden. The Land of the Dead cannot, however, retain Rosamond long, any more than it could retain her prototypes Persephone and Psyche, for these women carry the secret of freedom within themselves. That secret is faithful love. Through love's agency, Rosamond's escape is soon accomplished, and Salome, the wicked stepmother, is executed in her place. This is appropriate, for, unlike Rosamond, Salome loves no one whatsoever. She believes that she is subject to no power and is by herself in the world: a philosophy dangerous at best and, in this instance, fatal. Assured that Jamie is still alive, and full of hope and confidence, Rosamond sets off to find him and claim him for her own. The third moment has brought renewal of life through a love that knows its object truly. If anything has died, it is Rosamond's passion for the Bandit of the Woods. The death of that outmoded sentiment clears the way not only for reunion of the lovers but for the clear-eyed recognition by each of the other's true identity, shorn of disguise.

VI

In fairness to Jamie Lockhart it should be said that his guide in casting off his role as Bandit of the Woods was not the love of Rosamond alone. His reform was dramatically accelerated by seeing his seamy side personified as Little Harp, a man with a head "no larger than something off the orange tree . . ." and generally "just as ugly as it was possible to be." Jamie makes unconscious reference to himself when he tells Little Harp, "You are not the fool I took you to be, but another fool entirely, and I ought to break all your bones where you need them most." Probably it is too much to expect of a woman that she should maker her lover see himself as a person with a head the size of an orange. One may, on the other hand, doubt the wisdom of a woman who goes to the opposite extreme and makes it her business to protect a man not only from the truth about himself but from reality of every sort. In the scheme of values suggested by Miss Welty's fiction, recognition of reality holds a very high place, and it is interesting to see what Miss Welty envisions happening when habitual blindness to reality collides head-on with an inescapable stroke of fate. That is exactly what takes place in "The Ponder Heart."

One would anticipate that the result of the collision described above would be bathetic, and it is. Uncle Daniel Ponder, an advanced eccentric in his fifties, has for some time been separated from his wife, Bonnie Dee, aged 17, who unceremoniously "ran him off" from his own house in the country. Finally, he has been persuaded to cut off her allowance, and as a result she has summoned him and his niece, Edna Earle, to a conference. When they arrive, simultaneously with a fierce thunderstorm, Bonnie Dee is not at all glad to see her husband. This is hardly surprising, as she has never shown any sign of enthusiasm for him. Still this does not prevent Edna Earle from being enraged at Bonnie Dee for snubbing the man she has guarded "heart and soul" for a whole lifetime:

". . . he came into the parlor all beaming pleasure and went shining up to her to kiss her and she just jumped away when the storm went boom. Like he brought it . . . . she just looked at him with her little coon eyes, and would have sent him back if I hadn't been there."

But Uncle Daniel, in a world made safe by fantasy, shows no awareness that he is being ignored and humiliated. There is a flash of lightening and a burst of thunder. Bonnie Dee buries her face in a pillow and starts to cry. And

Uncle Daniel, to make her stop crying, begins to tickle her ankle with the tassel of an antimacassar. While the storm rages on and Bonnie Dee shrieks louder and louder, Uncle Daniel continues to play "creep-mousie" with the tassel all the way up to her neck and her ear,

> with the sweetest, most forbearing smile on his face, a forgetful smile. Like he forgot everything then that she ever did to him, how changeable she'd been.

It turns out that Bonnie Dee is not shrieking in fear of the storm but in reaction to the tickling. Then she is suddenly silent. She has always suffered from a weak heart, and now she has died laughing.

Faced with this bizarre horror, Uncle Daniel does nothing at all. He only sits absolutely still with his feet drawn up. All his life he has been oblivious to fatal or even threatening events:

> Oh, he hates sickness and death, will hardly come in the room with it! He can't abide funerals.

He had never mentioned his father's name since the old man died. It is impossible for him to react in any positive way to a reality which demands reaction. He has avoided believing in every species of reality—money, for example. His riches, says Edna Earle,

> were all off in the clouds somewhere—like true love is, I guess, like a castle in the sky, where he could just sit and dream about it being up there for him.

Safe with Edna Earle in her Beulah Hotel, he seemed quite content with being married *ex officio*. But now, as a ball of fire big as a man's head comes out of the fireplace, crosses the parlor and goes out through the beaded curtains into the hall, he is right up against a reality he can neither accept nor ignore—so he faints.

Edna Earle, on the other hand, does experience the horror that unfolds with the stroke of fate. Her first reaction to the catastrophe is anger at Bonnie Dee:

> I could have shaken her for it. She'd never laughed for Uncle Daniel before in her life. And even if she had, that's not the same thing as smiling; you may think it is, but I don't.

Even in retrospect, after Uncle Daniel's trial for the murder of Bonnie Dee, Edna Earle is still angry:

> . . . I wished that Uncle Daniel had just whipped out and taken a stick to Bonnie Dee . . . . He might have picked up Grandpa's trusty old stick . . . and whacked her one when she wasn't glad to see him.

But Edna Earle's anger is combined with a reaction of quite another sort. It is as though she and Uncle Daniel are being mocked—mocked by the dead. When she rushes into the bathroom for ammonia, she sees herself in Bonnie Dee's mail order magnifying mirror and gets the shock of her life: "Edna Earl, I said, you look old as the hills!" And when she returns to the parlor, neither her momentary absence, nor the ammonia she applies, nor the water she douses Bonnie Dee with, nor Uncle Daniel's presence, "still as a mouse," has the slightest effect on the laughter frozen on the dead girl's face.

Uncle Daniel remains unchanged. Edna Earle, who has lied at the trial about the actual circumstances of Bonnie Dee's death, will not permit Uncle Daniel, when he rises to recount those events himself, to get beyond a certain point, though she does have a moment of doubt: "You don't think I betrayed him by not letting him betray himself, do you?" Then Uncle Daniel begins giving his entire cash assets away to the crowd in the courtroom. "By that time," says Edna Earle, "I think that all he wanted was our approval."

VII

The psychology of feeling suggested in Miss Welty's fiction deserves careful attention. It is clear that feeling and perception of reality are closely interconnected and that both are essential to heroic action. Uncle Daniel does possess a capacity for strong feeling, but his almost total ignorance of reality so badly distorts his understanding of himself and of his relationships to others that his feelings are, for useful purposes, null and void. His heart, as Edna Earle repeatedly points out, is full of love; but the two women he loves—Edna Earle and Bonnie Dee—are actually strangers to him, just as Rosamond, for all her intimacy with Jamie, was at first a stranger to him and was obliged to remain one until she met the problem squarely and scrubbed away his disguise. Uncle Daniel knows nothing about Edna Earle except that he can depend upon her to support and protect him. That Edna Earle herself is aware of this comes out, with unintentional irony, in her account of her uncle's habit of appropriating other people's stories for his own:

> . . . he'd tell yours and his and the Man in the Moon's. Not mine: he wouldn't dream I had one, he loves me so. . . .

As for Bonnie Dee, her unreality for Uncle Daniel is epitomized by an incident during the trial when the Ponder heart begins beating wildly for Bonnie Dee's sister, Johnnie Ree, who does not resemble her sibling in the least but nevertheless soon attracts a Ponder-style proposal from Uncle Daniel simply because "she's got on rags and tags" of Bonnie Dee's clothing. One is reminded of Jamie Lockhart's initial preference for Rosamond's clothes over Rosamond herself. Love of this kind is not only blind; it is autonomous. Neither it nor the feelings associated with it requires anything more than a token object; and when this object does not respond to the love which it fortuitously inspires, the product of the impasse must be a marriage and no marriage like Uncle Daniel's to Bonnie Dee. "I'm sure Bonnie Dee and Uncle Daniel were as happy together as most married people," Edna Earle can say, but her thought as she passes in the line beside Bonnie Dee's coffin comes from a deeper level of her understanding: "When you saw her there, it looked like she could have loved *somebody*!"

A Welty character ideally ill-equipped for genuine heroic action would be one deficient both in feeling and in sense of reality and therefore all but incapable of love. As it happens, the character is not hypothetical. She appears in Miss Welty's most recent novel, "The Optimist's Daughter," and her name is Fay McKelva.

Several of Fay McKelva's qualities suggest the unreconstructed Perseus-hero to whom Miss Welty never accords heroic stature. Among these are her vanity, her belief in the efficacy of physical force and her allegiance to her own sovereign will. The bluntness of Fay's sensibilities is always painfully apparent. The immediate cause of Judge McKelva's death was her violent physical attack upon him as he lay helpless in his hospital bed. Yielding at last to Laurel McKelva's insistence that she give the reason for that brutal act, she replies, "I was trying to scare him into living! . . . . I tried to make him quit his old-man foolishness." Fay combines self-pity with an ominously defiant self-sufficiency: "I haven't got anybody to count on but me, myself, and I." The sentiment recalls Salome, the wicked stepmother of Rosamond, and also Gloria Renfro, although it must be said at once of Gloria that, unlike Salome and Fay, she is far from being a hopeless case of self-idolatry:

> "And what's your feelings now, Miss Gloria?" cried Miss Beulah.
> "They don't change! That I'm one to myself, and nobody's kin, and my own boss . . . ," she said.

At first glance, this insularity may seem to resemble the poised completeness of Virgie Rainey, but the likeness is superficial. Virgie is the calm center of something far greater than herself. The only thing she fears is the experience she has from time to time of feeling herself "at some moment callous over, go opaque . . . ." and lose touch with the realities outside as well as within herself.

For all of her blunt and corrosive self-assertion, Fay has little grasp of what is real. As Laurel observes of her, "Death in its reality passed her right over." Her "own life had not taught her how to feel." Such a person is not so much impervious to the horror of life as insensible to it. She is a member of "the great, interrelated family of those who never know the meaning of what has happened to them." The terrible irony of those whom Medusa turns to stone is that they do not know it.

The heroic task of Laurel McKelva is to meet with Fay and to resist her—not, as she comes close to doing, by physical violence, but by finding a way at last to pity her. As Laurel recognizes, her true peril lies not in anything Fay can do to her, "For Fay was without any powers of passion or imagination in herself. . . . She could no more fight a feeling person than she could love him." Laurel's peril lies in suffering an awful inner transformation into Fay's own likeness. When Laurel arrests the stroke of the weapon with which she intends to strike her enemy, the reason, she realizes, is that she has suddenly imagined Fay as she might once have been: "undriven, unfalsifying, unvindictive." Pity for Fay's lost self, the child within her, saves Laurel at the crucial instant. At the same time, it recalls to life her own past: her husband, killed in the war, her father and her mother. "Memory," she reflects, "lived not in initial possession but in the freed hands, pardoned and freed, and in the heart that can empty but fill again, in the patterns restored by dreams."

VIII

Like all of Miss Welty's novels, but with unequaled abundance, "Losing Battles" is supplied with landmarks of human existence: birth, marriage, death, separation, and related points of transition which mark "the lonesomeness and hilarity of survival. . . ." Within the time span covered by the action—thirty hours or so—the following events take place: Granny Vaughn's 90th birthday and the family reunion which commemorates it; the first anniversary of Grandpa Vaughn's death; the death, wake and funeral of Banner School's retired schoolmistress, Miss Julia Mortimer; the first day of the school year and the début of the school's new teacher; Jack Renfro's triumphant return from Parchman Penitentiary and his humiliating defeats by Curly Stovall and other agents of fate; Gloria Renfro's "second wedding day"; discovery of the identity of the orphaned Gloria's mother; the "engagement" of Ella Fay Renfro to Curly Stovall; the uttering by Miss Julia Mortimer of her last words ("What was the trip for?") and by Lady May Renfro of her first ones ("What you huntin', man?"); the blossoming and withering of the Renfros' night-blooming cereus; the rising of the full moon; and a rain-storm that ends a long season of drought.

Having equipped her story with a wealth of parallel and contrasting events, Miss Welty, with immense virtuosity, introduces on almost every page reference to irreconcilables whose confrontation provides for every feeling a counter-feeling, for every positive its negative and vice versa. The effect is that of a series of montages in which opposites stand face to face and, on occasion, merge into mysterious accord. To cite a few examples: the Renfros, gathered for a festive occasion, are told by Miss Julia, as from the grave, "You're all mourners." Mrs. Moody's Buick, because it is impaled on Uncle Nathan's inspirational sign, "Destruction Is At Hand," is saved from plunging over the cliff at Banner Top. Jack's horse, reportedly long since defunct at the hands of the renderer, comes into view alive and well, immediately after Miss Julia's funeral. And Brother Bethune, who had mistakenly thought that he was to preach Miss Julia's funeral sermon, waits for Jack and Gloria at the church, this time mistakenly believing that he is to conduct a wedding ceremony. Thus "Losing Battles" moves between Scylla and Charybdis, "swearing everything into being, swearing everything away—but telling it."

The axis upon which "Losing Battle" turns, spinning off evocative details, is the gradually unfolding life and death of Miss Julia Mortimer, followed by a dawning sense of her resurrection. The three moments of Miss Julia's life, which was a single, single-minded act of heroism parceled out in time, are re-created in the minds and emotions of her former pupils, and in this sharing they advance toward heroism of their own, each according to his lights. Their experience is accompanied every inch of the way by reluctance, protest and recrimination, all aimed at Miss Julia as she lived and now disconcertingly continues to live, beyond the grave. The very fact that she has died restores her memory to all who had been only glad to put her out of mind. As Miss Beulah points out, "the littler you wish to see of some people, the plainer you may come to remember 'em. . . . Even against your will." It soon becomes apparent that Miss Julia's spirit is indeed abroad and just as authoritarian as ever:

"Well," said Miss Beulah, "she may be dead and waiting in her coffin, but she hasn't given up yet. I see that. Trying to regiment the reunion into being part of her funeral!"

Miss Julia's will, read to the reunion by Judge Moody, gives explicit instructions for the proper conduct of her funeral and burial. It closes with the words, "And then, you fools—mourn me!"

> "If this ain't keeping after us!" Uncle Dolphus cried. "Following us to our graves."
> "You're following her," said Judge Moody.

And, taken in more ways than one, his remark is right.

As Miss Lexie reports, Miss Julia had told the children on her first morning at Banner School,

> "Nothing in this world can measure up to the joy you'll bring me if you allow me to teach you something."

But just at the end of her days, when she is dying of neglect, loneliness and despair, she admits in her uncompromising way that, although she has waged a lifelong battle against ignorance, "Except in those cases that you can count off on your fingers, I lost every battle." Uncle Noah Webster has a word for what he takes to have been her aim in teaching:

> "She thought if she mortified you long enough, you might have hope of turning out something you wasn't."

That is how some of her pupils felt and continue to feel. They are not so much losers of battles as the battles that are lost.

Not all of Miss Julia's battles, fortunately, ended in entire defeat. The rejection and neglect of Miss Julia by those who knew how much they owed her troubles the conscience of two characters in particular—Judge Moody and Gloria Renfro. Judge Moody's neglect of his old friend and sometime tutor seems originally to have been caused by his resentment of her tampering with his career. He had long put off a visit to Miss Julia. Then she wrote in desperation, summoning him; and the letter, written as it was at the cost of almost indescribable pain and difficulty, had immobilized the Judge with shame. "Men are the rankest cowards," Mrs. Moody tells him; and, if that is true of Judge Moody, he pays for it in full. He is obliged to suffer hearing every detail of Miss Julia's long ordeal, something which he calls, after all is said, "The complete and utter mortification of life!" Himself now in the grip of change, he awakens fully to the horror that had opened up in Julia Mortimer's life:

> "She knew exactly who she was. And what she was. What she didn't know till she got to it was what could *happen* to what she was."

As an austere, impartial man of law, Judge Moody had long been accustomed to deal with human misery impersonally, without emotion. Now, thanks to Miss Julia, he proves that Medusa has not robbed him of the power to feel. Of what has happened to his friend he says at last, "It could make a stone cry."

Gloria, who had planned to follow in Miss Julia's footsteps, still is bridling at the determined battle waged by that lady against her decision to marry Jack and by the wounding laughter with which she greeted Gloria's announcement that, for the future, she "wanted to give all [her] teaching to one." From Miss Lexie, who was Miss Julia's grudging nurse in her final days, we learn that her patient, when she "lay getting worse," daily expected Gloria to visit her:

"First she'd say, 'Gloria Short will be here soon now. She knows it's for her own good to get here on time.' Even in bed, she'd lean close to her window, press her face to the glass even on rainy mornings, not to miss the first sight of Gloria's coming."

To Aunt Cleo's question, "Where were you hiding, girl?" Gloria replies, "Hiding? I was having a baby. . . . That's what I was doing, and you can die from that." And Miss Beulah has her answer ready: "You can die from anything if you try good and hard." But Gloria remains unbending. Later, when Jack, taking the role of teacher in his turn, urges her not to "pity anybody you could love," she does admit that she "can think of one [she] can safely pity." She means Miss Julia; and pity, at least for the present, is the closest thing to love that Gloria can spare.

Of all the celebrants at Granny Vaughn's reunion, it is Jack Renfro who shares most generously and most fully in the heroic moments of Miss Julia's life. He has none of Gloria's resentment. Having suffered his own enforced separation from all he loved and all that he was meant to do, he is conditioned to understanding the anguish of another exile:

"Are you trying to say you could do better than pity her?" Gloria asked him. "You never laid eyes on her."

"I reckon I even love her," says Jack. "I heard her story."

In her letter to Judge Moody, Miss Julia pointed out that she had found, even in her deepest misery, a redeeming grace:

. . . the side that gets licked gets to the truth first. When the battle's over, something may dawn there—with no help from the teacher, no help from the pupil, no help from the book.

Now Jack has confirmed Miss Julia's paradox of losing battles. Like Miss Julia, he has lost them all—or nearly all. And, like her, he has gotten first to the truth. Death has not put an end to a lifetime of devoted teaching. Jack has listened to Miss Julia's story well. However many battles he has lost and still may lose, he has become truly a hero in the world given us by Eudora Welty.

Slightly revised from *The Virginia Quarterly Review* 51.4 (Autumn 1975): 605-27.

The Collected Stories of Eudora Welty 1980

The Fine, Full World of Welty

Anne Tyler

In Eudora Welty's small, full world, events float past as unexpectedly as furniture in a flood. A lady with her neck in a noose sails out of a tree; a stabbed woman folds in upon herself in silence; a child pushed off a diving board drops upright, seeming first to pause in the air before descending; a car rolls down an embankment, rocks in a net of grapevines, and arrives on the forest floor.

All violent acts, come to think of it—but not at first glance. They are so closely observed, so meticulously described, that they appear eerily motionless, like a halted film. That child falling off the diving board, for instance: The lifeguard hangs his bugle "studiously" on a tree and retrieves her from the lake. He lays her on a picnic table, alongside a basket of tin cups and cutlery, and while he resuscitates her, another child with her poison ivy patches bandaged in dazzling white, fans her with a towel, and Miss Lizzie Stark, Camp Mother, arrives with a little black boy bearing two watermelons like twin babies. ("You can put those melons down," Mrs. Stark tells him. "Don't you see the table's got somebody on it?")

Or a young boy, spying on a vacant house, observes the following: While the watchman sleeps upstairs, his hat upon the bedpost, a sailor and his girlfriend lie on a mattress eating pickles, and an ancient lady strings the first-floor parlor with strips of paper. At next glance, the watchman's hat is seen to have turned on the bedpost "like a weather-cock"; the sailor and his girlfriend are chasing each other in circles; the old woman holds a candle to the strips of paper, and two passing men, after breaking through a window, take a warmup jog around the dining room table, then charge on into the fire in the parlor.

Things happen, a girl in this story observes, like planets rising and setting, or like whole constellations spinning. And the town stays unsurprised; it simply watches people come and go, only hoping "to place them, in their hour or their street or the name of their mothers' people."

Placing, naming—isn't that why these stories work so well? Firmly pinned as butterflies, Eudora Welty's characters remain vivid after 30, 40 years, every dress fold and flash of eye caught perfectly: the deaf couple waiting in a railroad station, feeble-minded Lily Daw, and Phoenix Jackson traveling her eternal path through the pines. The running boards, rusty yard pumps, butter churns and powder-flash cameras have all but disappeared, but the people themselves remain so true that this volume, held in the hands, seems teeming with life. You can imagine that it's positively noisy, ringing as it does with voices laughing and scolding and gossiping, with the farmer calling out his buttermilk song and the Powerhouse band playing "Somebody Loves Me" and Virgie Rainey tinkling away on the Bijou picture-show piano.

The present collection contains all of Eudora Welty's published stories—four volumes' worth, along with two more recent stories not previously anthologized. *A Curtain of Green*, the first volume, was written in the 1930s. It contains some of her best-known pieces: "Why I Live at the P.O.," "Petrified Man" and "A Worn Path." *The Wide Net*, published in 1943, has for its motif the Natchez Trace, which runs alike through tales of the old-time outlaws, who traveled it and the modern townspeople now living near it. The effect is a kind of river of time—or perhaps, more accurately, timelessness. Place (always central to Eudora Welty's writing) makes insignificant the mere passage of years.

In *The Golden Apples* (1949), place again provides the link. Morgana, Mississippi, is the setting for six of its seven stories, and even in the one exception, Morgana is a presence so haunting—at least to us, the readers—that San Francisco, where a Morgana citizen has moved, seems foreign and bizarre and jarring. What a relief, upon finishing that story, to turn the page and find ourselves back in Morgana! And how poignant and oddly satisfying to see Snowdie's pesky twin boys change to ordinary, not-very-happy men, to watch the little girls from that camp on Moon Lake grow settled and brisk and domestic, while King MacLain becomes a senile old gentleman!

The stories in *The Bride of Innisfallen* (1955) move farther afield—to New Orleans, to Circe's Island, to a boat train passing through Wales and a steamer bound for Naples. It's worrisome at first (will she still be Eudora Welty? the *real* Eudora Welty?), but not for long. Just look at the title story, where on a speeding train "two greyhounds in plaid blankets, like dangerously ecstatic old ladies hoping no one would see them, rushed into, out of, then past the corridor door. . . ." Yes, it's still Eudora Welty.

In the two stories not previously anthologized—"Where Is the Voice Coming From?" and "The Demonstrators"— the movement is less in place than in time. Both deal with the racial unrest of the '60s. Introducing them, Eudora Welty says that they "reflect the unease, the ambiguities, the sickness and desperation of those days in Mississippi." They do indeed; and they prove her to be the most faithful of mirrors. She writes about what *is*, not what ought to be. The "niggers" and "colored" of her '40s stories give way to the civil-rights leaders of the '60s. It's a whole little social history, offered without comment.

Now: Is she, in fact, a Southern writer? (Someone will be bound to ask.) Well, assuming there is such a thing, I believe she qualifies—not only through accident of birth and her characters' rhythms of speech but also because, in telling a story, she concerns herself less with what happens than with whom it happens *to*, and where. Everything must have its history, every element of the plot its leisurely, rocking-chair-paced (but never dull) examination.

Unlike Flannery O'Connor, she is kind, viewing her characters with genuine sympathy and affection. Or if unkind events occur, one senses that that's simply what happened; it's not a result of any willful twist from the author. She tells stories like a friend, someone you're fond of—sitting on her porch shelling peas, you imagine, and speaking in a genteel murmur, but then startling you with sudden flashes of humor and perception.

For me as a girl—a Northerner growing up in the South, longingly gazing over the fence at the rich, tangled lives of the Southern neighbors—Eudora Welty was a window upon the world. If I wondered what went on in the country churches and "Colored Only" cafes, her writing showed me, as clearly as if I'd been invited inside.

But what seems obvious only now, with the sum total of these collected stories, is that Eudora Welty herself must once have felt the need for such a window. The children in her stories are all eyes, soaking up other people's lives, feeling for the slightest crack that might allow them to slip into another person's existence. Over and over, they observe and conjecture and catalog, file away their mental notes, have moments when they believe they're in somebody else's skin. It's tempting to link these children directly to their creator. Such unblinking watchfulness could, years afterward, lead to some uncannily wise story-telling.

"Making the jump," she calls it in her preface. "What I do in writing of any character," she says, "is to try to enter into the mind, heart and skin of a human being who is not myself. . . . It is the act of a writer's imagination that I set most high."

A jump it may be, but she knows better than anyone that it's a jump made by very small increments, requiring supreme patience. Tirelessly, unhurriedly she assembles her details: the frazzled peacock feather dangling from a lightbulb, the lost ball on the roof, ladies' luncheons of colored cream-cheese flowers, electric fans walking across the floor, cake plates decorated with "rowdy babies," Mother's Helper paregoric bottles, Sweet Dreams mosquito repellent. And the piano recitals where "some untalented little Maloney" hands out programs, the photographer's backdrop of "unrolled, yanked-down moonlight," the name of a long-dead woman spelled out across the lawn in narcissus bulbs, the movie-theater sign requiring a deposit for coming in to talk, the saucepan of zinnias in an open mailbox with a note attached to the handle.

And if that's still not enough, she will find a way to *make* you see. She will spin a phrase a certain way so you have to stop dead, astonished, and then think it over and nod and agree—and thinking it over, haven't you conjured up the scene for yourself? A thorny old rose twines around a pavilion "like the initial letter in a poetry book." On a spring day, the birds are "so busy you turned as you would at people as they plunged by." A woman passing a string of abandoned, boarded-up houses remarks that she is "walking in their sleep." A country man appears "home-made, as though his wife had self-consciously knitted or somehow contrived a husband when she sat alone at night." And a hat too big for the wearer "stood up and away from his head all around, and seemed only following him—on runners, perhaps, like those cartridges for change in Spight's store."

Then suddenness—an arresting incongruity—further convinces us that all this must be fact. (She couldn't just make these things up, you can hear a reader thinking.) In a crowded house where a death has occurred, a visiting relative pounces on a random child and tickles her violently—"speaking soberly over her screams. 'Now wait: You don't know who I am.'"

People are involved in strangely peripheral activities (tie-dying scarves, trying on lipstick) at crucial moments; or are caught by irrelevant sights, like the lavender soles of the lifeguard's feet or the black family's clothesline strung with cast-offs of the observer's relatives—his sister's golfing dress, wife's duster. More real than reality, these stories fairly breathe. We're taken in completely; we don't even raise an eyebrow, finally, when events as preposterous as miracles float by on the flood of her words.

The lighter stories are very, very funny—funny in their bones, as the best humor always is, so you'd have to read the entire story aloud from start to finish if someone asked why you were laughing. But how I'd love to be asked! Like a shot, I'd read "The Wide Net," with its motley collection of ne'er-do-wells joyfully assembling to drag the river. Yet on second thought, there's an undertone of sadness to that story, as there is to much of this collection. And some of the serious pieces can break your heart—the traveling salesman seeing, all at once, the vacancies in his life; or the little girl in "A Memory" constructing for herself, with infinite care a small circle of protection against the ugly and pathetic outside world.

A few years ago, introducing a book of photographs she'd taken during the Depression, Eudora Welty remarked that her photos must have been attended by an angel of trust. Trust did seem to shine from those subjects' faces—black and poor though most of them were. It was a mark of an innocent time, she suggested; but of course, it was more than that. People know, somehow, whom to open up to, and imaginary people know as surely as real ones. In Eudora Welty's stories, characters present themselves hopefully and confidingly, believing that she'll do right by them. Their faith is not misplaced. Eudora Welty is one of our purest, finest, gentlest voices, and this collection is something to be treasured.

From *Washington Evening Star* 26 October 1980, sec. D. p. 1, 7.

Songs of the South

Walter Clemons

Eudora Welty's first story, "Death of a Traveling Salesman," appeared in a small literary magazine nearly 45 years ago. Re-reading it, with all the others she has published since, in this big collected volume has strikingly altered my perception of a writer whose work I thought I knew. In a characteristically unassuming preface, Welty remarks: "In general, my stories as they've come along have reflected their own present time, beginning with the Depression in which *I* began" and progressing to two previously uncollected stories written during the 1960's that "reflect the unease, the ambiguities, the sickness and desperation of those days in Mississippi."

She presents herself—and we have tended to take her modest word for it—as the tiller of a small field. She has lived most of her life in her parents' house in Jackson, Miss., where she is "underfoot locally," as she long ago told an interviewer. I own a copy of a useful "Jackson Junior League Cookbook," to which she contributed a preface. At 71, she and Peter Taylor are surviving members of an extraordinary group of Southern storytellers, of whom William Faulkner and Katherine Anne Porter were the elders and Flannery O'Connor the youngster.

Mimic: Welty's rooted "Southernness" is attractive in a plasticized age, and everything she has produced is handmade. She is an expert mimic of excited Southern gossip, so adept that her early "Why I Live at the P.O." is irresistibly readable aloud: "I was getting along fine with Mama, Papa-Daddy and Uncle Rondo until my sister Stella-Rondo just separated from her husband and came back home again," its narrator begins, buzzing like an angry bee. "Mr. Whitaker! Of course I went with Mr. Whitaker first, when he first appeared here in China Grove, taking 'Pose Yourself' photos, and Stella-Rondo broke us up. Told him I was one-sided. Bigger on one side than the other, which is a deliberate, calculated falsehood: I'm the same. Stella-Rondo is exactly twelve months to the day younger than I am and for that reason she's spoiled." The family quarrel that ensues is so horrifically comic that a young actress enjoyed success in New York this year simply reciting it onstage.

Welty's best stories are densely specific, not only aurally but visually. Without a word, a tall Welshman in "The Bride of the Innisfallen" enters a crowded British railway carriage and takes "the one seat without question. . . . His hair was in two corner bushes, and he had a full eye—like that of the horse in the storm of old chromos in the West of America—the kind of eye supposed to attract lightning. In the silence of the dreary stop, he slapped all his pockets—not having forgotten anything, only making sure. His hands were powdered over with something fairly black." Her sense of smell is acute. A door-to-door cosmetics saleswoman produces "a golden lipstick which popped open like magic. A fragrance came out of it like incense, and Livvie cried out suddenly, 'Chinaberry flowers!' . . . 'Oh, no, not chinaberry flowers—secret ingredients,' said Miss Baby Marie. 'My cosmetics have secret ingredients—not chinaberry flowers'."

Local Color: These are the knowns in Welty's stories, along with her attentive renderings of Southern ceremonial occasions—the wake and funeral in "The Wanderers" (the last and best story in the linked collection published as "Golden Apples," to my mind Welty's least good book); the assemblage for an itinerant photographer in the enchanting story called "Kin"; the river dragging for a supposed suicide that turns into a fish fry in "The Wide Net"; the uproarious town gathering at the train station, complete with the Victory Civic Band, to send a mentally defective girl off to the state asylum in "Lily Daw and the Three Ladies."

What isn't so well known is that Welty is an experimental writer with access to the demonic. When she fails, as in "Asphodel," it is the failure of a far-reaching fantasist, not that of a humble regional realist. She ranges wider than usually believed. Three of her very best stories, "No Place for You, My Love," "The Bride of the Innisfallen" and "Going to Naples," describe journeys. The first of these is mistakable for a home-ground tale: it takes place, after all, in the American South. Two chance acquaintances, a married man and a young woman in the aftermath of an unhappy love affair, leave a New Orleans restaurant together and drive southward into the delta, where "there was a raging of insects from both sides of the concrete highway, not quite together, like the playing of separated marching bands." Heat, tentative human touch, unadmitted but palpable sexual attraction are the story's subject matter, shared solitude its theme. Welty, that nice Mississippi lady, is not generally thought to be acquainted with the passions represented here. "Going to Naples" recounts the robustly funny, heartbreaking shipboard romance of two Italian-Americans.

Sorceress: "Circe," told in first person by Odysseus's seductress, is another story of a kind we don't ordinarily think Welty capable of. The transformation of sailors into swine, the death of Elpenor, the sorceress's foreknowledge that her son by Odysseus will kill his father and her lonely puzzlement at her lack of human frailty—"I stood on my rock and wished for grief. It would not come"—are reimagined with Homeric confidence.

The publication of John Cheever's "Collected Stories" showed how mistaken we were to think of him as merely an acute chronicler of suburban discontent: gods, death angels, mythic satyrs board his commuter trains. Welty's Southern territory is similarly invaded. I would direct you to a story I read long ago but finished this week with the tremor with which one acknowledges greatness. In "A Still Moment" three figures converge in the wilderness: a murderer, a traveling preacher who is his chosen victim and the naturalist Audubon, who short-circuits the murder but slays, for his own artistic purposes, a white heron the three men watch. A real serpent, "giving out knowing glances," slithers through Welty's imaginary garden. Many pages of Audubon's marvelous journals are distilled in her observation that "he looked with care; great abundance had ceased to startle him, and he could see things one by one."

Then try two adjoining, not-often-noticed stories, "Livvie" and "At the Landing," one comic, one tragic, both tracing a young woman's progress from solitary, imprisoned safety to dangerous freedom. These show Welty as one of the most ambitious romancers, in Hawthorne's sense, in the history of American writing. Her "Collected Stories" give ample pleasure, but they inspire awe: she is bigger, and stranger, than we have supposed.

From *Newsweek* 96 (3 November 1980): 85-86.

Journeys out of Separateness

Jennifer Uglow

In the *New Yorker* in 1965 Eudora Welty defended "Where Is the Voice Coming From?", an exploration of bigotry in the form of a monologue delivered by the murderer of a civil rights leader, with the words "There is absolutely everything in fiction but a clear answer." Her assertion sums up the cumulative impression left by this splendid collected edition of her stories. They demonstrate such versatility that labels such as "Southern Gothic", "feminine", or "symbolist" seem partial and inadequate. Yet they all share a sense of strangeness, an enigmatic quality which stems both from the author's respect for the secret lives of individuals and from her concern with metaphysical mysteries—the question of where man can look for meaning in the arbitrary and uncaring processes of nature and time.

The edition contains four complete collections, plus two later stories inspired by the turmoil of the 1960s. The arrangement of the original volumes is unchanged—wisely, since each collection had its own shape and coherence. *A Curtain of Green* (1941) contains several stories of the Depression, but is often bitterly funny, with a gallery of characters whose outer grotesqueries won Welty her reputation as a Gothic writer. In *The Wide Net* (1943) the odd individuals remain, but the sardonic resignation gives way to a more romantic exploration of human loneliness and longing. *The Golden Apples* (1949), a cycle of stories with an extraordinary structural and symbolic unity, spanning forty years in a small town, pursues the oppositions of community and individual fulfilment, and the agony that accompanies a visionary openness to life. Finally, *The Bride of the Innisfallen* (1955), dedicated to Elizabeth Bowen, suggests that the acceptance of loneliness can be a condition of the strength required for clear perception and for entry into the world, "the lovely room full of strangers".

Between these collections she also wrote three novels, *The Robber Bridegroom*, *Delta Wedding*, and *The Ponder Heart*, and she has since written three more, *Losing Battles*, *One Time, One Place* and *Optimist's Daughter*. These, like her stories, are especially remarkable for their depiction of determined women, whose fate rarely corresponds to the stereotypes of female destiny. Yet although highly respected and critically acclaimed, her work has never won the popular readership it deserves. Her writing is immediate and direct; she pins down idiomatic speech with hilarious accuracy, and locates her stories with precise detail in time and place. But the detail itself also provides dense patterns of imagery, and there is perhaps something disconcerting in the way her realism suddenly becomes surreal, just as reality and fantasy continually blur in the minds of her characters:

> The cretonne pillows smelled like wet stones. . . . The curtains hung almost still, like poured cream, down the windows, but on the table the petals shattered all at once from a bowl of roses.

A hallucinatory vividness colours her picture of the South, which is often presented as a region of dreamers, floating in the backwater of time. As Dicey, the Yankee cousin in "Kin" says ". . . everybody I knew there lived as if they had never heard of anywhere else, even Jackson." The life and landscape of Mississippi—the hill farms, the sleepy towns, the expanse of the Delta, the luxuriance of the swamp, the old frontier road of the Natchez Trace—provide the subjects of nearly all the stories. Welty clearly understands the city exile's "Longing for that careless, patched land of Mississippi winter, trees in their rusty wrappers, slowgrown trees taking their time, the lost shambles of old cane, the winter swamp where his own twin brother, he supposed, still hunted". It is, of course, Welty's own country. Born in Jackson in 1909, she has lived there all her life, except for periods of study in Columbus Ohio, at the University of Wisconsin, a course in advertising at Columbia University, New York, and, later, trips to Europe. But, as she and her commentators have often pointed out, she has a measure of detachment, allowing her to escape the burden of guilt and regret for Southern history, since her father came from Ohio, and her mother from West Virginia. And although her early supporters included writers such as Cleanth Brooks, Robert Penn Warren and Katherine Anne Porter, who were grouped around the *Southern Review*, in Baton Rouge, she has never identified herself with any specific southern group.

This paradoxical combination of engagement and detachment is carried into her fiction, in the recurring narrative device of the journey and in the persona of the traveller. They appear in her first published story "Death of a Travelling Salesman", in which R. J. Bowman desperately struggles free from the longed for yet shocking security he discovers in a hill-top shack, "A marriage, a fruitful marriage. . . . Anyone could have had that", towards his car which "seemed to sit like a boat in the moonlight". And movement as a replacement for commitment is also a feature of Welty's last story. "The Demonstrators", in which a doctor broods in his car over the irrationality of violence between lovers, hatred between races, and the cruelty of chance which left his only daughter brain-damaged at birth.

All the stories hum with journeys and departures. One of the most impressive is the aptly named "No Place for You, My Love" which follows two Northerners, strangers to each other, on an impulsive trip from New Orleans to the very edge of the gulf, as they expose themselves to an unfamiliar world where the margins of the road are full of "crawling hides" with "grins that had come down from the primeval mud". And often the journey offers an escape from the South towards the fulfilment of a dream. This is a central theme of *The Golden Apples*, but an earlier instance is "The Key", in which two deaf mutes, Albert and Ellie, wait on a station platform for a train to Niagara—the ultimate honeymoon destination and also a place where "You listen with your whole self. You listen with your arms and your legs and your whole body—you'll never forget what hearing is, after that". Caught in the excitement revolving around a dropped key they miss their train, which they cannot hear. For Elsie, for whom the journey was a desperate bid to end her perpetual isolation, this is a disaster. But Albert, who has just come to realise the "enormity of the venture", transfers his dreams to the key itself:

> Perhaps he had even decided that it was a symbol not of happiness with Ellie, but of something else—something which he could have alone, for only himself, in peace, something strange and unlooked for which would come to him. . . .

Much of the elusiveness of the stories comes from the way Welty allows her characters to retain an inner life, hidden even from the omniscient author. Again this can involve the narrative structure itself. When events are described in the first person ("Why I live at the P.O.", "The Golden Shower", "Where Is the Voice Coming From?") or from the viewpoint of an individual or a closely-knit group ("The Petrified Man", "Keela, the Outcast Indian Maiden", "At the Landing", "The Whole World Knows"), the account may be so coloured by confusion, prejudice, ignorance or emotion that the reader is hard put to find a perspective from which to interpret them or to make moral judgments. Elsewhere the point of consciousness in the story may be a traveller who is in only partial possession of the facts ("The Hitch Hikers") or people wholly deprived of communication, such as deaf-mutes ("The Key", "First Love"), the inarticulate ("A Worn Path", "The Burning") or the insane ("Clytie").

The effect is to emphasize an alienation which the characters continually strive to overcome. They long, as the young girl Nina does in "Moon Lake", to merge the self with that of another. "To slip into them all—to change. To change for a moment into Gertrude, into Miss Gruenwald, into Twosie—into a boy. To *have been* an orphan." But the possibility of such union is not a real one. The most explicit statement of this preoccupation comes in the story "A Still Moment", in which the evangelist Lorenzo Dow reflects on his horror at Audubon's shooting of a white heron so that he may study its beauty:

> He could understand God's giving Separateness first and then giving Love to follow and heal its wonder; but God had reversed this, and given Love first and then Separateness, as though it did not matter to Him which came first. Perhaps it was that God never counted the moments of Time; Lorenzo did that, among his tasks of love. Time did not occur to God. Therefore—did he even know of it? How to explain Time and Separateness back to God, who had never thought of them, who could let the whole world come to grief in a scattering moment?

People adopt different defences, against this existential loneliness, and against the ravages of chance, whether mis-timed good fortune ("Flowers for Marjorie") or the accidental death of a beloved ("A Curtain of Green"). Some immerse themselves in daily life, and in the social rituals which figure repeatedly in these stories—concerts, parties, funerals. The numerous suicides belie their apparent success. Others become passive victims, finding contact in total surrender. Still others try to impose order, through love, through art, through an intense ecstatic moment of vision, or through the "willed reality" of fantasy and dream.

In the volume *The Golden Apples* the forces of love, sexuality, dream and art pull constantly against the small but remorseless demands of small-town life. We encounter a series of artist-wanderers, who, like Orpheus, may be either god or victim, or both. Their attempts to break out of the enchanted frozen existence of their town, Morgana, are enhanced by references to classical myth, Zeus and Danãe, Perseus and Medusa; to the folklore of natural fertility—"Tis the habit of Sir Rabbitt, To dance in the wood"; and to archetypal symbols of submersion, death and rebirth. Above all the stories are permeated by the echoes of Celtic mythology which cluster around Yeats's minstrel, the Wandering Aengus, driven on "Because a fire was in my head" to hunt perpetually for his vision of love.

Like Virgie Rainey, the pianist whose release from the community forms the climax to the cycle, Eudora Welty can convince us that she is in tune with the rain falling not only on "the whole South" but, "for all she knew, on the everywhere". Both character and author confront the terror of separateness and find solace in a tradition of the imagination which at once respects and transforms the violence of nature: "They heard through falling rain the running of the horse and bear, the stroke of the leopard, the dragon's crusty slither, and the glimmer and the trumpet of the swan." The publication of these *Collected Stories* allows us to celebrate the achievement of one of the most entertaining, evocative—and underrated—of American writers.

From *The Times Literary Supplement* 8 January 1982: 26.

A Visit with Eudora Welty

Anne Tyler

She lives in one of those towns that seems to have outgrown themselves overnight, sprouting—on reclaimed swampland—a profusion of modern hospitals and real estate officers, travel agencies and a Drive-Thru Beer Barn. (She can remember, she says, when Jackson, Miss., was so small that you could go on foot anywhere you wanted. On summer evenings you'd pass the neighbors' lawns scented with petunias, hear the pianos through the open windows. Everybody's life was more accessible.) And when her father, a country boy from Ohio, built his family a house back in 1925, he chose a spot near Belhaven College so he'd be sure to keep a bit of green around them, but that college has added so many parking lots, and there are so many cars whizzing by nowadays.

Still, Eudora Welty's street is shaded by tall trees. Her driveway is a sheet of pine needles, and her house is dark and cool, with high ceilings, polished floors, comfortable furniture and a wonderfully stark old kitchen. She has lived here since she was in high school (and lived in Jackson all her life). Now she is alone, the last of a family of five. She loves the house, she says, but worries that she isn't able to keep it up properly: A porch she screened with $44 from the *Southern Review*, during the Depression, needs screening once again for a price so high that she has simply closed it off. One corner of the foundation has had to be rescued from sinking into the clay, which she describes as "shifting about like an elephant's hide."

But the house seems solid and well tended, and it's clear that she has the vitality to fill its spare rooms. Every flat surface is covered with tidy stacks of books and papers. A collection of widely varied paintings—each with its own special reason for being there—hangs on wires from the picture rails. One of them is a portrait of Eudora Welty as a young woman—blond-haired, with large and luminous eyes.

Her hair is white now, and she walks with some care and wears an Ace Bandage around her wrist to ease a touch of arthritis. But the eyes are still as luminous as ever, radiating kindness and . . . attention, you would have to call it; but attention of a special quality, with some gentle amusement accompanying it. When she laughs, you can see how she must have looked as a girl—shy and delighted. She will often pause in the middle of a sentence to say, "Oh, I'm just enjoying this so much!" and she does seem to be that rare kind of person who takes an active joy in small, present moments. In particular, she is pleased by *words*, by ways of saying things, snatches of dialogue overheard, objects' names discovered and properly applied. (She likes to read technical manuals and diagrams with the parts labeled. Her whole face lights up when she describes how she heard a country woman confess to a "Gnawing and a craving" for something. "Wasn't that a wonderful way of putting it?" she asks. "A gnawing and a craving.")

Even in conversation, the proper word matters deeply to her and is worth a brief pause while she hunts for it. She searches for a way to describe a recent heat wave: The heat, she says, was like something waiting for you, something out to *get* you; when you climbed the stairs at night, even the stair railing felt like, oh, like warm toast. She shares my fear of merging into freeway traffic because, she says, it's like entering a round of hot-pepper in a jump-rope game: "'Oh, well,' you think, 'maybe the next time it comes by. . . .'" (I always did know freeways reminded me of something; I just couldn't decide what it was.) And when she re-read her collected stories, some of which date back to the 1930's: "It was the strangest experience. It was like watching a negative develop, slowly coming clear before your eyes. It was like recovering a memory."

A couple of her stories, she says, she really had wished to drop from the collection, but was persuaded not to. Others, the very earliest, were written in the days before she learned to rewrite ("I didn't know you *could* rewrite"), and although she left them as they were, she has privately revised her own printed copies by hand. Still others continue to satisfy her—especially those in *The Golden Apples*—and she laughs at herself for saying how much she loves "June Recital" and "The Wanderers." But her pleasure in these stories is, I think, part and parcel of her whole attitude toward writing: She sees it as truly joyful work, as something she can hardly wait to get down to in the mornings.

Unlike most writers she imposes no schedule on herself. Instead she waits for things to "Brood"—usually situations from her own life which, in time, are alchemized into something entirely different, with different characters and plots. From then on, it goes very quickly. She wakes early, has coffee and sets to work. She writes as long as she can keep at it, maybe pausing for a brief tomato sandwich at noon. (And she can tell you exactly who used to make the best tomato sandwiches in Jackson, back during her grade-school days when everybody swapped lunches. It was Frances MacWillie's grandmother, Mrs. Nannie MacWillie.)

What's written she types soon afterward; she feels that her handwriting is too intimate to re-read objectively. Then she scribbles revisions all over the manuscript, and cuts up parts of pages and pins them into different locations with dressmakers' pins—sometimes moving whole scenes, sometimes a single word. Her favorite working time is summer, when everything is quiet and it's "too hot to go forth" and she can sit next to an open window. (The danger is that any passing friend can interrupt her: "I saw you just sitting at your typewriter. . . .")

Describing the process of writing, she is matter-of-fact. It's simply her life's work, which has occupied her for more than 40 years. She speaks with calm faith of her own instincts, and is pleased to have been blessed with a visual mind—"the best shorthand a writer can have." When she's asked who first set her on her path (this woman who has, whether she knows it or not, set so many writers on *their* paths), she says that she doesn't believe she ever did get anything from other writers. "It's the experience of living," she says—leaving unanswered, as I suppose she must, the question of just how she, and not some next-door neighbor, mined the stuff of books from the ordinary experiences of growing up in Jackson, Miss., daughter of an insurance man and a schoolteacher; of begging her brothers to teach her golf; bicycling to the library in two petticoats so the librarian wouldn't say, "I can see straight through you," and send her home; and spending her honor roll prize—a free pass—to watch her favorite third baseman play ball.

And where (she wonders aloud) did she get the idea she was bound to succeed as a writer, sending off stories on her own as she did and promptly receiving them back? How long would she have gone on doing that?

Fortunately, she didn't have to find out. Diarmuid Russell—then just starting as a literary agent—offered to represent her. He was downright *fierce* about representing her, at one time remarking that if a certain story were rejected, the editor "ought to be horse-whipped." (It wasn't rejected). And there were others who took a special interest in her—notably the editor John Woodburn, and Katherine Anne Porter. (Katherine Anne Porter invited her to visit. Eudora Welty was so overwhelmed that she only got there after a false start, turning back at Natchez when her courage failed.) A photo she keeps from around this period shows a party honoring the publication of her first book: a tableful of admiring editors, a heartbreakingly young Diarmuid Russell, and in their midst Eudora Welty, all dressed up and wearing a corsage and looking like a bashful, charming schoolgirl. She does not admit to belonging to a literary community, but what she means is that she was never part of a formal circle of writers. You sense, in fact, that she would be uncomfortable in a self-consciously literary environment. (Once she went to the writers' colony at Yaddo but didn't get a thing done, and spent her time attending the races and "running around with a bunch of Spaniards." She'd suspected all along, she says, that a place like that wouldn't work out for her.)

Certainly, though, she has had an abundance of literary friendships, which she has preserved and cherished over the years. She speaks warmly of Robert Penn Warren; and she likes to recall how Reynolds Price, while still a Duke student, met her train in a pure white suit at 3 A.M. when she came to lead a workshop. But some other friends are gone now. Elizabeth Bowen was especially dear to her. Katherine Anne Porter's long illness and death have left her deeply saddened. And Diarmuid Russell, she says, is someone she still thinks of every day of her life.

In a profession where one's resources seem likely to shrink with time (or so most writers fear), Eudora Welty is supremely indifferent to her age. She says, when asked, that it does bother her a little that there's a certain depletion of physical energy—that she can't make unlimited appearances at colleges nowadays, much as she enjoys doing that, and still have anything left for writing. (Colleges keep inviting her because, she claims, "I'm so well behaved, I'm always on time and I don't get drunk or hole up in a motel with my lover.") But it's plain that her *internal* energy is as powerful as ever. She credits the examples she's seen around her: Elizabeth Bowen, who continued full of curiosity and enthusiasm well into her 70's; and V.S. Pritchett, now 80, whose work she particularly admires. In fact, she says, the trouble with publishing her collected stories is the implication that there won't be any more—and there certainly will be, she says. She takes it as a challenge.

She does not, as it turns out, go to those ladies' luncheons with the tinted cream cheese flowers that she describes so well in her stories. (I'd always wondered.) Her life in Jackson revolves around a few long-time friends, with a quiet social evening now and then—somebody's birthday party, say. Her phone rings frequently just around noon, when it's assumed that she's finished her morning's work. And one friend, an excellent cook, might drop off a dish she's prepared.

Nor is she entirely bound to Jackson. She loves to travel, and she positively glows when describing her trips. "Oh, I would hate to be confined," she says. Her only regret is that now you have to take the plane. She remembers what it was like to approach the coast of Spain by ship—to see a narrow pink band on the horizon and then hear the tinkling of bells across the water.

When she talks like this, it's difficult to remember that I'm supposed to be taking notes.

Is there anything she especially wants known about herself—anything she'd like a chance to say? Yes, she says, and she doesn't even have to think about it: She wants to express her thankfulness for all those people who helped and encouraged her so long ago. "Reading my stories over," she says, "brings back their presence. I feel that I've been very lucky."

From *The New York Times Book Review* 2 November 1980: 33-34.

The Loving Vision

Robert Drake

"I have been told, both in approval and in accusation, that I seem to love all my characters," writes Eudora Welty in the preface to her *Collected Stories*. And she continues: "What I do in writing of any character is to try to enter into the mind, heart, and skin of a human being who is not myself. Whether this happens to be a man or a woman, old or young, with skin black or white, the primary challenge lies in making the jump itself. It is the act of a writer's imagination that I set most high." I think every imaginative writer worth his salt would subscribe to this latter article of faith, but it is to Miss Welty's original observation that I should like to devote myself now—the *love* for her characters attributed to her. For that is precisely her attitude toward them, I've always felt—the same as that of Katherine Mansfield, a writer whom Miss Welty has admired and whom she once described to me as very "tough," toward her own creations. This has nothing to do with whether an author *likes* his creations; but he must honor them as entities, not just manipulate them as puppets. And it all involves a good deal of piety, a good deal of respect for both the act of creation and the fact of life.

A case in point: Miss Welty surely could not *like* the monstrous harridans of "Petrified Man," the story Katherine Anne Porter called a merciless exposure of vulgarity, funny and grotesque though they may be. But I think, in a way, she must have loved them, loved the terrifying, perverse vitality they embody, to have realized them so splendidly. Because Miss Welty, like any first-rate artist, is always, has got always to be, on the side of life. To vote for life involves for artist or layman or whomever an enormous exercise of love.

Often her very theme has been love. Robert Penn Warren has observed that a recurring motif in her work is that of love and separateness, which always seem to go hand in hand: the group and the outsider, the community and the individual, the family and the loner. Again and again, her stories—and her novels—reflect these polarities, these conflicts. And the recurring implication is that they constitute a sort of package deal: you can't have one without the other. Perhaps the terms define each other in the enormous complexity of human experience.

Considerations of the individual and the group lead one on to ponder the concept of *community*, which has been the third of the modern Southern writer's great assets, along with geography and history. Well, it's everywhere in Miss Welty's work, in the Delta plantations, in the small farms of the red-clay hills, in the large families that "can't be too close," in China Grove itself, which is "the next to smallest P.O. in the state of Mississippi." The individual ignores it or flouts it at his peril, of course. And it has given Miss Welty both setting and theme. The modern rage against context, evident in both modern literature and modern life, is simply inconceivable in both Miss Welty's world and her work. She has always a *there* and a *then*, always a *they* and a *you*. Ideas as such can take a back seat: *they're* not what literature is about.

My own conversion came about over twenty-five years ago, when I first read Miss Welty's comic masterpiece, "Why I Live at the P.O.," in *A Curtain of Green*, her first volume of stories and perhaps my favorite volume still, the one most abounding in those stories which a colleague of mine called "performances"—the great monologues and dialogues. And I relished particularly Miss Welty's enormous skill in taking the language of everyday Southern life (the language I'd always been hearing and speaking myself) and turning it into high art, usually comic art. (As in the case of many other Southern writers, one feels that underneath much of Miss Welty's work there lies as a foundation the oral tale and a powerful lot of listening.) But the oral resources weren't something she just "put in" to be colorful or quaint; they *worked* dramatically and thus became a part of the story's total design.

I admired also Miss Welty's ability to take the lowly, the humble, whether in character or locale and always without a shred of sentimentality or condescension, and use it as a microcosm for what one of her characters might have called "the whole wide world"—this proclivity particularly noticeable in her second volume of stories, *The Wide Net*. In that volume there emerges what was to flower, come to fruition in *The Golden Apples*, her third volume—that concern with folklore, with myth (again, in part the oral resource) as both inspiration and controlling form in the tale, sometimes set in rural Mississippi, sometimes not, but always in a country of wonder and awe. Even in her next (and latest) volume, *The Bride of the Innisfallen*, those qualities are present, though for me Miss Welty writes best when she writes about home, which is to say the country and towns of Mississippi. I've had other reservations about two uncollected stories here published in volume form for the first time: in general, literary artists should not report the news of the day, rather, the news from the human heart. And in all her best work Miss Welty has done just this.

Love, wonder, awe—I think these are Miss Welty's great concerns both in what stories she chooses (or is forced) to tell and in her attitude, as a craftsman, toward every aspect of her work. I think she's no less "tough" a writer than Katherine Mansfield, who, it should be noted, once wrote that she was very thankful she had been born in New Zealand and thus had Wellington (her birthplace) "to range about in." And I think that we in the South, and in all of America, have been lucky to have Miss Welty hold up her mirror to show us what we are, what our lives are, and thus provide, in the words of her story, "A Piece of News," that "eye in the world . . . looking in" on us, which is the artist's gift. Like many modern Southern writers, she often dramatizes a conflict between a new world and an old—present and past, "progress" and tradition; but these issues, though more sharply joined in the Southern context, are no less pertinent in the wider world. They are but another version of Faulkner's "human heart in conflict with itself," the writer's only real story ever. Miss Welty is honored in the publication of this book: all her stories here for us to read and savor, her ever developing artistry on display, yet her fundamental allegiances still intact after a long and distinguished career. But even more, we ourselves are honored and blessed in the loving vision which has been her work and is now, to us, her great gift.

From *Modern Age* 27.1 (Winter 1983): 96-97.

General Criticism 1980-1993

Family in Eudora Welty's Fiction

Sara McAlpin BVM

In one of many attempts made by a wide variety of writers to capture and explain the complex, yet clearly recognizable, characteristics of Americans labeled as "southern," John William Corrington and Miller Williams have written that the southerner

> feels first and foremost a bond inseverable and permanent with his family, his kindred, his immediate neighbors. There are things one does and things one may not do, and those things, whether in a larger context they seem good or bad, are chiefly determined by the collective authority of the people, those who owe him, and those he indisputably owes allegiance.

This emphasis on family, as one of several essential defining features among southerners, is consistently evident in the literature produced by authors whose origins lie in the American South; significant among these writers in the twentieth century is Eudora Welty of Mississippi. Like her southern colleagues, Welty repeatedly explores in her writing the nature of the family: its origins, structures, growth, influence, enmities, affections, and complexities.

Unlike certain of her contemporaries, however, Welty rarely engages in extensive, meditative searchings into the long, entangled past of family in order to discover forgotten secrets, to reveal unexpected and violent realities, or to interpret obscure facts about personal identity and familial relationships; nor is she primarily concerned with the burdens which family in the present must bear as the result of actions of family in the past. Although she is consistently *aware* of family development for several generations, she most often concentrates on family in the present involving, directly and typically, two generations and their immediate past. While interesting additional comparisons and contrasts can certainly be made between Welty's imaginative presentation of family and that of other southern writers, my concern here is simply to suggest the existence of such distinctions, before concentrating more fully and specifically on Welty's unique use of family in her fiction.

Although she focuses on family throughout her work and deals with it in a variety of ways, Welty's concentration on family is most explicit in two novels separated by a quarter of a century in her extensive, distinguished writing career: her first full-scale novel, *Delta Wedding*, published initially in the *Atlantic Monthly* in 1945 and her longest novel, *Losing Battles*, published in 1970.

Each of these novels concentrates not only on a single, extended family, but also on a traditional family occasion. *Delta Wedding* concerns the relatively commonplace but frenzied activities of the comfortable Fairchild family of Shellmound Plantation, located in the Delta community of Fairchilds, Mississippi; the action occurs in 1923 during the week leading up to the wedding of Dabney Fairchild, second oldest daughter in the family, to the plantation overseer, Troy Flavin, considered by several of the Fairchilds to be an unknown intruder and distinctly unworthy of such intimate admission into the family. *Losing Battles* concerns the incessant activity and talk of the large, impoverished Vaughn-Beecham-Renfro family, whose members live on or near a depleted farm just outside the northeastern hill community of Banner, Mississippi; they are gathered on an August Sunday in the 1930s for an annual reunion to celebrate the ninetieth birthday of the family matriarch, Elvira Jordan Vaughn, "the last Vaughn in the world."

In addition to the fact that both novels center on single families and demonstrate the gathering power of family rituals, many other similarities can be discovered in the two narratives. In *Delta Wedding*, for example, an incident occurring two weeks before the wedding week is returned to over and over in the novel as a focal point of individual characterization and familial response. The incident, which involves George Fairchild's rescue of his retarded niece who is trapped in a railroad trestle, is kept alive throughout the novel: the children delight in retelling the story about their uncle and cousin to fit their individual memories of the event; certain members of the family use the incident to underscore their already idolizing view of George as the noble hero of the family (second only to his brother, Denis, killed in France during the war); in radical contrast, George's wife, Robbie Reid Fairchild, sees the event totally from a viewpoint dominated by self rather than family. Since Robbie is characteristically defined by most of the family members as an outsider, because of her humble origins, her responses to this event only confirm "the family's" view of her.

In *Losing Battles*, on the other hand, an incident occurring months before the action of the novel is similarly and repeatedly brought forth for individual and familial evaluation. In this instance, the central male figure, Jack Jordan Renfro, struggles with his local opponent over the possession of a ring long treasured by the Renfro family; when Curly Stovall refuses to yield the ring, Jack reacts in a wildly comic, highly exaggerated manner. Hilarious as the episode is, the consequences are severe: for tying Curly up in a handy coffin and stealing his safe containing the ring, Jack is sentenced by an over-reacting local judge, Oscar Moody, to spend two years in the Parchman penitentiary. To his family, of course, Jack is an unqualified hero who suffers unjust punishment and whose absence from the farm causes inevitable hardship. As his story is told and retold by "the reunion," eagerly awaiting his return for Granny Vaughn's birthday celebration, only his maiden aunt, Miss Lexie Renfro, the one querulous, alienating member of the family, doubts that he will actually come, and only his young wife, Gloria, another clearly defined outsider, questions even tentatively Jack's heroic qualities.

These two incidents are significant for several reasons: structurally they serve as unifying devices in the novels and become the source of focal refrains for the families involved in each narrative; they also function as touchstones for individual characterization, in that people are to a considerable extent defined within the world of each novel by their responses to these events; most importantly, they underscore at the outset the significance of the family bond and of the individual's responsibility to family.

Several other obvious similarities between these novels can be noted briefly: Sam Dale Beecham and Denis Fairchild are both beloved sons and brothers lost in war; Grandpa and Granny Vaughn raised the seven Beecham children when their parents were mysteriously "carried off young" and "drowned . . . one black morning when the Bywy was high," just as Aunts Mac and Shannon raised the eight Fairchilds when their father was killed in a duel and their mother "died broken-hearted."

Like Dabney Fairchild, Jack Renfro chooses an outsider when he marries Gloria Short; Shelley Fairchild appears primarily in the shadow of her sister, Dabney, as Vaughn Renfro similarly fades in the light of his brother Jack; young, sensitive Laura McRaven who comes without her widowed father to Shellmound for the wedding, is in certain ways echoed in quiet, unobtrusive Vaughn Renfro; women in both novels (especially "the aunts") exert considerable influence in establishing family action and direction; Ellen Dabney

Fairchild and Beulah Beecham Renfro, though markedly different women, are clearly the mothers and leaders of their respective families.

Despite such evident and interesting similarities, however, each of the novels remains a unique presentation of a unique family. Although the presence of certain parallels illustrates Welty's continuing concern with particular relationships over a long period in the development of her fiction, simply to delineate resemblance between the two novels is to deny the richness and complexity of each.

I am more concerned with an exploration of precisely how Welty presents family, how family functions in her fiction, particularly in *Delta Wedding* and *Losing Battles*. Since family is obviously an influential force in her creation of fictional worlds, a limited investigation of its presentation and function in these novels should offer certain insights into Welty's more encompassing vision of reality.

One's initial response after reading *Delta Wedding* and *Losing Battles* is to conclude that family in Welty's fiction is basically a nurturing and supportive force for the group itself and for its individual members. Indeed, this impression is bolstered by countless features in both narratives, significant among them Welty's vivid demonstration that she shared with Jane Austen the gift which Welty described in her admiring essay on the earlier author's work as an awareness "that the interesting situations of life can take place, and notably do, at home."

With obvious relish, Welty brings to life the relatively commonplace activities of two unsensational families and celebrates their existence by emphasizing a variety of pleasing familial characteristics: enthusiasm and vigor with which families gather to celebrate; generous and thoughtful gift giving; lavish contributions of advice, assistance, and food to the success of family enterprises; expressions of genuine empathy of various family members for others in both joy and sorrow; stout defense for the actions of individual family members; constant communal awareness and sharing through direct conversations and subtle gestures. All of these dimensions of family existence, as well as others which might be noted, underscore Welty's presentation of the family as a truly caring, indeed loving, group and as a source of sustenance and affirmation.

Certainly, it is these features of Welty's portrayal of family which caused John Crowe Ransom to describe *Delta Wedding* as a "comedy of love"; Elmo Howell to label it a "comedy of manners" and to refer to Shellmound as a "gentle and happy" place; and Ruth Vande Kieft to describe the novel as a "gentle inquiry into the workings of human love." Similarly, Joyce

Carol Oates calls *Losing Battles* a "summery comedy" and Robert Griffen considers it "a mellow comic tale."

While not denying any of the warm, positive, celebratory aspects of family as presented by Welty, one is at the same time reminded, when reading these two novels, of Clement Musgrove's comment in *The Robber Bridegroom* that "all things are double," as well as of Welty's repeated emphasis both in her fictional and nonfictional works on the "mystery" of human existence. While on the one hand, that is, recognizing the abundant warmth of family in both novels, on the other hand, one recalls also, when reflecting on these narratives, Dabney Fairchild's judgment that "people are mostly layers of violence and tenderness—wrapped like bulbs." When exploring carefully Welty's portrayal of family in these works—unwrapping various layers—one becomes increasingly aware that the family is not *only* a nurturing and supportive force; just beneath the glowing, even mellow, surface of *Delta Wedding* and the exuberant, sometimes courageous, surface of *Losing Battles*, the family functions also as a decidedly restrictive and diminishing force.

One of the most obvious ways in which the family wields restrictive power is in its merciless categorizing of people, both implicitly and explicitly. As noted by several recent critics, especially Lucinda MacKethan and Carol Moore, both families tend to define certain people as insiders and others as outsiders. To the Vaughn-Beecham-Renfro clan, anybody not bearing one of those names is automatically a suspect stranger; such a character, like the valiant schoolteacher Julia Mortimer, is frequently reduced from a person to a mere label or to a communally created caricature, when seen from the self-protective viewpoint of the family.

Occasionally, certain members within the family are themselves recognized in terms of labels rather than of individual personalities. Laura McRaven is typically acknowledged as "the motherless child," and Vaughn Renfro is regularly dismissed by his mother with the curt statement: "He'll never be Jack." These characters are clearly, even though not radically, set outside the main group and forced to suffer the hurt of separation, an experience noted in early Welty criticism by Robert Penn Warren as "basic" in her fiction.

Other legitimate members of the family also often endure the condition of not "belonging." Like Robbie Reid Fairchild and Gloria Renfro, Troy Flavin will join the family through marriage but will never be totally accepted into it. One can be fairly certain in this judgment because even Ellen Fairchild, though she has been an extraordinarily devoted and loyal wife to Battle and borne him eight children with a ninth expected soon, remains to the end an outsider: "Not that Ellen hadn't changed . . . Ellen had come far, had yielded to much, for a Virginian, but still . . . a plantation was not her true home . . . she was in her original heart, she believed, a town-loving book-loving young lady of Mitchem Corners."

In both novels, moreover, there are finely calculated degrees of being inside and outside the family. Within the Vaughn-Beecham-Renfro clan the Beechams, descended from Granny Vaughn through her daughter, constitute the true inner circle. Among the seven Beechams, the only daughter, Beulah, has drawn the Renfros ("a big tribe to start with") into the extended family, though she clearly remains the dominant force in her family and sees herself as eventually filling Granny Vaughn's revered position. Though not a highlighted outsider, Beulah's husband, Ralph Renfro, characteristically stands quietly on the periphery of action. Among the Beechams aunts, a formidable group, Cleo has most recently married into the family and is told bluntly at the beginning of the narrative, in response to her curious questions about family activities: "If you don't know nothing to start with, I don't reckon we could tell you all that in a hundred years, Sister Cleo."

The tendency of the Fairchilds and Beechams to categorize people narrowly and absolutely is further stressed by their complacently limited conviction that the entire world is satisfactorily encompassed within their own geographical locations. Although Vaughn Renfro boasts of knowing the distance to Parchman and other remote places because, as he says, "I've been to school! I seen a map of the whole world!" the fact remains that he has "never been out of Banner!" When Judge Moody suggests that Jack and Gloria might move to Alabama, Jack replies incredulously: "Cross the state line! . . . You want me and Gloria and Lady May to leave all we hold dear and that holds us dear? Leave Granny and everybody else that's not getting any younger? . . . Why, it would put an end to the reunion."

Similarly, in *Delta Wedding* there is the conviction that "everything came to Shellmound. . . . When people were at Shellmound it was as if they had never been anywhere else." When Laura indicates to her cousins an awareness of a world outside the plantation, she receives a typical reaction: "In the great confines of Shellmound, no one listened." Obviously, knowledge of the world outside their residence is rare for these people, and when such knowledge is claimed it is often ignored or discredited by the family rather than encouraged and admired.

It is, in fact, Welty's emphasis on the tendencies of both families to limit, categorize, distort, even deny, certain realities, which causes a reader to reconsider the somewhat deceptive surface of the novels and to see family functioning in more negative ways than are perhaps at first perceived. Isolated and enclosed within itself, each family tends to view reality as it chooses; that is, the family as a unit demonstrates the collective power to ignore, alter, avoid, contradict, or accept reality according to its own view. In thus ordering reality, the family often functions as a restrictive and diminishing force for individual members of the group.

In *Losing Battles*, for instance, the family agreement that "now that Jack has come home to stay, everything's going to look up" and when he "jumps out in those fields tomorrow, he'll resurrect something out of nothing," simply denies the reality that the farm is dying and that no human effort can bring it to fruitful productivity. Familial expectations here decidedly do not acknowledge individual capacities.

In another case, the family's refusal to admit reality has genuinely repressive consequences for one of the Beecham brothers, Uncle Nathan, who wanders alone through his little world putting up crudely lettered signs warning of God's power and retribution. Urged by certain members of his family, in "strong, prohibitive tones," not to tell publicly the fact of his life which has haunted him for years, Nathan has carried his guilt deep within his lonely self. At this particular reunion, however, he blurts forth the truth: ". . . there's not but one bad thing either you or I or anybody else can do. And I already done it. That's kill a man. I killed Mr. Dearman with a stone to his head, and let 'em hang a sawmill nigger for it. After that, Jesus had to hold my hand." Other than shocked questioning, the only response to Uncle Nathan's wrenching admission is Beulah's reprimand: "Now what did you want to tell that for? . . . We could've got through one more reunion without that, couldn't we? Without you punishing yourself?"

The harshest attempt of family members to alter reality according to their desire occurs when they explore communally the parentage of Gloria, who defines herself as an orphan. In an effort to give her blood connection with the family, several of its members agree, on the basis of extremely questionable evidence, that Gloria is actually the child of Rachel Sojourner and the dead Sam Dale Beecham. Not wanting to be smothered in the family by accepting an identity fabricated by it, Gloria strongly resists this flimsy link: "I don't want to be a Beecham! . . . I won't be a Beecham." When the aunts and uncles move toward her with welcoming embraces and kisses she cries: "Go back! Please don't squeeze me!" Gradually, "all the aunts and some of the girl cousins" crowd in on Gloria, force her to the ground and, pushing a freshly opened watermelon into her face, engage in a primitively violent initiation ceremony:

> "Say Beecham!" they ordered her, close to her ear. They rolled her by the shoulders, pinned her flat, than buried her face under the flesh of the melon with its blood heat, its smell of evening flowers. Ribbons of juice crawled on her neck and circled it, as hands robbed of sex spread her jaws open.
>
> "Can't you say Beecham? What's wrong with being Beecham?"

"Say Beecham!" screamed Aunt Nanny.

"Don't you like watermelon?" screamed Aunt Cleo. "Swallow, then! Swallow!" . . .

"Say Beecham and we'll stop. Let's hear you say who's a Beecham!" . . .

"Come on, sisters, help feed her! Let's cram it down her little red lane! Let's make her say Beecham! *We* did!" came the women's voices.

Although this is a rather extreme example of the family compulsion to force reality into its desired mold, the Vaughn-Beecham-Renfro clan has several other means of bending truth to its liking, one of the most obvious and defensive of which is the long ritualistic recounting of family history, which is the core event of each annual reunion. Traditionally told by Grandpa Vaughn, now dead, the history this year has been entrusted to an admittedly poor substitute, Brother Bethune. "Giving us the family history?" Jack questions when hearing of the replacement; "He's licked to start with!" Throughout the elaborate telling of the history, various members of the family feel free to correct, challenge, expand, or minimize any details which fail to please them. The result is a carefully revised and edited version of history which, as critic Bessie Chronaki notes, members of the family have "colored to give a desired impression of themselves."

Although it is clear that the family thus adjusts reality to satisfy the group, though perhaps to limit and even hurt certain individuals, it seems important here to recall Welty's comments in her essay, "Some Notes on Time in Fiction," concerning the value of such remembering, inaccurate as it may be:

Remembering is so basic and vital a part of staying alive that it takes on the strength of an instinct of survival, and acquires the power of an art. Remembering is done through the blood, it is a bequeathment, it takes account of what happens before a man is born as if he were there taking part. It is a physical absorption through the living body, it is a spiritual heritage. It is also a life's work.

In *Losing Battles* talking, like remembering, also appears as a basic and vital aspect of staying alive. In this novel, even more than in *Delta Wedding*, talk is incessant. Consistent with her expressed desire "to *show* everything and not as an author enter the character's mind and say 'He was thinking so-and-so'," Welty presents the entire novel from outside her characters, allowing them to reveal everything we learn about them only through their conversation and action. Talking, however, like remembering, serves the family as a device for hiding or ignoring certain aspects of reality, and often reinforces the impression that family exerts a restrictive and negative influence. For all their talk and ostensible sharing with each other, for example, there is very little sense in the novel that individuals succeed in genuinely communicating with each other.

The one exception to this generalization occurs with Jack and Gloria. Although they do not view reality in precisely the same way, they *are* able to share their differing perspectives. While Jack sees all his actions in terms of "family duty," Gloria persistently reminds him of her opposing framework: ". . . we're going to get clear away from *everybody*, move to ourselves." Although they are clearly caught in the ambivalence of "being pulled two ways," they are thus far able only to express conflicting views; they do not yet fully understand the truth of Miss Beulah's summary of that inevitable dimension of human experience: "Life's given to tricks like that . . . You just have to be equal to the pulling."

While Gloria and Jack are able in their conversation to move toward some tentative mutual understanding of reality as it is, the more characteristic result of the cascade of talk throughout *Losing Battles* is to mold reality according to the speakers' desires. As Louis Rubin has commented, the people in this novel "do not talk *to*, they talk *at*. Part of the reason that they talk is to communicate, but part of the reason is to dissemble, to mask, to hide. They converse obliquely, chattering away all the time but never entirely revealing themselves or saying what they think; and the barrier, the mystery that results, lies at the center of the high art of Eudora Welty."

The same kind of oblique, masking talk pervades *Delta Wedding*. Like the Vaughn-Beecham-Renfro family, the Fairchild family has its own devices for ordering reality as it chooses, occasionally contributing to negative consequences for individual members. In *Delta Wedding*, however, primarily because the narrator has access to several minds and is not limited to dramatic presentation as in *Losing Battles*, the distortions of reality occasionally appear somewhat more subtle. Typically, though not exclusively, in *Delta Wedding* it is through the private reflections of a single character, rather than in overt conversations or actions, that we learn how the family functions to limit or alter reality.

In a minor but telling instance, for example, Ellen Fairchild reflects on Battle's "determined breaking of her children's lefthandedness," a specific suppressing of an individual characteristic under familial demand. A more general tendency of the family to fashion reality according to its wishes is underscored at the wedding dance toward the end of the novel, when Ellen considers her husband's insistent questioning of their daughter: "'Are you happy, Dabney?' Battle had kept asking over and over. How strange! Passionate, sensitive, to the point of strain and secrecy, their legend was *happiness*. 'The Fairchilds are the happiest people!' They themselves repeated it to each other. She could hear the words best in Primrose's gentle, persuading voice, talking to Battle or George or one of her little boys."

Just as the Fairchilds convince themselves of their general familial happiness, they also cast individuals into roles which are assuring to them. The most salient recipient of their efforts to mold, is George Fairchild. Although the reader never enters his mind, every significant character in the novel reflects upon George at one time or another, normally to glorify him, to emphasize his many virtues. The result is that the individuality of George is somewhat buried in familial expectations imposed upon him. Only his wife, Robbie, and his sister-in-law, Ellen, seem aware of complicated dimensions of his personality: "He appeared . . . infinitely simple and infinitely complex, stretching the opposite ways the self stretches and the selves of the ones we love . . . may stretch; but at the same time he appeared very finite in that he was wholly singular and dear, and not promisingly married, tired of being a lawyer, a smiling, intoxicated, tender, weatherworn, late-tired, beard-showing being."

While the family characteristically smothers George in positive responses, it just as regularly views Robbie with negative shading. The solidarity of familial reaction to her is overtly stressed on the occasion when Robbie returns to the plantation home to find George, after temporarily deserting him; after the family members sit uncomfortably in her presence for a brief time, they abruptly escape with relief to chase a "Bird in de house!" As they hastily leave, Ellen reflects: "It was not anything but pure distaste that made them run; there was real trouble in Robbie's face, and the Fairchilds simply shied away from trouble as children would do." In fact, as noted by Louis Rubin, the obvious tendency of the Fairchilds is to shy away from any reality which threatens to shake their world: "Death is denied, ignored; the family life goes on, organized, tranquil, ordered. Violence, agony, misery are kept removed from their lives. Occasionally one of the members of the group must deal with such things, but the family, as a family, shuts them from its consciousness. . . . For the Fairchilds everything is gentled, made human, a part of their ordered world."

Not often is their externally tranquil, serene world openly challenged. In one rare instance, however, Robbie rocks the complacent self-view of the family in an outburst which carries considerable truth: "You're all a spoiled, stuck-up family that thinks nobody else is really in the world! But they are! You're just one plantation. With a little crazy girl in the family, and listen at Miss Shannon. You're not even rich! You're just medium. Only four gates to get here, and your house needs a coat of paint!" Yet, Aunt Mac's only response is a mild "Get yourself a drink of water, child . . . You'll strangle yourself. And talk louder. Nobody's going to make me wear that hot ear-phone, not in September!" Clearly, the Fairchilds, like the Beechams, hear what they want to hear.

Although overt challenges to the family's ordering of reality are relatively rare in *Delta Wedding* and are largely unheeded, there are numerous suggestions that the family's eagerness to maintain its communal view of reality has restrictive, diminishing consequences for certain members of the family, forcing them to mask or deny their individual differences. Laura McRaven, for example, frequently reflects upon the pain and unhappiness caused by her isolation and the failure of the family to accept her fully; yet, when she is at last warmly invited to stay and live at Shellmound, she experiences ambivalent responses, feeling that "in the end she would go—go from all this, go back to her father. She would hold that secret, and kiss Uncle Battle now."

Shelley Fairchild similarly protects her own secrets; rather than reveal some of her most private and intimate reflections to others, she hides them for herself in her diary:

> We never wanted to be smart, one by one, but all together we have a wall, we are self-sufficient against people that come up knocking, we are solid to the outside. Does the world suspect? that we are all very private people? I think one by one we're all more lonely than private and more lonely than self-sufficient. I think Uncle G. takes us one by one. . . . but Papa takes us all together and loves us by the bunch, . . . I feel we should all be cherished but not all together in a bunch—separately, but not one to go unloved for the other loved.

Sharing some of Shelley's ambivalence, Dabney also reflects privately that she and others are seldom dealt with individually by members of the family, who tend, rather, to maintain an embracing, unruffled view of reality. As her wedding approaches, Dabney takes a fresh look at the family around her: "Now that she was so soon to be married, she could see her whole family being impelled to speak to her, to say one last thing before she waved good-bye. She would long to stretch out her arms to them, every one. But they simply never looked deeper than the flat surface of any tremendous thing, that was all there was to it. They didn't try to understand *her* at all." Later she reflects, "I am the first thing Papa has ever given up. Oh, he hates it!" but she concludes finally, "He would not tell her how he really felt about her going to Troy—nobody would. Nobody had ever told her anything—not anything very true or very bad in life."

Like her daughters, Ellen also wishes that the family would be more alert to the individuality of its members: "she, herself, wished they could all be a little different on occasion, more aware of one another when they were all so close. They should know of one another's rebellions, *consider* them."

Only then, Welty suggests, can the surface of ordered reality be pierced and the complexity of true reality be grasped; only then will the mystery of reality appear: "The outside did not change but the inside did; and iridescent life was busy within and under each alikeness."

So long as the family as a whole insists upon seeing exclusively the outside and fashioning reality according to corporate desires as is the case in both *Delta Wedding* and *Losing Battles*, little of the inner life of individuals is allowed to develop, emerge and reveal itself. In the tendency to avoid and adjust reality as it chooses, the family prevents its members from coming to the kind of realization gradually gained by Ellen Fairchild: "Not her young life . . . but her middle life . . . had shown her how deep were the complexities of the everyday, of the family, what caves were in the mountains, what blocked chambers, and crystal rivers that had not yet seen light." Insofar as the family stifles such realization, it may indeed function as a safe refuge and supportive force for its members, but it operates at the same time to restrict and to smother them. While the family may often be a restorative and nurturing force in Welty's world, then, she clearly demonstrates that it is also at times narrow, insensitive, selfish and limiting, even harsh, repressive, and cruel.

I have emphasized the latter function of family not in an effort to disprove the obvious fact that Welty celebrates the sustaining value of family, nor to undermine the validity of that presentation; rather, I have been concerned with demonstrating in this exploration that Welty's portrayal of family is much more ambivalent than is usually noted by readers. In *Delta Wedding* and *Losing Battles*, the family is both nurturing and stifling, affirming and negating, supportive and destructive.

Such ambivalence, however, enriches rather than diminishes Welty's final presentation of family, and emphasizes the fundamental conviction which she has consistently reiterated: "The sense of mystery in life we do well to be aware of." The fact that mystery in human existence, individual and familial, cannot be reduced to an easily explicable pattern, is persuasively reinforced in Welty's imaginative creation of family in these two novels.

Moreover, the vivid demonstration of overt and subtle ambivalence in her portrayal of family also underscores Welty's extraordinary sensitivity to the complexities of ordinary human beings, as well as her profound respect for the value of each individual person. Indeed, she thus illustrates in her own fiction a fact which she notes in *The Eye of the Story* about the work of both Cather and Chekhov: "In the whole population of Chekhov's characters," she writes, "Every single one, the least, the smallest, the youngest, the most obscure, has its clear identity. No life is too brief or too inconsequential for him to be inattentive to its own reality."

While it is clear in her rich creation of characters in both *Delta Wedding* and *Losing Battles* that no single life is unworthy of Welty's careful attention, however, in these two novels her primary focus remains on individuals within a group: her focus is on the family. "At all times," she says, "I'm interested in individuals . . . and in personal relationships, which to me are the things that matter; personal relationships matter more than any kind of generalizations about the world at large." Even more specifically, she declares, "Family relationships are the basis for all other relationships."

In her concentration on family relationships in *Delta Wedding* and *Losing Battles*, Welty implicitly juxtaposes herself to Willa Cather who, writes Welty admiringly, "*contended* for the life of the individual . . . This contending was the essence of her stories." In her own two novels, I think, Welty *contends* for the family. For her, as for numerous other southern authors, the family, linked by inseverable bonds, is the arbiter of behavior and action. Under the family the individual is to a large extent subsumed; what any individual ultimately does is chiefly determined by the collective authority of family.

Ambivalently wrapped like a bulb in "layers of violence and tenderness," then, the family functions in *Delta Wedding* and *Losing Battles* both to nurture and to suppress its individual members. As a force within each novel the family provides the source not just for viewing and ordering reality, but finally for *shaping* reality. Functioning with considerable ambivalence, which underscores the mystery of both the individuals within the family and the group itself, the family in each novel twists, trims, and expands reality sufficiently to understand it, cope with it, live with it, survive it.

"We come to terms as well as we can with our lifelong exposure to the world," wrote Welty in "One Time, One Place," in 1971, "and we use whatever devices we may need to survive." In *Delta Wedding* and *Losing Battles*, she vividly asserts that one of the devices we need most, with all its limitations and imperfections, is family.

From *Southern Review* 18.3 (1982): 480-94.

On Welty's Use of Allusion: Expectations and Their Revision in "The Wide Net," *The Robber Bridegroom* and "At The Landing"

Harriet Pollack

When Eudora Welty argues that Isak Dinesen's tales all had their "start in other tales—for a tale must have its 'start,' as a good bread must" and that those starts were most frequently from "fables . . . fairy tales, stories from the Bible and the Arabian Nights and Ancient Greece and Rome" (*Eye of the Story* 262), she applies a principle she had undoubtedly learned in her bedroom studio, at work. For Welty's own habit of telling "twice-told tales" is distinctive. Welty's fictions are built on allusions to well-known stories and story patterns—and on literary, more than autobiographical, memory. She has freely appropriated legend, history, fairy tale, folklore, myth, ballad and poetry. She also has reworked southern gothic, romantic and pastoral formulas. Critics sometimes think of her as a genial southern storyteller who knows numberless time-honored tales as well as how to combine them in curious amalgamation. Scholarly readers with the classics on their minds have sometimes paid more attention to Welty's sources than to her uses of them.[1] Source hunting in itself, however, is not an adequate critical response to Welty's allusions. What needs to be attended instead is the relationship of her sources to her new text: that is, the work performed when two or more narratives are simultaneously brought to a reader's mind. Could we not, then, see her as technical innovator, experimenting with readers' expectations through her use of allusion and, simultaneously, her mixing of genres?

The first step is to map out the process characteristically initiated by Welty's allusions and then examine the specific uses she makes of that process in three allusive fictions: "The Wide Net," *The Robber Bridegroom* and its story double, "At The Landing." Welty's fiction often evokes three types of allusion: (1) allusion that recollects a secondary literary genre and so mixes the genre of Welty's story—suggesting to a reader conflicting expectations (conflicting reading strategies) that interact; (2) allusion in its conventional sense—allusion to specific literary referents—which in Welty's case is often complicated as she calls up not one, but several, literary memories, again guiding her reader to shape conflicting expectations and to bring these into interaction; (3) interallusiveness among Welty's own fictions as another type of literary memory which her fiction evokes.

Welty's allusions, like all authors' allusions, bring together at least two texts or story patterns in readers' minds. Knowledge of the text-at-hand is modified by knowledge of a text evoked. This process has been analyzed as four discrete actions by Ziva Ben Porat: (1) recognizing the marker as closely related to—or from—a reference text; (2) identifying the evoked text, if it was not immediately recognized; (3) modifying the initial meaning of the marker to suit the next text; and (4) calling up the evoked text as a whole to form intertextual patterning. I would add a fifth process to Porat's series: (5a) calling up the entire genre to which the referent text belongs—the familiar class and pattern and all the recalled stories that belong to it—and (5b) situations in which a pattern, but no specific text, is recalled.

This revision of Porat's taxonomy suggests how allusions can do much more than alter the initial reading of a single element in the fiction-at-hand. They may alter the reader's experience and understanding of the text as a whole. Welty's reader, however, often is asked to do more, to work with the associations produced by several allusions, not just one.

When readers confront an allusion, they face something like a puzzle to be solved. They must decipher not only the reference itself, but also its relevance. Those readers are likely to ask certain predictable questions. They may want to know if the fictions involved run parallel, and if the referent texts act as either plot, genre, character or motif "pointers." They may wonder which of the adapted textual patterns will be reenacted, which will be reproduced with an ironic difference and which will be totally negated. They may look to see how the earlier text will complicate the meaning of the later one and if the later text will criticize or correct the earlier one. They may be attentive to submerged aspects of the text-at-hand which now take on new emphasis as a result of intertextual patterning, an interaction that brings the reader to realize effects hovering unarticulated in the juxtaposition of two articulated presences.

Characteristically, Welty disappoints predictions built on knowledge of referent texts. She relies on obstruction as a strategy for eliciting a desired response. When her allusions arouse expectations from which her tales diverge, meaning is located in the tension between the reader's literary memory and Welty's new text. That is, allusion emphasizes difference as well as similarity. Meaning is formulated in part by reference to and obstruction of expectations based on memory. These interactions sometimes silently comment on the source fictions and, in a sense, deconstruct them.

The process by which Welty leads the reader from allusion to a strategy for unraveling meaning can be seen clearly in "The Wide Net," a short work controlled by an allusive evocation of a genre other than the realistic short story, that is by mixing of genres. Genre is conventional; it is, as E.D. Hirsch put it, "a propriety which is, on the whole, socially considerate" of the author to observe (93). The reader who unexpectedly encounters a fiction extending generic conventions may feel as disoriented as a dinner guest whose host passes the evening without mentioning dinner. The visitor will not only be hungry but, like these readers, expectant and bewildered, too. To alter Hirsch slightly, readers also use their generic expectations as initial, prefabricated interpretive strategies. They may respond with irritation when genre expectations are frustrated, exactly as if they had been denied an expected courtesy. Welty's allusive evocation of more than one genre in a story, complicating a reader's interpretative process, is significant for a reader because, as Peter Rabinowitz has pointed out, "genres can be seen not only the traditional way as patterns or models that writers follow in constructing texts, but also from the other direction, as different packages of rules that readers apply in construing them, as ready-made strategies for reading" (177).

"The Wide Net" builds on a generic mixing; it is a vernacular tale about a back-country couple's marital squabble that slips into the mythic tradition of the heroic quest. As she often does, Welty leads a reader to begin making meaning within the context of a "primary framework"—a term borrowed from sociologist Irving Goffman's discussion of the contextuality of interpretation (21). Then Welty guides a reader to suspect that this initial framing has been a misframing and to readjust that first interpretive strategy. The reader's reworking adds a layer to the interpretation which is still attached to the first frame and its meanings; the layers created by these multiple frameworks may subsequently interact.[2]

A reader meeting "The Wide Net" for the first time begins what appears to be a realistic short story about William Wallace Jamieson's bemused reaction to his wife Hazel's first pregnancy. This father-to-be is troubled by a feeling that he has lost Hazel to some mystery; he feels excluded and resents her acting as though she were about to deliver, although she is only three months pregnant. In response to the situation, he has slipped away to a carnival in Carthage, Mississippi, and then stayed out all night with two boys down the road. But when he returns home, he does not find a chastened, more attentive Hazel. Instead he spots a little letter announcing her intention not to put up with him, but to drown herself. In his distress, William Wallace turns for help to his friend Virgil Thompson, who has sat "on his neck" with him all the previous night, "done as much as he done, and come home at the same time" (174). Together the two organize and conduct a river-dragging party.

Students of mine sometimes say that in their first encounter with the story they loved reading "The Wide Net," but they wonder why the tone of the story eventually seems genuinely celebratory when it might be expected to be full of comic grief. They echo Virgil's question to William Wallace: "Was you out catching cotton-tails, or was you out catching your wife?" (172). It is entirely reasonable that when Hazel's husband gorges himself with fresh-caught fried fish, lapses into a sated sleep and wakes to dance with a catfish hanging from his belt, initial readers may feel startled, and either pleased or puzzled depending on their flexibility and their range of literary experience.[3]

One way to understand the tale's mid-stream generic transformation from a realistic tale to something else is through its allusions. When it begins, William Wallace has, after all, just spent the night with Virgil. And like Vergil's Aeneas who wandered from his duty and his destiny in Queen Dido's Carthage, William Wallace has strayed from husbandly devotion at a carnival in Mississippi's Carthage.

Welty transforms a realistic short story into one lightly laced with the heroic epic, and then transforms the epic form that she lightly evoked. Susan Gubar has said[4] that while women writers tend to escape their strained relationships with some conventional literary forms through generic amalgamations, she found that in putting together *The Norton Anthology of Women's Literature* she had not come across a woman writing the heroic epic. But it is clear that Welty is revising that form, transforming it precisely as it is gendered.

Vergil's *Aeneid* is not a single, privileged reference that readers must find evoked by the text in order to appreciate it. Nor is it a single key allusion that all studious readers must inevitably find. Michael Kreyling, for example, is helped by memories of Dante taking Vergil as a companion in his search for Beatrice (and later of the attitude of the madonna in Hazel's final gesture) (*Eudora Welty* 19). It would be inaccurate to claim that Welty's tale recreates any one epic. Rather the story evokes the generic elements of the mythic, heroic quest. Its comic tone is in part the product of a reader's barely conscious awareness of parody and transformation.

Consider, for example, William Wallace's band of men. As if we were in a Homerian epic, we find the clans of Dover represented in it: the eight giant Malones, the Doyles and their noisy dogs, Grady and Brucie Rippen who are tied to this search by their history (their father had drowned in the Pearl River) and two black boys, Sam and Robbie Bell. These troops stomp and paw each other, eager to go, attending while their leaders apply to wise Old Doc for permission to use the wide net; Old Doc himself plays the part of oracle. He is a seer who could foretell the day's outcome, but instead he only obliquely hints at it, not quite revealing fate's decree. He waits patiently for the inevitable to come to pass, and for the order of the universe to become as clear to others as it is to him. As Ruth Vande Kieft points out (57-58), there are also the ordeals which the questing hero survives. Like Aeneas who voyaged into the underworld, William Wallace dives to the deepest spot on the Pearl River, a spot "so dark that it was no longer the muddy world of the upper river but the dark, clear world of deepness" and returns from "the gloom of such depths" with an intuition of the "true trouble that Hazel had fallen into" (180). Later he faces the inhabitant of these depths, that river creature, the King of Snakes, and he stares him down. Next he directs his men through a storm which steals the goldenness of the day. Lashing its tail "through the air," this tempest breaks the river "in a wound of silver," and fills the air with fragrance and a mystery reminiscent of Hazel's troubling mystery. Encountering this dragon-tailed storm, our hero founders on a sharp rock, opening a wound he later carries as a trophy of his quest. He reenters that town of Dover not obviously successful in his quest, but oddly triumphant.

Although the story shares several elements with the heroic epic, a reader making full sense of it must know that it also differs from them, and departs from expectations formed on knowledge of that genre. And this need to revise our expectations again, as in so many of Welty's works, brings us to the story's center. William Wallace, triumphant though he seems to be when he returns to Dover, has not in any obvious sense triumphed. That is, he has set out to find Hazel, but returns without her.

Unlike the traditional epic hero whose goal is clear, William Wallace's is not. For William Wallace needs, not to find Hazel, but to gain insight into what has possessed her and caused trouble between them. That is what Hazel, by writing her note, sends William Wallace to discover in the Pearl River. The effect of her suicide note is to send him into the natural world as it approaches its own "changing-time." And so Hazel leaves her husband to observe nature's cycle at this moment when, as Doc puts it, "any day now the change will come":

> It's going to turn from hot to cold, and we can kill the hog that's ripe and have fresh meat to eat. Come one of these nights and we can wander down here and trace a nice possum. Old Jack Frost will be pinching things up. Old Mr. Winter will be standing in the door. Hickory tree there will be yellow. Sweet-gum red, hickory yellow, dogwood

red, sycamore yellow. . . . Magnolia and live-oak never die. Remember that. Persimmons will all get fit to eat, and nuts will be dropping like rain all through the woods here. And run, little quail, for we'll be after you too. (176)

Standing on the verge of this ordered change and then immersing himself in the Pearl River, William Wallace intuits what Hazel must feel as she prepares to give birth: "the elation that comes of great hopes and changes, sometimes simply of the harvest time, that comes with a little course of its own like a tune to run in the head" (180). That is, he rediscovers the excitement that nature's changeful cycles can generate. This is what he celebrates finding. Welty has amalgamated the pattern of heroic epic to emphasize the powerful (and mysterious) cycles of nature over a powerful hero's conquest—and made a female revision of a literary form by blending elements of comic realism, pastoral and epic. This accommodation of forms, one to the other, is appropriate to the story's content in which William Wallace comes to accommodate something female and puzzling.

Welty makes William Wallace wander into a harmony with nature that causes him to rejoice when he intended to drag the river for his wife's body. As he returns home from this odd experience, he hears the music of "the Sacred Harp Sing"—female music that seems to evoke an oblique and comic transformation of the Sirens' songs that attracted previous wanderers. William Wallace associates this celestial music permeating the woods with nature's female principle. "He [smiles] faintly, as he would at his mother, and at Hazel, and at the singing women in his life, now all one young girl standing up to sing under the trees the oldest and longest ballads there were." Then in the night sky, he sees a rainbow which looks to him "in the light of the moon . . . small and of gauzy material, like a lady's summer dress, a faint veil through which the stars showed" (187). Affected by his glad knowledge of the Pearl River's depths, the night sky and the mysterious part that women play in mother nature's order, William Wallace walks back into his house. And there he finds Hazel awaiting his return from the ordeal she had conceived. Like some fairy-tale hero who has earned his heart's desire by successfully completing a series of tasks, William Wallace finds his life restored to routine domesticity. He feels relief, but also anger with Hazel who, coolly hidden in the closet, had watched him read her suicide note. Asserting himself against her mysterious and knowing superiority, he turns her upside down and spanks her. And she, responding unpredictably to his challenge, crawls into the crook of his arm. Then as she gazes into "the dark fields where the lightning bugs flickered," he stands beside her with a frown on his face, straining to see what she sees there in the natural world. And when, after a few minutes, she takes him by the hand and leads him into the house, "smiling as if she were smiling down on him" (188), a reader may feel that though William Wallace will never share Hazel's experience entirely, he may now better intuit the source and implication of her mystery.

Return then to the reader's initial notion that somehow in the course of the day William Wallace wandered from his purpose: to recover Hazel. That first impression needed revision, even though Welty appeared to confirm it in Virgil's question "was you out catching cottontails or was you out catching your wife?" As in the case of Aeneas, who to all first appearances was waylaid from his purpose and destiny in Carthage, the wandering of a hero may prove to be his destiny, the path by which he will arrive where he is going—in this case, by way of a river-dragging with the boys from the town.

Readers may not be entirely comfortable with "The Wide Net" until they consciously or, more probably, intuitively identify the genres which intertwine in it. This is not the case with *The Robber Bridegroom*, a fairy tale which evokes multiple sources and is more highly allusive than "The Wide Net." There, the tale does not discomfort the reader who neither senses nor recognizes its sources. But the reader who discovers the tale's allusiveness is rewarded when memories of fairy tale, history, legend and myth interact with the text, and that reader may find the tale considerably darker than the one who reads without these.

The list of allusions which critical readers of *The Robber Bridegroom* have compiled in their commentary is long indeed. J. A. Bryant, Jr. began a brief directory to these in his 1968 monograph, *Eudora Welty*:

> In addition to the general shape of Grimm's story, suggestions and reminiscences of a number of other tales are discoverable here, among them "The Little Goose Girl," "Rumpelstiltskin," "Little Snow White," "The Fisherman and His Wife," "Beauty and the Beast," Charles Perrault's "Cinderella," and the Hellenic myth of Cupid and Psyche. Moreover, a great deal of American folklore and near-folklore gets worked into the narrative, the stories of Davy Crockett and Mike Fink, the atrocities of Big Harpe and Little Harpe, and tall tales about Indians, frontiersmen and bandits of the Natchez Trace. (17)

Many of the allusions in this tale resemble dark threads that run through the fabric of a light, bright text. There, in the brightness where rape is obscured by the colors of love and murder by those of marriage, these dark threads running across the story's most obvious pattern are also a part of its look. A reader's overall impression may be that the tale's fabric is colorful and celebratory, while it holds in its background the darker hues of a lament for lost innocence (the nation's as well as Rosamond's).

As a fairy tale, *The Robber Bridegroom* belongs, by Welty's own definition, to a genre that is "not innocent," but has "been to the end of experience and back" ("And They All Lived Happily"). Some readers have argued that Welty's story is too dark to be called a fairy tale,[5] underestimating Welty's respect for the dark side of the fairy tale genre and the extent to which fairy tale allusions are sometimes directly responsible for the dark coloring of Welty's tale. The fairy tale, in spite of its conventional ending, is a genre that regularly offers dramatic instruction in man's dual nature and dark side. Welty herself has described the fairy tale genre in this way:

> ogres who enjoy eating people show children very well in fantasy what will threaten them later on. . . . We are all brothers, but some of us are loveless. If fairy tales stir the imagination toward benevolence with the "good" fairies, they can awaken respect for the power of the "bad" fairies. Without the old fairy tales, children today could easily think malice and ill will are nothing but a set of miniature, sanitized, plastic toys—"giants 'n' ogres"—that come free in boxes of cereal at the supermarket. ("And They All Lived Happily")

If fairy tales teach that "we are all brothers, but some of us are loveless," Welty's allusions in *The Robber Bridegroom*—to Grimm's and other old tales—are designed to carry news of this potential treachery. Her echoes of fairy tales emphasize familial lovelessness—the wife who does not love her husband, the mother who does not love her child. Her Salome, for instance, is an embodiment of the spirit of stepmotherliness. She is a composite of three characters by Grimm: the never-satisfied, husband-abusing old woman from "The Fisherman's Wife"; the unnatural mother of "Hansel and Gretel" who, because she is unwilling to share her food with her children, sends them into the forest hoping they will never return; and the jealous queen of "Little Snow White," that terrible replacement for a loving mother who demands that her stepdaughter's heart be brought to her. In Welty's retelling, Salome resembles that jealous queen as she poisons Rosamond's metaphoric heart by infecting it with suspicion. And Salome, again like the jealous stepmother in Grimm's "Snow White," pays for her crime when she is coerced to dance herself to death—a detail of Grimm's original version lost to those of us who grew up with altered retellings. But in the original, as in Welty' s tale, she "had to dance until she fell down dead to the ground" (*Frog King* 190). Allusions such as these act as character, plot and motif pointers, guiding the reader to recognize quickly Welty's variations on the archetype.

Welty also spins the tale's thread of doubleness "out of the times" (*Eye* 310), that is, out of the American past. Evoking an American literary tradition, she creates the wilderness as a place of anarchic, if sometimes liberating, lawlessness and then establishes a parallel between it and the morally ambiguous settlement where greed is sated legally. She calls up American literature, legend and history to darken the tapestry of her tale. She adapts, from the narratives of those who survived capture by Indians in the seventeenth and eighteenth centuries, a setting in which to uncover man's capacity for ungodly acts. She recreates the wilderness of the Natchez Trace where little Wiley Harpe, her "Little Harp," once carried the detached head of his own brother Micajah—wanted dead or alive—in preserving, blue Mississippi mud, as if it were a bank check to be cashed when needed. Welty also adapts southwestern humor, particularly those violent yet beguiling tales that chronicle the adventures of strutting, law-defying Mike Fink, half-horse, half-alligator. Merrill Maguire Skaggs and Melody Graulich have both written on Welty's adaptation of this genre. Skaggs argues that Welty's combination of southwestern humor with the fairy tale reveals the extent to which both genres are about the use of "extravagance . . . to confront basic fears and anxieties" (97) and an assertion of wished-for invulnerability. And Graulich, looking at how southwestern humor is itself a genre which breaks out of narrative conventions, discusses how Welty breaks its conventions by dropping the conventional framing narrator's voice, often used to constrain the voice of the roarer, and by allowing her narrator to speak the language of fantasy. In one especially provocative remark Graulich suggests that Welty revises the gender of this genre, creating a female tall tale in which "power comes through emotional rather than physical strength" (289), a view perhaps paralleling my reading of "The Wide Net."

These two types of allusion—to the fairy tales and to the American folklore named by Welty's various commentators and specifically cited in Welty's own essay, "Fairy Tale of the Natchez Trace"—murmur below the composition's most optimistic tones; they whisper distress. Distress, lament and the dark tones of this narrative have received much critical attention as the tale has been discussed as an American pastoral, "a putdown of mercantile probity" (French 186), a comic consideration of an historical change. Yet there is reason to give the female focus of Rosamond and her adolescent emotional discoveries centrality[6] and to emphasize three allusions which softly sound variations on the theme of the robber bridegroom. These allusions may be the most provocative of the group. For this fiction is one of Welty's many stories about a troubling love that reveals the need to transform a discovered separateness. Knowledge of these three source fictions, along with a perception of how Welty differs from these, can guide a reader's developing understanding.

First and most obvious among these sources is Grimm's "The Robber Bridegroom" (*German Popular Tales*). In that tale a young woman is engaged to, but ultimately saved from, a dangerous lover who threatens her innocence and her life. The heroine wanders into the forest one day to spy on her suitor. There she is warned by a bird and an old woman "to turn back my bonny, turn away home" (the refrain that Welty borrows). In spite of this warning the girl proceeds and discovers her betrothed, cutting other girls into pieces and salting them. A finger, chopped off for the wedding ring on it, flies into the observing girl's lap. She escapes undetected with this evidence of the danger approaching with her own wedding night. At her marriage ceremony, she produces the severed finger from her bodice, exposing her groom's violence. Then this loveless, lawless bridegroom, who is clearly associated with the sexual experience that cuts off childhood and threatens chastity, is ultimately restrained and arrested.

Ominous potential parallels occur to the reader familiar with Grimm's terrible robber bridegroom. And although the comedy of Welty's variant clearly promises that these predictions will be transformed, the allusion may alter the reader's perception of Jamie. For, having compared him to Grimm's bridegroom, a reader searches him for a sinister potential. And what does a reader find? Like the robber bridegroom, Jamie does away with a young girl—but by transforming her into the wife he takes. He accomplishes this when, robbing Rosamond of all her clothing, he awakens in her imagination visions of his return for "that which he . . . left her . . . before" (65), effectively ending her girlhood. He is not threatening as is Little Harp—the menacing double who covets Lockhart's success, then kills the girl he thinks is Jamie's and finally mounts her in sadistic conquest on a food-littered table. Harp personates the fearsome aspects of Grimm's character; rapacious, he slices off his victim's finger, and it pops into our hidden heroine's lap. But this doubling of robber bridegrooms whispers at least of a potential similarity between these two characters.

And that is the point that strikes Rosamond, although the reader who remembered Grimm may have felt it first. The severed finger, token of Harp's cruel passion, awakens in Rosamond, not only a terror of Harp, but a mistrust of her own Jamie's potential for lovelessness. In panic, she identifies so strongly with her violated double that she almost believes she is killed. This suddenly suspicious girl, daughter of Clement Musgrove, has been raised on the story of how her father's first loving mate gave way to another, selfish, jealous and insatiably greedy. Familiar with the danger of her father's spouse, Rosamond is concerned that she does not know Jamie's true identity. Perhaps the lover who comes to her wearing a mask is more robber than bridegroom.

Rosamond's fear is also underscored by allusion, overt but rarely identified,[7] to a ballad known as "Young Andrew," whose first stanzas Rosamond sings as she sits dreaming in her room and then again as she goes into the woods to meet Jamie:

> The moon shone bright, and it cast a fair light:
> "Welcome" says she, "my honey, my sweet!
> For I have loved thee these seven long year,
> And our chance it was we could never meet."
>
> Then he took her in his armes-two,
> And kissed her both cheek and chin,
> And twice or thrice he kissed this may
> Before they were parted in twin. (32)

Although these two stanzas are quoted in the text, the reader benefits who knows the unsung portion of this ballad. In it, Andrew persuades the girl who loves him to rob her father so they may marry. But later he unpredictably steals all her clothing as well as the money she has taken for his sake; abandoning her, he gives her the choice of going home naked or dying on the spot. When the jilted girl is sent off by the robber bridegroom who preferred to steal all she would have freely given, she returns home to her father. Her father, however, sets so much store on his gold that he leaves her to die naked on his doorstep, maimed by two loveless men.

Again, expectations based on this source will not be fulfilled. The ballad, like Grimm's fairy tale, will be transformed rather than recreated. But certainly the possibilities suggested by the ballad are evoked for a purpose. Although they do not accurately foreshadow Jamie Lockhart's behavior (since Jamie proves to be guilty of greed, but not of domestic treachery), they serve as motif pointers in another way. Rosamond's preoccupation with the ballad allows a reader to glimpse both her strategy for self-creation (that is, to fictionalize her way into her future) as well as her simultaneous yearning for romantic love and suspicion of it.

Rosamond at first uses the old ballad of betrayal to conjure up a lover (just as the ballad's heroine calls up her dream: "As I was cast in my ffirst slepe, / A dreadful draught in my mind I drew, / Ffor I was dreamed of a yong man, / Some men called him yonge Andrew." [Child 432]). Singing aloud, she rehearses the notion of a romantic adventure and imaginatively explores the risk of love. Jamie finds "Rosamond singing so sweetly, as if she had been practicing just for this" (45-46). Then he and she borrow their interchange from the ballad's storyline. Jamie's interest in each successive layer of clothing, Rosamond's appeal "were you born of a woman?" (48)

and Jamie's reply that he will have all, as well as Rosamond's story of the father and seven brothers who will want revenge, and her decision to go home naked rather than die on the point of a sword, all come from the original. In effect, when these two meet, they invent their lives along the ballad's lines. Singing the ballad and telling its story, Rosamond is educating herself to an idea of a potentially dangerous sexual union which she plans to disarm. This fictional exploration is part of the girl's education for marriage, and Welty's tale echoes Shakespearean comedies in which young men and women in forest settings educate themselves for union in plots rich in mistaken (that is, unrecognized) identities. This connection between Rosamond's singing of the ballad and her education for marriage is reinforced by Bernard Cook's discovery that in early southern Mississippi among families of means, the robber bridegroom fiction played a role in marriage ceremonies. After marriage was arranged, a ritualized abduction was enacted; the bridegroom and his party would ride on horseback to snatch the bride from her porch where she waited with her party. The ceremony, begun in ambush, would at last end in contractual vows.

On any reading it is obvious that Rosamond, filled with an adolescent eagerness for experience, is imaginatively set to turn whatever comes her way towards love. And that she—perhaps contradictorily—cannot help fearing the longed-for lover whom she cannot fully know. But the reader who misses Welty's allusion to "Young Andrew" of course does not recognize the couple's reenactment of the ballad, and so may not fully perceive Rosamond's habit of fitting her life to stories she knows. This character trait has earned her a reputation for lying, but the fictions that fall from her lips are neither snakes nor toads. They are instead the pearls of a romantic girl who lives with fantasy and reality interacting in her head. In this habit, she authors life while familiar with its literary sources and allusions, and uses her imagination (as it intersects with Jamie's) to transform robbery into love. The pessimistic expectations that a reader might base on "Young Andrew" are disappointed when Rosamond successfully recasts the melancholy ballad in a comic genre. And yet those discarded expectations are belatedly and unexpectedly fulfilled when her imagination, retaining the picture of love as separateness and vulnerability, generates suspicion and discord.[8]

The story's further development alludes to Apulieus's *The Golden Ass* and another tale that balances longing for love with the suspicion of love. There the story of Psyche and Eros is told to a frightened young woman who has dreamt of and feared being stolen from her bridal bed by a band of robbers. In the narrative told to calm and to instruct her, the young woman's fear is itself revealed to be more dangerous than the unknown lover.

In that story within a story, young Psyche is warned by her three jealous sisters that the mysterious lover who comes to her in the dark is a monster. The mortal girl allows this slander to breed suspicion. Soon she cannot overcome her apprehension. Her lover, Eros himself, warns her that he will leave her if she ever looks too closely at him. But Psyche, with her name that suggests that mind and its rationality, is unable to maintain unquestioning faith and turns a prying light onto Eros while he sleeps. When she does, a drop of her lamp's hot oil burns his shoulder, and the slumbering god of love awakens and departs. Only after arduous pursuit does Psyche regain Eros, to become his wife and a goddess.

In Welty's version, Salome[9] plays the jealous slanderer who seduces the young beloved to suspicion. Feeding Rosamond's mistrust of the masked lover who, for reasons of his own, is unwilling to reveal himself, Salome tells Rosamond:

> I fear, my dear, that you feel in your bosom a passion for a low and scandalous being, a beast who would like to let you wait on him and serve him, but will not do you the common courtesy of letting you see his face. It can only be for the reason that he is some kind of monster. (123)

Rosamond, who has attentively heard her father wonder if his loving wife and his selfish wife are not perhaps the same woman, whose beauty he loved so well at first that for a time it obliterated her ugliness, carefully attends Salome's words. She is alarmed by her ignorance of her lover and has not yet recognized that this mystery of identity has nothing to do with berry stains. When she leaves her father and stepmother and returns to Jamie's den to see Little Harp assume Jamie's place and then assault her by proxy, she is "torn as she had never been before with an anguish to know [her own lover's] name and true appearance" (134). She betrays her promise to Jamie by removing his mask, and watches him flee.

But for Rosamond, whose anxieties about betrayal, about the failure of love and about unknowable others have been released, this act of unmasking Jamie is not reassuring. And this is where Welty's tale surprises expectations based on a reader's knowledge of the Psyche/Eros story. Unlike Psyche, who finds Eros revealed beneath her lover's mask, Rosamond finds no answers in Jamie's face. Not the god of love, he is apparently robber, bridegroom and still unknown. Rosamond's unrelieved perplexity over Jamie's nature disappoints expectations based on allusion to *The Golden Ass*. This characteristic deviation from expectation, here as elsewhere in Welty's fiction, signals to us the scene's thematic importance.

Rosamond has met Jamie in the wooded wilderness of her imagination and loved him without knowing him at a time when she was herself caught in change and eager for love. She knew him so little that when she was reintroduced to him outside of the romantic forest, she did not recognize him, nor did he recognize her. She could not see her dark lover in the orthodox caller, nor could he see his beauty in the silly girl. Their romance, perhaps nourished by their repudiation of everyday identities, thrived on their ignorance of one another. But when they lived together, the question of Jamie's identity plagued Rosamond. In time she—who at first rejoiced in his successful theft of her love—grew disturbed by her inability to name her lover. Then "she would wake up out of her first sleep and study [Jamie's] sleeping face" only to find that "she did not know the language it was written in."

> She would look out the window and see a cloud put up a mask over the secret face of the moon, and she would hear the pitiful cries of the night creatures. Then it was enough to make her afraid, as if the whole world were circled by a band of Indian savages, and she would shake poor Jamie until he shouted up out of his sleep, and rouse him to see his eyes come open. (84-85)

Rosamond, who has uneasily come to dread her husband's unknown nature, does not precisely recognize what she fully feels—that her love has not so much been a discovery of another as a self-discovery. This is the rule rather than the exception in Welty's fictions. In "Livvie," for example, a girl is kissed by yet another robber bridegroom, one who steals her from a passionless marriage. Touched by him, she is "dazzled at herself . . . as he had been dazzled at himself to begin with" (236). Sexuality awakens Rosamond, like Livvie, not to her lover but to herself. Discoveries of sexual desire and personal identity mingle. In Welty's fiction, love often reveals the self's particular separateness as well as a similar quality intuited, but not exactly known, in the beloved.

Young Rosamond, however, knows little of such limitations and will not content herself to love the mysterious Jamie who is "visible and present" (86). She innocently feels she must know her lover's identity, which she assumes is simple and discernible, although hidden. But we readers, who know the complexity of his character more thoroughly than if he were an actual acquaintance, recognize that Jamie is not simple. He is robber and bridegroom, romantic and conventional, hero and businessman. When we first meet him, he simultaneously reveals himself as both hero and thief in the one gesture of saving Clement from Mike Fink. The fact of this doubleness is explained to Rosamond by her father, but she does not at first accept the explanation that Jamie is both bandit and lover. Only when in the course of time she removes Jamie's mask and sees for herself that faces reveal no mysteries and names untie no knots, does she, without another thought, accept the ambiguity she had resisted, only then does she decide to live with an imprecisely known, ambiguous nature, rather than live alone. She pursues the love that left her when she studied it too closely, regaining it in New Orleans, that city where "beauty and vice and every delight possible to the soul and body stood hospitably, and usually together, in every doorway" (182). And there she appropriately gives birth to Jamie's twins.

By having robbery and rape lead to fairy-tale love, Welty upsets those pessimistic expectations her reader may have built on knowledge of Grimm's "The Robber Bridegroom" and the ballad of "Young Andrew." Unlike Grimm's tale where the institution of marriage is dissolved by the threat of sexual violence, Welty's retelling seems to show lawlessness deferring to social order. The dangers discovered by Rosamond's literary predecessors seem at last resolved when her own romantic robber bridegroom kills his evil double "for the sake of [his] future and his love" (*Eye* 312). This done, the potentially predatory lover may become the prosperous husband and father of twins. Welty's fairy tale-rather than bringing news of lovelessness—seems again to be like a Shakespearean romance or a novel of manners in which lawlessness is eventually contained by a marriage contract.

But if this tale evokes older, more sinister tales only to transform them joyously, it also upsets whatever optimistic expectations may be built by allusions to *The Golden Ass*. Here fear cannot be cleared away by knowledge. The discomforting associations that are companions to this tale, the surprisingly dark contours that lurk in this coy fiction, are never wholly obliterated. For this tale about doubleness is neither simple, nor clearly optimistic. Its happily-ever-after resolution teases us, but leaves us with the problems of a love initiated by robbery and rape. And Jamie himself permits no one to ask of him what he is: a hero whose motto is "take first and ask afterward" (69) and who never alters his nature but only his appearance. If, at the story's conclusion, the bridegroom seems to part ways with the robber to become "a gentleman of the world . . . respected by all" (183), the fact is that Jamie has only washed his face and called on the thief to help the merchant, "enjoying all the same success he had ever had" (184-85). He is, then, as always, the hero inextricably entwined with the robber, "with the power to look both ways and to see a thing from all sides" (185).

Add to these ambivalences their context in a fairy tale so evidently built on stories that it reminds us that robbery and rape lead to love in fiction only, not in life.[10] Welty's allusions, having intensified the reader's awareness of being immersed in fiction, undercut the robber bridegroom's transformation with the aura of make-believe, and leave us uncertain of the fiction's optimism. This fairy tale, through the emphasis it places on human complexity, adjusts the genre it adapts. For as much as Welty respects Grimm's archetypal rendering of love and lovelessness, she finds his fairy-tale promise of evil's exile inadequate to her ambiguous America where good and evil are not so distinct as fairies and ogres. In her tale, resolution is ambiguous—another appearance which is not a reality.

If in *The Robber Bridegroom* Welty retells and implicitly comments on several old tales, "At The Landing," the closing story in the collection published next, is itself a retelling of her *The Robber Bridegroom*. For Welty not only alludes to twice-told tales, but also occasionally retells stories that she has herself told before, transposing plots used once, performing them again—with a difference—in other genres. When doubles such as these are brought to Welty's attention, she often seems rather dismayed; her "did-I-do-that" tone expresses a writer's concern for originality (a concern also disclosed in responses to questions about allusions). Her tone sometimes suggests that these remarkably original and yet related tales are semi-conscious variations. But story doubles—"double" here used unconventionally to suggest plots similar in situation but performed in different story genres—exist in Welty's canon and may be a mine for articles on the connectedness of her work. Pairs like "Flowers for Marjorie" and "The Wide Net"—which treat two husbands' uneasy responses to their wives' pregnancies—explore a single premise in two distinct genres. *Delta Wedding* and *Losing Battles* are another example of this sort of doubling; they each examine a family's use of story and ritual against change; the earlier fiction develops that premise in a modern novel of manners peopled with relatively sober southern gentry, while the later one, evoking the southern tall-tale tradition, develops country folk and broad comedy. *The Robber Bridegroom* and "At The Landing," written in fairly close sequence, are another interallusive pair.

The later story is the earlier tale's situational twin, but born outside of the fairy-tale genre. It too is set in and around Rodney's Landing, treats a rape received as love and its heroine is Jenny Lockhart (her last name appears on her mother's tombstone). This name—so close to Jamie Lockhart's—connects the two fictions, urging a consideration of their relationship, the patterns they share and how the later tale comments on the earlier one. This connectedness, then, is how allusion (even what may be unconscious allusion) leads a reader to create understanding "in relation to"—or in this instance, how the reader may understand "At The Landing" as not *The Robber Bridegroom*.

Jenny is another adolescent girl who, dreaming of love, is attracted to an unknown lover who rides through the woods on a red horse. And like Rosamond, Jenny has lost her mother. But unlike the fairy-tale parent who died romantically of a mother's grief when she lost her infant son, Jenny's parent more realistically died of a daughter's frustration when her father turned jailer. Raised by this severe grandfather who deprecated his daughter's raving as "a force of Nature and so beneath notice or mention" (242), young Jenny has grown within his confining restrictions and has had little enough to do with the female nature made emblematic by river water in this and other of Welty's fictions. (The river baptisms in "The Wide Net," "The Wanderers" and *Delta Wedding* all similarly emblematize an immersion in female nature.) When the story opens, the overly protective old man is himself dying. He comes to Jenny in his sleep to say that the river is rising ("It has come . . . ") and "made a complaint of it" (240). Anticipation of the day when she will be free to come and go trembles about her like "distant lightning" (242). She watches in the woods for a dreamt-of lover, but cannot imagine "what [is] to come" (244) until, like Rosamond when she sang "Young Andrew," Jenny conceives of separateness. Rosamond recognizes this potential source of pain from her father's stories and her favorite ballad. But Jenny perceives separateness in an observation of the life around her. Seeing Mag, she conceives of love, separateness and the possibility that these lie in store for her, too.

Once noticed, the counterpoint of similarity and difference between the two stories is obvious. When high water comes—with its overtones of passion, birth and baptism inextricably bound with change, danger and death—Floyd saves Jenny. Then when her eyes are "clear upon him, [he violates] her" (251). Like Rosamond, Jenny has longed for the violation of her isolation, and she attempts to use the power of her imagination to create love. But like the girl in "A Memory," Jenny invents a love that is challenged by Floyd's actual presence.

> If she could have followed and found him then, she would have started on foot. But she knew what she would find when she would come to him. She would find him equally real with herself—and could not touch him then. As she was living and inviolate, so of course was he, and when that gave him delight, how could she bring a question to him? . . . Nothing in Floyd frightened her that drew her near, but at once she had the knowledge come to her that a fragile mystery was in everyone and in herself, since it was there in Floyd, and that whatever she did, she would be bound to ride over and hurt, and the secrecy of life was the terror of it. (245)

Intuiting without fully knowing Floyd's otherness, and projecting onto Floyd the vulnerable position his separateness creates for her (as the girl of "A Memory" did as she "speculated endlessly on the dangers" [76] of her class-mate's home), Jenny hesitates to touch Floyd, fearing to find "him equally real with herself." She is drawn to something mythic rather than real in Floyd, who is for her—as Brookhart and Marrs have pointed out—"charged with the river country's vitality and mystery" (89). For Jenny, Floyd is a mythic wanderer who counterpoints her confinement. For her as for a Welty reader who is rereading or reading out of chronological sequence, Billy Floyd is as much an Aengus figure as King MacLain, and "At The Landing" may evoke *The Golden Apples* as well as *The Robber Bridegroom.* "In the long shadows," Floyd's figure appears with "the gleaming fish" (243)—an emblem of longing and desire whose name Jenny calls. But when Floyd finally grasps Jenny, she is taken not by the longed-for mythic lover, but by a wandering and dangerous beloved who "lived apart in delight" and about whom she has glimpsed something "used and worldly." Welty humorously underlines Floyd's doubleness when she juxtaposes Jenny's thought in the story before the flood that "there was something handled and used about Floyd, strong as an odor" (248), with the postmaster's comment aloud on flood slime.

Jenny Lockhart's encounter with Floyd echoes Rosamond's with Jamie Lockhart, but the contrast between Jenny who from her story's outset is confined in imagery of enclosure and Rosamond who roams outdoors, is critical.

> For all her life the shy Jenny could look, if she stayed in the parlor, back and forth between her mother's two paintings, "The Bird Fair" and "The Massacre at Fort Rosalie." Or if she went in the dining room she could walk around the table or sit on one after the other of eight needlepoint pieces, each slightly different, which her mother had worked and sewn to the chairs, or she could count the plates that stood on their rims in the closet. In the library she could circle an entirely bare floor and make up a dance to a song she made up, all silently, or gaze at the backs of the books without titles—books that had been on ships and in oxcarts and through fire and water, and were singed and bleached and swollen and shrunken, and arranged up high and nearly unreachable, like objects of beauty. (241)

Jenny is circumscribed by indoor spaces and limiting images, and then described with the language of passivity and obedience:

> Jenny was obedient to her grandfather and would have been obedient to anybody, to a stranger in the street if there could be one. She never performed any act, even a small act, for herself, she would not touch the prisms. It might seem that nothing began in her own heart. (242-43)

In the house she lives an object among objects, enclosed and protected as they are. She can be called to obedience even by her grandfather's "little murmur" (242), and yet her stillness initially contains an unsurrender paralleling "the stillness and unsurrender of the still and unsurrendering world" (243) before the flood. She contains longings that resemble the prisms with which she is associated,[11] prisms reflecting a trapped elusive light, glimmering, but not reached for. The image of her relationship to these prisms is promising but passive; Jenny hears their music, sees their color, but fears reaching to touch them.

> They gave off the faintest of musical notes when air stirred in any room or when only herself passed by, and they touched. It was her way not to touch them herself, but to let the touch be magical, a stir of the curtain by the outer air, that would also make them rainbows. (241)

Her attraction to these prisms implicitly resembles her attraction to Floyd, for whom she also fears to reach. There is, however, a contrast between the magical touch of the prisms—creating a faint music—and Floyd's touching of her—creating a slowly building cacophony.

The very heart of the contrast between Rosamond and Jenny is in their voices. Rosamond has the power to sing aloud, to retell old stories, to make them hers in ways she wishes, reshaping them to yield her story. From Rosamond's mouth, adventurous, authoritative lies fall "like diamonds and pearls" (39) while Jenny's is marked with silence. Jenny composes and sings a song "all silently." When she and Floyd walk together they hold berries in their mouths, not words. Jenny hardly speaks in this tale; her infrequent speech is characteristically reported. She only has three brief direct speeches, first to say "wake up, Grandpa" (240), next to say "go back" (244) to Floyd in an early encounter and lastly to deny the accusation that she has been offensively silent: "I speak to you, Mag" (254). In the landing store, others pointedly speak to her in a conversational "exchange," but she does not respond. We are told that she knew she was not supposed to speak, and that eventually "in a kind of haste she whispered to the five old men" (249) of her grandfather's death. At a critical moment she is reported to have said Billy Floyd's name. Later she is not able to speak to Floyd.

> "I . . ." she began, and stopped. . . .
> She would like to tell him some strange and beautiful thing, if she could speak at all, something to make him speak. Communication would be telling something that is all new, so as to have more of the new told back. The dream of that held her spellbound. . . (251)

After "he violated her," Jenny attempts what the fairy-tale Rosamond comes closer to achieving: she attempts to transform the violation of her separateness with a story of love. Jenny's violation is as ambiguous as the flood that Floyd's name suggests, at once life's rush and violence. (This is the story of living "At The Landing"—that is, of living on high ground, out of life's water, until that water rises dangerously; the title, "At The Landing," and the town's name, "The Landing," suggest being *caught* on high ground rather than saved by it.) But unlike Rosamond's fairy-tale "rape," Jenny's violation indeed turns out to be rape. When Jenny attempts to speak and so to shape her story as Rosamond does by bringing her ballad to life, Jenny whispers over the sound of the lapping water. "Her words came a little louder and in shyness she changed them from words of love to words of wishing. . . . 'I wish you and I could be far way. I wish for a little house'"(251). But to communicate her desire to her mythic wanderer might be to confine him; she has already uncomfortably imagined him "caught and cornered in a little store," "trapped in the confined space with her between him and the door" (248). So Jenny does not speak too loudly and Floyd does not look around: "ideas of any different thing from what was in his circle of fire might never have reached his ears, for all the attention he paid to her remarks" (251). Unlike Rosamond's, Jenny's hesitant words have no transforming powers.

When Jamie Lockhart leaves Rosamond in the woods, that heroine goes home and scours her house until she is ragged and dirty. Having in that manner ordered her thoughts, she soon sets out after her lover. When in time she recognizes his nature as more complex and less perfect than she had pictured, she nevertheless claims him as he is. Jenny, when Floyd leaves her, also returns home to obsessively clean house and to put her feelings in place. Unlike Rosamond, however, Jenny hides, feeling troubled by beauty and ugliness alike because she is unwilling to discover the closeness of the two in Floyd. Her eventual response to this "shock of love" (253) is to shut down like a house with all its rooms darkened. The narrator tells us that to help her "someone would have to go slowly from room to room, slowly and darkly, leaving each one lighted behind, before going to the next" (254). Damaged, darkened and yet without having admitted Floyd's double nature, Jenny sets out to follow him because she is unable to make "any way alone" (256). Jenny wonders:

> what more love would be like. Then of course she knew. More love would be quiet. She would never be so quiet as she wished until she was quiet with her love. . . . It had been enough to make her desperate in her heart, the long search for Billy Floyd to give quiet to. (255)

When Jenny wanders among the fishermen asking for her lover, they are not concerned for her love, but put her inside a grounded boathouse. One by one they come in to rape her:

she called out, she did not call any name; it was a cry with a rising sound, as if she said "Go back," or asked a question, and then at the last protested. A rude laugh covered her cry, and somehow both the harsh sounds could easily have been heard as rejoicing, going out over the river in the dark night. (258)

Jenny's final cry is an inarticulate echo of her first words to Floyd, "go back," and her long silence is overwhelmed at the story's conclusion by the boatman's callous laughter. Their rude noise, shades distinct from a joyful noise, again conveys the ambiguity of Jenny's experience with Floyd, a missed celebration. Unlike Rosamond, Jenny does not unmask emotional violence to recognize it as a real danger that she can nonetheless manage in a world where she had hoped to escape guardedness. Unfortunately the world that Jenny's grandfather had wanted her to fear and to withdraw from, proves to be worthy of fear. With no defenses other than evasion, Jenny can only extinguish all the lights in the house of her mind and hope the threat at its door will go away. In this state, Jenny "waits for Billy Floyd," her face hung with a smile "no matter what was done to her, like a bit of color that kindles in the sky after the light has gone" (258). Where Rosamond, who exists in a fairy-tale universe, can transform violation into deliverance, Jenny is overcome by the story of love with which she tries to shape experience. And she is silenced. The sound that readers are left with is not Rosamond's voice assuring her father that her story as she now authoritatively tells it, "is the truth" and not a lie ("all true but the blue canopy") (184). It is instead the inhumanly inarticulate "dull *pit*" (258) of boys' knives thrown at a tree, the sound of casual, unconcerned violence.

The Robber Bridegroom and "At The Landing," then, are variations written in the same time period. *The Robber Bridegroom* saw earlier publication, but "At The Landing" grew from a draft called "The Children" and dated 1934.[12] The two finished fictions significantly evoke one another in ways that emphasize difference. Welty has repeatedly worked toward this pattern with allusion, using it not only for the sake of building accurate character, plot or motif predictors, but for establishing expectations that need adjustment and revision. As she leads readers to consider the difference between a literary memory and the fiction-at-hand, she pushes them toward a discovery of meaning. Her use of allusion does not create correspondence so much as transformation, which habitually restructures the intentions of the source fictions, causing the reader to revise initial predictions based on the allusion.

NOTES

[1]Here I am thinking of insightful works that nevertheless fit a category Welty commented on by saying, "Anyone who attributes my stories to myths very specifically and thoroughly is overshooting it. I would rather suggest things" (Gretlund 203).

[2]See Dawn Kendig's article for another application of Goffman to Welty.

[3]Having noticed this response in readers, I was interested to see that the made-for-television version of *The Wide Net* offered an interpretive performance of William Wallace's catfish dance that was wild-with-grief. This interpretation is not, I think, true to the text, but to initial expectations that the text moves beyond.

[4]In a keynote address for "Women, Society, and The Arts," Susquehanna University, 3 November 1989.

[5]Kreyling, for one, citing folklorist Francis Lee Utlty, argues that "this novel is properly a 'local legend' and not simply a 'fairy tale' because it has 'a cruelty and a directness . . . glossed over in the fairy tale'" ("Clement" 33). Marilyn Arnold is another who argues that Welty's tale is in conflict with "the shallowness of the fairy tale vision" (16). Arnold, however, shrewdly suggests the role that generic allusion may play in the reader's construction of the text, stating that "*Welty creates standard expectations in the reader, but she does not fulfill them. Instead, she subverts, reverses, burlesques, and just generally scatters asunder* the fairy tale's sacrosanct notions about the agenda for happily-ever-after living" (16).

[6]Those who have given Rosamond rather more emphasis include Skaggs and Graulich. Skaggs's article extends Bruno Bettelheim's notions that fairy tales provide "a cultural escape valve" and that "the most important ingredient of all fairy tales is the promise of success," to the genre of southwestern humor and to Welty's tale. In making this extension, Skaggs tends to brighten Rosamond's story, suggesting that her happy ending transforms the anxieties suggested by the older plots of Grimm, Psyche and Eros or frontier humor—a conclusion with which I cannot agree entirely.

[7]"Young Andrew" appears as ballad no. 48 in Francis James Child's *The English and Scottish Popular Ballads*. vol. 1. New York: Houghton, 1904. Gordon E. Sleuthang (in "Initiation in Eudora Welty's *The Robber Bridegroom*." *Southern Humanities Review* 7 [Winter 1973]: 77-78) is the only other critic I know who discusses Welty's use of this ballad.

[8]The education which stories can provide is also a subject of Welty's autobiographical essay, "The Little Store." In it she remembers the moment when her own developing imagination, made bold by the news of "some act of violence" concerning the people who ran the neighborhood grocery store, strayed beyond her family's supervision.

[9]Salome's name refers us to the Biblical character who traded a dance for the decapitated head of "the only man [she] ever loved" (this line from Oscar Wilde's version), a girl simultaneously awakened to sexuality and to a dangerously evil willfulness. The name strikes another allusive note.

[10]As Rabinowitz points out in his discussion of narrative conventions, "undermining a conventional ending tends to stress the conventionality of that closure" (162-63), emphasizing the fictionality of that closure.

[11]Is it coincidence that in *The Robber Bridegroom* "the *prism* light of day" diverts a redbird into his old song just before Jamie Lockhart rides up to rob Rosamond "of that which he had left her the day before" (63)?

[12]Brookhart and Marrs discuss the development in their essay, "More Notes on River Country."

WORKS CITED

Apulieus, Lucius. *The Golden Ass*. New York: Marvin, 1931.

Arnold, Marilyn. "Eudora Welty's Parody." *Notes on Mississippi Writers* 2 (Spring 1978): 15-22.

Brookhart, Mary Hughes, and Suzanne Marrs. "More Notes on River Country." *Welty: A Life in Literature*. Ed. Albert J. Devlin. Jackson: UP of Mississippi, 1987. 82-95.

Bryant, J.A. *Eudora Welty*. Minnesota Pamphlet No. 66. Minneapolis: U of Minnesota P, 1968.

Child, James Francis. *The English and Scottish Popular Ballads*. vol. 1. New York: Houghton, 1904.

Cook, Bernard. "Ritual Abduction in Early Mississippi." *Mississippi Quarterly* 36.1 (1982-83): 72-73.
French, Warren. "'All Things Are Double': Eudora Welty as a Civilized Writer." *Eudora Welty: Critical Essays*. Jackson: UP of Mississippi, 1983. 77-87.
Goffman, Irving. *Frame Analysis*. New York: Harper Colophon, 1974.
Graulich, Melody. "Pioneering the Imagination: Eudora Welty's *The Robber Bridegroom*." *Women and Western American Literature*. Ed. Helen Winter Stauffer and Susan J. Rosowski. Troy, NY: Whitson, 1982. 283-96.
Gretlund, Jan Nordby. "An Interview with Eudora Welty." *Southern Humanities Review* 14 (Summer 1980): 193-208.
Grimm, Jacob, and Wilhelm Grimm. "Little Snow White." *The Frog King and Other Tales of the Brothers Grimm*. New York: New American Library, 1964.
Grimm, Jacob Ludwig Karl. *German Popular Tales*. Philadelphia: Porter, 1869.
Gubar, Susan. Keynote address at "Women, Society, and the Arts." Susquehanna U, Selinsgrove, PA. Nov. 1989.
Hirsch, E. D. *Validity in Interpretation*. New Haven: Yale UP, 1967.
Kendig, Daun. "Realities in Sir Rabbit: A Frame Analysis." *Eudora Welty: Eye of the Storyteller*. Ed. Dawn Trouard. Kent, OH: Dent State UP, 1989. 119-32.
Kreyling, Michael. *Eudora Welty: The Achievement of Order*. Baton Rouge: U of Louisiana P, 1980.
___. "Clement and the Indians: Pastoral and History in *The Robber Bridegroom*." *Eudora Welty: A Form of Thanks*. Jackson: UP of Mississippi, 1979. 25-45.
Porat, Ziva Ben. "The Poetics of Literary Allusion." *PTL: A Journal* 1 (1976): 105-28.
Rabinowitz, Peter. *Before Reading: Narrative Conventions and the Politics of Interpretation*. Ithaca: Cornell UP, 1987.
Skaggs, Merrill Maguire. "The Uses of Enchantment in Frontier Humor and *The Robber Bridegroom*." *Studies in American Humor* 3 (Oct. 1976): 96-102.
Vande Kieft, Ruth M. *Eudora Welty*. Rev. ed. Boston: Twayne, 1987.
Welty, Eudora. "And They Lived Happily Ever After." *New York Times Book Review*. Part II. 10 Nov. 1963: 3.
___. "At The Landing." *Collected Stories*. 240-58.
___. *The Collected Stories of Eudora Welty*. New York: Harcourt, 1982.
___. *The Eye of the Story*. New York: Random, 1977.
___. "Livvie." *Collected Stories*. 228-39.
___. "A Memory." *Collected Stories*. 75-80.
___. *One Time, One Place*. New York: Random, 1971.
___. *The Robber Bridegroom*. New York: Harcourt, 1942.
___. "The Wide Net." *Collected Stories*. 169-88.
Yeats, William Butler. *Selected Poems and Two Plays of William Butler Yeats*. Ed. M. L. Rosenthal. New York: Collier, 1962.

From *The Southern Quarterly* 29.1 (Fall 1990): 5-31.

Diverting Swine: The Magical Relevancies of Eudora Welty's Ruby Fisher and Circe

Dawn Trouard

"A Piece of News" (1941; [1937]) and "Circe" (1955; [1949]) would appear to have little in common. Separated by 10 publishing years plus in their respective narratives, Ruby Fisher and Circe do not even hail from the same southern state of things—one a legendary sorceress, albeit doomed to single parenthood and seduced and abandoned by the philandering Odysseus, the other critically tagged as a slow-witted, faithless hick who screws the Folger man for a sample pack of coffee; one viewed as tragically abandoned by her hero lover, the other swatted by the balding Clyde in "semi-comic" spousal discipline for her afternoon indiscretion. Instead of viewing these women as lost and lonely victims of the dark, I will contend that what they share are radical strategies of survival, enabling reservoirs of vitality, life-altering powers of determination; they also have shared a readership loath to acknowledge the textual evidence of female authority. Culturally uncomfortable with incarnations of female sufficiency, readers have too often viewed Ruby Fisher and Circe as hostage to the males who, in fact, on close examination, play mere supporting roles in female dramas.

Until recently, neither story has received much focused critical attention. Ann Romines, in examining the tactics of first-person narrators Sister ("Why I Live at the P.O.") and Circe, has done the most extensive analysis of Welty's most mythic, and as I will argue, most feminist story, "Circe." Finding both females failed storytellers, Romines's analysis of "Circe" attends delightfully to the rituals of domesticity and female cyclical time pervading the story; narrative success depends on mortal appreciation and perceptions, and so, for Romines, Circe's narrative disappoints since this goddess "will never be satisfied" (103), a victim paradoxically of her limiting immortality. But by and large, Circe has been relegated to brief mention, and Alfred Appel, Jr. most dramatically illustrates the dulling power of entrenched analysis: "her magic is useless, and she is as helpless as any of those human lovers" (242).

"A Piece of News" has received critical short-shrift despite W.U. McDonald's appeal for attention in his helpful 1970 study of the story's evolution through its revisions; its deceptive briefness within Welty's provocatively lush short story canon has perhaps led to its all-too-summary treatment by theme. Ruth Vande Kieft and Louise Westling note its comic details, and Elizabeth Evans articulates a view of Ruby "left empty and lonely, her life as vague and dark as the night outside" (55). Marie-Antoinette Manz-Kunz reads the story somewhat more optimistically, viewing Ruby's experience as an exciting fantasy interlude, but finds Ruby ultimately hovel-bound, "incapable of assessing the magnitude of the power which has revealed itself to her as being part of herself despite its puissant allurement" (112). Carol Hollenbaugh suspects that the "unfulfilled" Ruby may be offering the news of her desire to Clyde with the paper (63, 67). Appel, similarly, acknowledges Ruby's eroticism, but undermines his reading by harping on her loneliness and isolation (13). If not quite a victim, Ruby has through the years received her share of critical condescension.

In 1988, however, Ruby and her readers had their consciousness raised courtesy of Patricia Yaeger's sweeping political and revisionary text *Honey-Mad Women*. Yaeger, in a book that devotes only a dozen pages to Welty, provides a dazzling reconsideration of this story. She reads against Ruby's marginality, finding "pleasure" and liberating unpredictability in Ruby's repossession of her twice-appropriated story: once by "A Piece of News"'s mysterious narrator and a second time, by the plot-galvanizing version discovered in the Tennessee newspaper's account of one Ruby Fisher shot.[1] Yaeger sees in Welty's story "a desire for a 'cultural revolution'" (262) and uses it as evidence of a text laden with successful liberatory coups against a dominant discourse that Yaeger refuses to see as stifling (114-48). Peter Schmidt's 1991 *The Heart of the Story*, devoted entirely to Welty's short fiction, capaciously rereads both "A Piece of News" and "Circe." Like Yaeger's work, this study has a feminist agenda; focused exclusively on Welty, however, Schmidt has room to consider textual revision and stylistics, as well as limn the material culture that Welty's fiction renders—worlds of masculine authority and female negotiations within it.

Having spent forty-plus years as wall flowers, these two stories can hardly be worn-out by even the exquisitely choreographed occasions created for them by Schmidt and Yaeger. In fact, I would like to extend these analyses, and locate connections in these two stories of latent power, since I share a critically congenial view of these apparently dissimilar stories. But I would like to offer an elaboration that *aggressively* locates powers in each of the characters: Yaeger, for instance, views the text as liberating primarily *for readers*, women in particular, who are in dire need of discovering tactics of release from domination; and Schmidt, though he finds the powers of Welty's women unbounded, suggests that her stories often present an ambivalent view of this power and its implications for gender. I maintain that both Ruby and Circe exist as full and potent constructions in a "woman's imaginary." I hope to demonstrate in the process that the next frontier for feminist readers is not to flinch at the possibility of texts that marginalize male experience. If fiction is not required to crusade, neither is it obligated to be fair. In fact, old lessons offering to instruct us about the delight to be had from disorder, need to be applied and relished. And I am of the persuasion that Welty licenses herself in these two examples of *jouissance* to consider not so much Adrienne Rich's imagined "*world where men are absent*" ("Natural Resources"), but a world where men's proper place is ancillary. When readers are given permission to discover in imaginative constructions patterns of masculine deflation as normative, to see self-important male readings as smokescreens against a greater likelihood that masculine performance will be recognized as less powerful, "almost ridiculous," then many cultural models that disempower women will be subverted. Then women, and men, will be forced to imagine redistributions of powers that do not invest Prufrockian attendant lords who merely swell progresses or start a scene with greater prominence than they deserve. Easy tools are easy tools regardless of high sentence and should not be confused with sites of absolute power, though coercive traditions in reading practice have resulted in this. In dismantling the tradition of male dignity, Welty's two stories open up the possibility, at least for me, of women seizing the power of their convictions and the too-often-suppressed view of independence that is not loneliness, of the energy which need not be deployed in nurture. Margaret Atwood has reported that men's greatest fear when it comes to women is that they will be laughed at (413); my reading seeks to articulate this very comedy in these stories and explore it as an instrument of liberation. Atwood's survey further revealed that women's concomitant fear was being killed (413). The key to remedying this heinous inequity based in power distortions is to give permission to readers, especially female readers, to discover the literal and figurative pleasure of their sex. Since Ruby Fisher and Circe, courtesy of Welty's wand, are already in possession of this secret, they can be our guides.

Carolyn Heilbrun has sought such guides for and from the fictional territories for some time. Specifically in "What Was Penelope Unweaving?" she poses a version of this quest: "The question women must all ask is how to be freed from the marriage plot and initiated into the quest plot. How many women today find a script, a narrative, a story to live by?" (127). This I agree is a crucial direction for feminist writers—how to invent stories that are not contaminated since as Heilbrun further notes, "the power of the phallocracy is appalling. We invent as we go along . . . and recognize, as we must, that our choice is as Florence Nightingale long ago told us, between pain and paralysis" (127). But in this I think she is wrong—her fervor luring her into a dire and false binarism that will participate in the same captive imagination that has traditionally trapped women. A necessary interim step would be not to turn women who are not victims into victims. In Ruby's story and Circe's, Welty presents methods of circumvention and disruption of male ideological control. At least some of the possible plots Heilbrun seeks are already available—and Welty is a spinner of such yarns—if we will only see what is in her text. If male culture has taught us to read consistently the approved, unified, and solid patriarchal ideology, then it will take a kind of blurring of vision; or to put it otherwise, if the spell of female thralldom has been cast, let the counter reading de-spell and recuperate what has calcified and sedated our perception.[2] Such a counter-spell could free women to read and hear what has always been in the stories of sibyls like Welty. Welty has made this point another way in her essay "On Writing": "Discovery, not being a matter of writing our name on a wall, but of seeing what that wall is, and what is over it, is a matter of vision" (129).

It is important to note that I am not claiming comfort comes from finding strident politics in Welty's fiction; nor do I view Welty as a doctrinaire champion of the oppressed woman, or even as a social commentator on the plight of women trapped by poverty or trapped in brutal marriages or on mythic islands. I offer a feminist reading, specifically indebted to Luce Irigaray's *This Sex Which Is Not One*,[3] that asks one to read against the ingrained lessons of patriarchal culture, to see these two female figures not as semi-comic, least of all as tragic, but instead as sites of instruction, subversive figures challenging culturally determined identities and narrative familiarization. Judith Fetterley has long since alerted us to the necessity of resistant reading; now it is time to be suspiciously be-mused readers. What we have assumed was in the text has too often been provided by a conditioned politeness, a desire to fit the fiction to the ideological lie of dominance.

Peter Schmidt is not alone in his view that Ruby sexually outstrips her husband in desire (34). And Louise Westling has produced a reading of Ruby that approaches the perimeters of Irigaray's "exterritoriality," a zone where women's experience of their own pleasure remains outside the authorized dis-course on women's desire produced by men (Irigaray 158).[4]

Westling observes that Ruby Fisher "simply enjoys her body and stretches dreamily . . . unapologetic about her sexual adventures" (67). She asserts further that "By induction, the story defines an autonomous female sexuality that has only an oblique relation to patriarchal institutions defining the traditional bonds between women and men. Ruby Fisher is able to pleasure herself without endangering her relationship to her husband" (67). But Welty has invested Ruby with more than a healthy freedom from the traditional bonds of fidelity. And her powers do not merely reside in her Tom Sawyerish fantasies about her own death. What appears to be a pathetic afternoon of an intellectually and socially disadvantaged woman, barely able to read and reason, becomes, through Welty's intercessions, an allusive and mythic encounter with the feminine dimension of fluids that "jam the works" (Irigaray 107). And while most readings tend to observe her containment in The House of Clyde, Ruby's ability to produce "ek-stasy" when alone confirms the conditions Irigaray deems necessary for "any subject to form his/her/its desires" (101), conditions that technically seem unavailable to women, but which Ruby demonstrates are ubiquitous if only claimed. Even the act of reading the story in this spirit involves the reader contagiously in the play of *jouissance*. Readings that see Ruby oppressed and marginally embedded in her own text, or see Circe woefully abandoned on her Aeaean island, occlude details that are aesthetically irrelevant in male-dominated economies. The trick is to read for the relevancy of what has traditionally been seen as irrelevant. There is one story for the male-identified reader, another for the resisting anti-idealist of literary experience.

For instance, "A Piece of News" opens in defiance of sanity, reason—Ruby Fisher, Welty's narrator tells us, "has been *out in the rain*" and is shaking off the rain "crossly like a cat reproaching herself for not knowing better" (12).[5] Immediately, conventional wisdom is dealt a double blow—cats substitute for the proverbial chicken and everything in Ruby's carriage suggests that she is in a state of SELF-possession—legs wide, bending and shaking and warming herself at the fire. She is a study in conscious pleasure—if not ecstatic, she is "quite rosy" and most certainly not a bedraggled victim of her own sexuality. The story is thick with appearances that direct us one way but in fact accumulate to suggest their very opposite: *"like a cat reproaching itself."* Still further, her talk is to herself, the proper and inevitable direction for women to talk in a world where "the sex which is one" refuses to hear the whisper of two lips in perpetual touch with each other (Irigaray 29). By not privileging the narrator's speculations, Welty has deliciously complicated our experience of Ruby, enhanced her independence and her unavailability. The expectation that she is easy to understand, simple, predictable is immediately overturned when the narrator's pretensions to authority topple in the opening paragraph where Ruby's talk eludes the narrative presence since it is "hard to lay hold of" (12).[6] According to Irigaray, "Woman never speaks the same way. What she emits is flowing, fluctuating. Blurring" (112). The narrator gestures toward possible meaning, seeks to make Ruby's story familiar and Same—so Ruby's sounds are heard and shaped into something "like a song"—about "The pouring down rain" (12).

After centering the coffee sample, she expresses a startling but telling mystification at male behavior—"why how come he wrapped it in a newspaper!" This response becomes the occasion for the narrative voice to encourage the assumption that "she must have been lonesome and slow all her life, the way things would take her by surprise." Notice there is no specific textual clue to indicate Ruby is more surprised than she is exasperated—only an asking *WHY*. But the narration suggests that not immediately fathoming male motive, in fact questioning at all the decision of the wrapper (revising for containment), constitutes deficiency *and* neediness in Ruby. The reader participates in the judgment that Ruby must be dim not to see the need to wrap the sample against the rain—though we have no information as to whether it rained when she received "the gift," nor that the package itself needed this extra protection. The inclination is to find against the woman. If querying why men do things the way they do them constitutes slowness then who sentient is not slow?

If we resist the urge to confer authority on the narrator, many of the patently negative judgments of Ruby are countered by particulars of the text. In fact, what the story goes on to reveal is that Ruby may be barely literate, but she is more than sufficient in the ways of invention and pleasure and desire. The narrative voice's judgments of her are consistently predicated on the idea that to be alone is a bad thing—a sad thing, a state filled with pathos. The same judgment is rendered on Circe by her literary critics. This view dominates response despite ample and explicit evidence that both women experience satisfaction and delight when alone, and further, there is a great deal of active choosing and inventing unleashed when they are manless.

The next scene is marked by dream, hallucination, and happiness. Ruby crosses the floor dreamily; she sings—her exclamations which the narrative voice has only been able to speculate on are now reassessed and become "a preliminary, only playful pouting with which she amused herself when she was alone" (12). As she arranges herself before the fire the narrator determines: "She was pleased with herself now" (12). She commences to fall into a trancelike state—"Her mouth fell into a deepness, into a look of unconscious cunning. Yet in her very stillness and pleasure she seemed to be hiding there, all alone" (12). From her rest, she begins an examination of the newspaper—and a winking line I think gives us the proper orientation for Ruby: "Her lips trembled, as if looking and spelling so slowly had stirred her heart" (13). *Spelling so slowly*, Ruby Fisher is making magic for herself, conjuring. When she utters her own name, cited in the newspaper—printed in the language of cultural identity—she evidences, according to the narrator, a "look of fright": "what eye in the world did she feel looking in on her?" (13). Schmidt maintains that Ruby has granted the newspaper's text "unlimited authority over her life, much like the authority she concedes Clyde when he is present," and so is made to feel guilty for the dalliance with the salesman earlier (35). Since Clyde is familiar with Ruby's hobbies and even jokes about her afternoon recreation, I find the notion of her guilt unlikely. I do however think she is disconcerted to confront herself in the extremity of her private pleasure as a public figure in printed tragedy, shot in the leg; she adjusts herself in a temporary concession to her awareness of the gaze that has pinned her in print. Her brief anxiety, marked by pulling down her dress—straightening up—gives way to formality and as she reads through the report she significantly subverts the message, saving the long word "misfortune" until the end. We are biased to assume she saves up hard words till the end—but just possibly she is not compelled by linearity, takes meaning in her own time and way. Rearranging the event, drawing support from the power of nature's pounding rain, raging lightening and thunder, and a roaring fire, Ruby Fisher, fresh from her rest, has all the materials for a drama she can make at home. She races to the door and framed in the doorway with elements in full, discordant play, presents a dramatic tableau. And the narrator reports that she waits, with lightening flashing, "As *if* she half thought that would bring him in, a gun leveled in his hand" (13; stress mine), as if to utter theatrically "Where are you, Clyde Fisher?" will serve as cue for her newly scripted antagonist to enter, ready to participate in the spectacle she is re-making, generating out of a news narrative too sparse and meager to contain her.[7]

Like a director fretting the no-show of a principal, Ruby Fisher begins to compose. Alternating pacing with pausing, the narrator claims that "When she was still, there was a passivity about her, or a deception of passivity, that was not really passive at all. There was something in her that never stopped" (13). At this moment she is creative, invested, and transcendent—in the throes of weaving her own narrative in response to the one generated in the newspaper, Ruby Fisher is a heroine and author of her life. The question for great actors is always—what to do with a melodramatic script. Shot in the leg indeed!

Gazing into the fire, the narrator suggests it functions as her "mirror, mirror" giving herself back to her and the inevitable "Clyde *coming* up behind her" (13; stressed pun mine). A "voluble" dialogue with herself ensues and Ruby sorts through the want of probability in the news story. Her conclusion: Clyde "fraid-of-lightening" Fisher, like his fellow cuckold Junior Holifield, is no shooter. As she begins to dream, she instantly revises the "mistaken" and prosaic story from the paper.[8] When she imagines herself dying—her heart would ache mightily from the bullet in it, under her nightgown—the pain would outstrip the pain of Clyde's slappings—and Clyde in "her lethal imaginings" would be an attractive version of his old self—reinstated with handsomeness and strength and long black hair. As her fantasy continues, I submit wryly, Clyde utters a version of every woman's fantasy: I was wrong. Assuming responsibility for her death, she affirms him and lets him know he is speaking "truth." This is either the function of bad scriptwriting, or Ruby's efforts to mark off true statements from untrue. Getting the last word, she dies. Are we willing to imagine a woman *not* somewhat happy, even in death, if the men she knows would finally say they were wrong, *and* responsible?

Then like her avenging female forebear, Faulkner's Addie Bundren, she directs her fantasy toward revenge—revenge sweeter because it is enjoyed in the fine private space of female fantasy for Ruby, in the coffin for Addie (*AILD* 116). It consists of personal charges and duties for the bereaved spouse. In state, "beautiful, desirable, and dead," Clyde is busy—buying her dress, digging the grave—and deranged: he would never be able to "touch her" again. These delicious speculations are made still sweeter by the "tears of some repentance" her death would wring from him. Ruby in front of the warm fire with a storm still raging is suffused with the corporeal pleasure of her fireside thoughts all exponentially raised when she is able to recognize "the pity and beauty and power of her death." On cue, with Ruby swollen like a tic with her surfeitity, the thunder rolls.

Welty supplies a narrative pause, and the textual break allows for the melodramatic entrance Ruby has been preparing for—not of the villain, but a supporting player. Clyde, drenched, "pokes" Ruby with the butt of his gun and begins to complain and demand. The phallic inversion of the language gives power to the idea of what makes certain plates lucky—the driver of those cars may just know which end is up, so to speak. Clearly drenched, with his dribbling gun, Clyde, by the time he takes his seat, seems a curiously porous bit of iconography (a poster child for Irigaray's mechanics of fluids): "Small streams began to flow from him everywhere" (15).

The ritual of dinner commences with Ruby knowing that tonight she will usurp center stage from the Consuming Male. Clyde finally grumbles the question that apparently opens the scene—where has she been? Her formulaic reply, "nowheres special" provokes his enjoinment not to "talk back" and "almost chuckling," he asserts the probability of hitchhiking. But Ruby will not have this scene stolen and she defies his efforts to control, dominate, or minimize the production she has under way. Looking him straight in the eyes, concentrating entirely on the vitality within her "that never stopped," she has "not even heard him." In her ecstasy of anticipation, "filled with happiness," she even splashes him with coffee (15). When the meal is over she delightedly brings the paper: "It excited her even to touch the paper with her hand, to hear its quiet secret noise when she carried it, the rustle of surprise" (16). Clyde reacts with force, maintaining it must be a lie, asking to see, in the tradition of *Tristram Shandy*, the place where she has been wounded. Significantly, the narrator doesn't bother to invoke the standard against Clyde that was so recently employed against Ruby: has Clyde Fisher been lonesome and slow all his life? I ask the reader to take note of such a marked absence and to ask why a comparable diminution of a man befuddled sparks no editorial justification. Instead, Clyde's interrogation of Ruby leads to an epiphanic moment, suggesting certain resemblances between this story and several other stories in this collection, especially "The Key" and "The Whistle." The couple freezes in an encounter with "doubleness" that takes into account the possibility of murder, death, agency, and consequence. Immediately, Clyde puts the paper in the fire and finally notices its out-of-town banner. Righteously, albeit good humoredly, he charges Ruby with trying to fool him. Her simple response is to declare passionately that "'It was Ruby Fisher'"; and she is Ruby Fisher (16).

As the domestic curtain falls, she remains trembling at the window until the quiet that finally follows the storm is found within her too: "the storm had rolled away" (16). McDonald and Appel find the end of the storm an end to her "emotional tumult" (McDonald 246), though Appel locates "quiet desperation" in her ordinary state and views the "subsiding" storm (16) as having been a temporary respite from "the lonely reality of her life" (15). Periodically blue, yes, but has this girl ever been lonely? For me, the story's finale invokes Kate Chopin's "The Storm," another story of marital infidelity, disturbing and transgressive in its utterly non-retributive, even sanguine response to female passion. Chopin's Calixta renews an affair of the heart with Alcée while her cuckolded husband and child are obliviously waiting out the storm in town. The story ends with "So the storm passed and everyone was happy" (87). Welty's significant variation goes Chopin one better and allows the storm to provide orchestration for a woman deliciously alone, spinning a tale of punishment and consequence for her very disappointing husband as a kind of post-coital *divertisement*. Ruby does something akin to what William Faulkner said he was doing: improving on God who had "no sense, no feeling for, theater" (Blotner 532). The delights of the storm are Ruby's. The sexual encounter with the coffee salesman is reduced to mere "hitchhiking" in the *Michelin* guide to their marriage vows; and the partner with the lucky plates has ceased to be any consideration at all, not even sufficiently compelling to figure anywhere into her reverie. When she has leisure and aloneness and can direct her world imaginatively, she is the center of her thoughts. There is a strong sense that Clyde has never been better than when she imagines him penitent, and supporting her centrality. He is reduced to a bit part in this rural one-woman production. Welty creates men who function as props in Ruby's little theater, and the readers' pleasure, as well as Ruby's, emanates from her ability to determine her own pleasure, the delight of self-absorption. "A Piece of News" is flanked by two stories with other clear lessons about life in the patriarchy. The first is "Lily Daw and the Three Ladies," a story exploring a marriage of community convenience which re-poses Adrienne Rich's question about Jane Eyre—"how and why is this [a marriage] a happy ending?" (*Lies* 104). And "A Piece of News" is followed by "Petrified Man," a gruesome tale of male violence and grotesqueness retailed in the realm of female fixity—the beauty salon.[9]

Part of what Luce Irigaray's thinking seeks to challenge is the frightening accuracy of Robert Grave's opening line in "To Juan at the Winter Solstice": "There is one story and one story only." And if there was ever a story that has been retold it is Odysseus's, told mostly by men[10] and for men as proof of the talents and wonders of maleness, and an instrument for insuring the privileges of patriarchal control. Virtually all critics of Welty's version of this legend employ the word "daring" in their praise of Welty's 1955 handling of Odysseus's encounter with Circe. Even in its 1949 incarnation, "Put Me in the Sky!" and in a draft called "The Wand," Welty had already settled on Circe herself for narrator. I wish to argue that Welty has created a story that asks you not to believe your ears about a story you may know by heart, a story so well told that you may have learned about it without ever choosing to have read it. Welty's Circe is no simple diversion for a wandering Odysseus. She has her own version; she speaks in her own voice; she draws her own conclusions. Daring may be the word that best describes Welty's Circe, but her subtle heresy against the ideal Odysseus is an even greater dare. In many ways, to Circe, a busy goddess, Odysseus is simply a big-budget Clyde, demanding, egomaniacal, and irresolute. The few commentators on the story have sparked more to its final passages where they see a forlorn and abandoned Circe bereft of her wandering hero.[11] Not surprising, of course, since this is a culture that insists on seeing women without men as somehow defective; a woman *deserted by a man* is guaranteed contempt. It is assumed that she is necessarily grief stricken. But Alice Walker's Celie offers another version of female "abandonment" that may come closer to the truth of women left alone: "One good thing bout the way he never do any work round the place, us never miss him when he gone" (46). To read this story in the tradition of passion betrayed runs counter to the very spirit of Welty's daring venture. Would she foreground Circe, let her have her say out of and against the tradition of Homer's tale, only to have her languish without him? Again, as I have claimed for Ruby in "A Piece of News," many of the "new" narratives Heilbrun believes women need to live by are already in place; but we must learn to read them. Ever in search of female victims, even on Aeaean, critics to date have wanted to smirk, much like Circe's serving girls who have yet to "learn that unmagical people are put into the world to justify and serve the magical—not to smile at them!" (532). The fact that there has been little commentary on this story and the majority view sees Circe pining away at her story's end needs to be closely examined.

Though I realize that in arguing against the view of humanity's charming frailty, I make myself odd-reader out, I still would like to pose a perverse alternative: does mortality have to be the desire of every fictive creation? Much commentary on "Circe" depends on privileging the human. Vande Kieft, for instance, finds Welty's Circe "envious" of the human "instrument of air," a metaphor for human sensitivity and frailty at the heart of mortal mystery (34). Circe is admittedly curious, covetous of "the secret." Another version of this persuasive argument comes from Danièle Pitavy-Souques who argues that Circe's "lust for power" stems from her failure to view Odysseus's tale properly: his narrative is not "sheer arrogance . . . [but] his ultimate attempt at denying death. For what is a legend-making exploit but a refusal to be reduced to mere body?" (146). As siren-tempting as Pitavy-Souques's position is, she collaborates in service of a patriarchal vision that requires suffering to attend love and journeys towards the other in the pursuit of transcendence and understanding. Elegantly defending the courage required for creation, she is ultimately mounting an argument that would restore Odysseus to the center of the narrative. Both critics are reluctant to grant the enchantress her donnée, to imagine her values, when her values are not confined by this world. Would Welty really be writing a story to give Circe a come-uppance—teach her a lesson in the best country-western tradition about cheating and loving and losing?

If it were possible to engage enchanted Circe on her terms, inhabiting a world where romantic love does not dominate the economy, then it would be possible to consider and reconsider other Welty stories where the price of love is exorbitant, even crippling to women who are seduced by its mythology.[12] Stories in which this ideology appears most explicitly have, I think, proved least attractive as subjects for Welty critics. Why is there so much ease in celebrating the message in "Death of a Traveling Salesman" and such critical silence about the unnerving power of a story like "At the Landing"? Equal partner in the legend, Circe is fighting for power and control of the narrative; but since the mortal community has preserved this legend in the "idiom of man," she has been unfairly diminished. Welty's Circe is revising the canon. And in goddess idiom, there is no need for a vocabulary of love. This is not to say she is without passion, and, in fact, this is the communicative ground she inhabits with Odysseus (534). The disappointment about Odysseus's loveless departure resides in the criticism, not in this island girl who has different concerns. But in an effort to bring her in line with dominant expectations, critics have skillfully focused on the familiar when it is available: Romines's artful study of housekeeping ritual represents one tactical approach. And Appel typifies another by manifesting what Irigaray regards as the phallocratic urge to Sameness (33, 72). Unable to tolerate Circe's resistance to commodification, he prefers to argue that her story is like other stories where female determination is less threatening. He deflects "Circe"'s energy by sweeping it into a category of the familiar: it is "not so far from 'Kin'" (241), he claims. But "Kin" is a very different story exploring engagement, marriage, and female community. I would like to offer a more specific critical counter to these two readings which neglect emphases in the story that suggest Welty viewed Circe in a different light than her critics. In the approach stressing Circe as a domestic harridan, she is unnecessarily and inappropriately demystified. Her special powers are made impotent and the rhetorical victory must go to Odysseus by default. In dispelling the reading of Circe as Cranky Housewife, I hope to remedy the related myopic view that Circe's power is subordinate to Odysseus at any juncture of her dealings with him.

As hostess, Circe makes wicked observations about the squalor produced by her greedy and untidy guests. Her comments serve to validate her conviction that men are swine—yes, there they are eating up all the food ungratefully; and yes, there they are tracking the floor. Yet I see no evidence in the text that Circe is doomed to clean house—her servant girls apparently do the scut work on Aeaean. Circe simply marks monarchically, and somewhat disingenuously, the disruption and chaos attending unexpected guests. In fact, when all has been said and claimed, Odysseus appears a diversion. His inconveniences are offset by the occasion he offers to satisfy her opportunistic curiosity re: mortals—mortals specifically known for having the Right Stuff, at least in their own legendizing.

All critics of the story note that Circe is engaged with needle "making" at the story's start. Even in draft, Welty's Circe has never been merely waiting. In fact, her absorbing activity is arrested by the intrusion of Odysseus's disembarking crew. Further, Circe's creativity in needlework is just one of many versions of creation and transformation detailed in the story. I stress as well that both creation and transformation are under her control. Less a story of love and loss, odyssey and abandonment, "Circe" is a story of female occupation beatified, verified, and vindicated. Unlike traditional and ubiquitous versions of male occupation and conquest literature, Welty's rendition does not involve masculine conquest of virgin territory.[13] When Odysseus's rude crew steps inside, Circe withdraws; but to appreciate Welty's emphasis and empowerment of Circe see the very sentence: "*I left them thus*, and withdrew to make the broth" (531; stress mine). Privileging and indulging her goddess sense of whimsy, Circe serves her transforming broth certain to yield metamorphoses that only "the gods really like." Gods, according to Circe, have the capacity mortals lack—to take in all the wonder, thus justifying the trouble (531).

At this point, the swine-men are evicted and the instructive nature of housekeeping is revealed: "In the end, it takes phenomenal neatness of housekeeping to put it through the heads of men that they are swine" (531). Notice that the essence of housekeeping is a matter of fact in the world, easily grasped by Circe; but the object of the lesson is the difficulty men have in getting it though their skulls. Ingratitude and slovenliness are the conditions of having men in the house—goddess or not. That Circe is "bothered" by this seems to me a purely human female construction—suspecting empathy where none exists. This is the first, last, and only comment made by Circe on the subject of untidiness until the men prepare to depart. Action shifts to the situation where Odysseus's men are welcomed again, this time by their peer group, the prior swine, stationed outside.

Circe, confident in the efficacy of her magic, assumes herself alone and reveals the story's crucial secret—the point lost on the critics: she draws "back into [her] privacy—deathless privacy that heals everything" (532). At this moment she suddenly realizes extrasensorily that she is in fact not alone: and from behind she feels "the press like the air of heaven before a storm" (532). Ruby's expectation during the storm that Clyde would surprise her from behind is realized in the residual lingering of one Odysseus, herbisized, and so protected from the potion his fellow-travellers have succumbed to. In revealing the restorative wonders of privacy, Circe gives the second crucial clue to Welty's conception of her character. Realizing that Odysseus is still under foot, Circe responds to this aberration tellingly—"Before everything, I think of my power" (532). I think it is important to see

Welty's foregrounding of Circe's priorities. Pleasure from these transformations comes from their affirmation of her broth-making skills, its infallible consistency, its amusing effects. She notes that such an exception had been foretold; and she is off guard only since nothing in this *here* has warned her that this is the *moment*. The language of her explanation is particularly worth noting: "If a man remained, unable to leave that magnificent body of his, then enchantment had met with a hero" (532). Too bad the prophecies had not included another fact: the magic inhered in the herb and not the man. The charm has functioned to fortify his mortality—and he is unable to leave that body, thus resisting run-of-the goddess transformation.

Circe unrobes and sports with Odysseus of the empty gaze. She removes his sword, sends his tunic out for laundry and not until she assumes a human female's voice and informs him she knows his name is there any indication that he is aware of her actual presence. All these amazing events, known even to mortal readers—men turned to swine, garments vanishing, even Odysseus's role in what will become his own epic story—have happened to him while he has been oblivious to their magical agent. In fact, until the moment she makes their appointment with destiny known, Odysseus's story has been her private spectacle. Like Ruby's Clyde, Odysseus enters stage left and she employs him in her narrative. In a sense, he has been appropriated, or rather cast. The lines preserved in the story are for the most part hers. I am not suggesting he does not speak—wondrous though that transformation might be. I am simply saying that in Welty's imaginings, Odysseus is not granted significant voice until his first effort to depart. Then, as if in mannerly instruction, setting right centuries of Homeric ingratitude (a text in which Circe's ample hospitality and assistance with his future voyage is taken entirely for granted), Welty's Odysseus finally takes his cue: "'Thank you, Circe, for the hospitality we have enjoyed beneath your roof'" (535).

The issue even more pronounced in "Circe" than in "A Piece of News" is who controls the story, and so though Odysseus's voice is contained he is hardly silent. Following mythic foreplay, magical sedation, and undisclosed pleasures, Odysseus foreshortens his erotic adventures by bursting into speech. His narration seems to function, by her account, as the proverbial cigarette after. Awash in newness, he wants routine; he needs to tell a story. A tired story, one even the owl knows by heart. And in a frank admission of desire Circe solves the riddle at least of what women don't want: "I didn't want his story" (533). But Odysseus is insensible and proceeds to talk himself into a dreamy stupor from the time he declares the day done till Venus is sighted in the sky. Not even Circe can rouse the snoring hero who has indulged himself terrifically on his own wind. Not willing to spare herself the full experience of taking a hero to bed, Circe tactfully spares her real audience the long-winded narration which like that owl, and in something akin to foreknowledge, we already know.

While he sleeps, Circe contrasts her magical and unmysterious world with the mortal world marked by mystery which is "only uncertainty" (533). What is not mystifying in her calculus is the fact that "Men are swine." Circe translates this article of faith instantly into action: "let it be said, and no sooner said than done" (533). Exempt from mortal Addie Bundren's lament that "words go straight up" and deeds move "terribly" along the ground (*AILD* 117), Circe presides over a world where there is intimate connection between woman's utterance and action. And this is the trufflish root of the story's comedy: the swine to man syllogism. Swept up in her own rhapsodizing on human mystery, frailty, "instrument made of air," she makes the Faustian trade—she would become "a harmless dove for the rest of eternity" to possess that "one trifling secret" (533). This is a transformation contract that seems utterly insincere given what we have learned about Circe's values to date: "I think of my power. One man was left."

Unable to resist seizing a rhetorical occasion, Circe confirms the hero's irrelevancy to her own magical meditations when she admits she "had nearly forgotten he would move again" (533). When Odysseus leaps up, he seems to her a veritable hibiscus amongst weeds, something she has seen on walks "apart" (533). Odysseus declines the tempting offer of dinner in a godlike vessel until Circe agrees to restore his men. Again Circe's different system of values emerges and she marks another limitation of mortals: "he cared nothing for beauty that was not of the world, he did not want the first taste of anything new" (533). While transforming them again, she reports that Odysseus, a mock Aeaean Adam, names each and egocentrically asks, "'Do you know me?'" Given the traditional power granted to the prerogative of naming and the traditional sanctity of male identity, Welty's Odysseus is further undermined; "'Do you know me?'" (534) is hardly the sort of question you expect a hero to ask. But in the domain of a female "god," Odysseus must depend on her to *Let there be men* and so reconfer identity and relationship to all of them. With the men "staggering up on their hind legs," he tediously counts each of them and embraces the old familiar. Even this feeble exercise in reasserting his heroic self is thwarted since Welty's Circe accents her privilege and power by stepping on his attempts at tribal reunion. Each time, she names him herself to "spoil the moment" (534). Circe watches the celebration with ethnocentric contempt: all of the festivity brings home the only sure fact about the unmysterious mystery of mortals: "But the pigsty was where they belonged" (534).

Circe and Odysseus wile away the time before sleep talking shop—"signs, omens, premonitions"—and she credits and privileges his relentless nature with a passion like her own. Morning finds his sailors "full of themselves and stories" (534); Circe has maintained her control over the restoration by bringing the sailors back younger and, in her view, more "winsome than they ever could have been before," though they are predictably unappreciative of her alteration. But Odysseus's presence is proving compensation for any stress or inconvenience the household is suffering. But Circe, not Odysseus, is in charge of departures. The Aeaean version of *High Noon* appears in the text when Odysseus announces that "A year's visit is visit enough" (535). Since time has been subverted throughout the story, we have no way of knowing how frequently this announcement may have occurred. What we do know is that she corrects his provocatively ambiguous claim that she "has done too much" with her version: "'I undid as much as I did! . . . That was hard'" (535). She further counters his "recapitulating" kiss with four kisses of her own, looks into his eyes and he is broken. Informing his troops "tomorrow,"[14] Odysseus is clearly under Circe's spell as his men disperse, sadder in human shape than they would have been in their true identity snarfing acorns and trotting (535). Welty breaks the narrative and her pause finds us absorbed in Circe's languid depiction of time passing. With her command to store this season's wine, we are alerted to the fact that Circe has always been in charge. The period of freeloading is at an end, and so apparently is Odysseus's usefulness[15] to her projects in the making. Circe is not the least inclined to discomfit herself or jeopardize her world: "I made clear to the servants, [this wine harvest] was to store. Hospitality is one thing, but I must consider how my time is endless" (535). In her "Put Me in the Sky!" version, she elaborates this sense of proportion and priority even further: "Even while wine can get at the memory, I never forget that I must live. So, then, magic is stronger than intoxication, just as the tree is stronger than the little bird that perches in it to sing and fly away" (8). "Before everything, *I think* of my power" (532).

But as she surveys her domain, she is clearly altered herself—and I posit that morning sickness for a goddess may be something like that for mortal women—she would rather kiss death than the man who has impregnated her. She taunts the constellation of Cassiopeia for her stalwartness and the terrain is entirely mournful. Most critics use these passages to argue her despair over the departure of Odysseus. But she has already declared that his presence is "displeasing"; his welcome worn out. Her knowledge of his inevitable death in the "menacing world," by the very son she is now carrying, makes her a highly suspect portrait of a woman in love. Her biological misery, hostess now for this half-mortal child, is more likely the source of her entire complaint. In this dark night of the soul, she must evaluate the trade she has in fact made—goddess pregnant, she must at least feel some compromise in her magic, in the new version of "making" that is underway. Believing herself "in disgrace," she wakes in the pigsty.

Crucially, her resolve to terminate Odysseus's stay does not yield; she has undermined Odysseus's command and purpose before. She could again if she chose to. She chooses not: remember her need for "endless wine." They depart scurrying, abandoning the companion they should have been burying, laden with gifts they do not appreciate or acknowledge. We are told that she does not watch the houseguests depart for Hades, since she already has seen it (foreknowledge), has always known what was to be. In "Sky," she has made herself invisible since "only vanishing prevents ugly farewells" (10). In fact, she counts on the restorative powers of "deathless privacy" to heal the ruptures past and coming from transformation. For now, the only stormy sound is the Kiplingesque grumbling "like summer thunder" of her pet swine. Now she identifies herself with Cassiopeia—consigned to a position, less pleasant since she is tied by her pregnancy. If Odysseus's ship is like an ejaculation, "a moment's gleam on a wave," her state is a "rim of fire, a ring on the sea" (537). Making metaphors, Circe marks the transitoriness of voyages, storytelling, even stories. She, however, is for eternity. Humanity's diminished capacity to take in all the wonder makes the story enough for mankind. The need to tell it, the most repetitive of tales, as we have seen, will be the mortal compensation for these men who will soon die. Circe knows that they must take their "felicity" from the chance to enter narrative, endlessly but terminally, since mortals are without alternatives to death and oblivion. "Who has *not* seen a horrid man with one eye?" ("Sky" 8).

In the story's final paragraph, she stages a drama akin to Ruby's. Posed on her rock, she longs for grief—but it is not a possibility; she considers shrieking at the Moon, and melodramatically rhapsodizes on the elusive nature of grief. Poor Circe! The cultural scripts have told us she should feel great grief—but she doesn't. Unable to muster a proper bereavement, or even melancholy, Circe opts to play her curtain scene as a sulky oracle. Spared grief and death, she explains why welcome is such a dangerous word. Grief is guaranteed Odysseus; in fact, it is waiting on him—foretold—because here "foretold" is the same as the last word. Her world is complete without him; the magic of her world is sufficient. Outliving, or rather living forever, coupled with the retributive knowledge that she will bear the agent of this ungrateful hero's undoing works a radical revision of the legend and invests with delicious power the idea that biology is destiny. In fact, Welty literally buries the traditional notion of romance by having

Circe suggest Elpenor's epitaph be "His tomb was love" in "The Wand." In "Circe" she proposes the more cynical version, "He died of love" (536). She anticipates the lesson Alice Walker's Gloria offers in "At First": "'Really, / You've got to be kidding. Other / women have already done this / sort of suffering for you, / or so I thought'"(15). Foreknowledge may in fact be better than the last word and the goddess who laughs last laughs a medusa's laugh.[16]

NOTES

[1]114-23. Yaeger's wide-ranging study offers a lucid and profound consideration of women writers and their relation to language/speech/dominance. Yaeger seeks to "define an alternate mythology of feminine speech" (4), finding subversion, victory, terror, espionage, resistance and liberation implicit in texts we have too quickly accepted as documents of oppression. Though Welty's "A Piece of News" serves Yaeger as an illustration of a process and is not her principle subject, she discovers heretofore unappreciated drama in the story and reminds us of Welty's persistent doubling aesthetic—there is never just surface, however compelling the surface may be.

Carey Wall's call for papers for the American Literature Association in 1990 asked for readings of Welty's fiction that demonstrated power and creativity despite patriarchal oppression, readings that discovered resources in female figures that accounted for their singular vitality amidst often unsatisfying, even miserable circumstance. Since my presentation of an earlier version of this essay at this conference, I discovered Yaeger's amazing book, and much of my revision is indebted to what I learned from it.

[2]Kenneth Burke's *A Rhetoric of Motives* (Berkeley: U of California P, 1969). In his discussion of the etymology of "glamour," Burke links the word to the corrupted "gramarye," which meant magic and stemmed from days when the power to read and write granted status. Burke's focus is the "hierarchic motive" that influences perception and may grant "radiance due to . . . place in the social order." As he extends connotations for the word, he ties it to weakness of sight, charms that alter sight, even "a kind of haze in the air, causing things to appear different from what they really are; any artificial interest in, or association with, an object, through which it appears delusively magnified or glorified" (210). I invoke Burke as a way to remedy the syndrome Virginia Woolf identified whereby women "reflect the figure of man at twice his natural size." If this is what the cultural practice of glamorizing maleness has done (inflation), feminist readers must read and resist the aura; in effect, they must counter the distorting tradition with a compensatory and liberating blurring of the dominant images and investing "deviant" female activity with new versions of glamor. I am grateful to Daryl Palmer for alerting me to Burke's reading of glamour.

[3]Though there is dispute as to whether or not Irigaray's writings "qualify" as legitimate feminism or philosophy, I have found her perspectives on desire, philosophical dissent, and sexuality essential. For application of her insights to a canonical author see my essay on Faulkner's Eula Varner in *Mississippi Quarterly*, 42.3 (1989): 281-97. For a lucid and engaging reading of Irigaray's career and thought see Margaret Whitford's *Luce Irigaray: Philosophy of the Feminine* (London: Routledge, 1991).

[4]Irigaray goes on to argue that "feminine pleasure is the greatest threat of all to masculine discourse" (157). Functioning only as a commodity in this masculine economy, women, according to Irigaray, may disrupt the power in such a system by expressing their own desires going "to market alone" (158). Ruby, of course, sings, talks, and even takes herself to "market" with the driver of the car with lucky Tennessee plates. Irigaray's analysis of what threatens male pleasure proves a dark corollary to Atwood's discovery that above all men fear being laughed at by women.

[5]Yaeger observes that Ruby's "dampness" at the story's opening is the only interesting feature in a minimal opening (135); but she does not particularly pursue the role of water, since her central argument focuses on Ruby's relationship to the newspaper, and her subsequent use of it to give "birth to herself" (117). I find Hollenbaugh's view of the weather and Ruby's "intense experience of self" more satisfying on this point (63). W.U. McDonald, Jr.'s invaluable collation of Welty's revisions of this story stresses that the emergence of the storm is a specific device by which Welty has made Ruby more "vulnerable and sensuous" (235); but McDonald shares the view of Ruby as ultimately lonely and sees Clyde, though not the focus of the story, certainly more "stolid" and "dignified" than I, in this far less generous reading of him, do. I resist Schmidt's view that Welty revised Clyde to make him more "ironic" as well (36).

All references to Welty's stories are parenthetically documented and keyed to *The Collected Stories of Eudora Welty* unless otherwise specified.

[6]For discussion of the ideological consequences of "the sovereign *authority*" of the privileged narrator see Gennette (258-59). Also, I ask readers to consider the alteration in this line from its 1937 published version which reads, "She was always lonesome and slow; things would take her by surprise" (90). When a writer like Welty makes a point about seeming vs. being then it is altogether likely that she is playing with "spelling" mysteries and negotiating perception as well. (For more discussion of this kind of textual problem see Daun Kendig's essay on "Sir Rabbit.")

[7]Though McDonald's sensitive reading of Ruby is wonderfully illuminating, he is most effective for me in his recognitions about her capacity to luxuriate in her play. I am less persuaded by his inclination to see Ruby as hopeful of resuscitating "some new responsiveness from" Clyde (243). In line with Robert Penn Warren's ideology of love in Welty, McDonald finds the story invested with this dominant view of Welty's fiction that routinely yields the precious, human "communion," albeit transient, between two people (244-45). Sometimes it does, and sometimes it doesn't. I suspect the "rare and wavering" possibility that rises up between Ruby and Clyde, extravagantly marked by its exponentially raised rhetorical doubleness, is totally unassigned and indeterminate, especially since what constitutes shame and pleasure for each is deeply rooted in their differences.

[8]I want to provide an alternative to Schmidt's compelling reading that sees Ruby's fantasy rooted in a tradition of female passive power that can assert itself only through death (35). She is working with an existing text—a report of her much exaggerated wound to be certain—and what she does is speculate on the traditional economy and succeed in preserving herself. The elaboration of the funeral seems to fit in with what Irigaray has designated as the "masquerade of femininity" wherein a woman fulfills the image, achieves value in a male-assigned role; her only "compensation" would be the dubious privilege of being selected for "consumption" (84). But the only consumer for this scene is Ruby (and how does the narrator know this is her fantasy anyway?), and Welty's revisions show an underlining of Twain's tradition of attending one's funeral: in the *SR* version, she composes her face "so as not to look ugly like her mother. She would look beautiful and desirable" and Clyde moves from "mirthless, violent, distraught" to "wild, shouting, and all distracted" (McDonald 240-41).

[9]For excellent treatments of these Welty's stories featuring examinations of female containment in culture see Weston on "Lily Daw and the Three Ladies" and Schmidt on "Petrified Man."

[10]Graves also wrote a poem "Ulysses" (as did Tennyson and many, many others), worth noting in the context of this argument since it is distinguished by its sexism and revolting treatment of its subject: "Penelope and Circe seemed as one: / She like a whore made his lewd fancies run, / and wifely she a hero to him bore" (*Norton* 551.3-4). Efforts to consider other points of view occur in Wallace Stevens's "The World as Meditation" which focuses on Penelope's wait, but still portrays her desire as singleminded: "She wanted nothing he could not bring her by coming / alone" (*The Collected Poems of Wallace Stevens* 520-21). The most important attempt to re-vision Circe is Katherine Anne Porter's "A Defense of Circe" which Joan Givner in her 1982 biography (*Katherine Ann Porter: A Life*. [New York: Simon and Schuster]) claims Porter regarded as "the only original idea she ever had" (412). Porter narrates from the third-person and is unabashedly supportive of Circe, "a beautiful, sunny-tempered, merry-hearted young enchantress" (133).

[11]Elizabeth Evans characterizes Circe's language as "more suited to a determined domestic than an immortal enchantress" (38-39) and views the story as comic because of "the goddess's fanatic domesticity and insistence on cleanliness from travel-weary men about to be turned into swine" (110). The comedy is broken for Evans at the end when Circe is left "with child and full of grief" (110).

[12]Noel Polk, working with other stories in *The Bride of the Innisfallen*, comes, I think, to the right conclusion; but since his argument finally collaborates with the traditional Warren-Vande Kieft-et.al of "ah love, ah humanity!" school of Welty reading, I think it needs special scrutiny. For Polk, the lesson in "No Place for You, My Love" and "The Bride of the Innisfallen," and in novels like *The Optimist's Daughter* has to do with Welty's reckoning of the price of love and relationship against the reality of freedom and isolation. Polk acknowledges that the price of relationship is often "a heavy burden" and that love seeks out "alterations to make" (122). The idea that struggle is a necessary good leads Polk to some traditional and sentimental claims: Judge McKelva marries Fay because her love is cheaply bought (she makes no spiritual demands); or that the strangers in "No Place" come to a mutual recognition, share "an apostrophe to love" at the story's end. Welty's uniqueness for me consists in the fact that I believe she entertains all possibilities of desire in fiction and so does not privilege communion; in fact, characters like Miss Eckhart and Virgie, and Mrs. Larkin may well mark outposts in fictional territory where "free and helpless," as Polk frames the alternative to fraught and fulfilling community, begin to seem inappropriately paired.

[13]See Annette Kolodny's landmark study *The Lay of the Land* (Chapel Hill, NC: Duke UP, 1975).

[14]In "Put Me in the Sky!" two significant differences mark this scene: Circe initially responds to Odysseus's announcement with anger and shock: "Not to seize him by the heart had made me grind my teeth, but. . . . His self-protection never prepared me for being abandoned" (7). Furthermore, he changes his mind after he gives her a single kiss. In the 1955 version, Circe kisses more and regrets less.

Another shift in emphasis occurs in the revision of her equation about foreknowledge. The 1949 treatment includes a self-satisfied "nevertheless." Moreover, in "The Wand," Circe explicitly deems the grief she desired beneath consideration—even "less than ungrateful man." In the later version, Circe's phrasing becomes more oracular and haunting and less petulant.

I wish to thank Eudora Welty for permission to quote from her manuscript "The Wand" in the Harry Ransom Humanities Research Center at the University of Texas at Austin.

[15]In an exceptionally rich reading of this story, Schmidt rightfully insists that Circe "needs no rescuer and feels no grief" (190). He also negotiates the problems of the critical tradition that finds Circe inadequate as a narrator because she cannot experience grief, time, and mystery; he proposes that she is "'beyond'" narrative and that Welty is offering a critique of the limitations of the narrative tradition that celebrate the male rescuer. In proposing that her capacity for revising narrative may be symbolized in her wand, Schmidt links her to several other women artists in Welty. Though he succeeds entirely in his claim that she is successful in freeing herself from "the inherited bonds of male-centered narrative," I think he mutes the power of Welty's message somewhat by emphasizing Circe as "immortal and inhuman" (191). I think her immortal extra-ordinariness is deliberately complicated by Welty's decision to invoke the most biologically determined revision of *The Odyssey* possible: when Welty makes Circe pregnant, she transforms both the goddess and the legend, opening even wider the door for readers to consider Circe's responses to men and relationship as genuine possibilities—new scripts for women, granting them authority and power regardless of affiliation. As a mother-to-be, Circe will have all the leisure required to continue her inquiry into human mystery—without the continued involvement with Odysseus.

[16]Schmidt posits an ingenuous reading of the Perseus myth, suggesting elements of Medusa's story are being worked out in "Circe" (191). As tantalizing as I find all of Schmidt's readings of Welty's fiction, I was merely invoking Cixous's Medusa as a way of recuperating the proverb about who gets the last laugh.

WORKS CITED

Appel, Alfred, Jr. *A Season of Dreams: The Fiction of Eudora Welty*. Baton Rouge: Louisiana State UP, 1965.

Atwood, Margaret. "Writing the Male Character." *Second Words*. Boston: Beacon Press, 1982. 412-30.

Blotner, Joseph. *Faulkner: A Biography*. Vol. 1. New York: Random House, 1974.

Chopin, Kate. "The Storm." *Literature: An Introduction to Fiction, Poetry and Drama*. Ed. X. J. Kennedy. 5th ed. New York: Harper Collins, 1990. 83-87.

Evans, Elizabeth. *Eudora Welty*. New York: Frederick Ungar, 1981.

Faulkner, William. *As I Lay Dying*. In *Novels 1930-35*. New York: Library of America, 1985.

Fetterley, Judith. *The Resisting Reader: A Feminist Approach to American Fiction*. Bloomington: Indiana UP, 1978.

Genette, Gérard. *Narrative Discourse: an Essay in Method*. Trans. Jane E. Lewin. Ithaca, New York: Cornell UP, 1972.

Graves, Robert. "To Juan at the Winter Solstice." *The Norton Anthology of Modern Poetry*. Ed. Richard Ellmann and Robert O'Claire. New York: Norton, 1973. 554.

Heilbrun, Carolyn G. "What Was Penelope Unweaving?" *Hamlet's Mother and Other Women*. New York: Ballantine, 1991. 120-30.

Hollenbaugh, Carol. "Ruby Fisher's Demon Lover." *Notes on Mississippi Writers* 7.2 (1974): 63-67.

Irigaray, Luce. *This Sex Which Is Not One*. Trans. Catherine Porter. Ithaca, NY: Cornell UP, 1985.

Kendig, Daun. "Realities in 'Sir Rabbit': A Frame Analysis." Trouard 119-32.
Manz-Kunz, Marie-Antoinette. *Eudora Welty: Aspects of Reality in her Short Fiction*. Swiss Studies in English 63. Bern: Francke Verlag, 1971.
McDonald, W.U., Jr. "Eudora Welty's Revisions of 'A Piece of News.'" *Studies in Short Fiction* 7 (1970): 232-47.
Pitavy-Souques, Danièle. "Of Suffering and Joy: Aspects of Storytelling in Welty's Short Fiction." Trouard 142-50.
Polk, Noel. "Water, Wanderers, and Weddings: Love in Eudora Welty." *Eudora Welty: A Form of Thanks*. Ed. Louis Dollarhide and Ann J. Abadie. Jackson: UP of Mississippi, 1979. 104-10.
Porter, Katherine Anne. "In Defense of Circe." *The Collected Essays and Occasional Writings of Katherine Anne Porter*. New York: Dell, 1973. 133-40.
Rich, Adrienne. "Jane Eyre: The Temptations of a Motherless Woman." *On Lies, Secrets and Silence: Selected Prose 1966-1978*. New York: Norton, 1979. 89-106.
___. "Natural Resources." *Dream of a Common Language*. New York: Norton, 1978. 60-65.
Romines, Ann. "How Not to Tell A Story: Eudora Welty's First-Person Tales." Trouard 94-104.
Schmidt, Peter. *The Heart of the Story: Eudora Welty's Short Fiction*. Jackson: UP of Mississippi, 1991.
___. "Sibyls in Eudora Welty's Stories." Trouard 78-93.
Trouard, Dawn, ed. *Eudora Welty: Eye of the Storyteller*. Kent, OH: Kent UP, 1989.
Vande Kieft, Ruth M. *Eudora Welty*. 1962. Rev. ed. Boston: Twayne, 1987.
Walker, Alice. *The Color Purple*. New York: Simon & Schuster, 1985.
___. "At First." *Good Night Willie Lee. I'll See You in the Morning*. New York: HBJ, 1979.
Welty, Eudora. *The Collected Stories of Eudora Welty*. New York: HBJ, 1980.
___. "On Writing." *The Eye of the Story*. New York: Vintage, 1979.
___. "Put Me in the Sky!" *Accent* 10.1 (Autumn 1949): 3-10.
___. "A Piece of News." *Southern Review* 3 (1937-38): 80-84.
Westling, Louise. *Eudora Welty*. Totowa, NJ: Barnes & Noble, 1989.
Weston, Ruth D. "American Folk Art, Fine Art, and Eudora Welty: Aesthetic Precedents for 'Lily Daw and the Three Ladies.'" Trouard 3-13.
Yaeger, Patricia. *Honey-Mad Women: Emancipatory Strategies in Women's Writing*. New York: Columbia UP, 1988.

Selected Other Readings

Appel, Alfred, Jr. *A Season of Dreams: The Fiction of Eudora Welty*. Baton Rouge: Louisiana State UP, 1965.

Arnold, Marilyn. "Images of Memory in Eudora Welty's *The Optimist's Daughter*." *Southern Literary Journal* 14.2 (1982): 28-38.

Bradford, M.E. "Miss Eudora's Picture Book." *Mississippi Quarterly* 26 (1973): 659-62.

Brantley, Fredrick. "*A Curtain of Green*: Themes and Attitudes." *American Prefaces* 7 (1942): 241-51.

Bryant, James A., Jr. *Eudora Welty*. Minneapolis: U of Minnesota P, 1968.

____. "Eudora Welty." *Fifty Southern Writers after 1900*. Ed. Joseph M. Flora and Robert Bain. New York: Greenwood, 1987. 516-25.

____. "Seeing Double in *The Golden Apples*." *Sewanee Review* 82 (1974): 300-15.

Buckley, William F., Jr. "The Southern Imagination: An Interview with Eudora Welty and Walker Percy." *Mississippi Quarterly* 26 (1973): 493-516.

Carson, Barbara Harrell. "In the Heart of Clay: Eudora Welty's *The Ponder Heart*." *American Literature* 59 (1987): 609-25.

Carson, Franklin D. "'The Song of Wandering Aengus': Allusions in Eudora Welty's *The Golden Apples*." *Notes on Mississippi Writers* 6 (1973): 14-17.

Clark, Charles C. "*The Robber Bridegroom*: Realism and Fantasy on the Natchez Trace." *Mississippi Quarterly* 26 (1973): 625-38.

Daniel, Robert. "The World of Eudora Welty." *Southern Renascence: The Literature of the Modern South*. Eds. Louis D. Rubin, Jr. and Robert D. Jacobs. Baltimore: John Hopkins Press, 1953. 306-15.

Davis, Charles E. "The South in Eudora Welty's Fiction: A Changing World." *Studies in American Fiction* 3 (1975): 199-209.

Devlin, Albert J. *Eudora Welty's Chronicle*. Jackson: UP of Mississippi, 1983.

____. "Eudora Welty's Historicism: Method and Vision." *Mississippi Quarterly* 30 (1977): 213-34.

____, ed. *Welty: A Life in Literature*. Jackson: UP of Mississippi, 1987.

Dollarhide, Louis, and Ann J. Abadie, eds. *Eudora Welty: A Form of Thanks*. Jackson: UP of Mississippi, 1979.

Donaldson, Susan V. "Recovering Otherness in *The Golden Apples*." *American Literature* 63 (1991): 489-506.

Drake, Robert Y., Jr. "Comments on Two Eudora Welty Stories." *Mississippi Quarterly* 13 (1960): 123-131.

____. "The Reasons of the Heart." *Georgia Review* 11 (1957): 420-26.

Eisinger, Charles E. "Eudora Welty and the Triumph of the Imagination." *Fiction of the Forties*. Ed. Eisinger. Chicago: U of Chicago P, 1963. 258-83.

Evans, Elizabeth. *Eudora Welty*. New York: Ungar, 1981.

____. "Eudora Welty: The Metaphor of Music." *Southern Quarterly* 20.4 (1982): 92-100.

Fleischauer, John F. "The Focus of Mystery: Eudora Welty's Prose Style." *Southern Literary Journal* 5.2 (1973): 64-79.

Glenn, Eunice. "Fantasy in the Fiction of Eudora Welty." *A Southern Vanguard*. Ed. Allen Tate. New York: Prentice, 1947. 78-91.

Griffin, Robert J. "Eudora Welty's *A Curtain of Green*." *The Forties: Fiction, Poetry, Drama*. Ed. Warren French. Deland, FL: Everett/Edwards, 1969. 101-10.

Gossett, Louise Y. "Eudora Welty's New Novel: The Comedy of Loss." *Southern Literary Journal* 3.1 (1970): 122-37.

Gross, Seymour L. "Eudora Welty's Comic Imagination." *The Comic Imagination in American Literature*. Ed. Louis D. Rubin, Jr. New Brunswick, NJ: Rutgers UP, 1973. 319-28.

Gygax, Franziska. *Serious Daring from Within: Female Narrative Strategies in Eudora Welty's Novels*. Westport, CT: Greenwood, 1990.

Hardy, John Edward. "The Achievement of Eudora Welty." *Southern Humanities Review* 2 (1968): 269-78.

____. "*Delta Wedding* as Region and Symbol." *Sewanee Review* 60 (1952): 397-417.

Heilman, Robert B. "Salesmen's Deaths: Documentary and Myth." *Shenandoah* 20 (1969): 20-28.

Hicks, Granville. "Eudora Welty." *English Journal* 41 (1952): 461-68.

Hoffman, Frederick J. "Eudora Welty and Carson McCullers." *The Art of Southern Fiction*. By Hoffmann. Carbondale: Southern Illinois UP, 1967. 51-73.

Holland, Robert B. "Dialogue as a Reflection of Place in *The Ponder Heart*." *American Literature* 35 (1963): 352-58.

Isaacs, Neil. *Eudora Welty*. Austin, TX: Steck-Vaughn, 1969.

Jones, Alun R. "The World of Love: The Fiction of Eudora Welty." *The Creative Present*. Eds. Nona Balakian and Charles Simmons. Garden City: Doubleday, 1963. 175-92.

Kreyling, Michael. *Author and Agent: Eudora Welty and Diarmuid Russell*. New York: Farrar, 1991.

____. *Eudora Welty*. Jackson: Mississippi Library Commission, 1976.

____. *Eudora Welty's Achievement of Order*. Baton Rouge: Louisiana State UP, 1980.

____. "Modernism in Welty's *A Curtain of Green and Other Stories*." *Southern Quarterly* 20.4 (1982): 40-53.

____. "The Natchez Trace in Eudora Welty's Fiction." *Southern Quarterly* 29.4 (1991): 161-70.

Ladd, Barbara. "Coming Through: The Black Initiate in *Delta Wedding*." *Mississippi Quarterly* 41 (1988): 541-51.

Landess, Thomas H. "The Function of Taste in the Fiction of Eudora Welty." *Mississippi Quarterly* 26 (1973): 543-57.

Manning, Carol S. *With Ears Opening Like Morning Glories: Eudora Welty and the Love of Storytelling*. Westport, CT: Greenwood, 1985.

Marrs, Suzanne. *The Welty Collection: A Guide to the Eudora Welty Manuscripts and Documents at the Mississippi Department of Archives and History*. Jackson: UP of Mississippi, 1988.

____. "'The Treasure Most Dearly Regarded': Memory and Imagination in *Delta Wedding*." *Southern Literary Journal* 25.2 (1992): 79-91.

McDonald, W. U. "Works by Welty: A Continuing Checklist." *Eudora Welty Newsletter* 1-16 (1986-1993).

McHaney, Pearl. "Checklist of Welty Scholarship." *Eudora Welty Newsletter* 1-16 (1986-1993).

____. "A Eudora Welty Checklist: 1973-1986." *Mississippi Quarterly* 39 (1986): 651-97.

McHaney, Thomas L. "Eudora Welty and the Multitudinous Golden Apples." *Mississippi Quarterly* 26 (1973): 589-624.

McMillan, William E. "Conflict and Resolution in *Losing Battles*." *Criticism* 15 (1973): 110-24.

Mortimer, Gail L. "Image and Myth in Eudora Welty's *The Optimist's Daughter*." *American Literature* 62 (1990): 616-33.

Pei, Lowry. "Dreaming the Other in *The Golden Apples*." *Modern Fiction Studies* 28 (1982): 415-33.

Percy, Walker. "Eudora Welty in Jackson." *Shenandoah* 20 (1969): 37-38.

Peterman, Gina D. "*A Curtain of Green*: Eudora Welty's Auspicious Beginning." *Mississippi Quarterly* 46.1 (1992-93): 91-114.

Phillips, Robert L. "Patterns of Vision in Welty's *The Optimist's Daughter*." *Southern Literary Journal* 14.1 (1981): 10-23.

Pickett, Nell A. "Colloquialism as a Style in the First-Person-Narrator Fiction of Eudora Welty." *Mississippi Quarterly* 26 (1973): 559-76.

Polk, Noel. "A Eudora Welty Checklist." *Mississippi Quarterly* 26 (1973): 663-93.

____. *Eudora Welty: A Bibliography of Her Work*. Jackson: UP of Mississippi, 1993.

Porter, Katherine Anne. Introduction. *A Curtain of Green*. By Eudora Welty. New York: Doubleday, 1941. ix-xix.

Prenshaw, Peggy Whitman, ed. *Conversations with Eudora Welty*. Lafayette: Mississippi UP, 1984.

____. "Cultural Patterns in Eudora Welty's *Delta Wedding* and 'The Demonstrators.'" *Notes on Mississippi Writers* 3 (1970): 51-70.

____. "Eudora Welty." *American Women Writers: Bibliographical Essays*. Ed. Maurice Duke, Jackson R. Bryer, and M. Thomas Inge. Westport, CT: Greenwood, 1983. 233-67.

____, ed. *Eudora Welty: Critical Essays*. Jackson: UP of Mississippi, 1979.

Price, Reynolds. "The Onlooker Smiling: An Early Reading of *The Optimist's Daughter*." *Shenandoah* 20 (1969): 58-73.

Randisi, Jennifer. "Eudora Welty and the Fairy Tale." *Southern Literary Journal* 23.1 (1990): 30-44.

Ransom, John Crowe. "Delta Fiction." *Kenyon Review* 8 (1946): 503-07.

Reynolds, Larry J. "Enlightening Darkness: Theme and Structure in Eudora Welty's *Losing Battles*." *Journal of Narrative Technique* 8 (1978): 113-40.

Rupp, Richard H. "Eudora Welty: A Continual Feast." *Celebration in Postwar American Fiction 1945-1967*. By Rupp. Coral Gables, FL: U of Miami P, 1970. 59-75.

Russell, Diarmuid. "First Work." *Shenandoah* 20 (1969): 16-19.

Saunders, James Robert. "'A Worn Path': The Eternal Quest of Welty's Phoenix Jackson." *Southern Literary Journal* 25.1 (1992): 62-73.

Schmidt, Peter. *The Heart of the Story: Eudora Welty's Short Fiction*. Jackson, UP of Mississippi, 1991.

Seaman, Gerda, and Ellen L. Walker. "'It's All in a Way of Speaking': A Discussion of *The Ponder Heart*." *Southern Literary Journal* 23.2 (1991): 65-76.

Slethaug, Gordon E. "Initiation in Eudora Welty's *The Robber Bridegroom*." *Southern Humanities Review* 7 (1973): 77-87.

Snyder, Lynn. "Rhetoric in *The Ponder Heart*." *Southern Literary Journal* 21.2 (1989): 17-26.

Stuckey, William J. "The Use of Marriage in Welty's *The Optimist's Daughter*." *Critique* 17.2 (1975): 36-46.

Swearingen, Bethany C. *Eudora Welty: A Critical Bibliography, 1936-1958*. Jackson: UP of Mississippi, 1984.

Thompson, Victor H. *Eudora Welty: A Reference Guide*. Boston: Hall, 1976.

____. "The Natchez Trace in Eudora Welty's 'A Still Moment.'" *Southern Literary Journal* 6.1 (1973): 59-69.

Trouard, Dawn, ed. *Eudora Welty: Eye of the Storyteller*. Kent, OH: Kent State UP, 1990.

Turner, Craig W., and Lee Harding Emling, eds. *Critical Essays on Eudora Welty*. Boston: Hall, 1989.

Vande Kieft, Ruth. *Eudora Welty*. Boston: Twayne, 1962.

____. "Eudora Welty and the Right to Privacy." *Mississippi Quarterly* 43 (1990): 475-84.

____. "The Mysteries of Eudora Welty." *Georgia Review* 15 (1961): 343-57.

____. "The Vision of Eudora Welty." *Mississippi Quarterly* 26 (1973): 517-45.

Walker, Ellen L., and Gerda Seaman. "*The Robber Bridegroom* as a Capitalist Fable." *Southern Quarterly* 26.4 (1988): 57-68.

Warren, Robert Penn. "The Love and Separateness in Miss Welty." *Kenyon Review* 6 (1944): 246-59.

Weiner, Rachel V. "Eudora Welty's *The Ponder Heart*: The Judgment of Art." *Southern Studies* 19 (1980): 261-73.

Welty, Eudora. *The Eye of the Story: Selected Essays and Reviews*. New York: Random House, 1978.

____. "How I Write." *Virginia Quarterly Review* 31 (1955): 240-51.

____. *One Time, One Place: Mississippi in the Depression, A Snapshot Album*. New York: Random House, 1971.

____. *One Writer's Beginnings*. Cambridge, MA: Harvard UP, 1984.

Westling, Louise. "Food, Landscape and the Feminine in *Delta Wedding*." *Southern Quarterly* 30.2-3 (1992): 29-40.

____. *Sacred Groves and Ravaged Gardens: The Fiction of Eudora Welty, Carson McCullers, and Flannery O'Connor*. Athens, GA: U of Georgia P, 1985.

Wolff, Sally. "'Among Those Missing': Phil Hand's Disappearance from *The Optimist's Daughter*." *Southern Literary Journal* 25.1 (1992): 74-78.

____. "Some Talk about Autobiography: An Interview with Eudora Welty." *Southern Review* 26 (1990): 81-88.

Yaeger, Patricia S. "'Because a Fire Was in My Head': Eudora Welty and the Dialogic Imagination." *PMLA* 99 (1984): 955-73.

____. "Toward a Feminine Sublime." *Gender and Theory: Dialogues on Feminist Criticism*. Ed. Linda Kauffman. Oxford, UK: Basil Blackwell, 1989. 191-212.

Index

About the Editor

LAURIE CHAMPION is a Ph.D candidate at the University of North Texas. Her articles have appeared in *The Southern Literary Journal* and *The Explicator.* She is the editor of *The Critical Response to Mark Twain's Huckleberry Finn* (Greenwood Press, 1991).